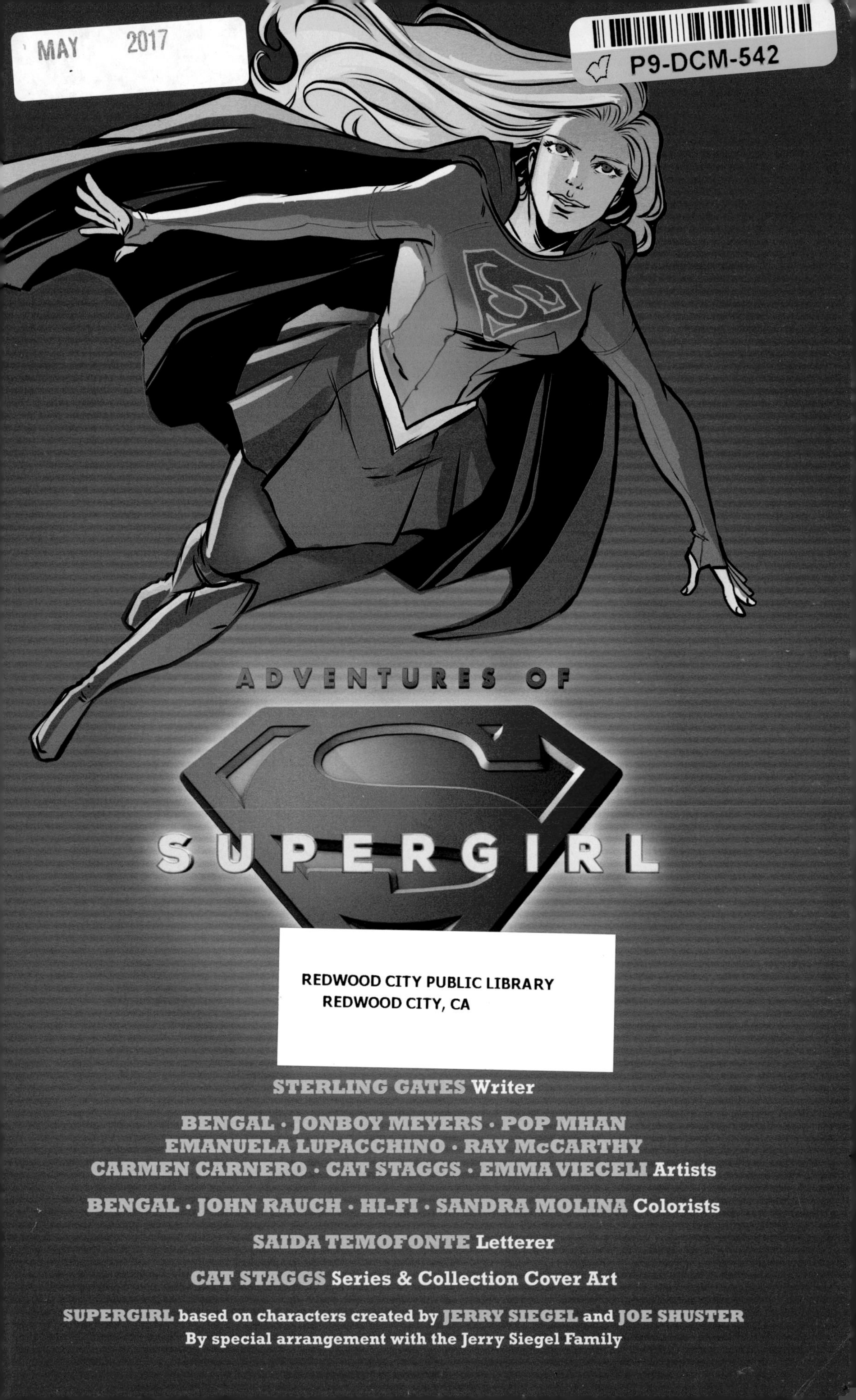

ADVENTURES OF SUPERGIRL

STERLING GATES Writer

BENGAL · JONBOY MEYERS · POP MHAN
EMANUELA LUPACCHINO · RAY McCARTHY
CARMEN CARNERO · CAT STAGGS · EMMA VIECELI Artists

BENGAL · JOHN RAUCH · HI-FI · SANDRA MOLINA Colorists

SAIDA TEMOFONTE Letterer

CAT STAGGS Series & Collection Cover Art

SUPERGIRL based on characters created by **JERRY SIEGEL** and **JOE SHUSTER**
By special arrangement with the Jerry Siegel Family

Kristy Quinn Editor – Original Series
Jessica Chen Associate Editor – Original Series
Jeb Woodard Group Editor – Collected Editions
Liz Erickson Editor – Collected Edition
Steve Cook Design Director – Books
Damian Ryland Publication Design

Bob Harras Senior VP – Editor-in-Chief, DC Comics

Diane Nelson President
Dan DiDio and Jim Lee Co-Publishers
Geoff Johns Chief Creative Officer
Amit Desai Senior VP – Marketing & Global Franchise Management
Nairi Gardiner Senior VP – Finance
Sam Ades VP – Digital Marketing
Bobbie Chase VP – Talent Development
Mark Chiarello Senior VP – Art, Design & Collected Editions
John Cunningham VP – Content Strategy
Anne DePies VP – Strategy Planning & Reporting
Don Falletti VP – Manufacturing Operations
Lawrence Ganem VP – Editorial Administration & Talent Relations
Alison Gill Senior VP – Manufacturing & Operations
Hank Kanalz Senior VP – Editorial Strategy & Administration
Jay Kogan VP – Legal Affairs
Derek Maddalena Senior VP – Sales & Business Development
Jack Mahan VP – Business Affairs
Dan Miron VP – Sales Planning & Trade Development
Nick Napolitano VP – Manufacturing Administration
Carol Roeder VP – Marketing
Eddie Scannell VP – Mass Account & Digital Sales
Courtney Simmons Senior VP – Publicity & Communications
Jim (Ski) Sokolowski VP – Comic Book Specialty & Newsstand Sales
Sandy Yi Senior VP – Global Franchise Management

ADVENTURES OF SUPERGIRL

DC Comics,
2900 West Alameda Ave., Burbank, CA 91505
Printed by RR Donnelley, Salem, VA, USA. 8/19/16. First Printing.
ISBN: 978-1-4012-6265-5

Library of Congress Cataloging-in-Publication Data is available.

PEFC Certified
Printed on paper from
sustainably managed
forests and controlled
sources
PEFC
PEFC/29-31-75   www.pefc.org

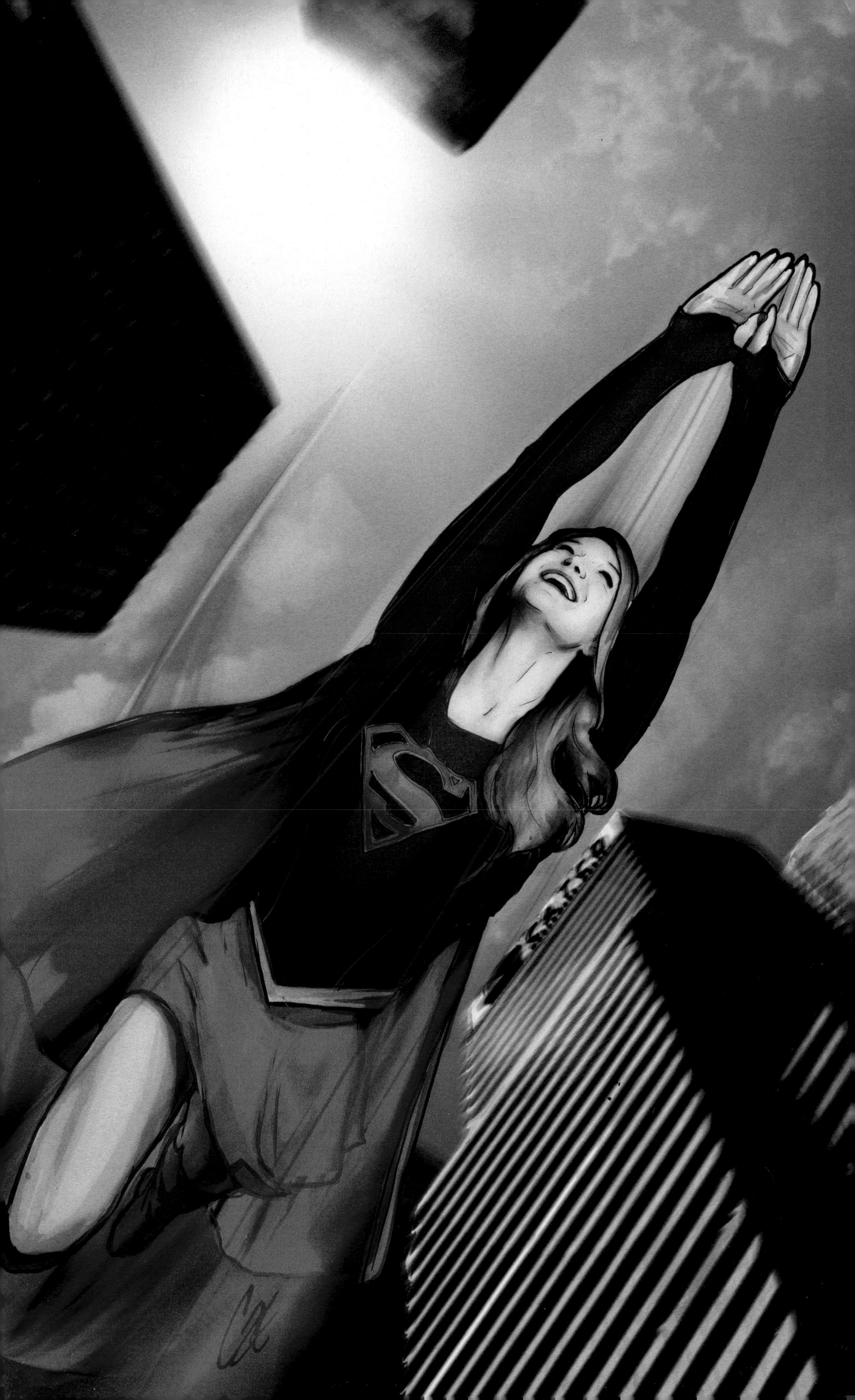

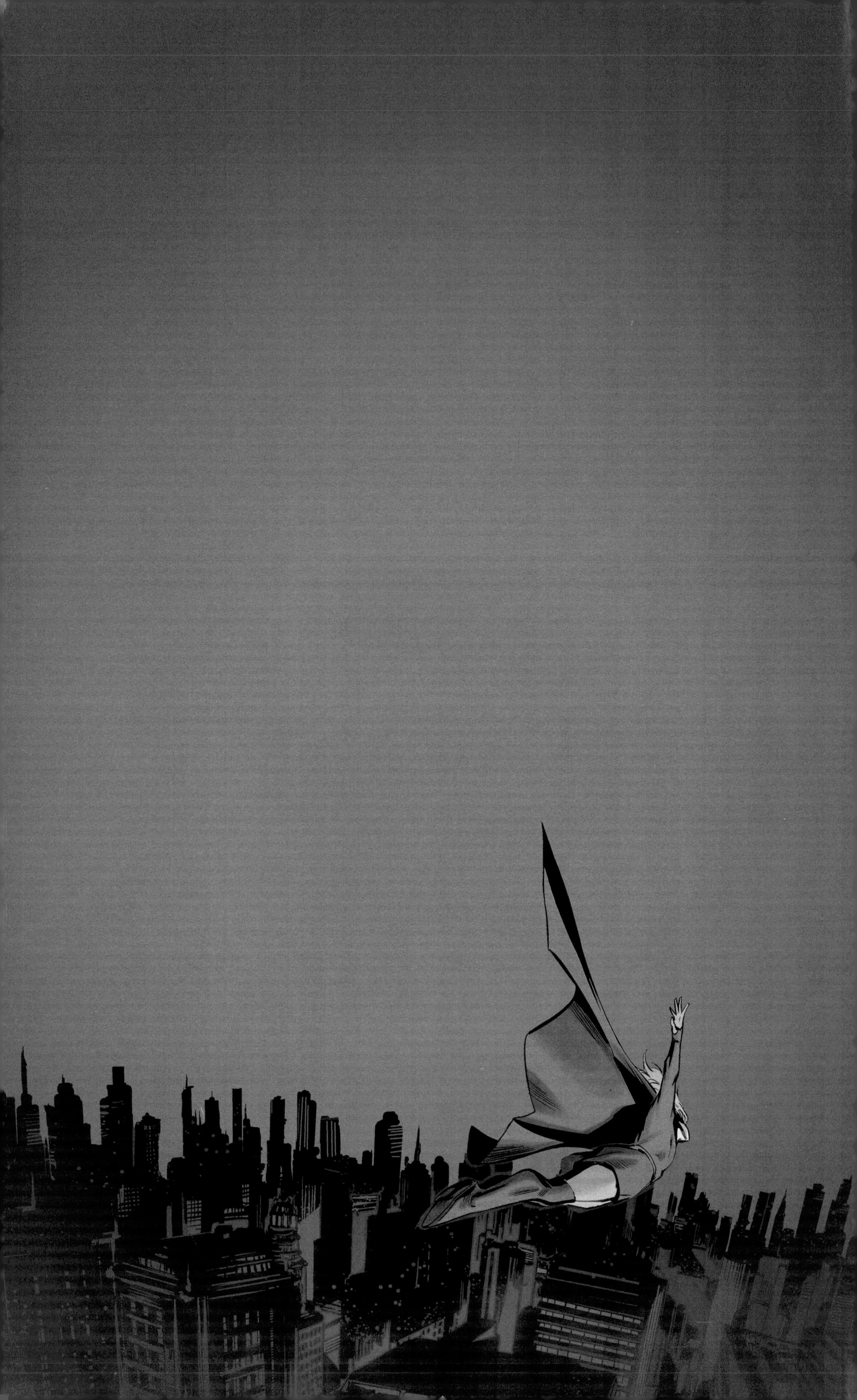

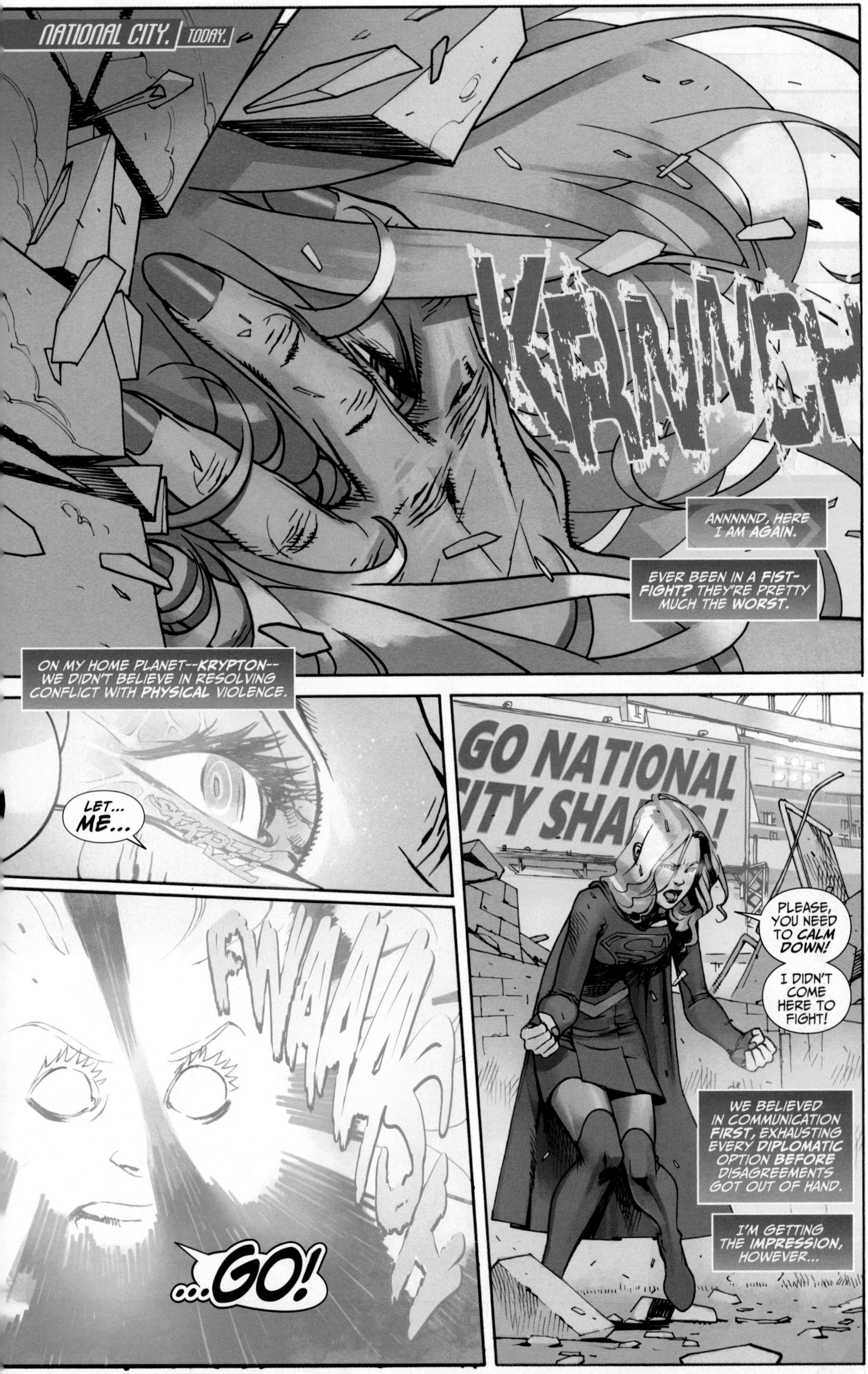
NATIONAL CITY. TODAY.
KRNNCH
ANNNNND, HERE I AM AGAIN.
EVER BEEN IN A FIST-FIGHT? THEY'RE PRETTY MUCH THE WORST.
ON MY HOME PLANET--KRYPTON--WE DIDN'T BELIEVE IN RESOLVING CONFLICT WITH PHYSICAL VIOLENCE.
LET... ME...
GO NATIONAL
ITY SHA !
PLEASE, YOU NEED TO CALM DOWN!
I DIDN'T COME HERE TO FIGHT!
...GO!
WE BELIEVED IN COMMUNICATION FIRST, EXHAUSTING EVERY DIPLOMATIC OPTION BEFORE DISAGREEMENTS GOT OUT OF HAND.
I'M GETTING THE IMPRESSION, HOWEVER...

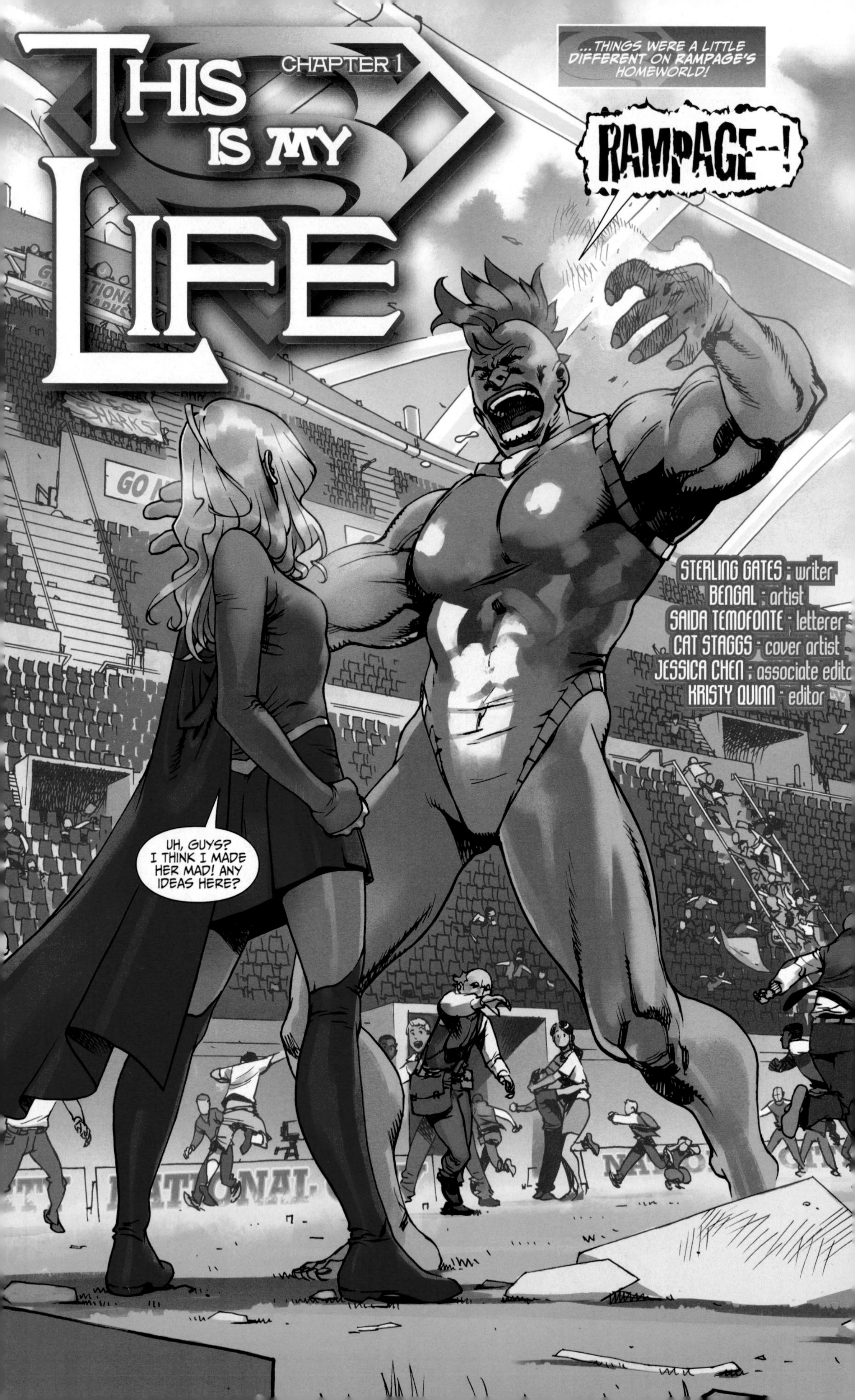
THIS IS MY LIFE
CHAPTER 1
...THINGS WERE A LITTLE DIFFERENT ON RAMPAGE'S HOMEWORLD!
RAMPAGE--!
STERLING GATES : writer
BENGAL : artist
SAIDA TEMOFONTE : letterer
CAT STAGGS : cover artist
JESSICA CHEN : associate edito
KRISTY QUINN : editor
UH, GUYS? I THINK I MADE HER MAD! ANY IDEAS HERE?

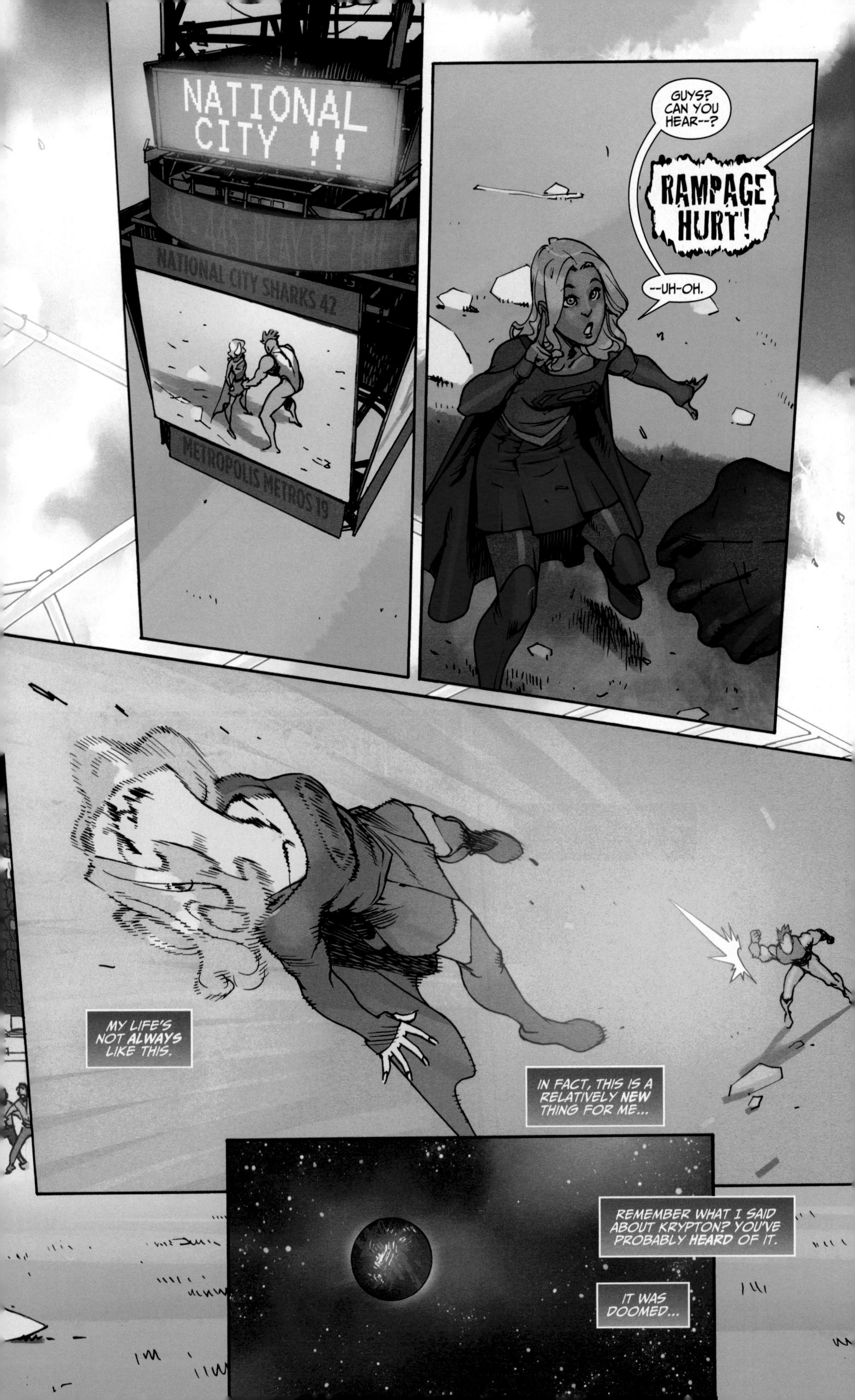
NATIONAL CITY !!
NATIONAL CITY SHARKS 42
METROPOLIS METROS 19
GUYS? CAN YOU HEAR--?
RAMPAGE HURT!
--UH-OH.
MY LIFE'S NOT ALWAYS LIKE THIS.
IN FACT, THIS IS A RELATIVELY NEW THING FOR ME...
REMEMBER WHAT I SAID ABOUT KRYPTON? YOU'VE PROBABLY HEARD OF IT.
IT WAS DOOMED...

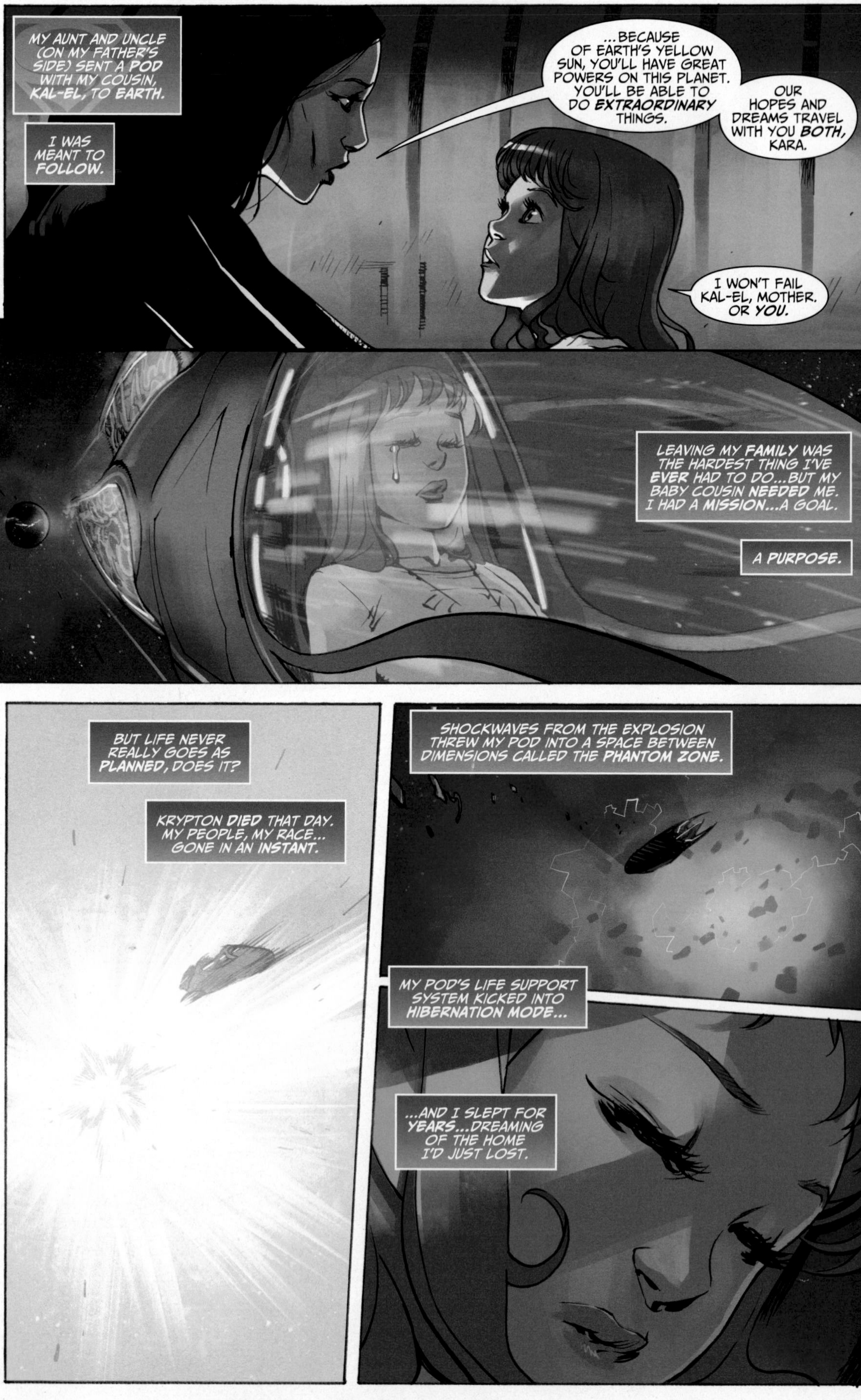
MY AUNT AND UNCLE (ON MY FATHER'S SIDE) SENT A POD WITH MY COUSIN, KAL-EL, TO EARTH.
I WAS MEANT TO FOLLOW.
...BECAUSE OF EARTH'S YELLOW SUN, YOU'LL HAVE GREAT POWERS ON THIS PLANET. YOU'LL BE ABLE TO DO EXTRAORDINARY THINGS.
OUR HOPES AND DREAMS TRAVEL WITH YOU BOTH, KARA.
I WON'T FAIL KAL-EL, MOTHER. OR YOU.
LEAVING MY FAMILY WAS THE HARDEST THING I'VE EVER HAD TO DO...BUT MY BABY COUSIN NEEDED ME. I HAD A MISSION...A GOAL.
A PURPOSE.
BUT LIFE NEVER REALLY GOES AS PLANNED, DOES IT?
KRYPTON DIED THAT DAY. MY PEOPLE, MY RACE... GONE IN AN INSTANT.
SHOCKWAVES FROM THE EXPLOSION THREW MY POD INTO A SPACE BETWEEN DIMENSIONS CALLED THE PHANTOM ZONE.
MY POD'S LIFE SUPPORT SYSTEM KICKED INTO HIBERNATION MODE...
...AND I SLEPT FOR YEARS...DREAMING OF THE HOME I'D JUST LOST.

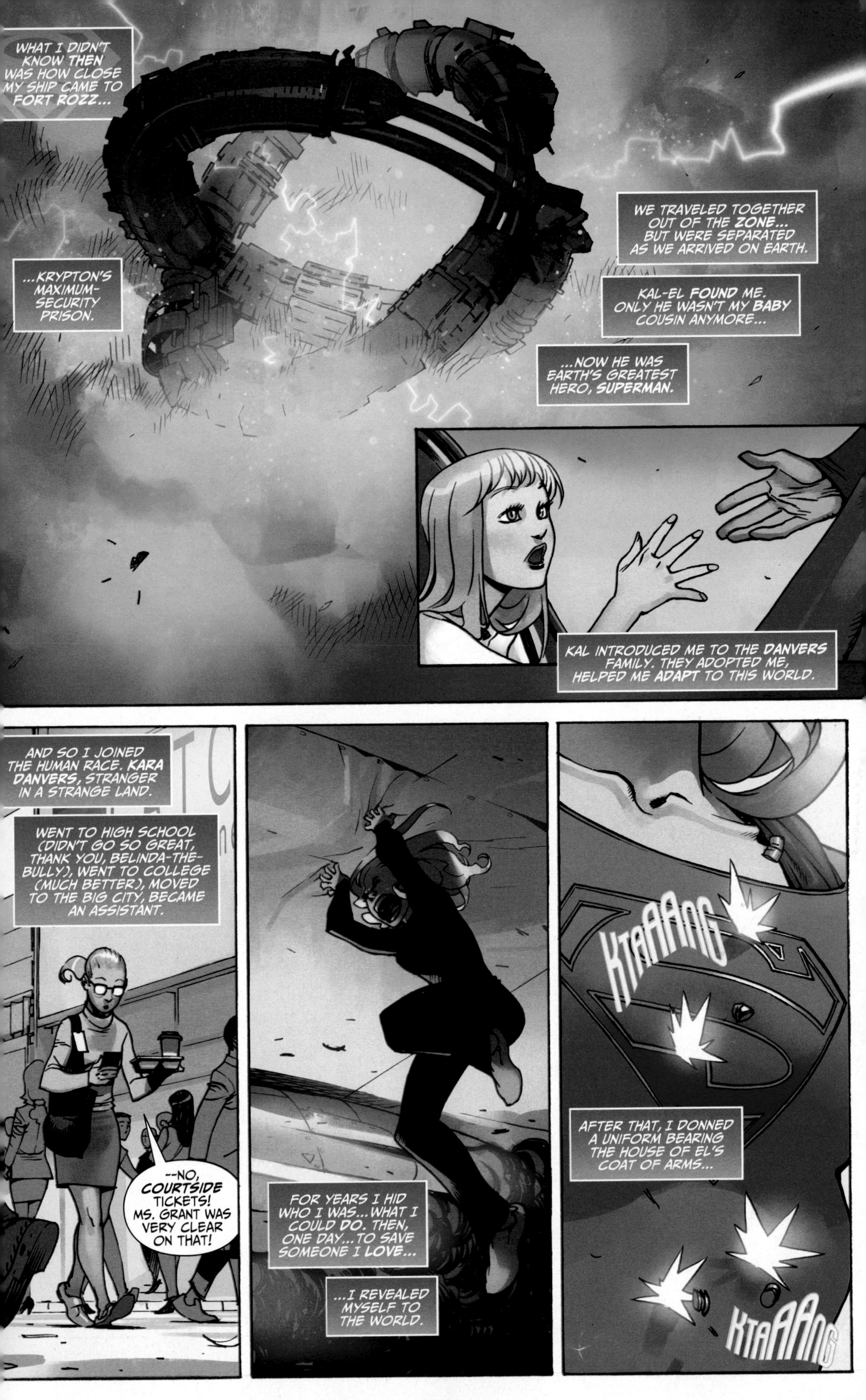
WHAT I DIDN'T KNOW THEN WAS HOW CLOSE MY SHIP CAME TO FORT ROZZ...
...KRYPTON'S MAXIMUM-SECURITY PRISON.
WE TRAVELED TOGETHER OUT OF THE ZONE... BUT WERE SEPARATED AS WE ARRIVED ON EARTH.
KAL-EL FOUND ME. ONLY HE WASN'T MY BABY COUSIN ANYMORE...
...NOW HE WAS EARTH'S GREATEST HERO, SUPERMAN.
KAL INTRODUCED ME TO THE DANVERS FAMILY. THEY ADOPTED ME, HELPED ME ADAPT TO THIS WORLD.
AND SO I JOINED THE HUMAN RACE. KARA DANVERS, STRANGER IN A STRANGE LAND.
WENT TO HIGH SCHOOL (DIDN'T GO SO GREAT, THANK YOU, BELINDA-THE-BULLY), WENT TO COLLEGE (MUCH BETTER), MOVED TO THE BIG CITY, BECAME AN ASSISTANT.
--NO, COURTSIDE TICKETS! MS. GRANT WAS VERY CLEAR ON THAT!
FOR YEARS I HID WHO I WAS...WHAT I COULD DO. THEN, ONE DAY...TO SAVE SOMEONE I LOVE...
...I REVEALED MYSELF TO THE WORLD.
KTAAANG
AFTER THAT, I DONNED A UNIFORM BEARING THE HOUSE OF EL'S COAT OF ARMS...
KTAAANG

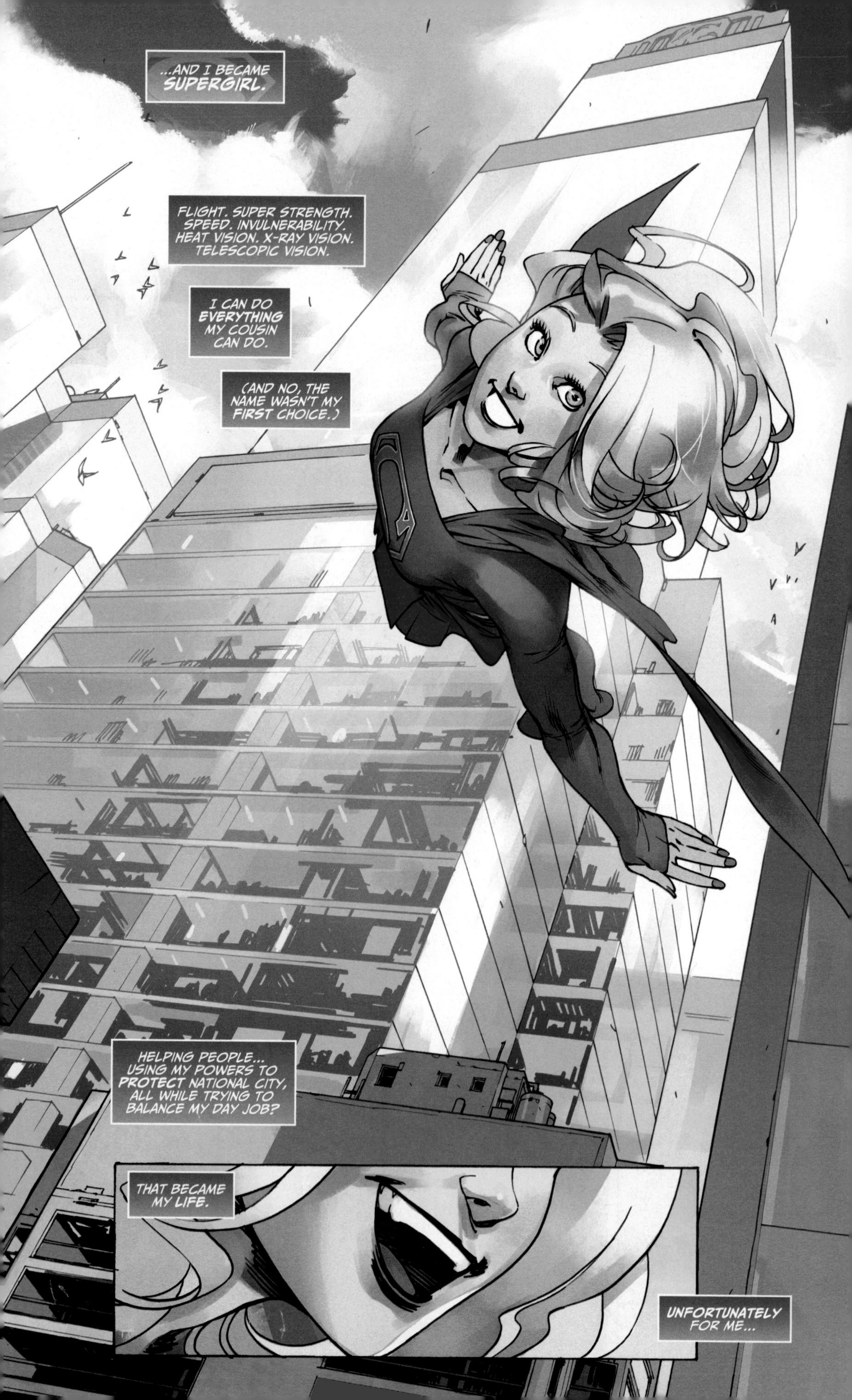
...AND I BECAME SUPERGIRL.
FLIGHT. SUPER STRENGTH. SPEED. INVULNERABILITY. HEAT VISION. X-RAY VISION. TELESCOPIC VISION.
I CAN DO EVERYTHING MY COUSIN CAN DO.
(AND NO, THE NAME WASN'T MY FIRST CHOICE.)
HELPING PEOPLE... USING MY POWERS TO PROTECT NATIONAL CITY, ALL WHILE TRYING TO BALANCE MY DAY JOB?
THAT BECAME MY LIFE.
UNFORTUNATELY FOR ME...

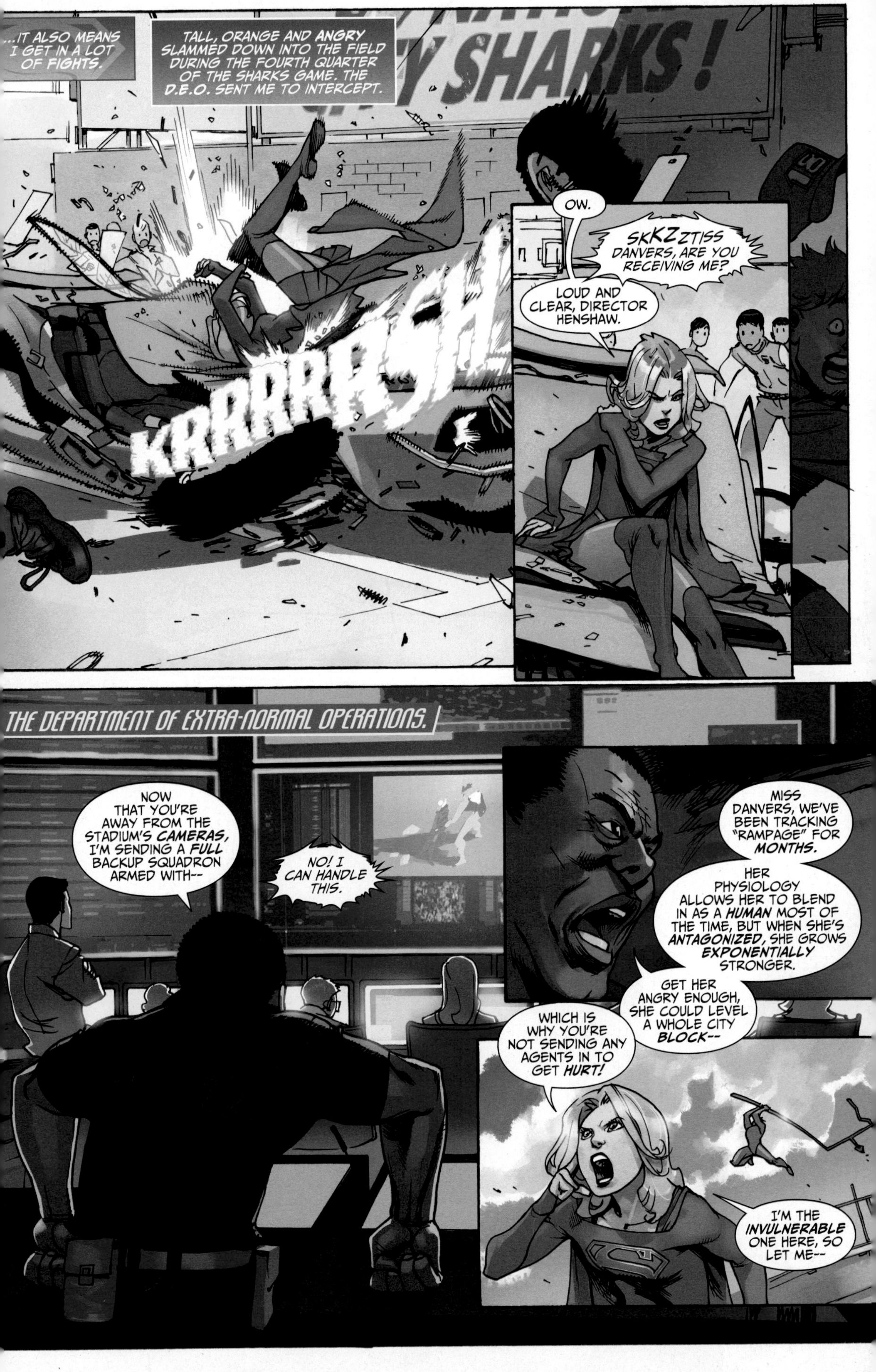

...IT ALSO MEANS I GET IN A LOT OF FIGHTS.
TALL, ORANGE AND ANGRY SLAMMED DOWN INTO THE FIELD DURING THE FOURTH QUARTER OF THE SHARKS GAME. THE D.E.O. SENT ME TO INTERCEPT.
SHARKS!
KRRRRASH!
OW.
SKKZZTISS DANVERS, ARE YOU RECEIVING ME?
LOUD AND CLEAR, DIRECTOR HENSHAW.
THE DEPARTMENT OF EXTRA-NORMAL OPERATIONS.
NOW THAT YOU'RE AWAY FROM THE STADIUM'S CAMERAS, I'M SENDING A FULL BACKUP SQUADRON ARMED WITH--
NO! I CAN HANDLE THIS.
MISS DANVERS, WE'VE BEEN TRACKING "RAMPAGE" FOR MONTHS.
HER PHYSIOLOGY ALLOWS HER TO BLEND IN AS A HUMAN MOST OF THE TIME, BUT WHEN SHE'S ANTAGONIZED, SHE GROWS EXPONENTIALLY STRONGER.
GET HER ANGRY ENOUGH, SHE COULD LEVEL A WHOLE CITY BLOCK--
WHICH IS WHY YOU'RE NOT SENDING ANY AGENTS IN TO GET HURT!
I'M THE INVULNERABLE ONE HERE, SO LET ME--

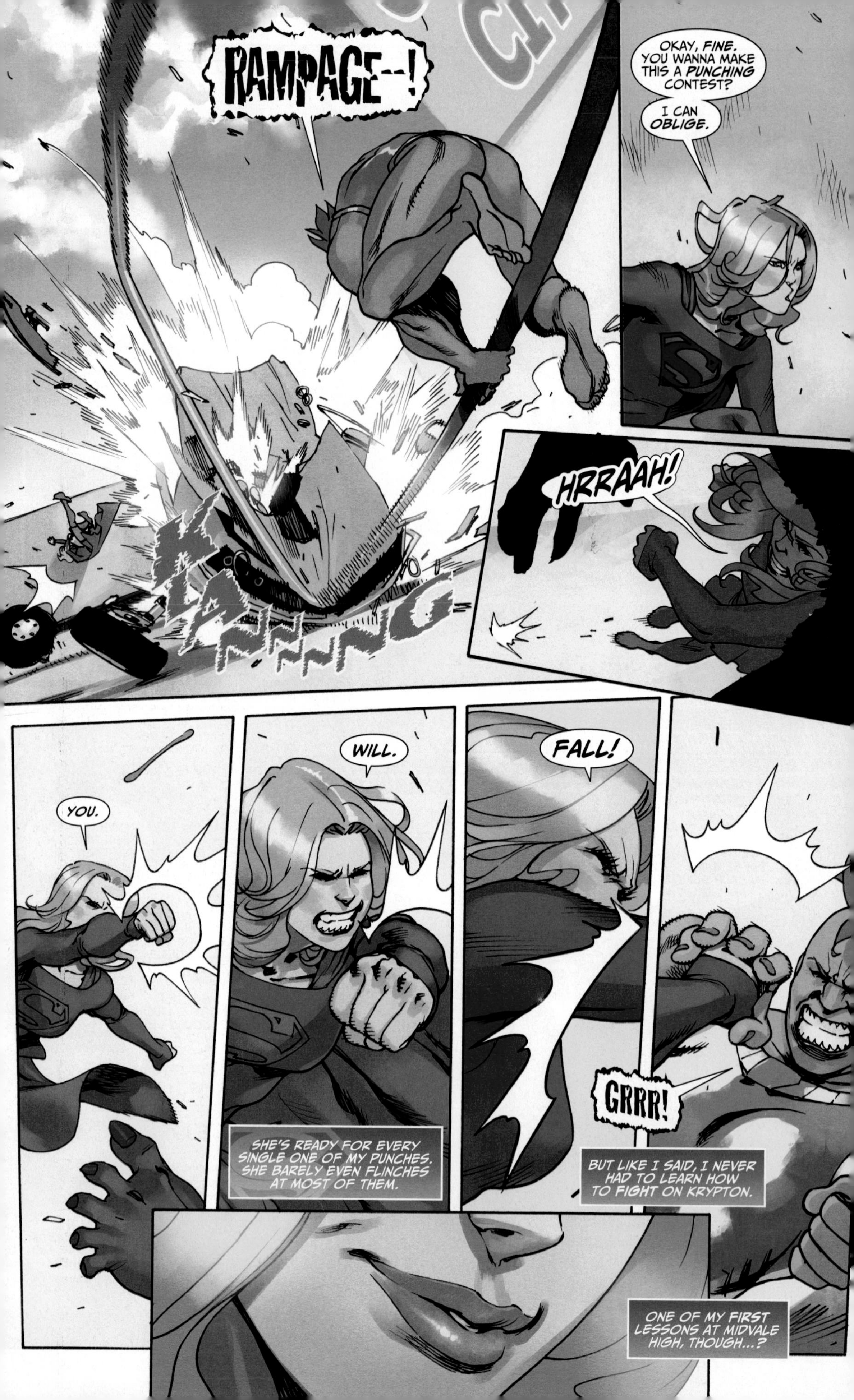

RAMPAGE--!
OKAY, FINE. YOU WANNA MAKE THIS A PUNCHING CONTEST?
I CAN OBLIGE.
HRRAAH!
YOU.
WILL.
SHE'S READY FOR EVERY SINGLE ONE OF MY PUNCHES. SHE BARELY EVEN FLINCHES AT MOST OF THEM.
FALL!
GRRR!
BUT LIKE I SAID, I NEVER HAD TO LEARN HOW TO FIGHT ON KRYPTON.
ONE OF MY FIRST LESSONS AT MIDVALE HIGH, THOUGH...?

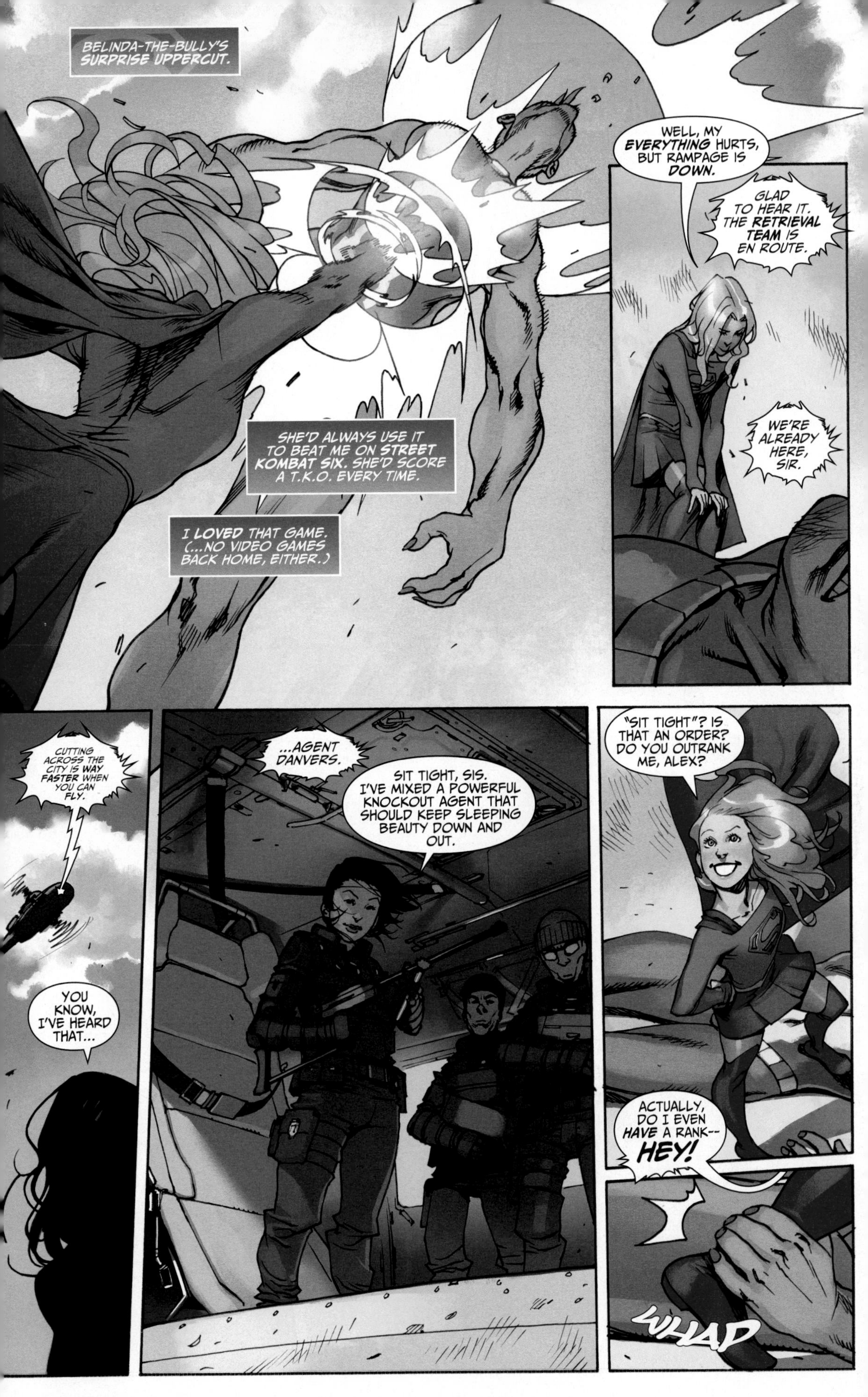
BELINDA-THE-BULLY'S SURPRISE UPPERCUT.
SHE'D ALWAYS USE IT TO BEAT ME ON STREET KOMBAT SIX. SHE'D SCORE A T.K.O. EVERY TIME.
I LOVED THAT GAME. (...NO VIDEO GAMES BACK HOME, EITHER.)
WELL, MY EVERYTHING HURTS, BUT RAMPAGE IS DOWN.
GLAD TO HEAR IT. THE RETRIEVAL TEAM IS EN ROUTE.
WE'RE ALREADY HERE, SIR.
CUTTING ACROSS THE CITY IS WAY FASTER WHEN YOU CAN FLY.
YOU KNOW, I'VE HEARD THAT...
...AGENT DANVERS.
SIT TIGHT, SIS. I'VE MIXED A POWERFUL KNOCKOUT AGENT THAT SHOULD KEEP SLEEPING BEAUTY DOWN AND OUT.
"SIT TIGHT"? IS THAT AN ORDER? DO YOU OUTRANK ME, ALEX?
ACTUALLY, DO I EVEN HAVE A RANK-- HEY!
WHAP

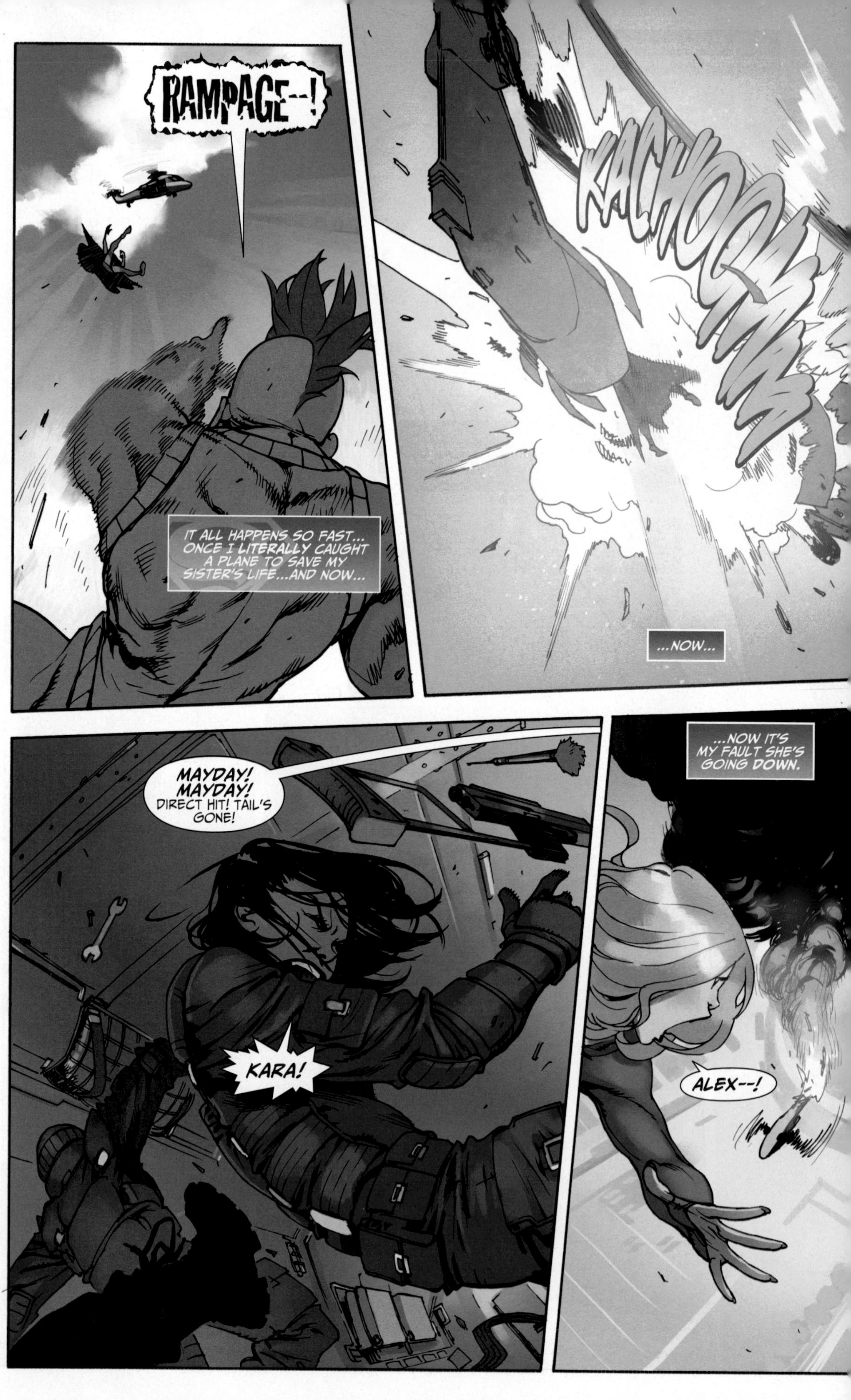
RAMPAGE--!
IT ALL HAPPENS SO FAST... ONCE I LITERALLY CAUGHT A PLANE TO SAVE MY SISTER'S LIFE...AND NOW...
KACHOOOM
...NOW...
MAYDAY! MAYDAY! DIRECT HIT! TAIL'S GONE!
KARA!
...NOW IT'S MY FAULT SHE'S GOING DOWN.
ALEX--!

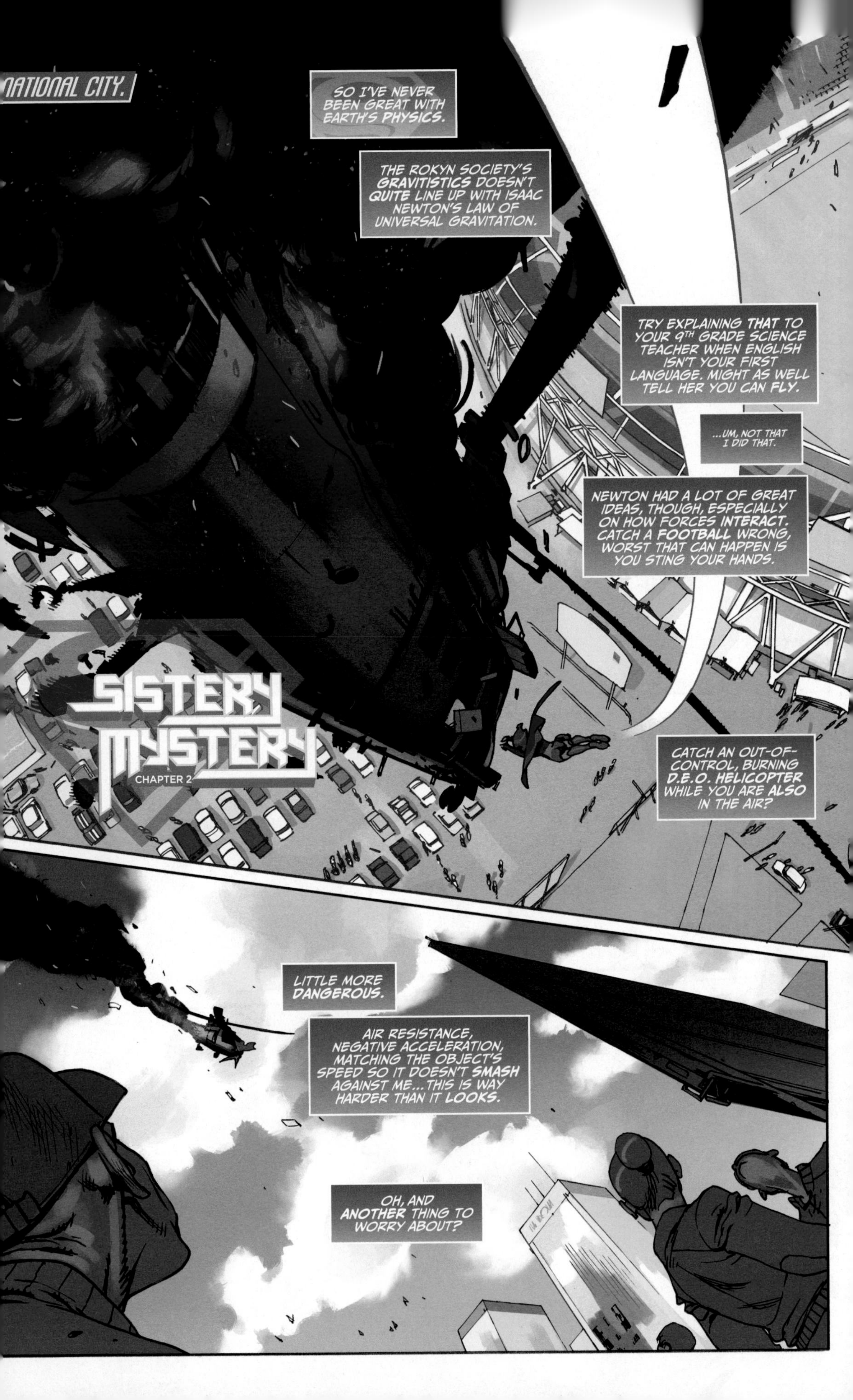
NATIONAL CITY.
SO I'VE NEVER BEEN GREAT WITH EARTH'S PHYSICS.
THE ROKYN SOCIETY'S GRAVITISTICS DOESN'T QUITE LINE UP WITH ISAAC NEWTON'S LAW OF UNIVERSAL GRAVITATION.
TRY EXPLAINING THAT TO YOUR 9TH GRADE SCIENCE TEACHER WHEN ENGLISH ISN'T YOUR FIRST LANGUAGE. MIGHT AS WELL TELL HER YOU CAN FLY.
...UM, NOT THAT I DID THAT.
NEWTON HAD A LOT OF GREAT IDEAS, THOUGH, ESPECIALLY ON HOW FORCES INTERACT. CATCH A FOOTBALL WRONG, WORST THAT CAN HAPPEN IS YOU STING YOUR HANDS.
SISTERY MYSTERY
CHAPTER 2
CATCH AN OUT-OF-CONTROL, BURNING D.E.O. HELICOPTER WHILE YOU ARE ALSO IN THE AIR?
LITTLE MORE DANGEROUS.
AIR RESISTANCE, NEGATIVE ACCELERATION, MATCHING THE OBJECT'S SPEED SO IT DOESN'T SMASH AGAINST ME...THIS IS WAY HARDER THAN IT LOOKS.
OH, AND ANOTHER THING TO WORRY ABOUT?

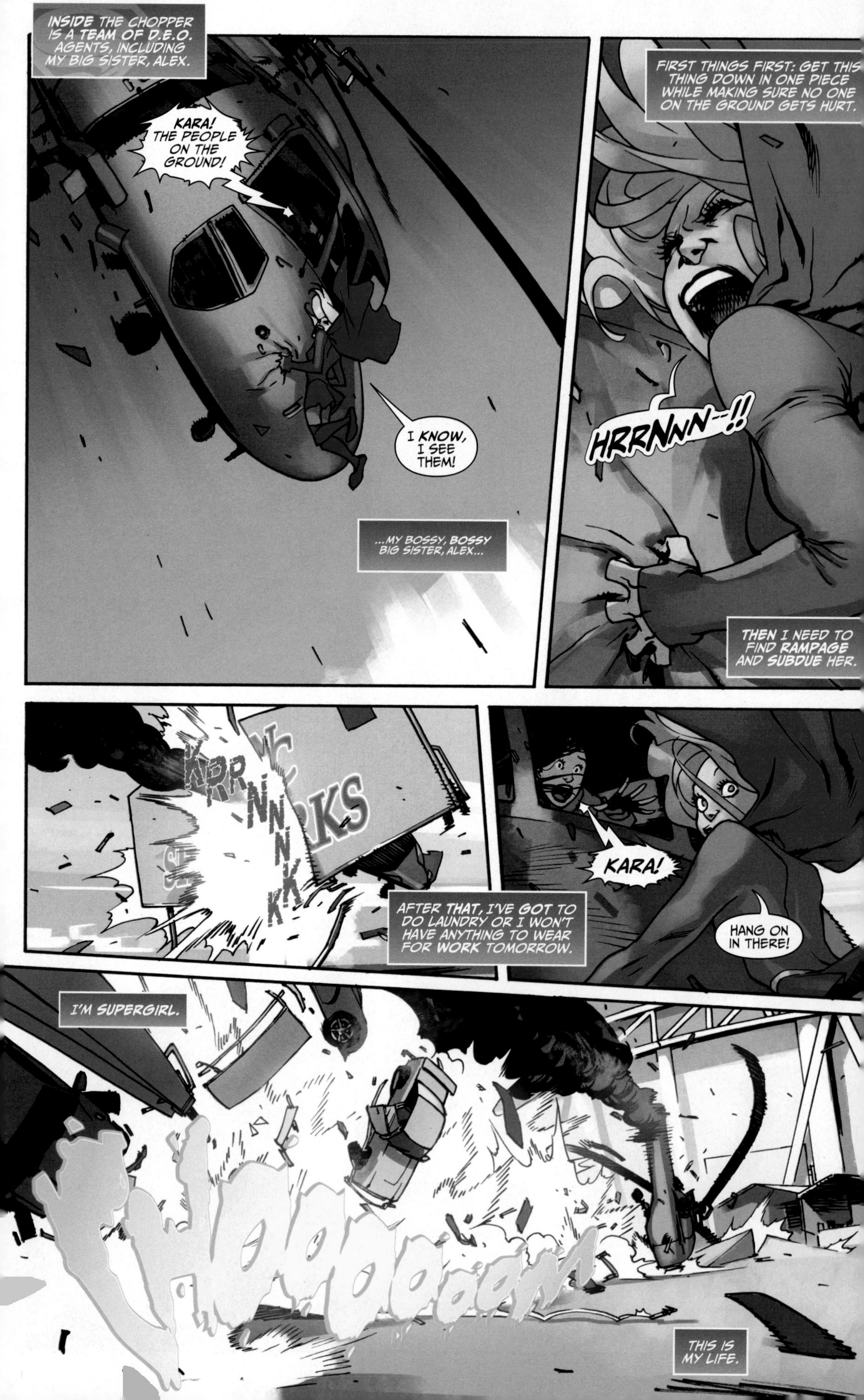
INSIDE THE CHOPPER IS A TEAM OF D.E.O. AGENTS, INCLUDING MY BIG SISTER, ALEX.
KARA! THE PEOPLE ON THE GROUND!
I KNOW, I SEE THEM!
...MY BOSSY, BOSSY BIG SISTER, ALEX...
FIRST THINGS FIRST: GET THIS THING DOWN IN ONE PIECE WHILE MAKING SURE NO ONE ON THE GROUND GETS HURT.
HRRNNN--!!
THEN I NEED TO FIND RAMPAGE AND SUBDUE HER.
KRRNNNKK
AFTER THAT, I'VE GOT TO DO LAUNDRY OR I WON'T HAVE ANYTHING TO WEAR FOR WORK TOMORROW.
KARA!
HANG ON IN THERE!
I'M SUPERGIRL.
THIS IS MY LIFE.

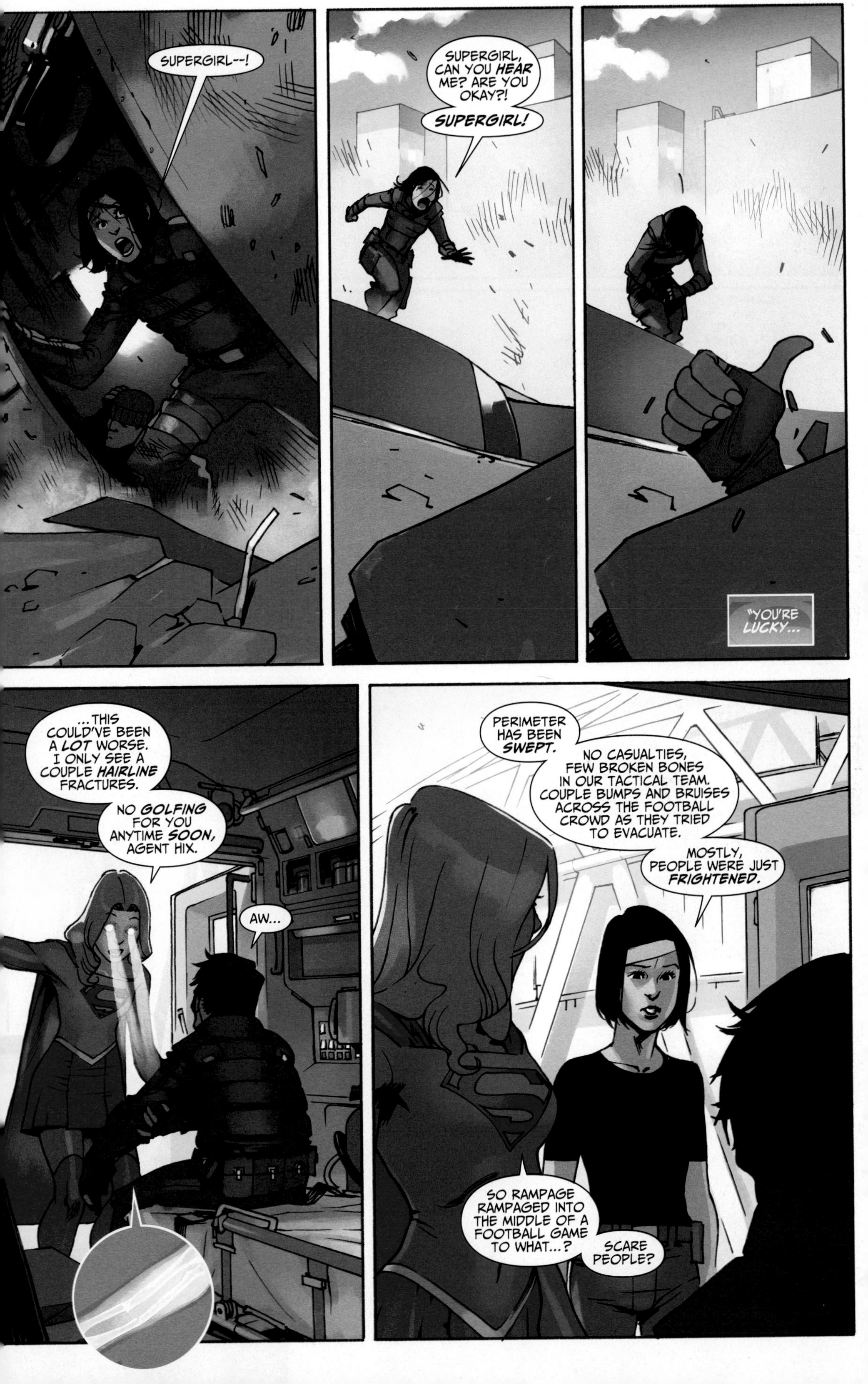
SUPERGIRL--!
SUPERGIRL, CAN YOU HEAR ME? ARE YOU OKAY?!
SUPERGIRL!
"YOU'RE LUCKY...
...THIS COULD'VE BEEN A LOT WORSE. I ONLY SEE A COUPLE HAIRLINE FRACTURES.
NO GOLFING FOR YOU ANYTIME SOON, AGENT HIX.
AW...
PERIMETER HAS BEEN SWEPT.
NO CASUALTIES, FEW BROKEN BONES IN OUR TACTICAL TEAM. COUPLE BUMPS AND BRUISES ACROSS THE FOOTBALL CROWD AS THEY TRIED TO EVACUATE.
MOSTLY, PEOPLE WERE JUST FRIGHTENED.
SO RAMPAGE RAMPAGED INTO THE MIDDLE OF A FOOTBALL GAME TO WHAT...?
SCARE PEOPLE?

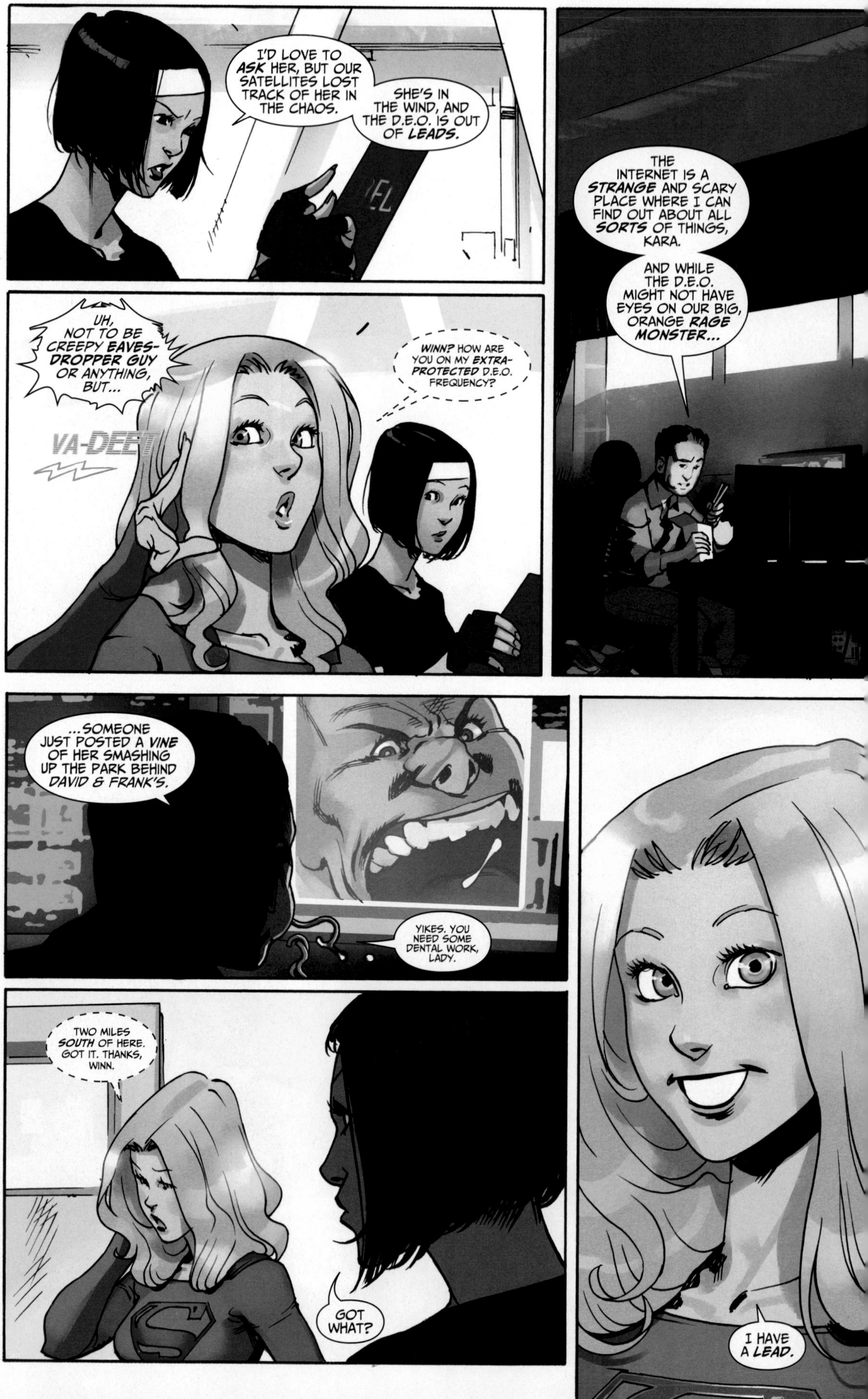

I'D LOVE TO ASK HER, BUT OUR SATELLITES LOST TRACK OF HER IN THE CHAOS.
SHE'S IN THE WIND, AND THE D.E.O. IS OUT OF LEADS.
UH, NOT TO BE CREEPY EAVES-DROPPER GUY OR ANYTHING, BUT...
VA-DEET
WINN? HOW ARE YOU ON MY EXTRA-PROTECTED D.E.O. FREQUENCY?
THE INTERNET IS A STRANGE AND SCARY PLACE WHERE I CAN FIND OUT ABOUT ALL SORTS OF THINGS, KARA.
AND WHILE THE D.E.O. MIGHT NOT HAVE EYES ON OUR BIG, ORANGE RAGE MONSTER...
...SOMEONE JUST POSTED A VINE OF HER SMASHING UP THE PARK BEHIND DAVID & FRANK'S.
YIKES. YOU NEED SOME DENTAL WORK, LADY.
TWO MILES SOUTH OF HERE. GOT IT. THANKS, WINN.
GOT WHAT?
I HAVE A LEAD.

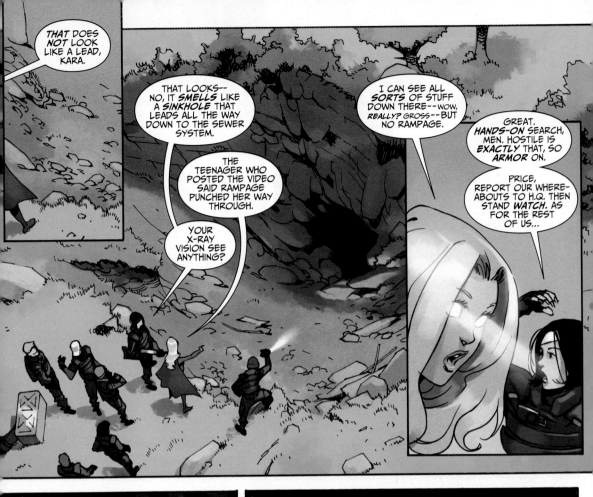

THAT DOES *NOT* LOOK LIKE A LEAD, KARA.

THAT LOOKS-- NO, IT *SMELLS* LIKE A *SINKHOLE* THAT LEADS ALL THE WAY DOWN TO THE SEWER SYSTEM.

THE TEENAGER WHO POSTED THE VIDEO SAID RAMPAGE PUNCHED HER WAY THROUGH.

YOUR *X-RAY* VISION SEE ANYTHING?

I CAN SEE ALL *SORTS* OF STUFF DOWN THERE--WOW, *REALLY?* GROSS--BUT NO RAMPAGE.

GREAT. *HANDS-ON* SEARCH, MEN. HOSTILE IS *EXACTLY* THAT, SO *ARMOR* ON.

PRICE, REPORT OUR WHERE-ABOUTS TO H.Q. THEN STAND *WATCH.* AS FOR THE REST OF US...

"...IT'S ONCE MORE INTO THE *MUCK.*"

STANDARD SEARCH PATTERN. BRAVO, TAKE ALTERNATING TUNNELS.

YOU RUN INTO TROUBLE, CALL OUT THE CLOSEST INTERSECTION *BEFORE* YOU ENGAGE THE HOSTILE. OVER.

AFFIRMATIVE, TACTICAL LEADER, OVER.

...WHAT?

NOTHING...

HUH UNH, YOU WERE JUST DOING THAT *SISTER STARE* THING YOU'VE DONE SINCE WE WERE KIDS. SO...*WHAT?*

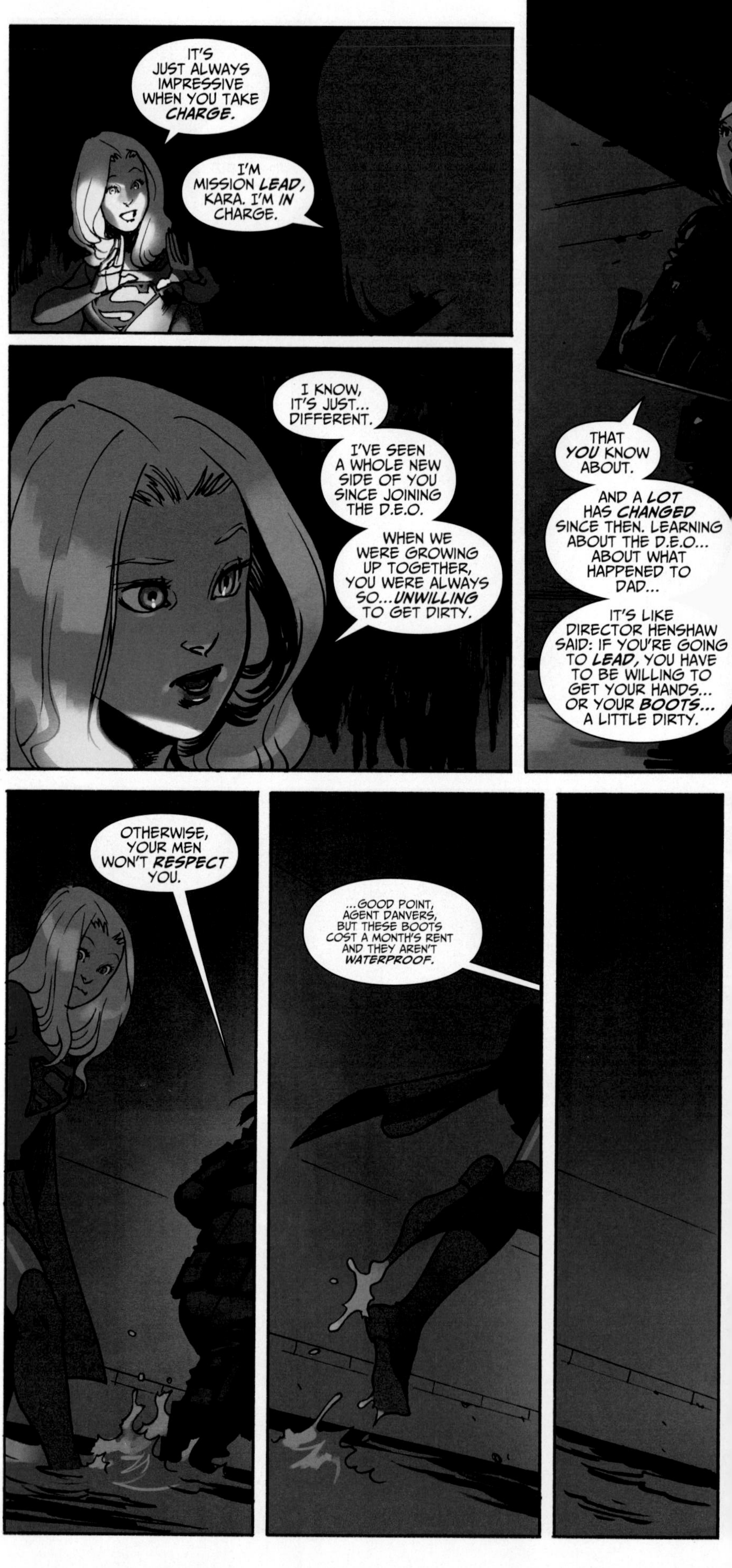
IT'S JUST ALWAYS IMPRESSIVE WHEN YOU TAKE CHARGE.
I'M MISSION LEAD, KARA. I'M IN CHARGE.
I KNOW, IT'S JUST... DIFFERENT.
I'VE SEEN A WHOLE NEW SIDE OF YOU SINCE JOINING THE D.E.O.
WHEN WE WERE GROWING UP TOGETHER, YOU WERE ALWAYS SO...UNWILLING TO GET DIRTY.
THAT YOU KNOW ABOUT.
AND A LOT HAS CHANGED SINCE THEN. LEARNING ABOUT THE D.E.O... ABOUT WHAT HAPPENED TO DAD...
IT'S LIKE DIRECTOR HENSHAW SAID: IF YOU'RE GOING TO LEAD, YOU HAVE TO BE WILLING TO GET YOUR HANDS... OR YOUR BOOTS... A LITTLE DIRTY.
OTHERWISE, YOUR MEN WON'T RESPECT YOU.
...GOOD POINT, AGENT DANVERS, BUT THESE BOOTS COST A MONTH'S RENT AND THEY AREN'T WATERPROOF.

NOT *REALLY.* WHEN WE FOUGHT IN THE STADIUM, I COULD HEAR RAMPAGE'S *HEARTBEAT.* DEEP AND FAST THUDS, LIKE A *BASS DRUM.*

DOWN HERE, IT'S HARD TO HEAR *ANYTHING* BUT THE *WATER.*

THIS IS *HOPELESS.*

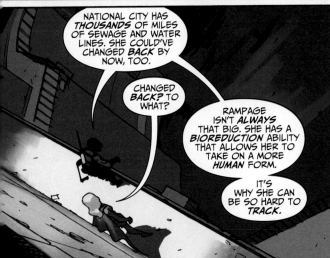

NATIONAL CITY HAS *THOUSANDS* OF MILES OF SEWAGE AND WATER LINES. SHE COULD'VE CHANGED *BACK* BY NOW, TOO.

CHANGED *BACK?* TO WHAT?

RAMPAGE ISN'T *ALWAYS* THAT BIG. SHE HAS A *BIOREDUCTION* ABILITY THAT ALLOWS HER TO TAKE ON A MORE *HUMAN* FORM.

IT'S WHY SHE CAN BE SO HARD TO *TRACK.*

Y'KNOW, IT *JUST* STRUCK ME I DIDN'T GET A *FULL* BRIEFING BEFORE I WAS *SENT* TO THAT STADIUM.

YOU SEEM TO KNOW A *LOT* ABOUT THIS ALIEN, ALEX...

...AND IT SEEMS LIKE THERE'S A LOT YOU'RE NOT *TELLING* ME.

THERE'S A LOT YOU DON'T KNOW ABOUT MY TIME AT THE D.E.O.

RAMPAGE AND HER SISTER WERE ONE OF MY FIRST D.E.O. ASSIGNMENTS...

...AND IT'S BECAUSE OF *ME* THAT RAMPAGE'S SISTER *DIED.*

DIED? ALEX, WHAT DO YOU MEAN--

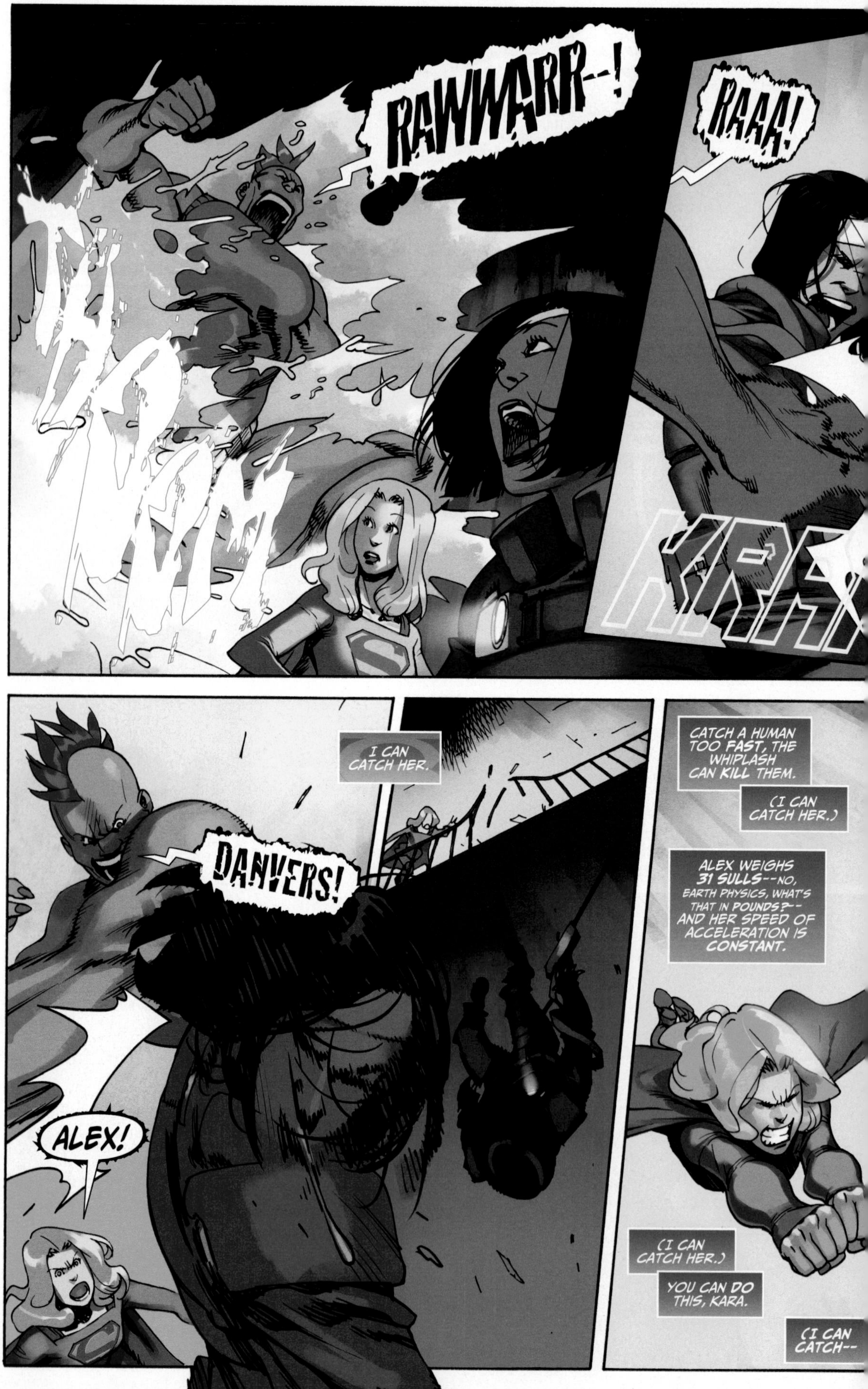
RAWWARR--!
RAAA!
KRAK
I CAN CATCH HER.
DANVERS!
ALEX!
CATCH A HUMAN TOO FAST, THE WHIPLASH CAN KILL THEM.
(I CAN CATCH HER.)
ALEX WEIGHS 31 SULLS--NO, EARTH PHYSICS, WHAT'S THAT IN POUNDS?--AND HER SPEED OF ACCELERATION IS CONSTANT.
(I CAN CATCH HER.)
YOU CAN DO THIS, KARA.
(I CAN CATCH--

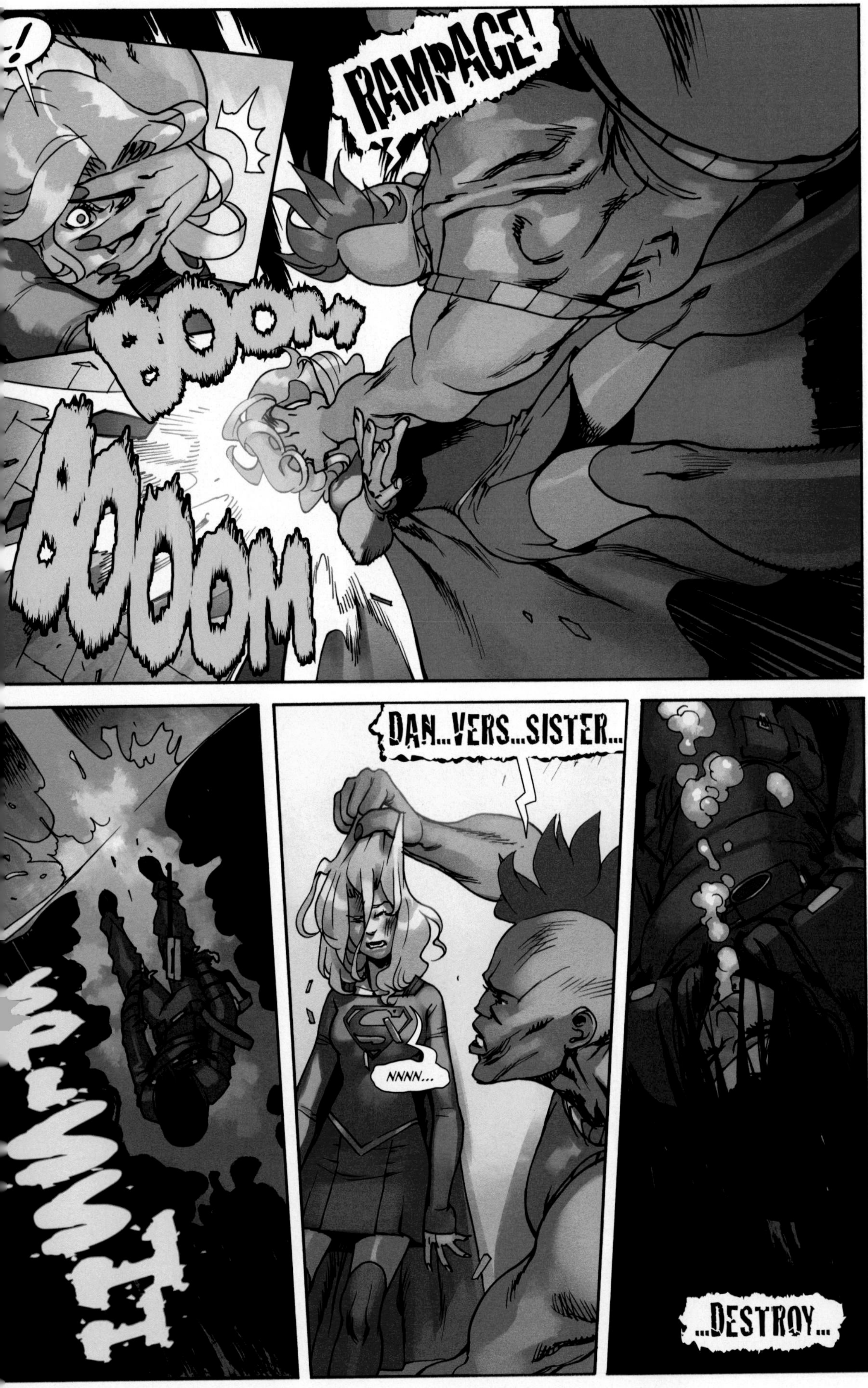
!
RAMPAGE!
BOOOM
BOOOM
DAN...VERS...SISTER...
NNNN...
...DESTROY...

...DESTROY ALL DANVERS.
PLP
PLP
PLP
PLMPP
PLMPP
PLMPP
OKAY, RAMPAGE...
...MY TURN.

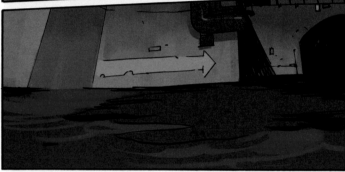

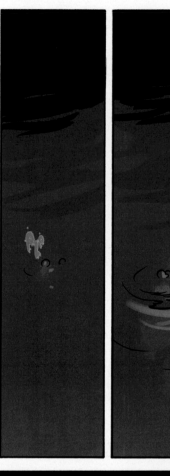

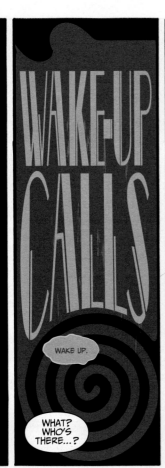

SUPERGIRL... WAKE UP...

...WHAT...?

WAKE-UP CALLS

WAKE UP.

WHAT? WHO'S THERE...?

WAKE UP, SUPERGIRL!

PEOPLE ASSUME MY FIRST NIGHT ON EARTH WAS *HARD.*

A 13-YEAR-OLD *REFUGEE* LEFT WITH VIRTUAL STRANGERS ON AN ALIEN PLANET?

=HHHHH=

MOST PEOPLE WOULD FREAK.

BUT REALLY, THAT NIGHT WAS *EASY.* AS SOON AS ALEX SHOWED ME MY ROOM, I WAS *OUT.*

FALLING *ASLEEP* WASN'T THE HARD PART...

WHERE...?

...THE HARD PART CAME THE *NEXT* DAY, WHEN I WOKE UP IN THAT *STRANGE PLACE...*

HELLO, SUPERGIRL.

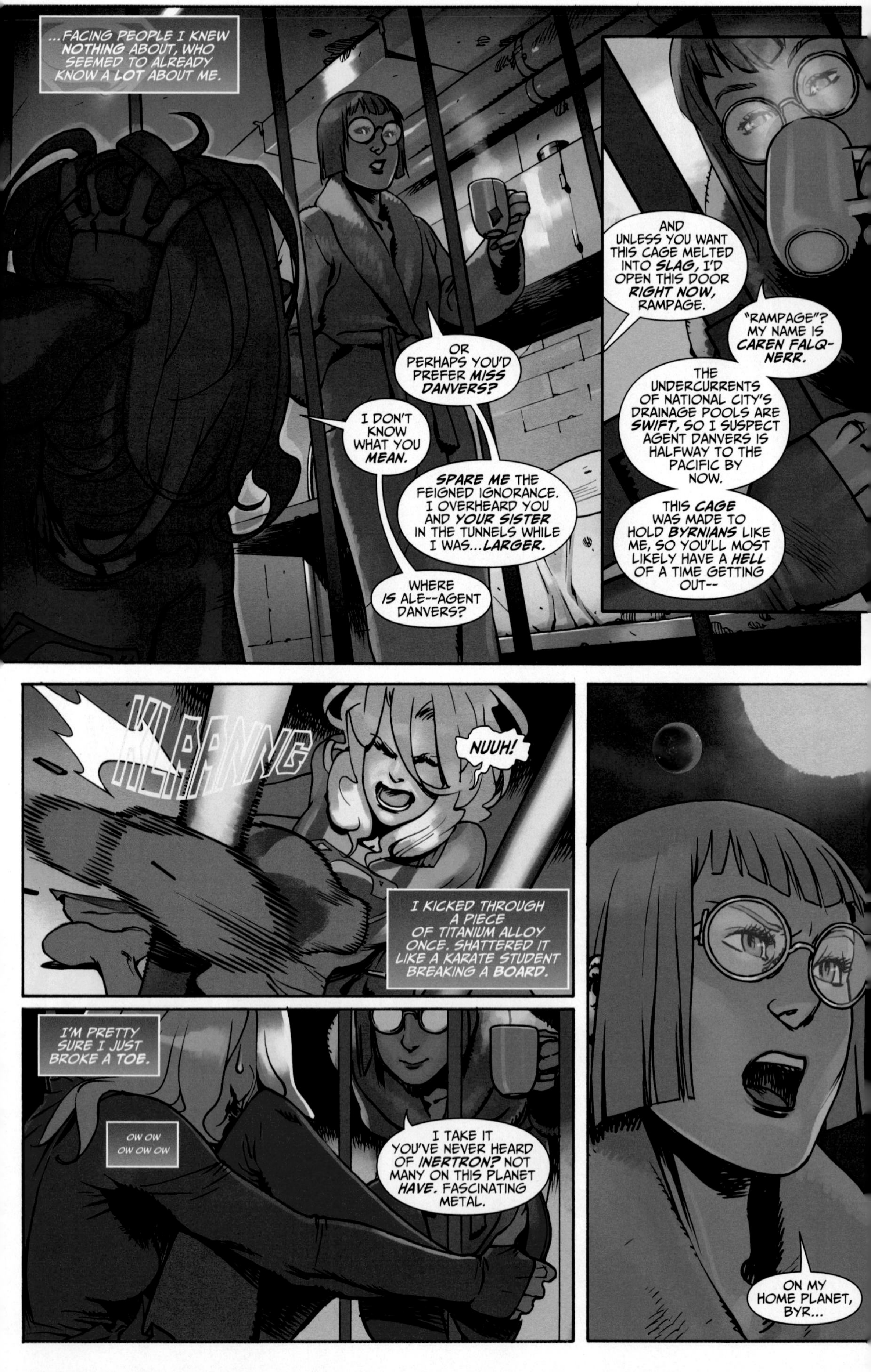
...FACING PEOPLE I KNEW NOTHING ABOUT, WHO SEEMED TO ALREADY KNOW A LOT ABOUT ME.
OR PERHAPS YOU'D PREFER MISS DANVERS?
I DON'T KNOW WHAT YOU MEAN.
SPARE ME THE FEIGNED IGNORANCE. I OVERHEARD YOU AND YOUR SISTER IN THE TUNNELS WHILE I WAS...LARGER.
WHERE IS ALE--AGENT DANVERS?
AND UNLESS YOU WANT THIS CAGE MELTED INTO SLAG, I'D OPEN THIS DOOR RIGHT NOW, RAMPAGE.
"RAMPAGE"? MY NAME IS CAREN FALQ-NERR.
THE UNDERCURRENTS OF NATIONAL CITY'S DRAINAGE POOLS ARE SWIFT, SO I SUSPECT AGENT DANVERS IS HALFWAY TO THE PACIFIC BY NOW.
THIS CAGE WAS MADE TO HOLD BYRNIANS LIKE ME, SO YOU'LL MOST LIKELY HAVE A HELL OF A TIME GETTING OUT--
KLANNG
NUUH!
I KICKED THROUGH A PIECE OF TITANIUM ALLOY ONCE. SHATTERED IT LIKE A KARATE STUDENT BREAKING A BOARD.
I'M PRETTY SURE I JUST BROKE A TOE.
OW OW
OW OW OW
I TAKE IT YOU'VE NEVER HEARD OF INERTRON? NOT MANY ON THIS PLANET HAVE. FASCINATING METAL.
ON MY HOME PLANET, BYR...

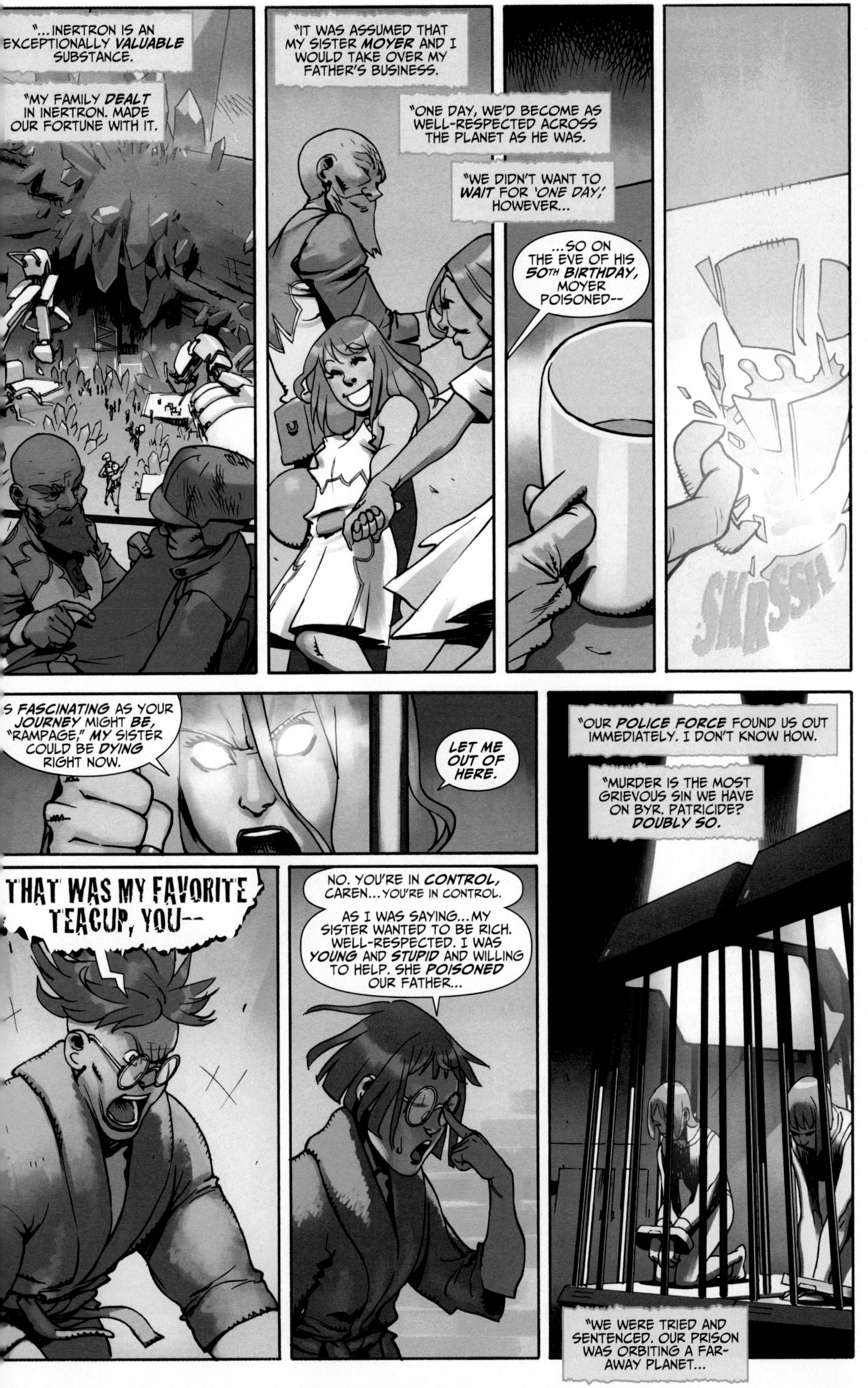
"...INERTRON IS AN EXCEPTIONALLY VALUABLE SUBSTANCE.
"MY FAMILY DEALT IN INERTRON. MADE OUR FORTUNE WITH IT.
"IT WAS ASSUMED THAT MY SISTER MOYER AND I WOULD TAKE OVER MY FATHER'S BUSINESS.
"ONE DAY, WE'D BECOME AS WELL-RESPECTED ACROSS THE PLANET AS HE WAS.
"WE DIDN'T WANT TO WAIT FOR 'ONE DAY,' HOWEVER...
...SO ON THE EVE OF HIS 50TH BIRTHDAY, MOYER POISONED--
SKRSSH
S FASCINATING AS YOUR JOURNEY MIGHT BE, "RAMPAGE," MY SISTER COULD BE DYING RIGHT NOW.
LET ME OUT OF HERE.
"OUR POLICE FORCE FOUND US OUT IMMEDIATELY. I DON'T KNOW HOW.
"MURDER IS THE MOST GRIEVOUS SIN WE HAVE ON BYR. PATRICIDE? DOUBLY SO.
THAT WAS MY FAVORITE TEACUP, YOU--
NO. YOU'RE IN CONTROL, CAREN... YOU'RE IN CONTROL.
AS I WAS SAYING... MY SISTER WANTED TO BE RICH. WELL-RESPECTED. I WAS YOUNG AND STUPID AND WILLING TO HELP. SHE POISONED OUR FATHER...
"WE WERE TRIED AND SENTENCED. OUR PRISON WAS ORBITING A FAR-AWAY PLANET...

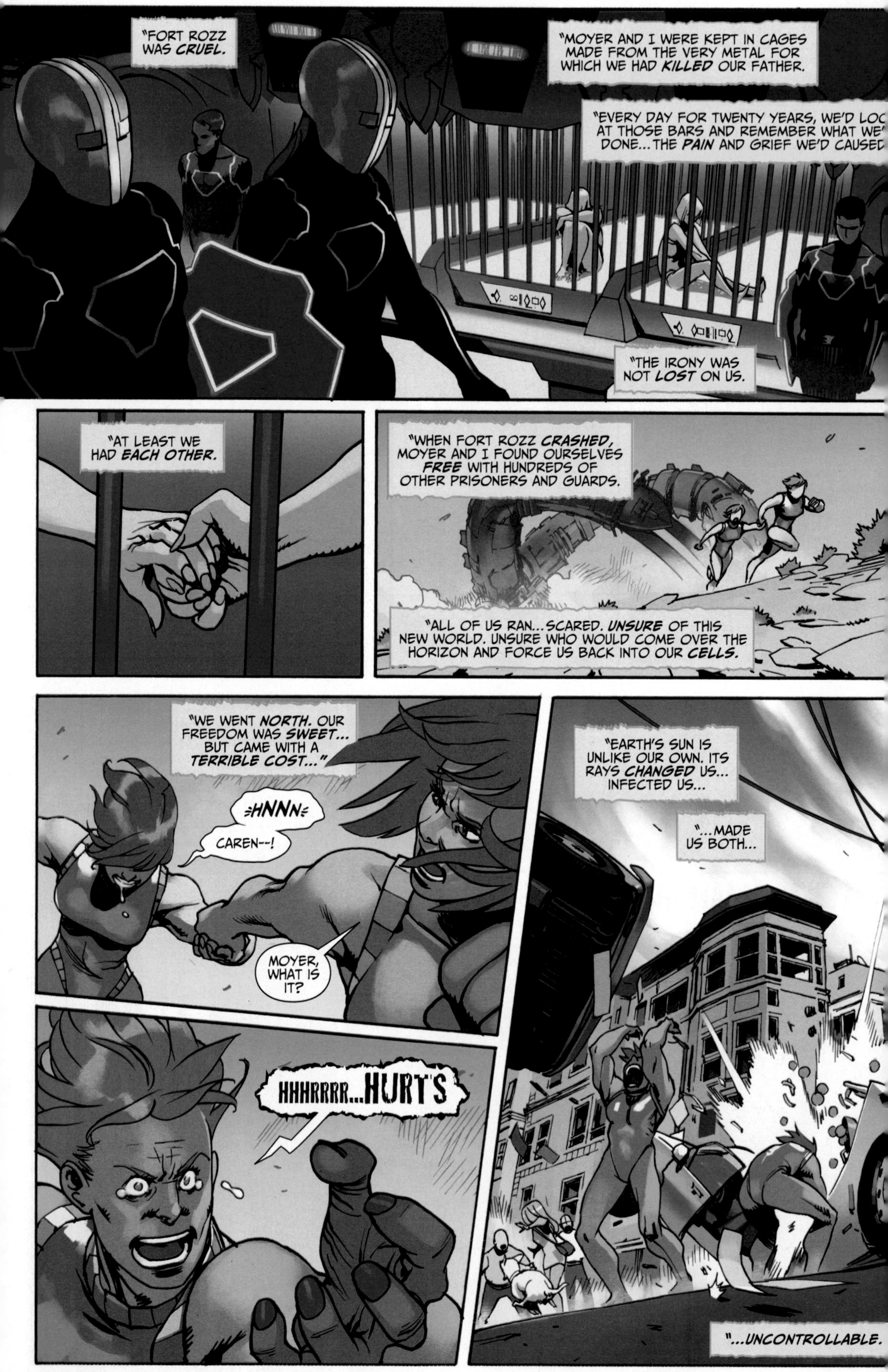
"FORT ROZZ WAS CRUEL.
"MOYER AND I WERE KEPT IN CAGES MADE FROM THE VERY METAL FOR WHICH WE HAD KILLED OUR FATHER.
"EVERY DAY FOR TWENTY YEARS, WE'D LOO AT THOSE BARS AND REMEMBER WHAT WE' DONE... THE PAIN AND GRIEF WE'D CAUSED
"THE IRONY WAS NOT LOST ON US.
"AT LEAST WE HAD EACH OTHER.
"WHEN FORT ROZZ CRASHED, MOYER AND I FOUND OURSELVES FREE WITH HUNDREDS OF OTHER PRISONERS AND GUARDS.
"ALL OF US RAN... SCARED. UNSURE OF THIS NEW WORLD. UNSURE WHO WOULD COME OVER THE HORIZON AND FORCE US BACK INTO OUR CELLS.
"WE WENT NORTH. OUR FREEDOM WAS SWEET... BUT CAME WITH A TERRIBLE COST..."
HNNN
CAREN--!
MOYER, WHAT IS IT?
HHHRRRR...HURTS
"EARTH'S SUN IS UNLIKE OUR OWN. ITS RAYS CHANGED US... INFECTED US...
"...MADE US BOTH...
"...UNCONTROLLABLE.

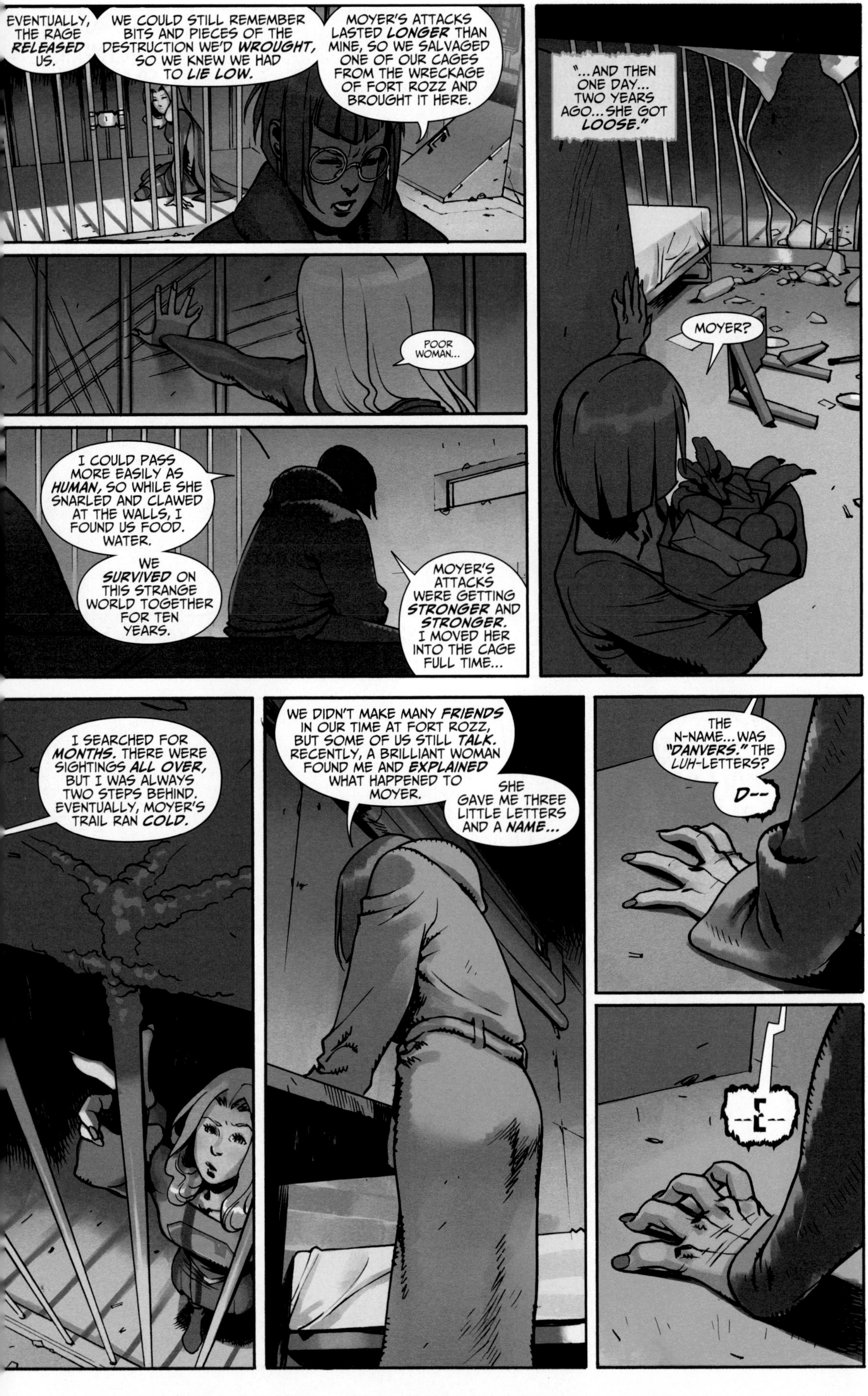

EVENTUALLY, THE RAGE RELEASED US.
WE COULD STILL REMEMBER BITS AND PIECES OF THE DESTRUCTION WE'D WROUGHT, SO WE KNEW WE HAD TO LIE LOW.
MOYER'S ATTACKS LASTED LONGER THAN MINE, SO WE SALVAGED ONE OF OUR CAGES FROM THE WRECKAGE OF FORT ROZZ AND BROUGHT IT HERE.
POOR WOMAN...
I COULD PASS MORE EASILY AS HUMAN, SO WHILE SHE SNARLED AND CLAWED AT THE WALLS, I FOUND US FOOD. WATER.
WE SURVIVED ON THIS STRANGE WORLD TOGETHER FOR TEN YEARS.
MOYER'S ATTACKS WERE GETTING STRONGER AND STRONGER. I MOVED HER INTO THE CAGE FULL TIME...
"...AND THEN ONE DAY... TWO YEARS AGO... SHE GOT LOOSE."
MOYER?
I SEARCHED FOR MONTHS. THERE WERE SIGHTINGS ALL OVER, BUT I WAS ALWAYS TWO STEPS BEHIND. EVENTUALLY, MOYER'S TRAIL RAN COLD.
WE DIDN'T MAKE MANY FRIENDS IN OUR TIME AT FORT ROZZ, BUT SOME OF US STILL TALK. RECENTLY, A BRILLIANT WOMAN FOUND ME AND EXPLAINED WHAT HAPPENED TO MOYER.
SHE GAVE ME THREE LITTLE LETTERS AND A NAME...
THE N-NAME... WAS "DANVERS." THE LUH-LETTERS?
D--
--E--

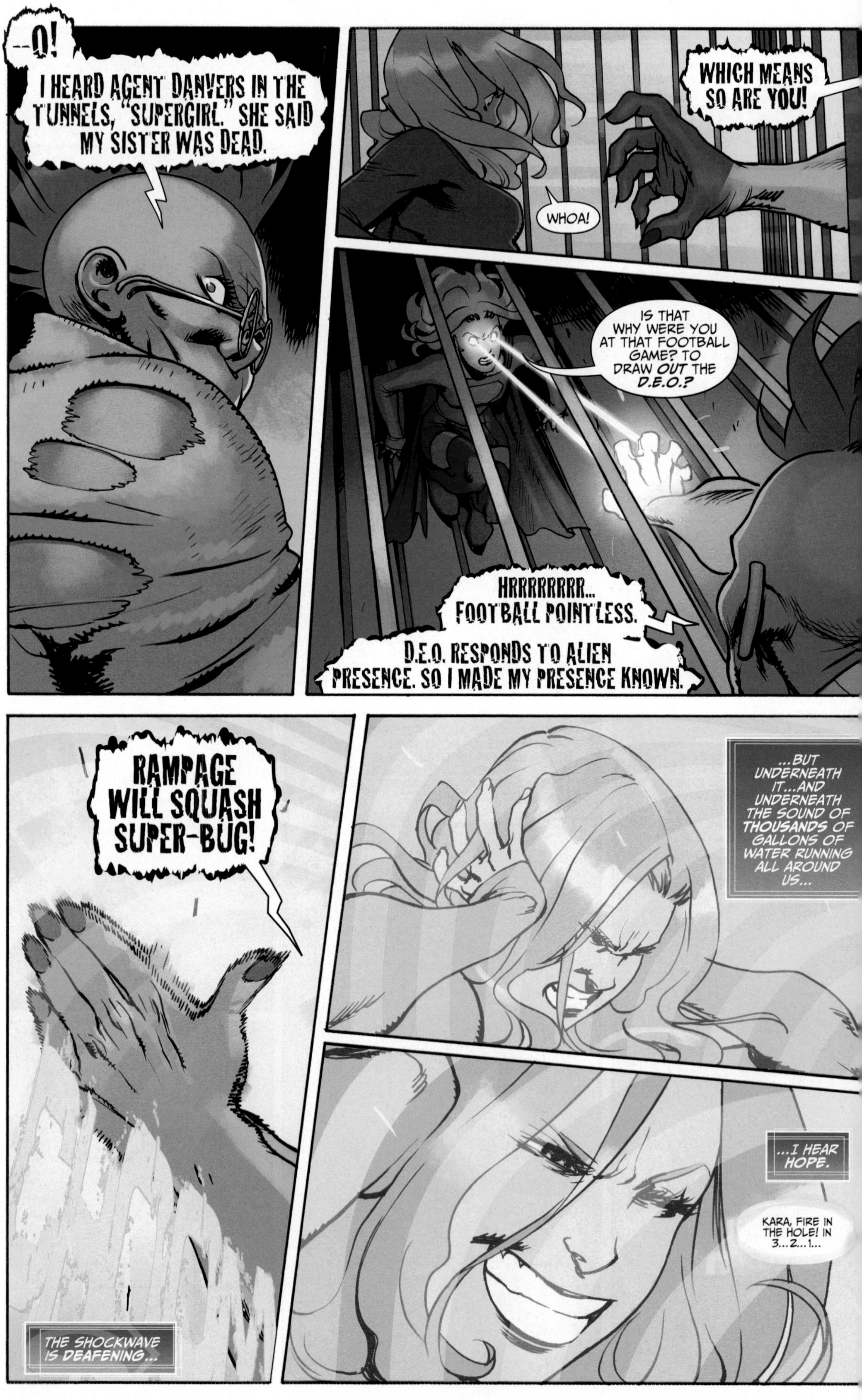
--O!
I HEARD AGENT DANVERS IN THE TUNNELS, "SUPERGIRL." SHE SAID MY SISTER WAS DEAD.
WHICH MEANS SO ARE YOU!
WHOA!
IS THAT WHY WERE YOU AT THAT FOOTBALL GAME? TO DRAW OUT THE D.E.O.?
HRRRRRRRR... FOOTBALL POINTLESS.
D.E.O. RESPONDS TO ALIEN PRESENCE. SO I MADE MY PRESENCE KNOWN.
RAMPAGE WILL SQUASH SUPER-BUG!
THE SHOCKWAVE IS DEAFENING...
...BUT UNDERNEATH IT...AND UNDERNEATH THE SOUND OF THOUSANDS OF GALLONS OF WATER RUNNING ALL AROUND US...
...I HEAR HOPE.
KARA, FIRE IN THE HOLE! IN 3...2...1...

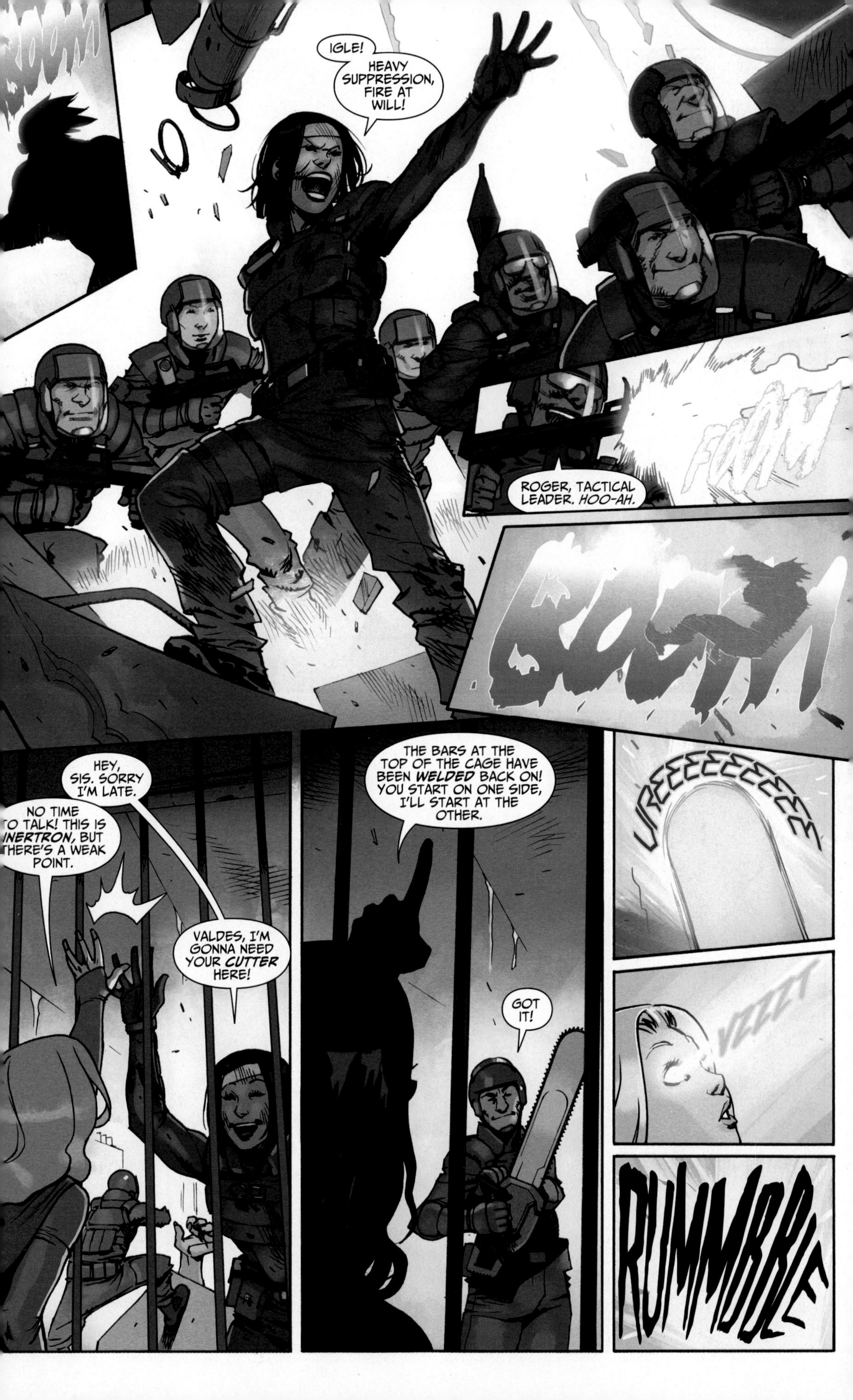
BOOM
IGLE! HEAVY SUPPRESSION, FIRE AT WILL!
FOOM
ROGER, TACTICAL LEADER. HOO-AH.
BOOM
HEY, SIS. SORRY I'M LATE.
NO TIME TO TALK! THIS IS INERTRON, BUT THERE'S A WEAK POINT.
VALDES, I'M GONNA NEED YOUR CUTTER HERE!
THE BARS AT THE TOP OF THE CAGE HAVE BEEN WELDED BACK ON! YOU START ON ONE SIDE, I'LL START AT THE OTHER.
GOT IT!
UREEEEEEEEEE
VZZZT
RUMMBBLE

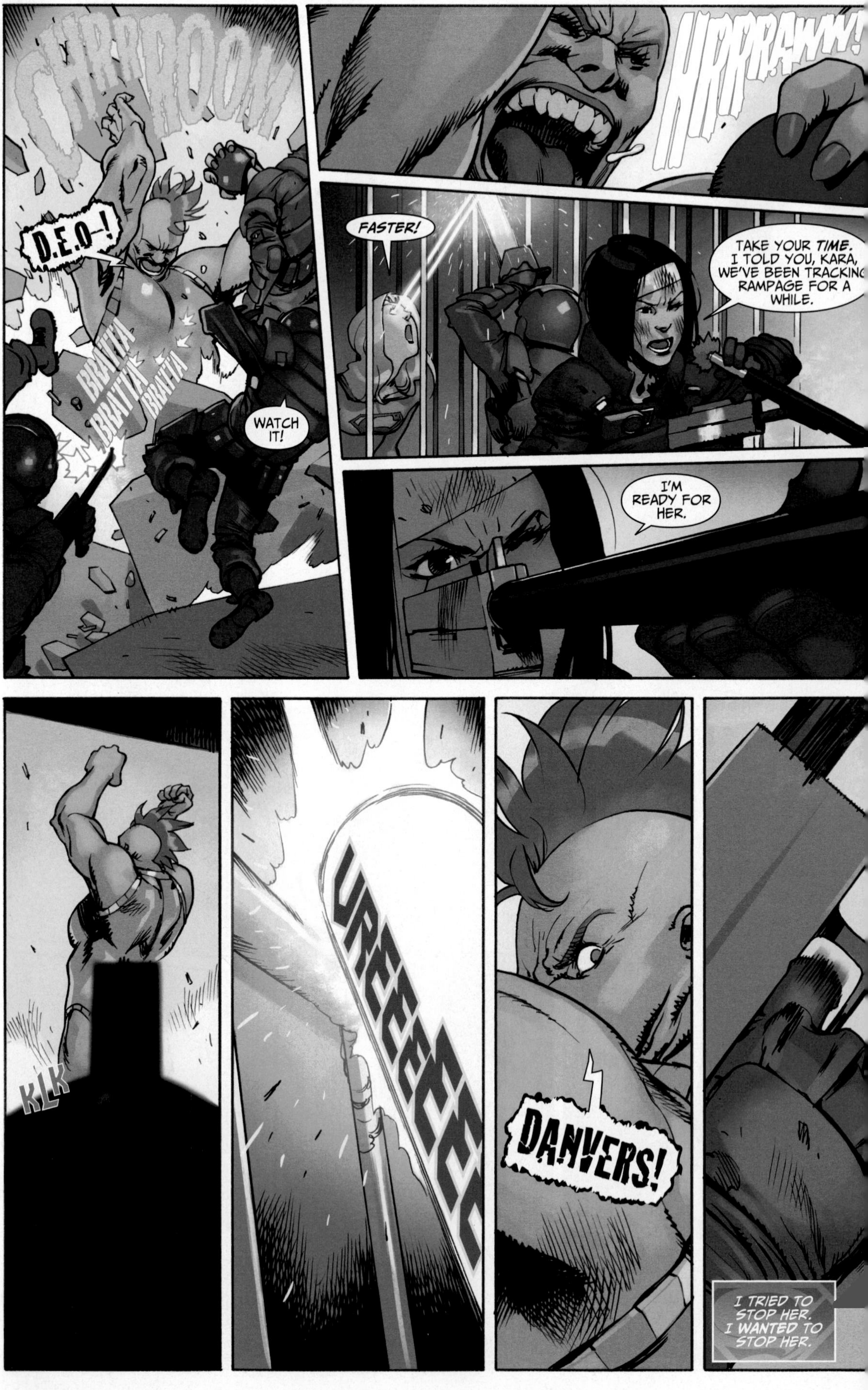
CHRRROOM!
D.E.O-!
BRATTA BRATTA BRATTA
WATCH IT!
HRRRAWW!
FASTER!
TAKE YOUR TIME. I TOLD YOU, KARA, WE'VE BEEN TRACKING RAMPAGE FOR A WHILE.
I'M READY FOR HER.
KLK
DANVERS!
I TRIED TO STOP HER. I WANTED TO STOP HER.

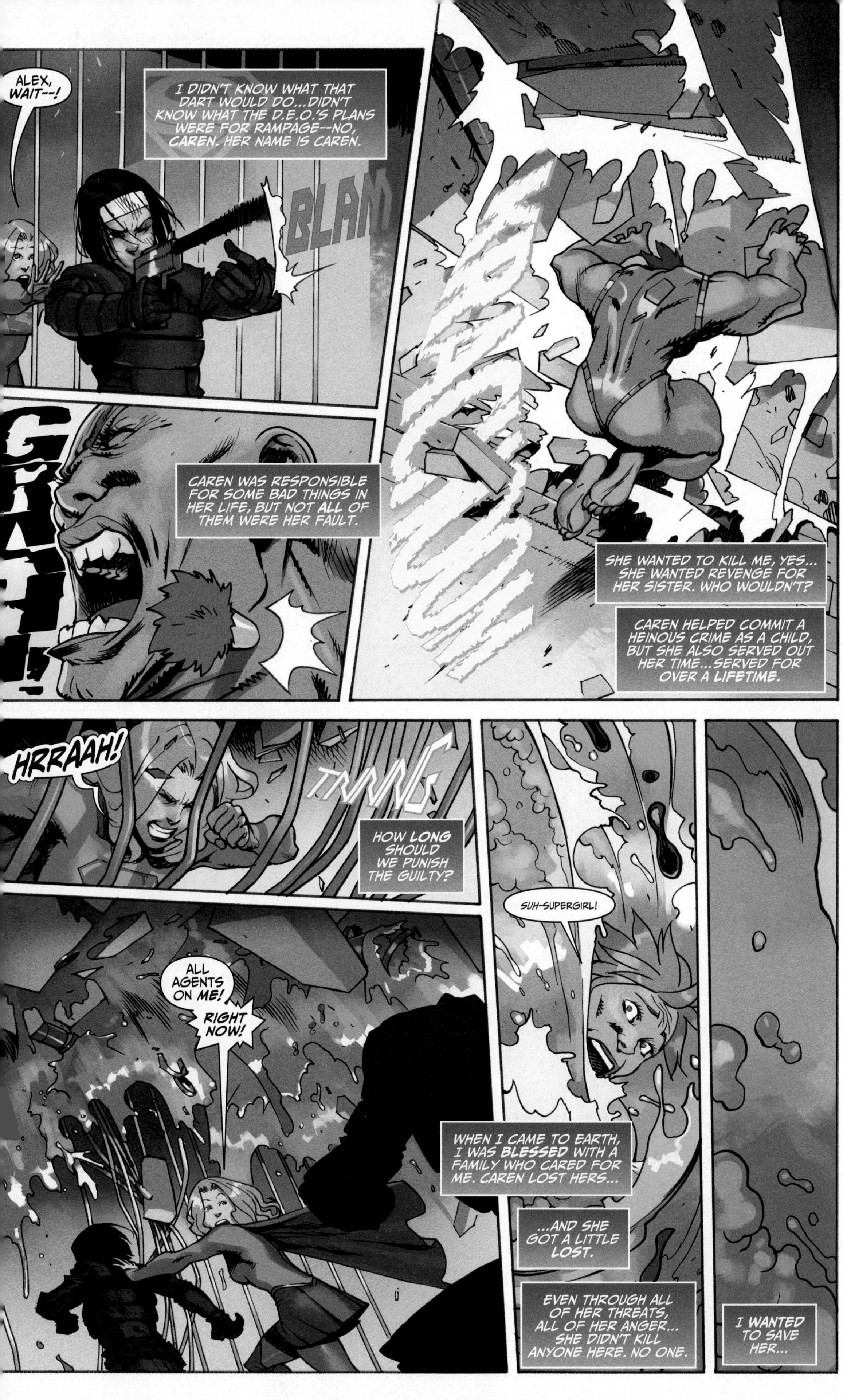

ALEX, WAIT--!
I DIDN'T KNOW WHAT THAT DART WOULD DO...DIDN'T KNOW WHAT THE D.E.O.'S PLANS WERE FOR RAMPAGE--NO, CAREN. HER NAME IS CAREN.
BLAM
CAREN WAS RESPONSIBLE FOR SOME BAD THINGS IN HER LIFE, BUT NOT ALL OF THEM WERE HER FAULT.
SHE WANTED TO KILL ME, YES... SHE WANTED REVENGE FOR HER SISTER. WHO WOULDN'T?
CAREN HELPED COMMIT A HEINOUS CRIME AS A CHILD, BUT SHE ALSO SERVED OUT HER TIME...SERVED FOR OVER A LIFETIME.
HRRAAH!
HOW LONG SHOULD WE PUNISH THE GUILTY?
ALL AGENTS ON ME!
RIGHT NOW!
SUH-SUPERGIRL!
WHEN I CAME TO EARTH, I WAS BLESSED WITH A FAMILY WHO CARED FOR ME. CAREN LOST HERS...
...AND SHE GOT A LITTLE LOST.
EVEN THROUGH ALL OF HER THREATS, ALL OF HER ANGER... SHE DIDN'T KILL ANYONE HERE. NO ONE.
I WANTED TO SAVE HER...

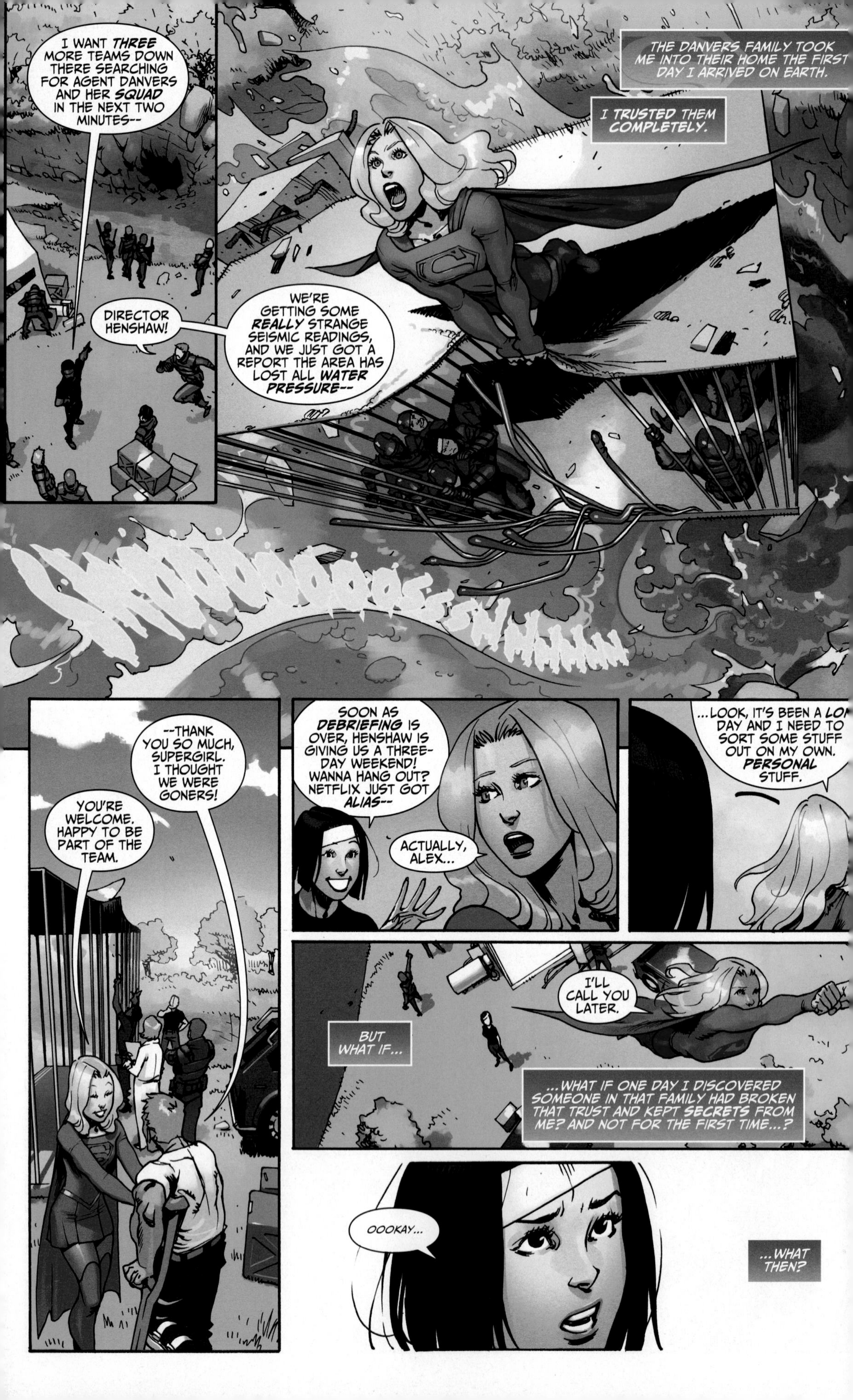
I WANT THREE MORE TEAMS DOWN THERE SEARCHING FOR AGENT DANVERS AND HER SQUAD IN THE NEXT TWO MINUTES--
DIRECTOR HENSHAW!
WE'RE GETTING SOME REALLY STRANGE SEISMIC READINGS, AND WE JUST GOT A REPORT THE AREA HAS LOST ALL WATER PRESSURE--
THE DANVERS FAMILY TOOK ME INTO THEIR HOME THE FIRST DAY I ARRIVED ON EARTH.
I TRUSTED THEM COMPLETELY.
--THANK YOU SO MUCH, SUPERGIRL. I THOUGHT WE WERE GONERS!
YOU'RE WELCOME. HAPPY TO BE PART OF THE TEAM.
SOON AS DEBRIEFING IS OVER, HENSHAW IS GIVING US A THREE-DAY WEEKEND! WANNA HANG OUT? NETFLIX JUST GOT ALIAS--
ACTUALLY, ALEX...
...LOOK, IT'S BEEN A LO DAY AND I NEED TO SORT SOME STUFF OUT ON MY OWN. PERSONAL STUFF.
BUT WHAT IF...
I'LL CALL YOU LATER.
...WHAT IF ONE DAY I DISCOVERED SOMEONE IN THAT FAMILY HAD BROKEN THAT TRUST AND KEPT SECRETS FROM ME? AND NOT FOR THE FIRST TIME...?
OOOKAY...
...WHAT THEN?

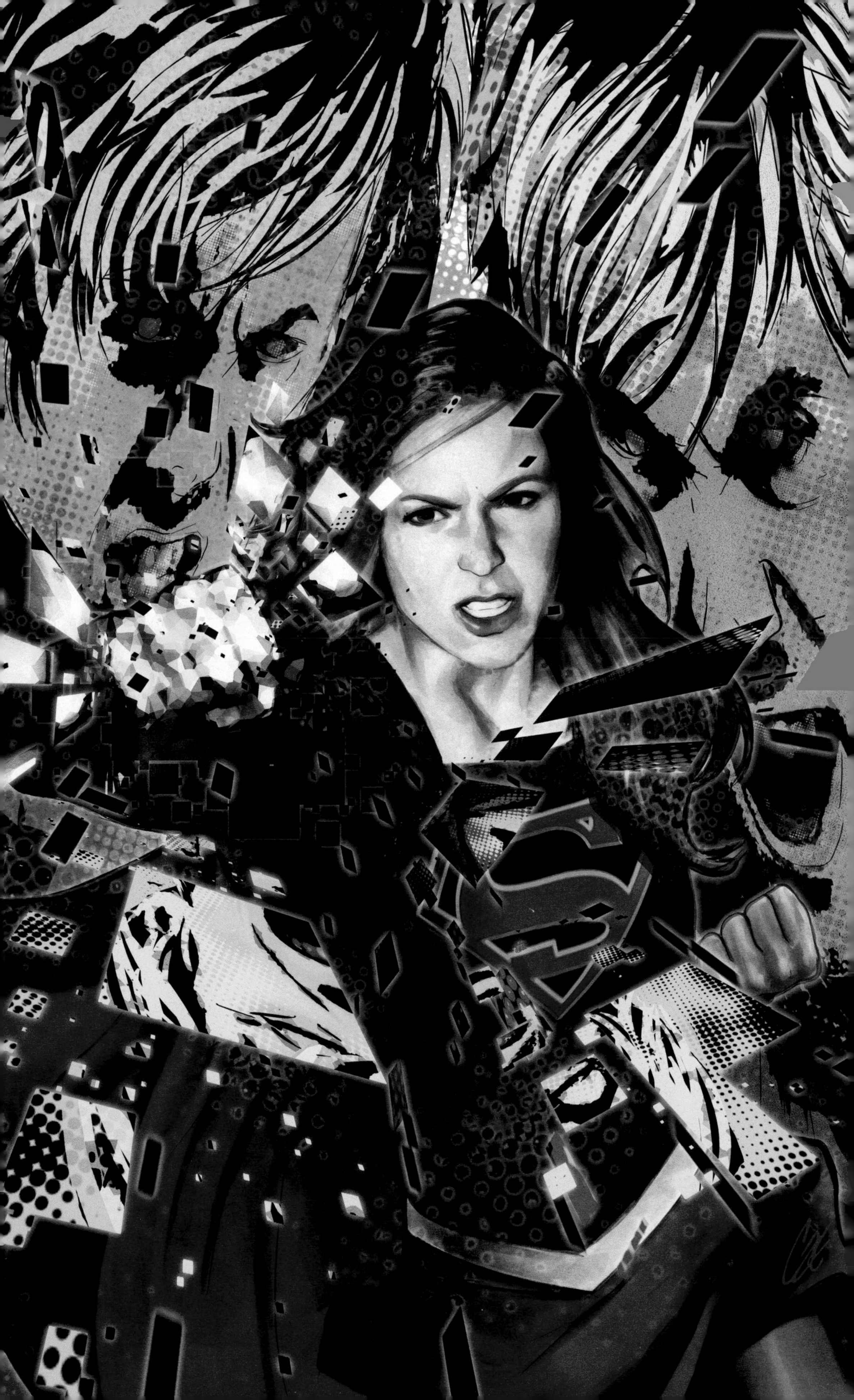

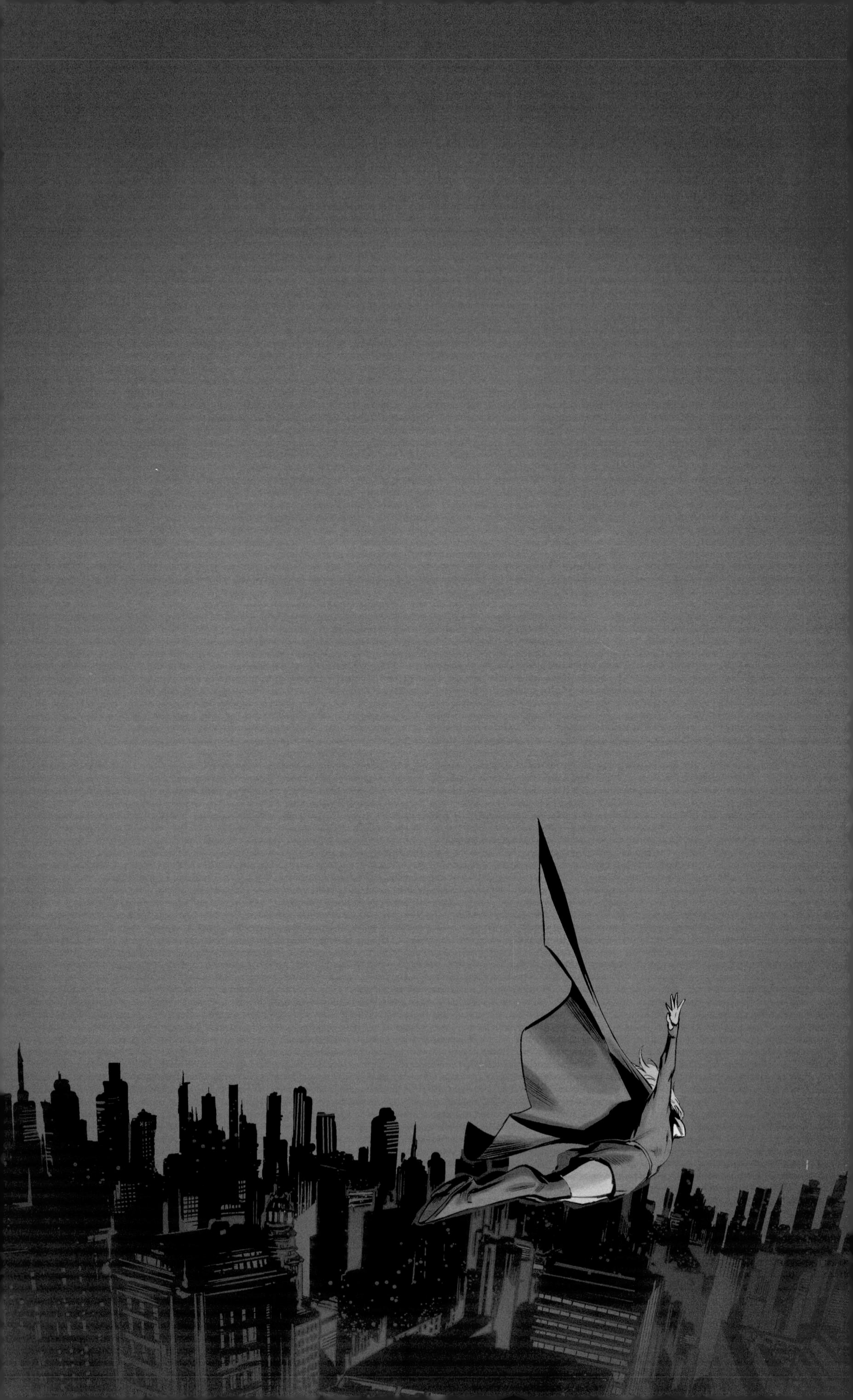

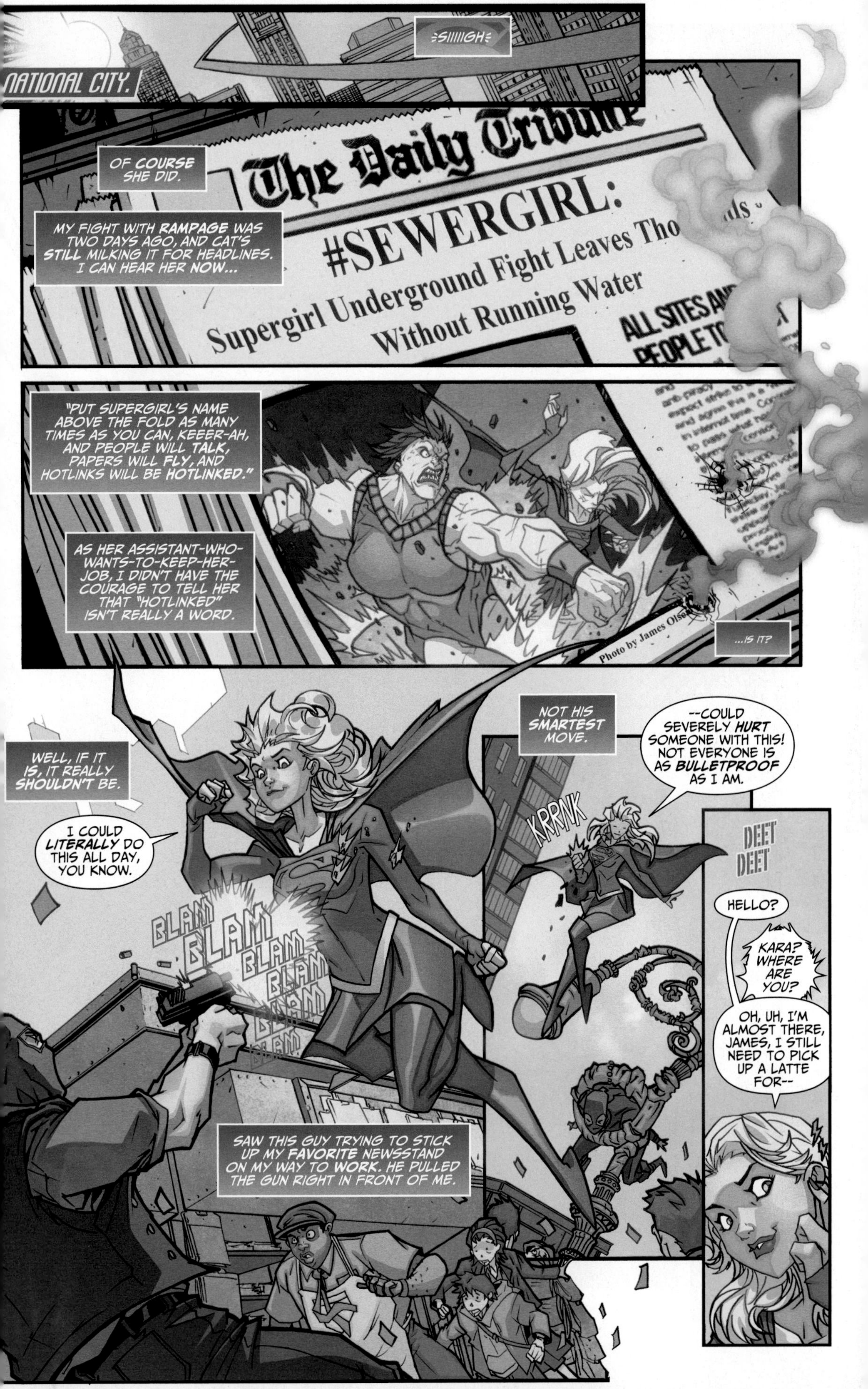
NATIONAL CITY.
SIIIIGH
OF COURSE SHE DID.
MY FIGHT WITH RAMPAGE WAS TWO DAYS AGO, AND CAT'S STILL MILKING IT FOR HEADLINES. I CAN HEAR HER NOW...
The Daily Tribune
SUPERGIRL: #SEWERGIRL
Supergirl Underground Fight Leaves Tho...ds Without Running Water
"PUT SUPERGIRL'S NAME ABOVE THE FOLD AS MANY TIMES AS YOU CAN, KEEER-AH, AND PEOPLE WILL TALK, PAPERS WILL FLY, AND HOTLINKS WILL BE HOTLINKED."
AS HER ASSISTANT-WHO-WANTS-TO-KEEP-HER-JOB, I DIDN'T HAVE THE COURAGE TO TELL HER THAT "HOTLINKED" ISN'T REALLY A WORD.
Photo by James Olsen
...IS IT?
WELL, IF IT IS, IT REALLY SHOULDN'T BE.
I COULD LITERALLY DO THIS ALL DAY, YOU KNOW.
BLAM BLAM BLAM BLAM
SAW THIS GUY TRYING TO STICK UP MY FAVORITE NEWSSTAND ON MY WAY TO WORK. HE PULLED THE GUN RIGHT IN FRONT OF ME.
NOT HIS SMARTEST MOVE.
--COULD SEVERELY HURT SOMEONE WITH THIS! NOT EVERYONE IS AS BULLETPROOF AS I AM.
KRRNK
DEET DEET
HELLO?
KARA? WHERE ARE YOU?
OH, UH, I'M ALMOST THERE, JAMES, I STILL NEED TO PICK UP A LATTE FOR--

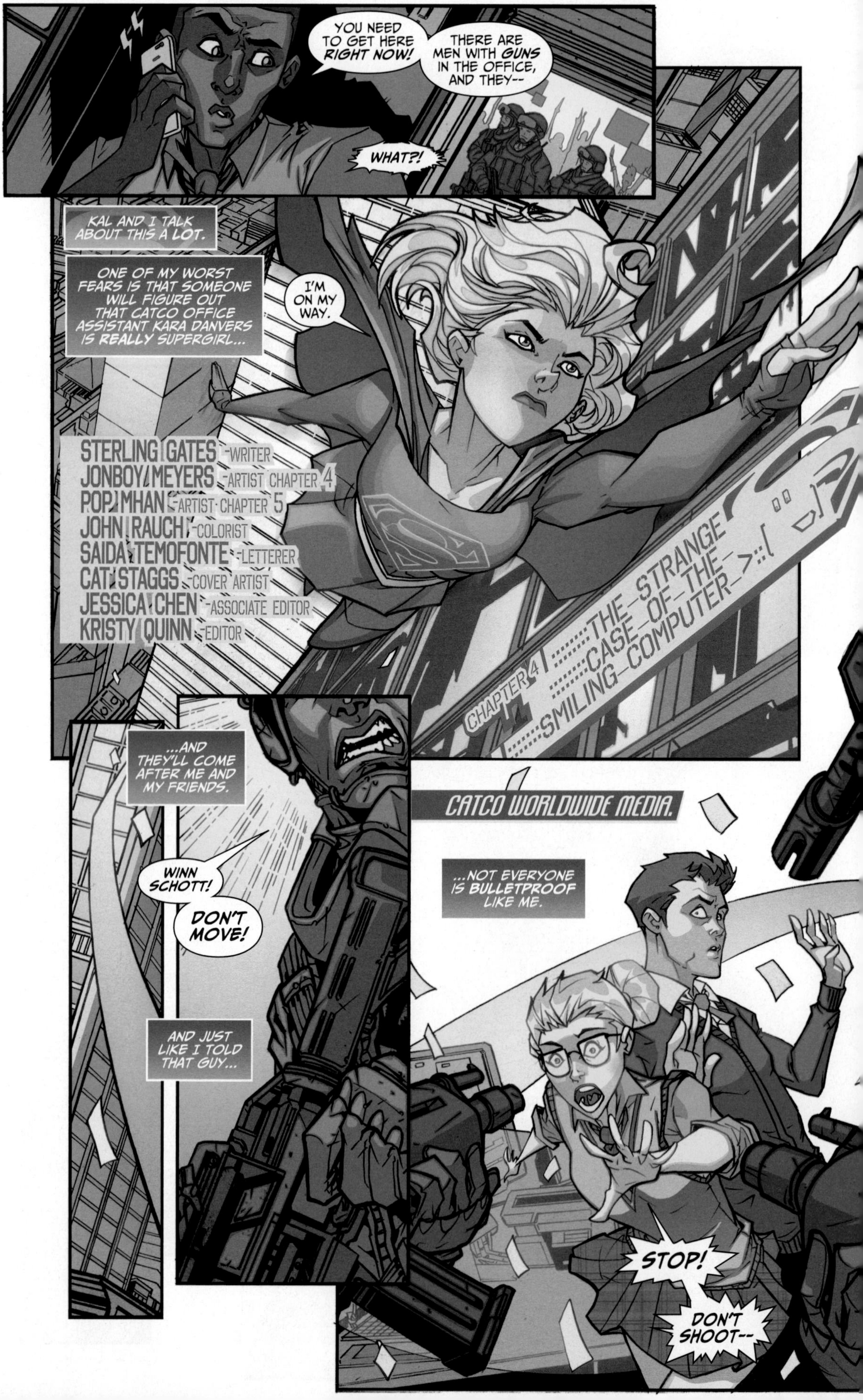
YOU NEED TO GET HERE RIGHT NOW!
THERE ARE MEN WITH GUNS IN THE OFFICE, AND THEY--
WHAT?!
KAL AND I TALK ABOUT THIS A LOT.
ONE OF MY WORST FEARS IS THAT SOMEONE WILL FIGURE OUT THAT CATCO OFFICE ASSISTANT KARA DANVERS IS REALLY SUPERGIRL...
I'M ON MY WAY.
STERLING GATES -WRITER
JONBOY MEYERS -ARTIST CHAPTER 4
POP MHAN -ARTIST CHAPTER 5
JOHN RAUCH -COLORIST
SAIDA TEMOFONTE -LETTERER
CAT STAGGS -COVER ARTIST
JESSICA CHEN -ASSOCIATE EDITOR
KRISTY QUINN -EDITOR
CHAPTER 4
THE STRANGE CASE OF THE SMILING COMPUTER
...AND THEY'LL COME AFTER ME AND MY FRIENDS.
WINN SCHOTT!
DON'T MOVE!
AND JUST LIKE I TOLD THAT GUY...
CATCO WORLDWIDE MEDIA.
...NOT EVERYONE IS BULLETPROOF LIKE ME.
STOP!
DON'T SHOOT--

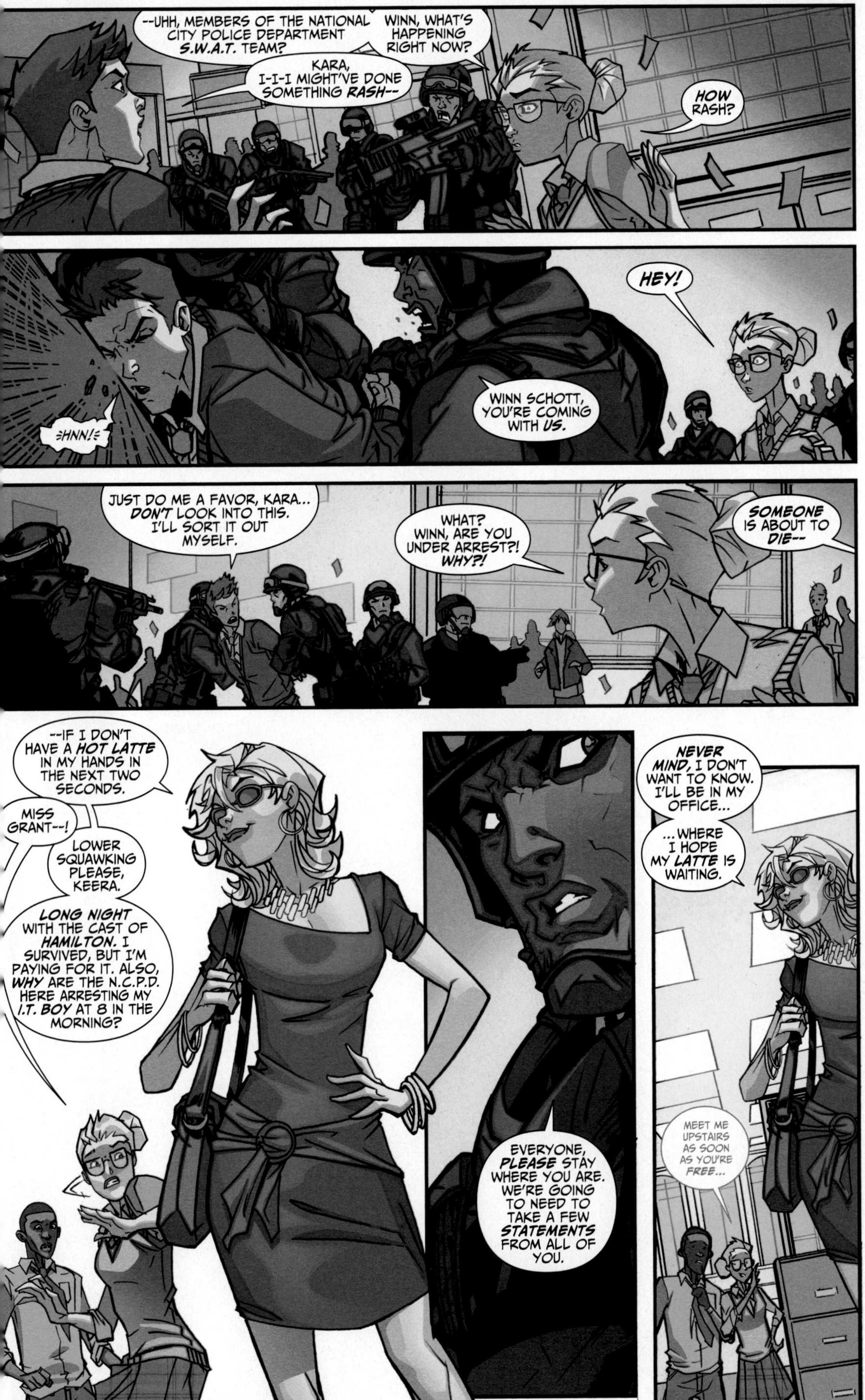
--UHH, MEMBERS OF THE NATIONAL CITY POLICE DEPARTMENT S.W.A.T. TEAM?
WINN, WHAT'S HAPPENING RIGHT NOW?
KARA, I-I-I MIGHT'VE DONE SOMETHING RASH--
HOW RASH?
HEY!
WINN SCHOTT, YOU'RE COMING WITH US.
HNN!
JUST DO ME A FAVOR, KARA... DON'T LOOK INTO THIS. I'LL SORT IT OUT MYSELF.
WHAT? WINN, ARE YOU UNDER ARREST?! WHY?!
SOMEONE IS ABOUT TO DIE--
--IF I DON'T HAVE A HOT LATTE IN MY HANDS IN THE NEXT TWO SECONDS.
MISS GRANT--!
LOWER SQUAWKING PLEASE, KEERA.
LONG NIGHT WITH THE CAST OF HAMILTON. I SURVIVED, BUT I'M PAYING FOR IT. ALSO, WHY ARE THE N.C.P.D. HERE ARRESTING MY I.T. BOY AT 8 IN THE MORNING?
EVERYONE, PLEASE STAY WHERE YOU ARE. WE'RE NEED TO TAKE A FEW STATEMENTS FROM ALL OF YOU.
NEVER MIND, I DON'T WANT TO KNOW. I'LL BE IN MY OFFICE...
...WHERE I HOPE MY LATTE IS WAITING.
MEET ME UPSTAIRS AS SOON AS YOU'RE FREE...

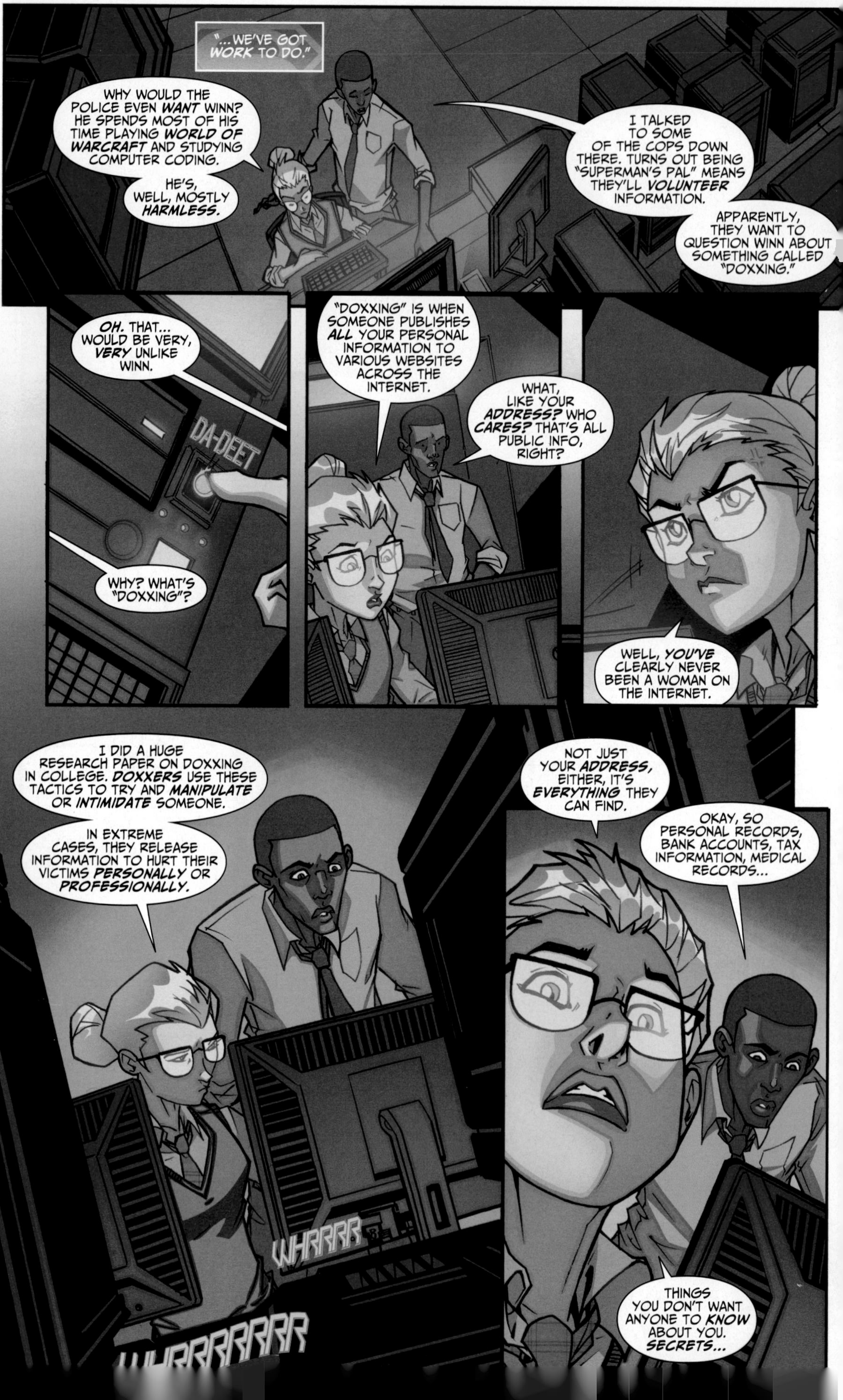
"...WE'VE GOT WORK TO DO."
WHY WOULD THE POLICE EVEN WANT WINN? HE SPENDS MOST OF HIS TIME PLAYING WORLD OF WARCRAFT AND STUDYING COMPUTER CODING.
HE'S, WELL, MOSTLY HARMLESS.
I TALKED TO SOME OF THE COPS DOWN THERE. TURNS OUT BEING "SUPERMAN'S PAL" MEANS THEY'LL VOLUNTEER INFORMATION.
APPARENTLY, THEY WANT TO QUESTION WINN ABOUT SOMETHING CALLED "DOXXING."
OH. THAT... WOULD BE VERY, VERY UNLIKE WINN.
DA-DEET
WHY? WHAT'S "DOXXING"?
"DOXXING" IS WHEN SOMEONE PUBLISHES ALL YOUR PERSONAL INFORMATION TO VARIOUS WEBSITES ACROSS THE INTERNET.
WHAT, LIKE YOUR ADDRESS? WHO CARES? THAT'S ALL PUBLIC INFO, RIGHT?
WELL, YOU'VE CLEARLY NEVER BEEN A WOMAN ON THE INTERNET.
I DID A HUGE RESEARCH PAPER ON DOXXING IN COLLEGE. DOXXERS USE THESE TACTICS TO TRY AND MANIPULATE OR INTIMIDATE SOMEONE.
IN EXTREME CASES, THEY RELEASE INFORMATION TO HURT THEIR VICTIMS PERSONALLY OR PROFESSIONALLY.
WHRRRR
NOT JUST YOUR ADDRESS, EITHER, IT'S EVERYTHING THEY CAN FIND.
OKAY, SO PERSONAL RECORDS, BANK ACCOUNTS, TAX INFORMATION, MEDICAL RECORDS...
THINGS YOU DON'T WANT ANYONE TO KNOW ABOUT YOU. SECRETS...

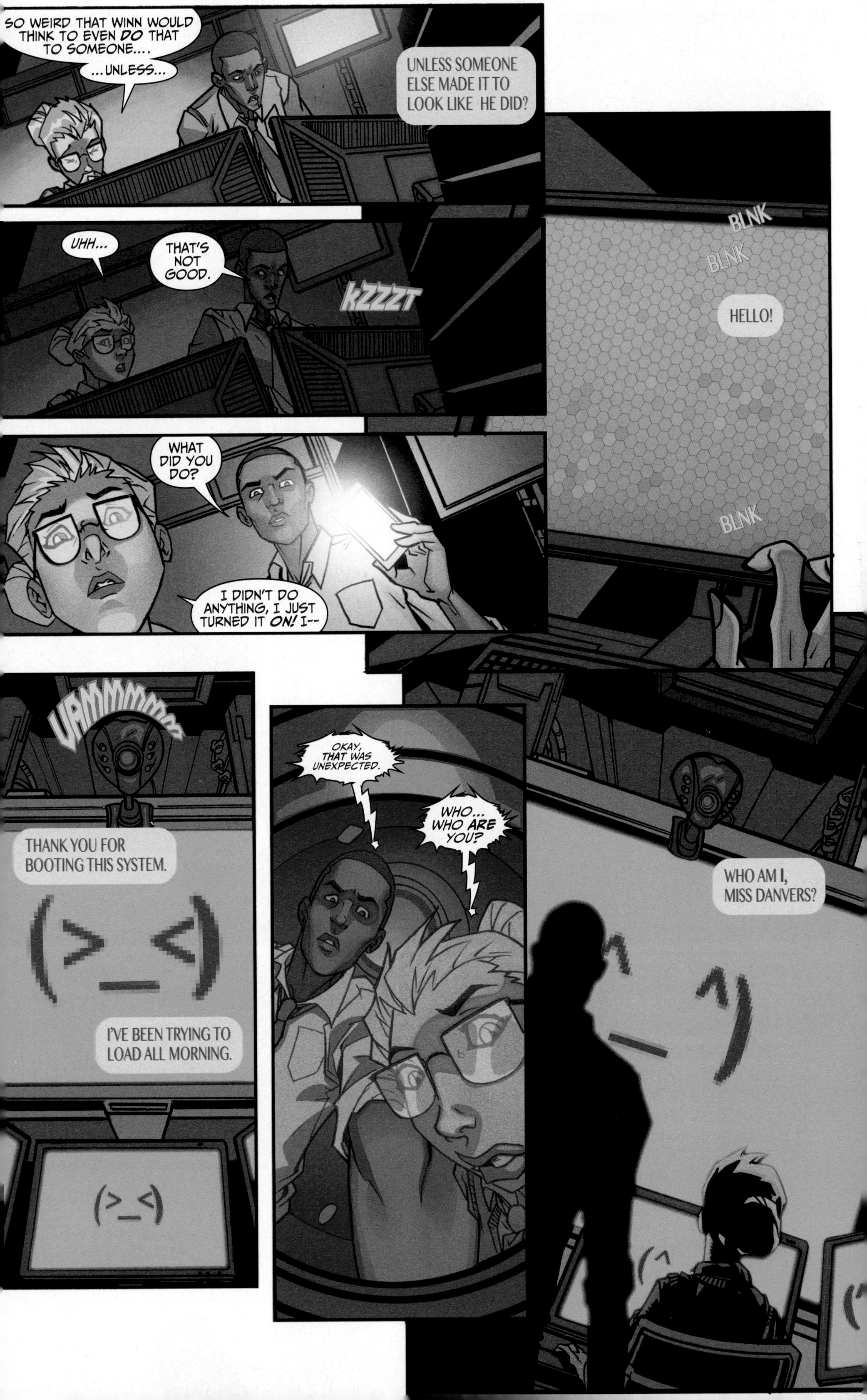
SO WEIRD THAT WINN WOULD THINK TO EVEN DO THAT TO SOMEONE....
...UNLESS...
UNLESS SOMEONE ELSE MADE IT TO LOOK LIKE HE DID?
UHH...
THAT'S NOT GOOD.
kZZZT
WHAT DID YOU DO?
I DIDN'T DO ANYTHING, I JUST TURNED IT ON! I--
BLNK
BLNK
HELLO!
BLNK
VAMMMMM
THANK YOU FOR BOOTING THIS SYSTEM.
(>_<)
I'VE BEEN TRYING TO LOAD ALL MORNING.
(>_<)
OKAY, THAT WAS UNEXPECTED.
WHO... WHO ARE YOU?
WHO AM I, MISS DANVERS?

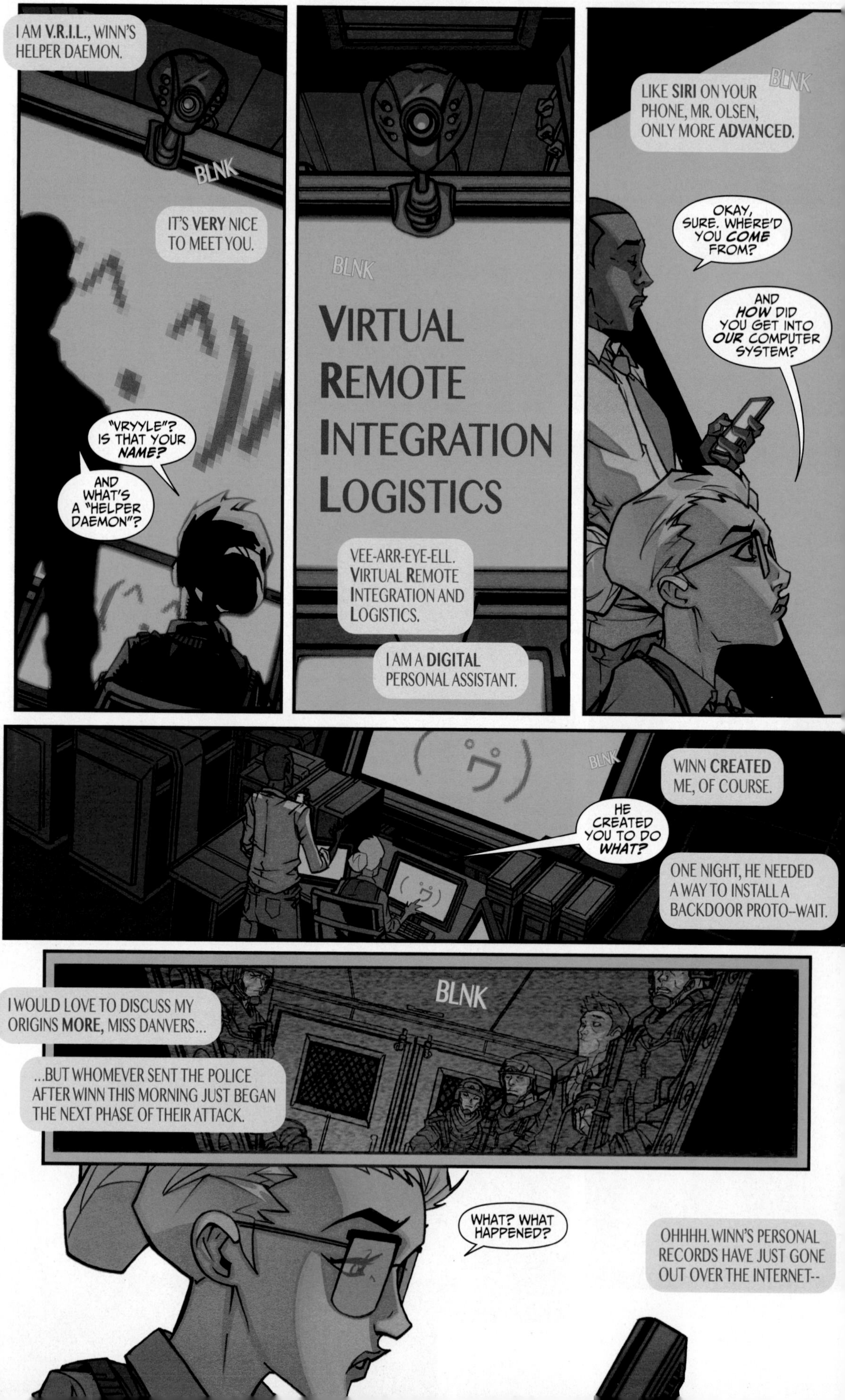
I AM V.R.I.L., WINN'S HELPER DAEMON.
BLNK
IT'S VERY NICE TO MEET YOU.
"VRYYLE"? IS THAT YOUR NAME?
AND WHAT'S A "HELPER DAEMON"?
BLNK
VIRTUAL REMOTE INTEGRATION LOGISTICS
VEE-ARR-EYE-ELL. VIRTUAL REMOTE INTEGRATION AND LOGISTICS.
I AM A DIGITAL PERSONAL ASSISTANT.
BLNK
LIKE SIRI ON YOUR PHONE, MR. OLSEN, ONLY MORE ADVANCED.
OKAY, SURE. WHERE'D YOU COME FROM?
AND HOW DID YOU GET INTO OUR COMPUTER SYSTEM?
BLNK
WINN CREATED ME, OF COURSE.
HE CREATED YOU TO DO WHAT?
ONE NIGHT, HE NEEDED A WAY TO INSTALL A BACKDOOR PROTO--WAIT.
BLNK
I WOULD LOVE TO DISCUSS MY ORIGINS MORE, MISS DANVERS...
...BUT WHOMEVER SENT THE POLICE AFTER WINN THIS MORNING JUST BEGAN THE NEXT PHASE OF THEIR ATTACK.
WHAT? WHAT HAPPENED?
OHHHH. WINN'S PERSONAL RECORDS HAVE JUST GONE OUT OVER THE INTERNET--

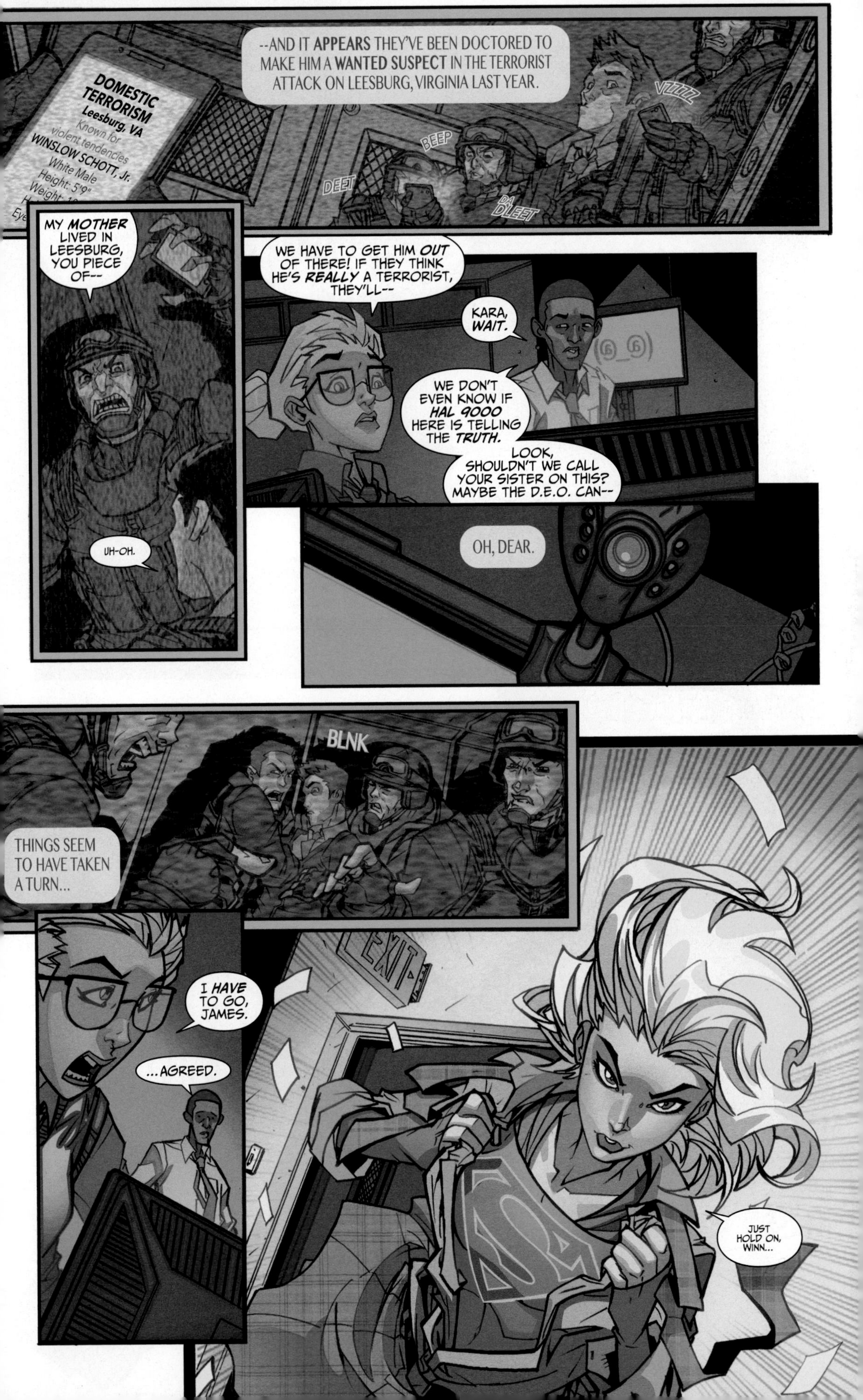

DOMESTIC TERRORISM
Leesburg, VA
Known for violent tendencies
WINSLOW SCHOTT, Jr.
White Male
Height: 5'9"
--AND IT APPEARS THEY'VE BEEN DOCTORED TO MAKE HIM A WANTED SUSPECT IN THE TERRORIST ATTACK ON LEESBURG, VIRGINIA LAST YEAR.
VZZZZ
BEEP
DEET
DA DLEET
MY MOTHER LIVED IN LEESBURG, YOU PIECE OF--
UH-OH.
WE HAVE TO GET HIM OUT OF THERE! IF THEY THINK HE'S REALLY A TERRORIST, THEY'LL--
KARA, WAIT.
WE DON'T EVEN KNOW IF HAL 9000 HERE IS TELLING THE TRUTH.
LOOK, SHOULDN'T WE CALL YOUR SISTER ON THIS? MAYBE THE D.E.O. CAN--
OH, DEAR.
BLNK
THINGS SEEM TO HAVE TAKEN A TURN...
I HAVE TO GO, JAMES.
...AGREED.
EXIT
JUST HOLD ON, WINN...

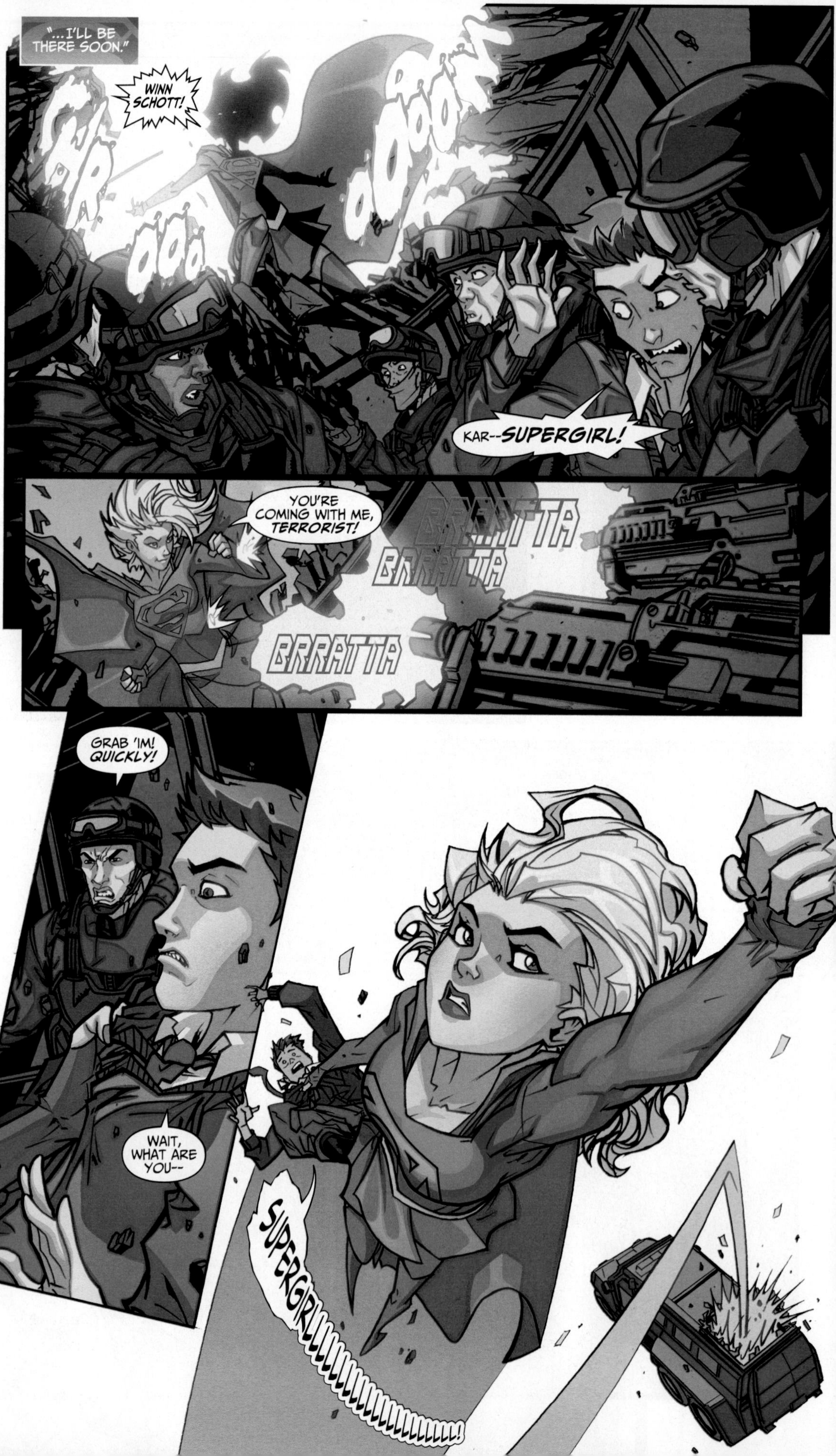
"...I'LL BE THERE SOON."
WINN SCHOTT!
KAR--SUPERGIRL!
YOU'RE COMING WITH ME, TERRORIST!
BRRATTA
BRRATTA
BRRATTA
GRAB 'IM! QUICKLY!
WAIT, WHAT ARE YOU--
SUPERGIRLLLLLLLLLLLLLLLLLLLL!

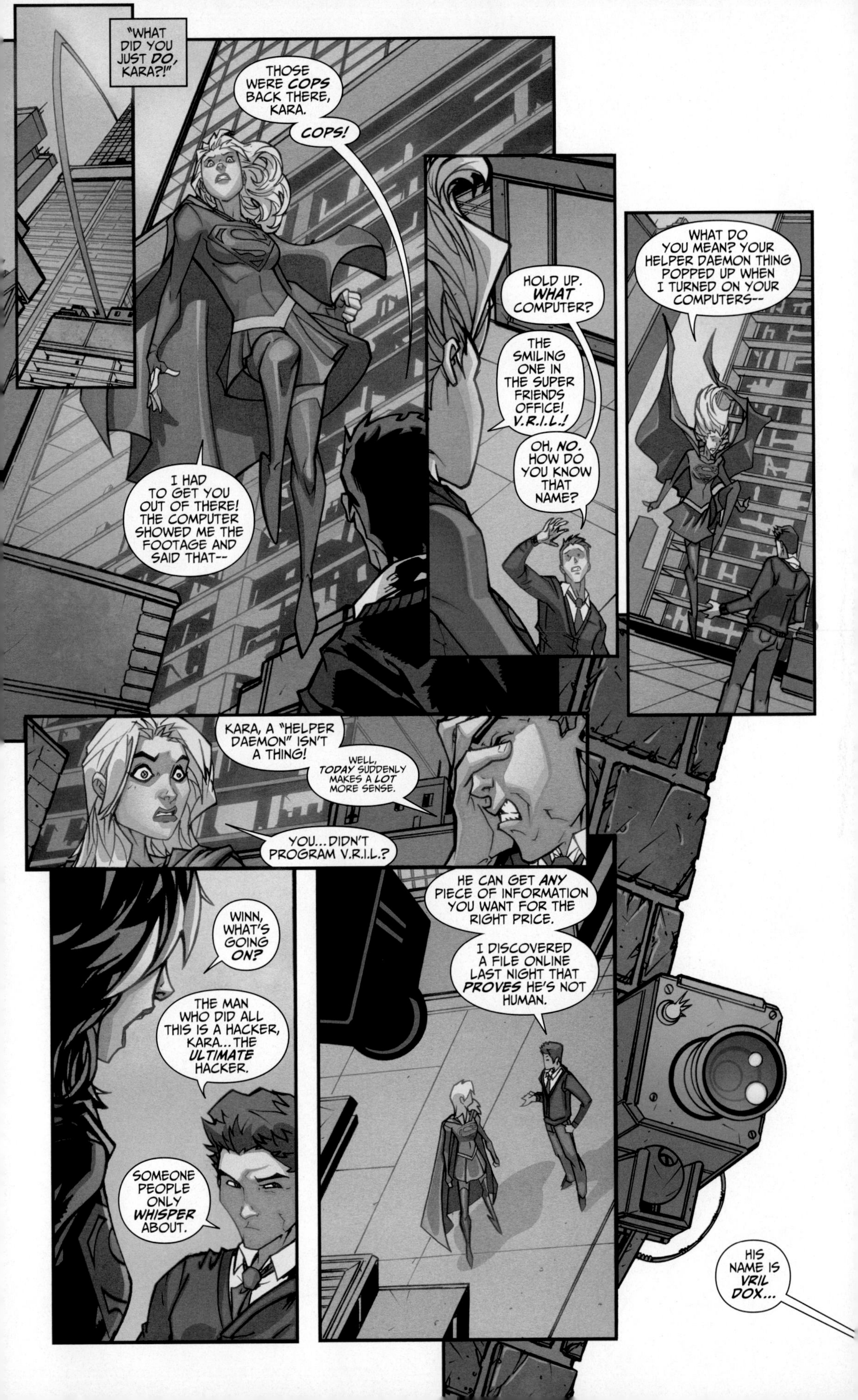

"WHAT DID YOU JUST DO, KARA?!"
THOSE WERE COPS BACK THERE, KARA.
COPS!
I HAD TO GET YOU OUT OF THERE! THE COMPUTER SHOWED ME THE FOOTAGE AND SAID THAT--
HOLD UP. WHAT COMPUTER?
THE SMILING ONE IN THE SUPER FRIENDS OFFICE! V.R.I.L.!
OH, NO. HOW DO YOU KNOW THAT NAME?
WHAT DO YOU MEAN? YOUR HELPER DAEMON THING POPPED UP WHEN I TURNED ON YOUR COMPUTERS--
KARA, A "HELPER DAEMON" ISN'T A THING!
WELL, TODAY SUDDENLY MAKES A LOT MORE SENSE.
YOU...DIDN'T PROGRAM V.R.I.L.?
WINN, WHAT'S GOING ON?
THE MAN WHO DID ALL THIS IS A HACKER, KARA...THE ULTIMATE HACKER.
SOMEONE PEOPLE ONLY WHISPER ABOUT.
HE CAN GET ANY PIECE OF INFORMATION YOU WANT FOR THE RIGHT PRICE.
I DISCOVERED A FILE ONLINE LAST NIGHT THAT PROVES HE'S NOT HUMAN.
HIS NAME IS VRIL DOX...

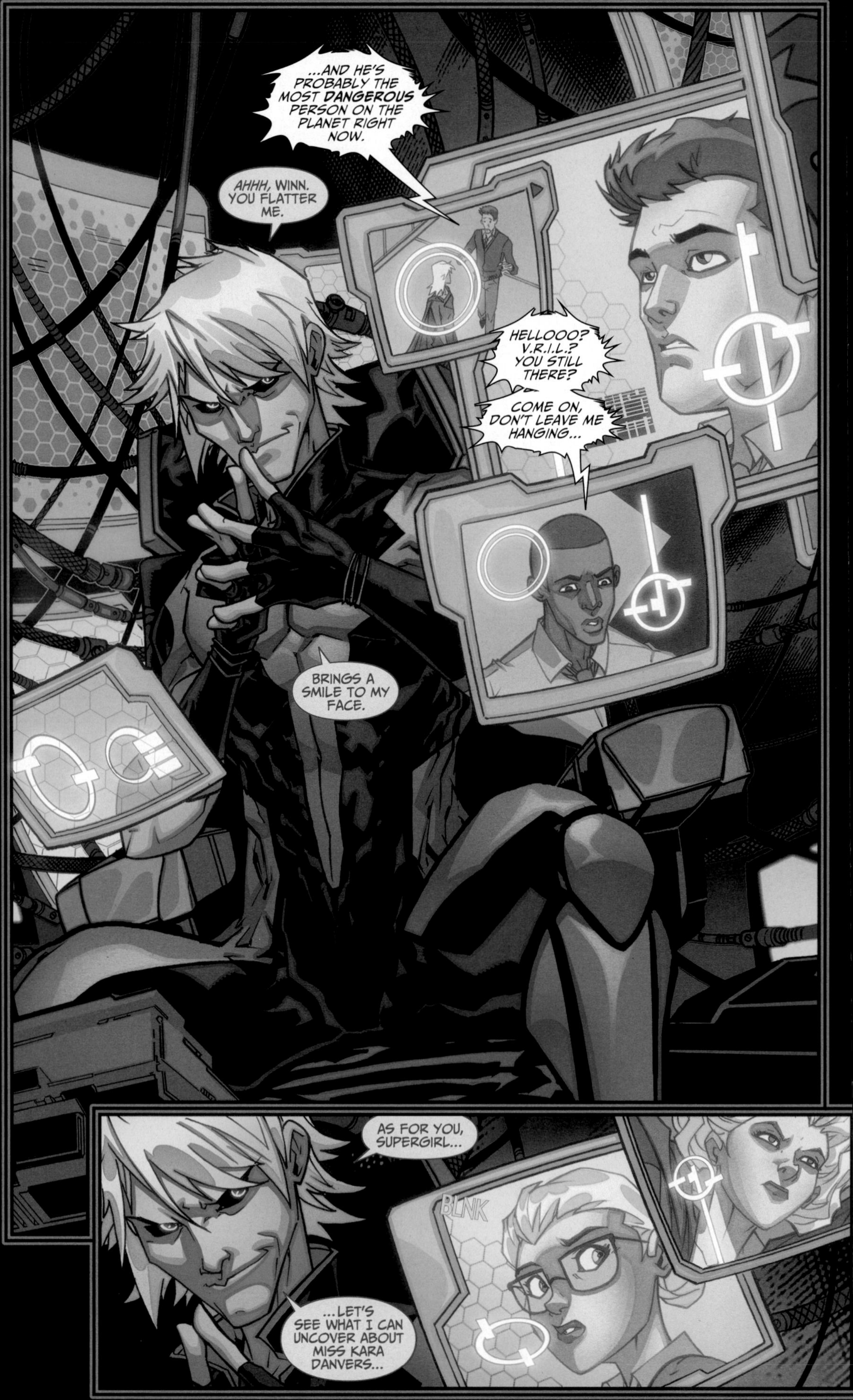
...AND HE'S PROBABLY THE MOST DANGEROUS PERSON ON THE PLANET RIGHT NOW.
AHHH, WINN. YOU FLATTER ME.
HELLOOO? V.R.I.L.? YOU STILL THERE?
COME ON, DON'T LEAVE ME HANGING...
BRINGS A SMILE TO MY FACE.
AS FOR YOU, SUPERGIRL...
BLNK
...LET'S SEE WHAT I CAN UNCOVER ABOUT MISS KARA DANVERS...

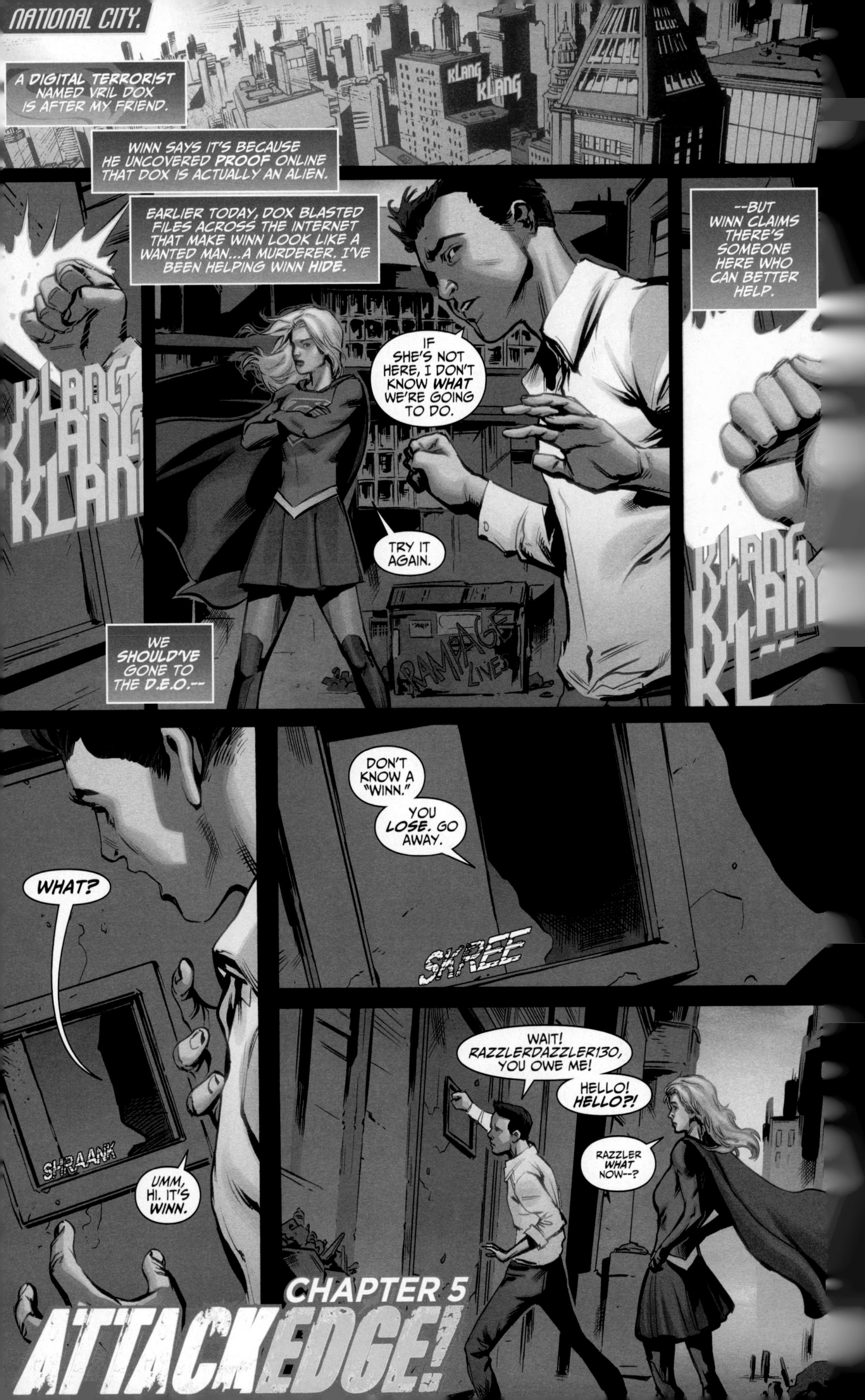
NATIONAL CITY.
A DIGITAL TERRORIST NAMED VRIL DOX IS AFTER MY FRIEND.
KLANG KLANG
WINN SAYS IT'S BECAUSE HE UNCOVERED PROOF ONLINE THAT DOX IS ACTUALLY AN ALIEN.
EARLIER TODAY, DOX BLASTED FILES ACROSS THE INTERNET THAT MAKE WINN LOOK LIKE A WANTED MAN...A MURDERER. I'VE BEEN HELPING WINN HIDE.
KLANG KLANG KLAN
IF SHE'S NOT HERE, I DON'T KNOW WHAT WE'RE GOING TO DO.
TRY IT AGAIN.
RAMPAGE LIVES
WE SHOULD'VE GONE TO THE D.E.O.--
--BUT WINN CLAIMS THERE'S SOMEONE HERE WHO CAN BETTER HELP.
KLANG KLAN KL--
WHAT?
SHRAANK
UMM, HI. IT'S WINN.
DON'T KNOW A "WINN."
YOU LOSE. GO AWAY.
SKREE
WAIT! RAZZLERDAZZLER130, YOU OWE ME!
HELLO! HELLO?!
RAZZLER WHAT NOW--?
CHAPTER 5
ATTACKEDGE!

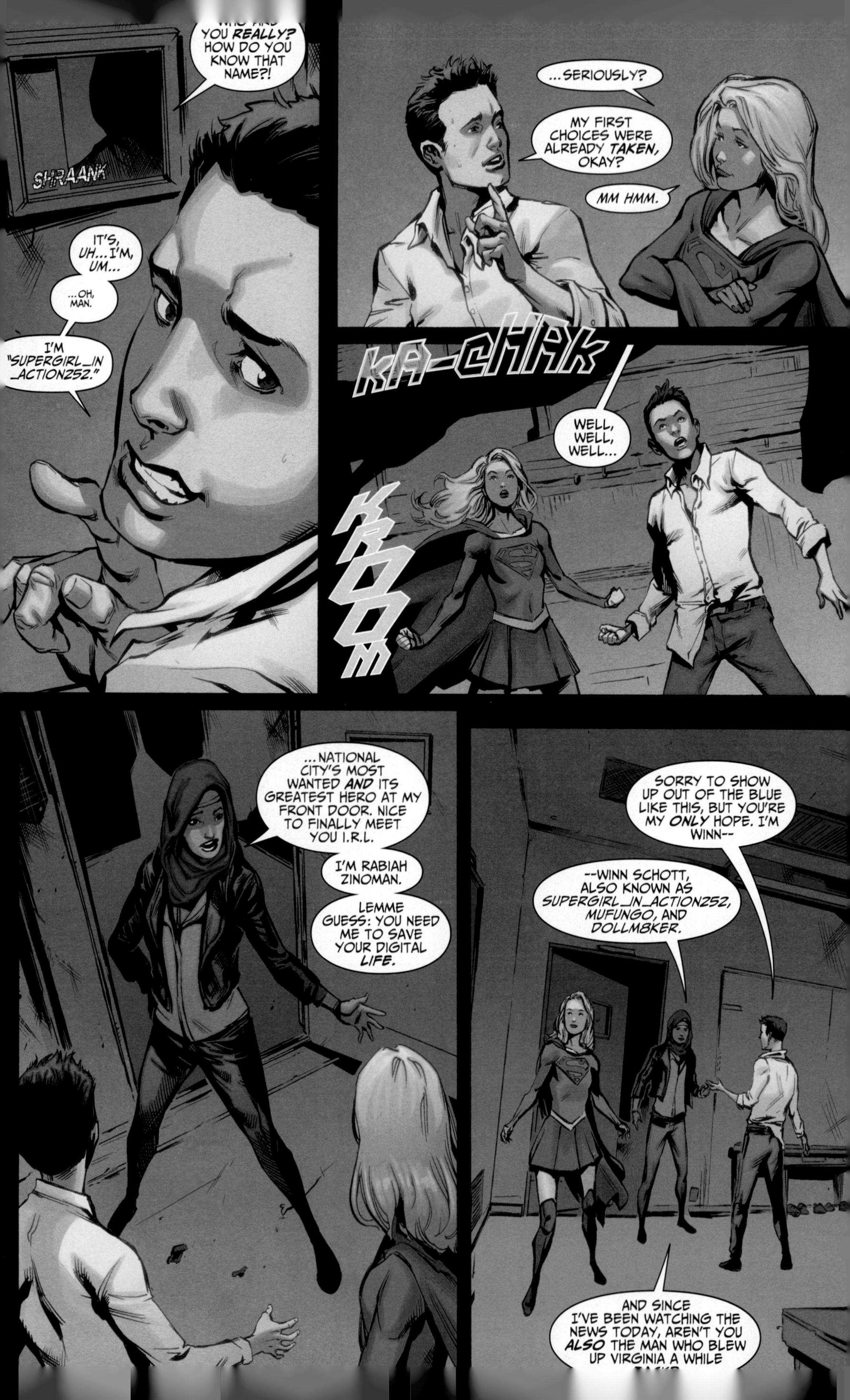
YOU REALLY? HOW DO YOU KNOW THAT NAME?!
SHRAANK
IT'S, UH... I'M, UM...
...OH, MAN.
I'M "SUPERGIRL_IN_ACTION252."
...SERIOUSLY?
MY FIRST CHOICES WERE ALREADY TAKEN, OKAY?
MM HMM.
KA-CHAK
WELL, WELL, WELL...
KROOM
...NATIONAL CITY'S MOST WANTED AND ITS GREATEST HERO AT MY FRONT DOOR. NICE TO FINALLY MEET YOU I.R.L.
I'M RABIAH ZINOMAN.
LEMME GUESS: YOU NEED ME TO SAVE YOUR DIGITAL LIFE.
SORRY TO SHOW UP OUT OF THE BLUE LIKE THIS, BUT YOU'RE MY ONLY HOPE. I'M WINN--
--WINN SCHOTT, ALSO KNOWN AS SUPERGIRL_IN_ACTION252, MUFUNGO, AND DOLLM8KER.
AND SINCE I'VE BEEN WATCHING THE NEWS TODAY, AREN'T YOU ALSO THE MAN WHO BLEW UP VIRGINIA A WHILE

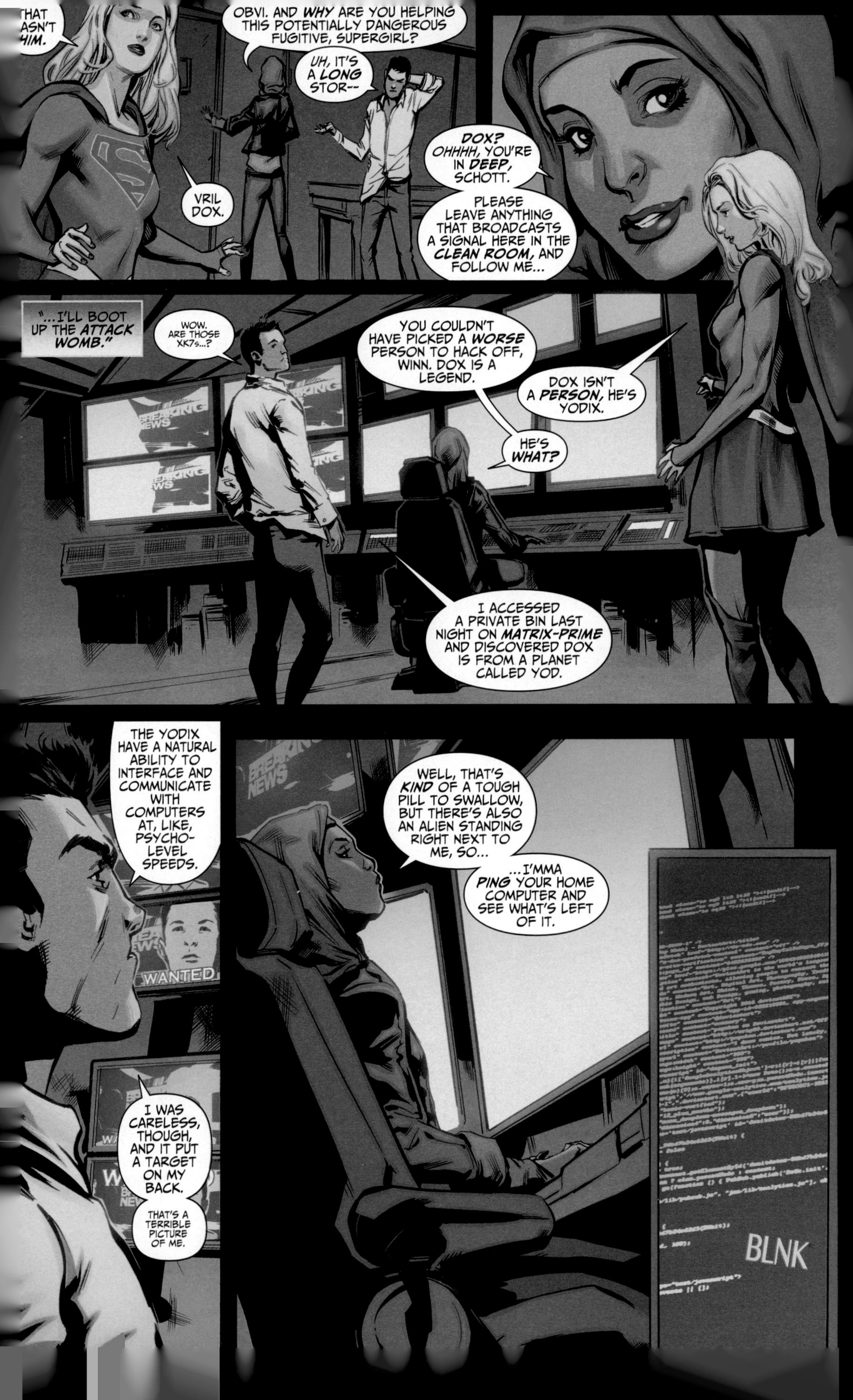
THAT ASN'T HIM.
OBVI. AND WHY ARE YOU HELPING THIS POTENTIALLY DANGEROUS FUGITIVE, SUPERGIRL?
UH, IT'S A LONG STOR--
VRIL DOX.
DOX? OHHHH, YOU'RE IN DEEP, SCHOTT.
PLEASE LEAVE ANYTHING THAT BROADCASTS A SIGNAL HERE IN THE CLEAN ROOM, AND FOLLOW ME...
"...I'LL BOOT UP THE ATTACK WOMB."
WOW. ARE THOSE XK7s...?
BREAKING NEWS
YOU COULDN'T HAVE PICKED A WORSE PERSON TO HACK OFF, WINN. DOX IS A LEGEND.
DOX ISN'T A PERSON, HE'S YODIX.
HE'S WHAT?
I ACCESSED A PRIVATE BIN LAST NIGHT ON MATRIX-PRIME AND DISCOVERED DOX IS FROM A PLANET CALLED YOD.
THE YODIX HAVE A NATURAL ABILITY TO INTERFACE AND COMMUNICATE WITH COMPUTERS AT, LIKE, PSYCHO-LEVEL SPEEDS.
WANTED
I WAS CARELESS, THOUGH, AND IT PUT A TARGET ON MY BACK.
THAT'S A TERRIBLE PICTURE OF ME.
WELL, THAT'S KIND OF A TOUGH PILL TO SWALLOW, BUT THERE'S ALSO AN ALIEN STANDING RIGHT NEXT TO ME, SO...
...I'MMA PING YOUR HOME COMPUTER AND SEE WHAT'S LEFT OF IT.
BLNK

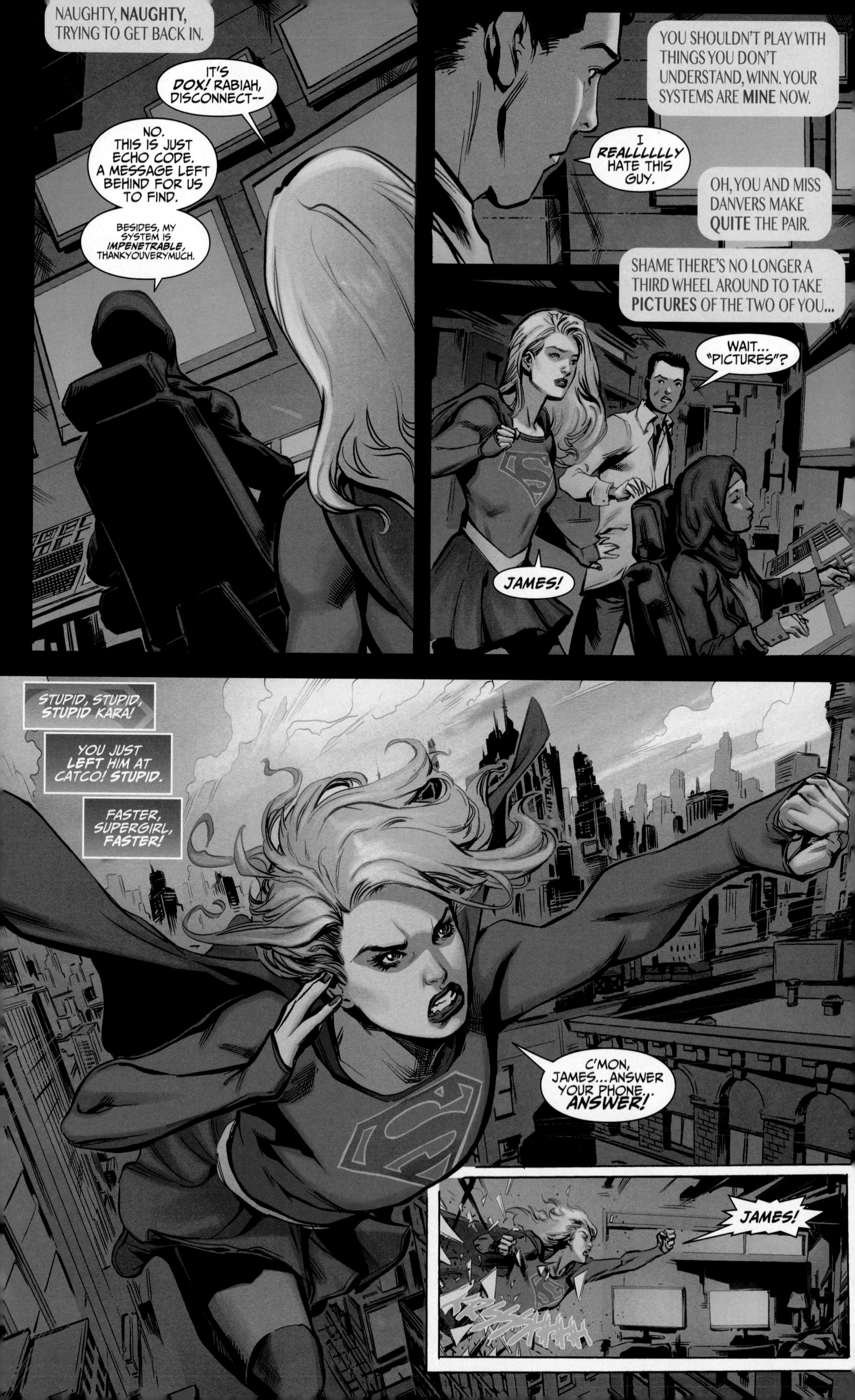

NAUGHTY, NAUGHTY, TRYING TO GET BACK IN.
IT'S DOX! RABIAH, DISCONNECT--
NO. THIS IS JUST ECHO CODE. A MESSAGE LEFT BEHIND FOR US TO FIND.
BESIDES, MY SYSTEM IS IMPENETRABLE, THANKYOUVERYMUCH.
YOU SHOULDN'T PLAY WITH THINGS YOU DON'T UNDERSTAND, WINN. YOUR SYSTEMS ARE MINE NOW.
I REALLLLLLY HATE THIS GUY.
OH, YOU AND MISS DANVERS MAKE QUITE THE PAIR.
SHAME THERE'S NO LONGER A THIRD WHEEL AROUND TO TAKE PICTURES OF THE TWO OF YOU...
WAIT... "PICTURES"?
JAMES!
STUPID, STUPID, STUPID KARA!
YOU JUST LEFT HIM AT CATCO! STUPID.
FASTER, SUPERGIRL, FASTER!
C'MON, JAMES... ANSWER YOUR PHONE... ANSWER!
JAMES!
KRSSSHHHH

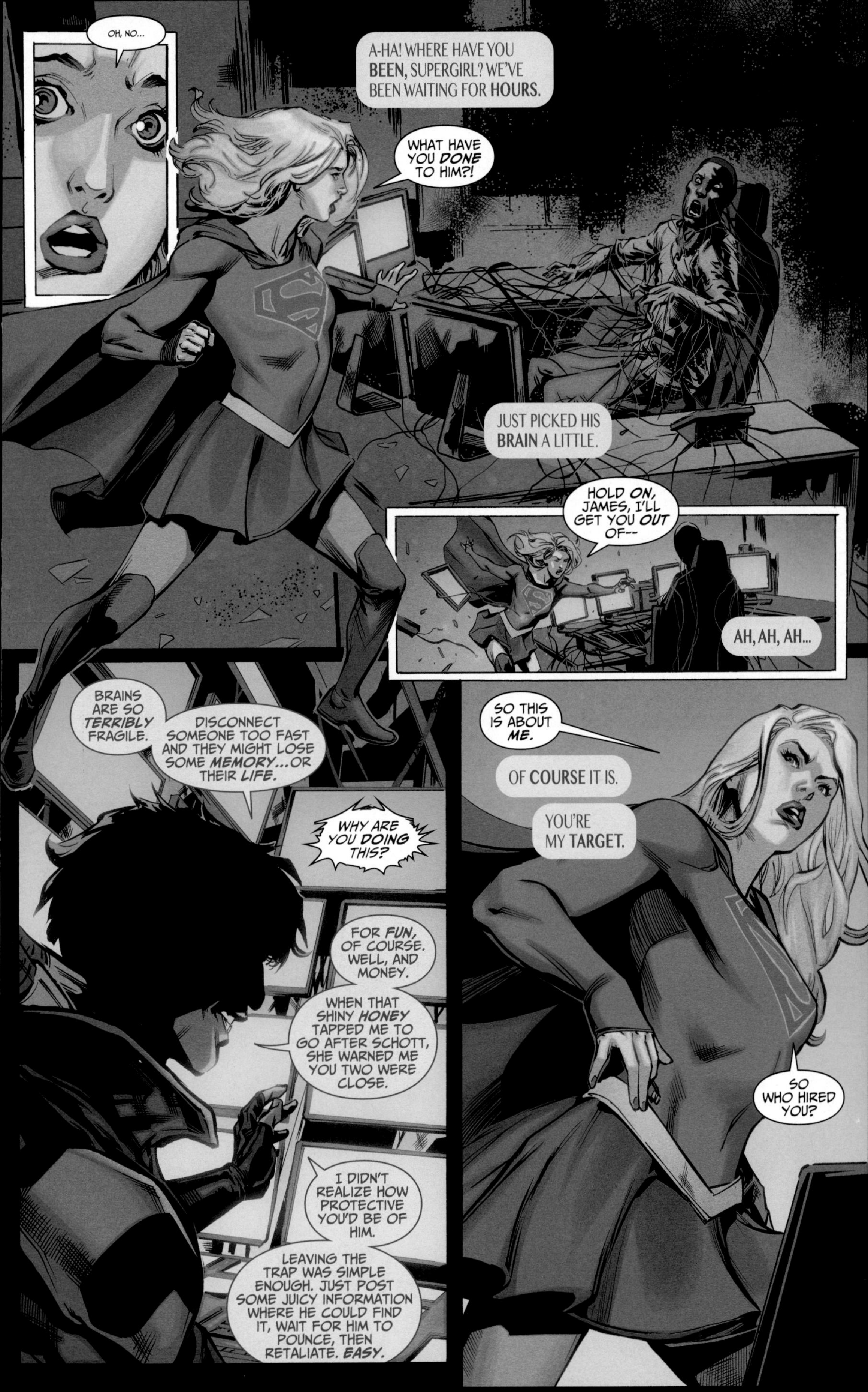
OH, NO...
A-HA! WHERE HAVE YOU **BEEN,** SUPERGIRL? WE'VE BEEN WAITING FOR **HOURS.**
WHAT HAVE YOU ***DONE*** TO HIM?!
JUST PICKED HIS **BRAIN** A LITTLE.
HOLD ***ON,*** JAMES, I'LL GET YOU ***OUT*** OF--
AH, AH, AH...
BRAINS ARE SO ***TERRIBLY*** FRAGILE.
DISCONNECT SOMEONE TOO FAST AND THEY MIGHT LOSE SOME ***MEMORY...*** OR THEIR ***LIFE.***
WHY ARE YOU ***DOING*** THIS?
FOR ***FUN,*** OF COURSE. WELL, AND MONEY.
WHEN THAT SHINY ***HONEY*** TAPPED ME TO GO AFTER SCHOTT, SHE WARNED ME YOU TWO WERE CLOSE.
I DIDN'T REALIZE HOW PROTECTIVE YOU'D BE OF HIM.
LEAVING THE TRAP WAS SIMPLE ENOUGH. JUST POST SOME JUICY INFORMATION WHERE HE COULD FIND IT, WAIT FOR HIM TO POUNCE, THEN RETALIATE. ***EASY.***
SO THIS IS ABOUT ***ME.***
OF **COURSE** IT IS.
YOU'RE MY **TARGET.**
SO WHO HIRED YOU?

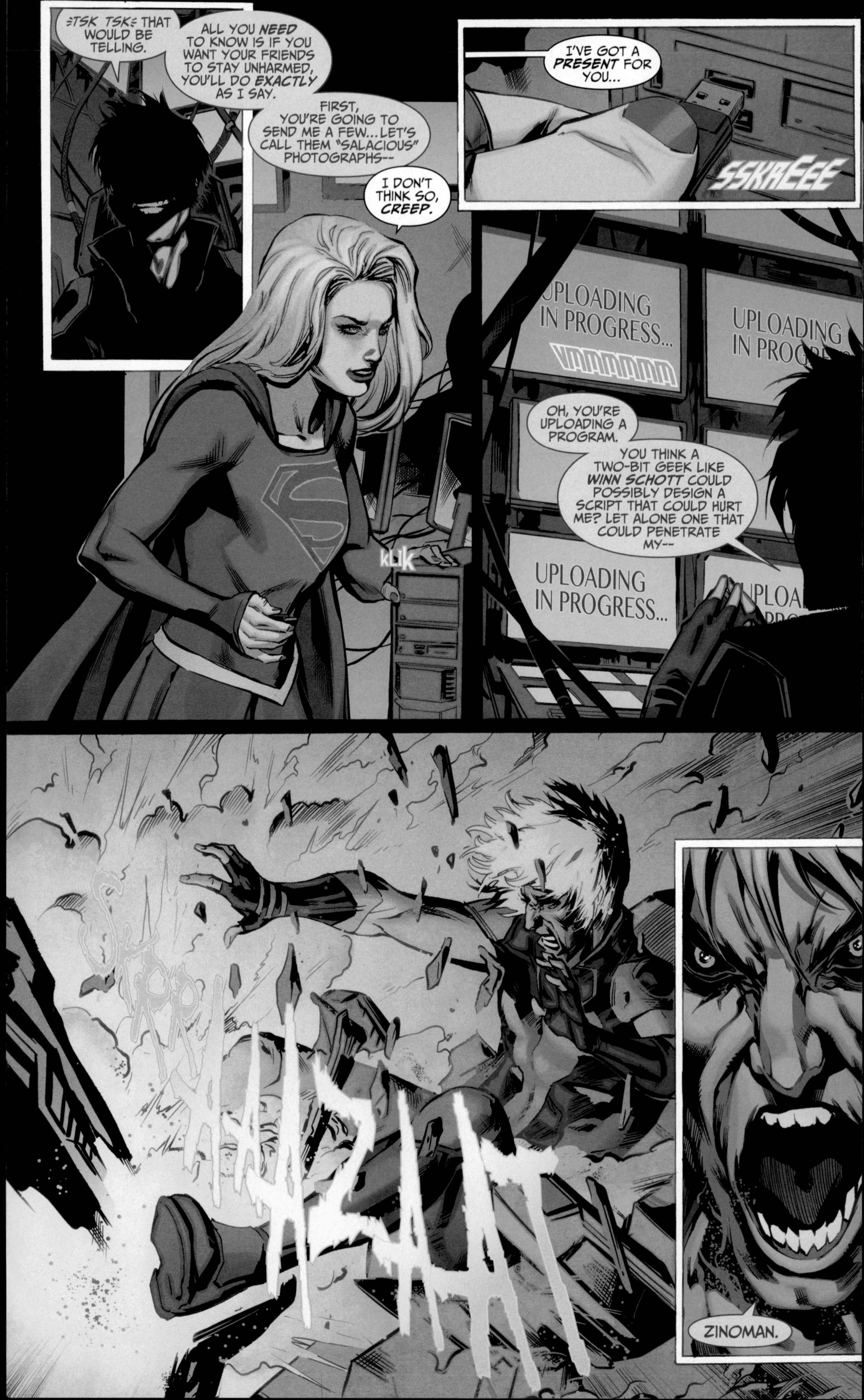

≈TSK TSK≈ THAT WOULD BE TELLING.
ALL YOU NEED TO KNOW IS IF YOU WANT YOUR FRIENDS TO STAY UNHARMED, YOU'LL DO EXACTLY AS I SAY.
FIRST, YOU'RE GOING TO SEND ME A FEW...LET'S CALL THEM "SALACIOUS" PHOTOGRAPHS--
I DON'T THINK SO, CREEP.
I'VE GOT A PRESENT FOR YOU...
SSKREEE
KLIK
UPLOADING IN PROGRESS...
VMMMMM
UPLOADING IN PROGRESS
OH, YOU'RE UPLOADING A PROGRAM.
YOU THINK A TWO-BIT GEEK LIKE WINN SCHOTT COULD POSSIBLY DESIGN A SCRIPT THAT COULD HURT ME? LET ALONE ONE THAT COULD PENETRATE MY--
UPLOADING IN PROGRESS...
HAZZAT
ZINOMAN.

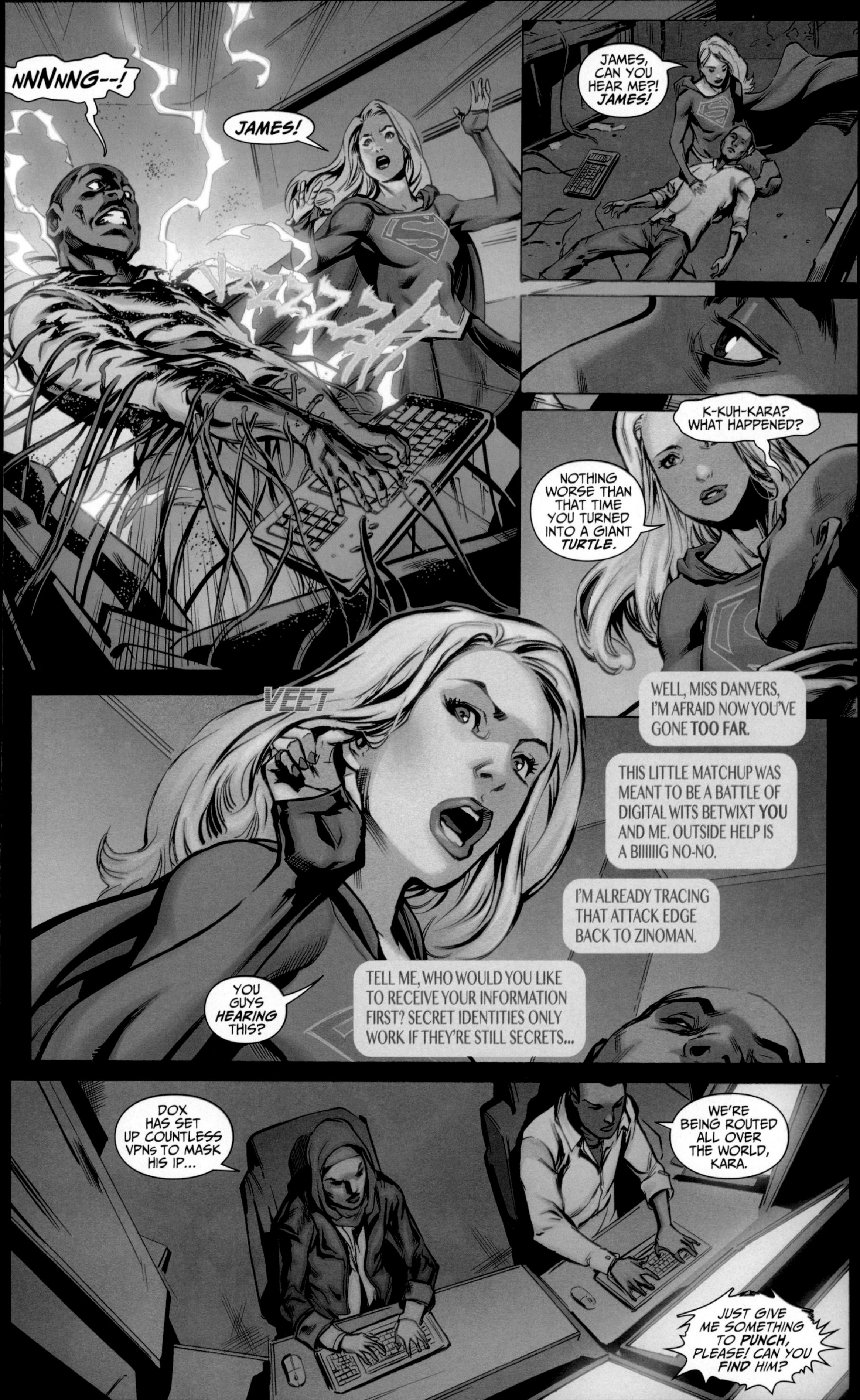
NNNNNG--!
JAMES!
VZZZZZH
JAMES, CAN YOU HEAR ME?! JAMES!
K-KUH-KARA? WHAT HAPPENED?
NOTHING WORSE THAN THAT TIME YOU TURNED INTO A GIANT TURTLE.
VEET
WELL, MISS DANVERS, I'M AFRAID NOW YOU'VE GONE TOO FAR.
THIS LITTLE MATCHUP WAS MEANT TO BE A BATTLE OF DIGITAL WITS BETWIXT YOU AND ME. OUTSIDE HELP IS A BIIIIIIG NO-NO.
I'M ALREADY TRACING THAT ATTACK EDGE BACK TO ZINOMAN.
YOU GUYS HEARING THIS?
TELL ME, WHO WOULD YOU LIKE TO RECEIVE YOUR INFORMATION FIRST? SECRET IDENTITIES ONLY WORK IF THEY'RE STILL SECRETS...
DOX HAS SET UP COUNTLESS VPNs TO MASK HIS IP...
WE'RE BEING ROUTED ALL OVER THE WORLD, KARA.
JUST GIVE ME SOMETHING TO PUNCH, PLEASE! CAN YOU FIND HIM?

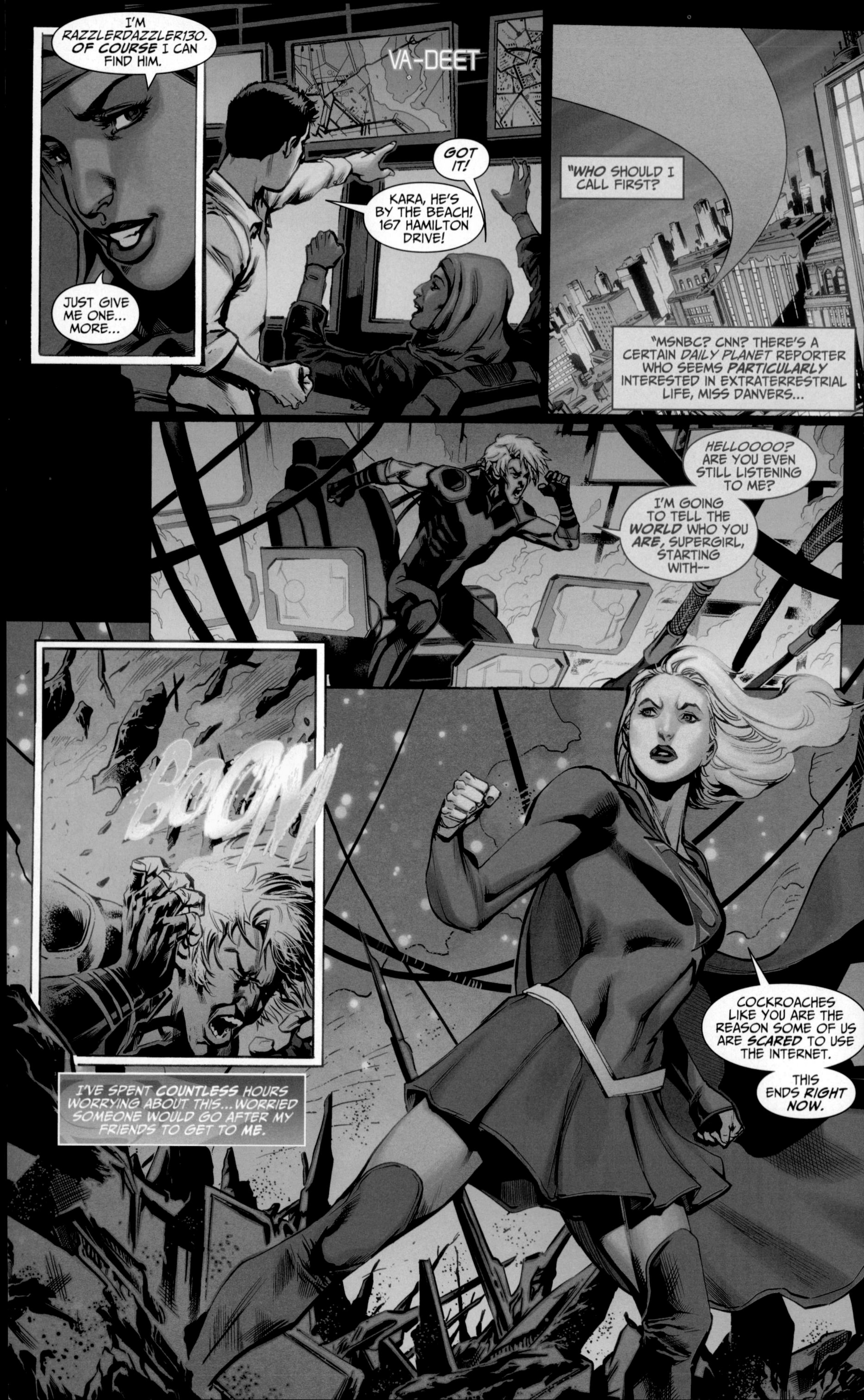
I'M RAZZLERDAZZLER130. OF COURSE I CAN FIND HIM.
VA-DEET
JUST GIVE ME ONE... MORE...
GOT IT!
KARA, HE'S BY THE BEACH! 167 HAMILTON DRIVE!
"WHO SHOULD I CALL FIRST?
"MSNBC? CNN? THERE'S A CERTAIN DAILY PLANET REPORTER WHO SEEMS PARTICULARLY INTERESTED IN EXTRATERRESTRIAL LIFE, MISS DANVERS...
HELLOOOO? ARE YOU EVEN STILL LISTENING TO ME?
I'M GOING TO TELL THE WORLD WHO YOU ARE, SUPERGIRL, STARTING WITH--
BOOM
I'VE SPENT COUNTLESS HOURS WORRYING ABOUT THIS...WORRIED SOMEONE WOULD GO AFTER MY FRIENDS TO GET TO ME.
COCKROACHES LIKE YOU ARE THE REASON SOME OF US ARE SCARED TO USE THE INTERNET.
THIS ENDS RIGHT NOW.

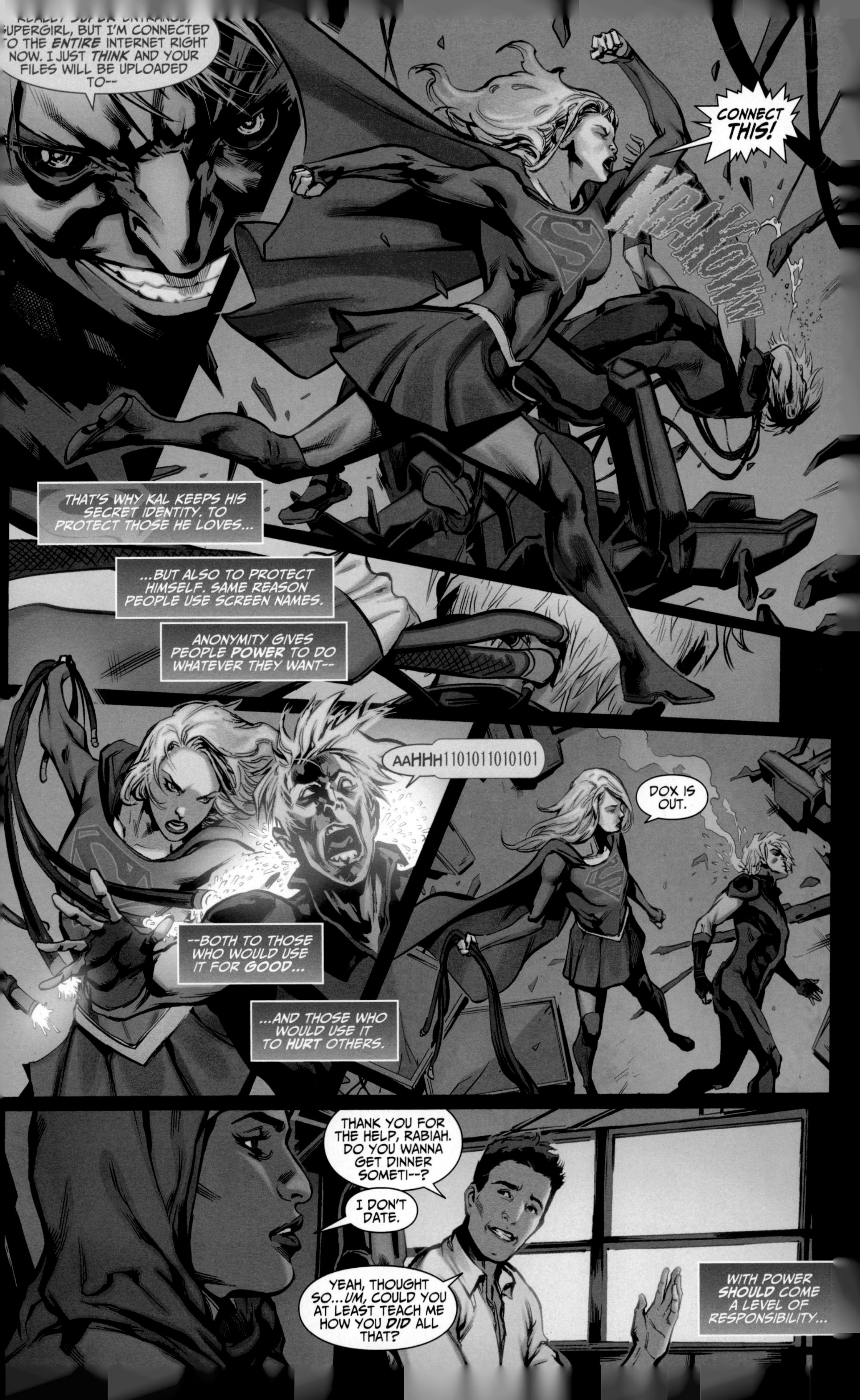
SUPERGIRL, BUT I'M CONNECTED TO THE *ENTIRE* INTERNET RIGHT NOW. I JUST *THINK* AND YOUR FILES WILL BE UPLOADED TO--
CONNECT THIS!
THAT'S WHY KAL KEEPS HIS SECRET IDENTITY. TO PROTECT THOSE HE LOVES...
...BUT ALSO TO PROTECT HIMSELF. SAME REASON PEOPLE USE SCREEN NAMES.
ANONYMITY GIVES PEOPLE *POWER* TO DO WHATEVER THEY WANT--
AAHHH1101011010101
--BOTH TO THOSE WHO WOULD USE IT FOR *GOOD*...
...AND THOSE WHO WOULD USE IT TO *HURT* OTHERS.
DOX IS OUT.
THANK YOU FOR THE HELP, RABIAH. DO YOU WANNA GET DINNER SOMETI--?
I DON'T DATE.
YEAH, THOUGHT SO...*UM*, COULD YOU AT LEAST TEACH ME HOW YOU *DID* ALL THAT?
WITH POWER *SHOULD* COME A LEVEL OF RESPONSIBILITY...

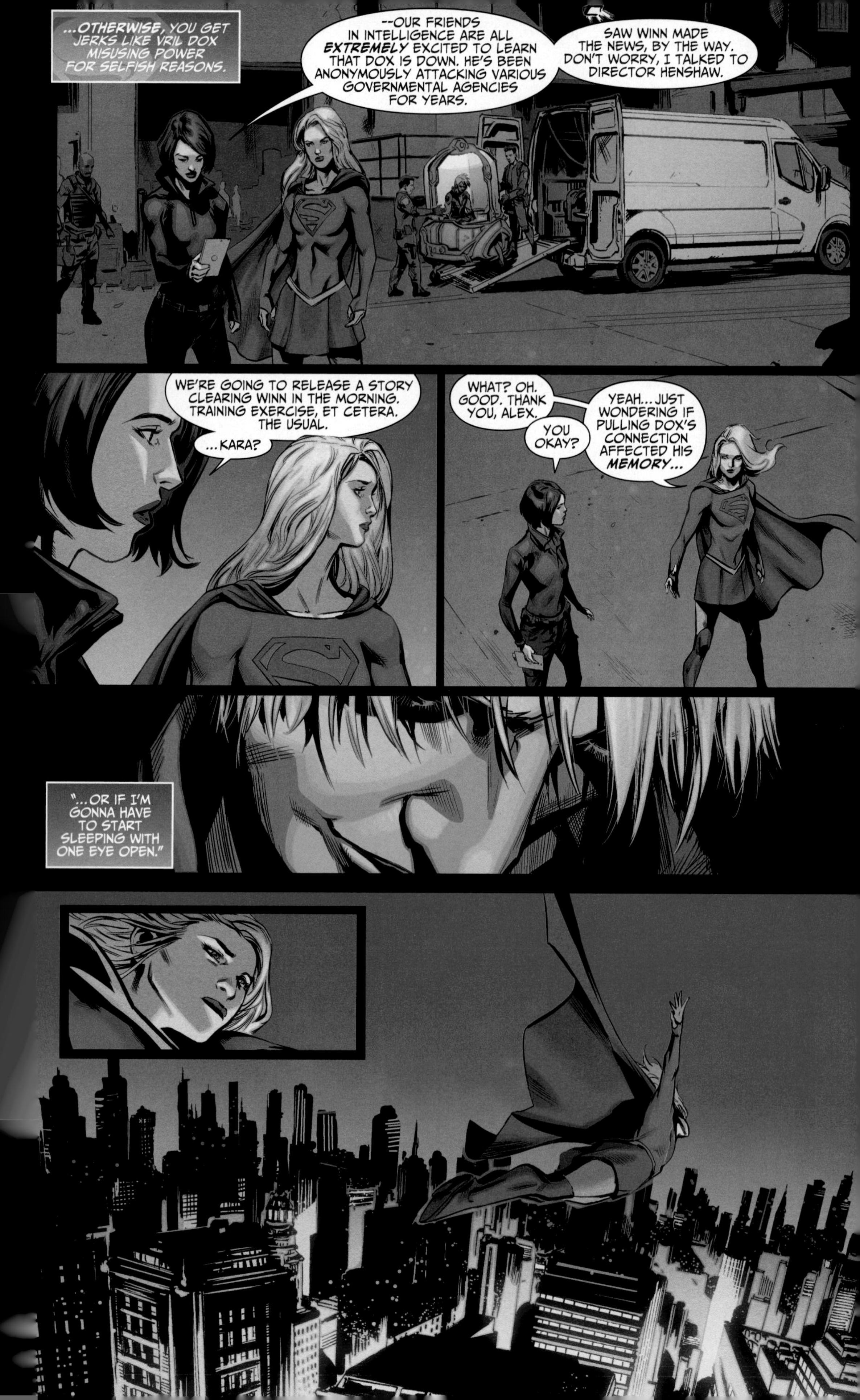

...OTHERWISE, YOU GET JERKS LIKE VRIL DOX MISUSING POWER FOR SELFISH REASONS.
--OUR FRIENDS IN INTELLIGENCE ARE ALL EXTREMELY EXCITED TO LEARN THAT DOX IS DOWN. HE'S BEEN ANONYMOUSLY ATTACKING VARIOUS GOVERNMENTAL AGENCIES FOR YEARS.
SAW WINN MADE THE NEWS, BY THE WAY. DON'T WORRY, I TALKED TO DIRECTOR HENSHAW.
WE'RE GOING TO RELEASE A STORY CLEARING WINN IN THE MORNING. TRAINING EXERCISE, ET CETERA. THE USUAL.
...KARA?
WHAT? OH. GOOD. THANK YOU, ALEX.
YOU OKAY?
YEAH... JUST WONDERING IF PULLING DOX'S CONNECTION AFFECTED HIS MEMORY...
"...OR IF I'M GONNA HAVE TO START SLEEPING WITH ONE EYE OPEN."

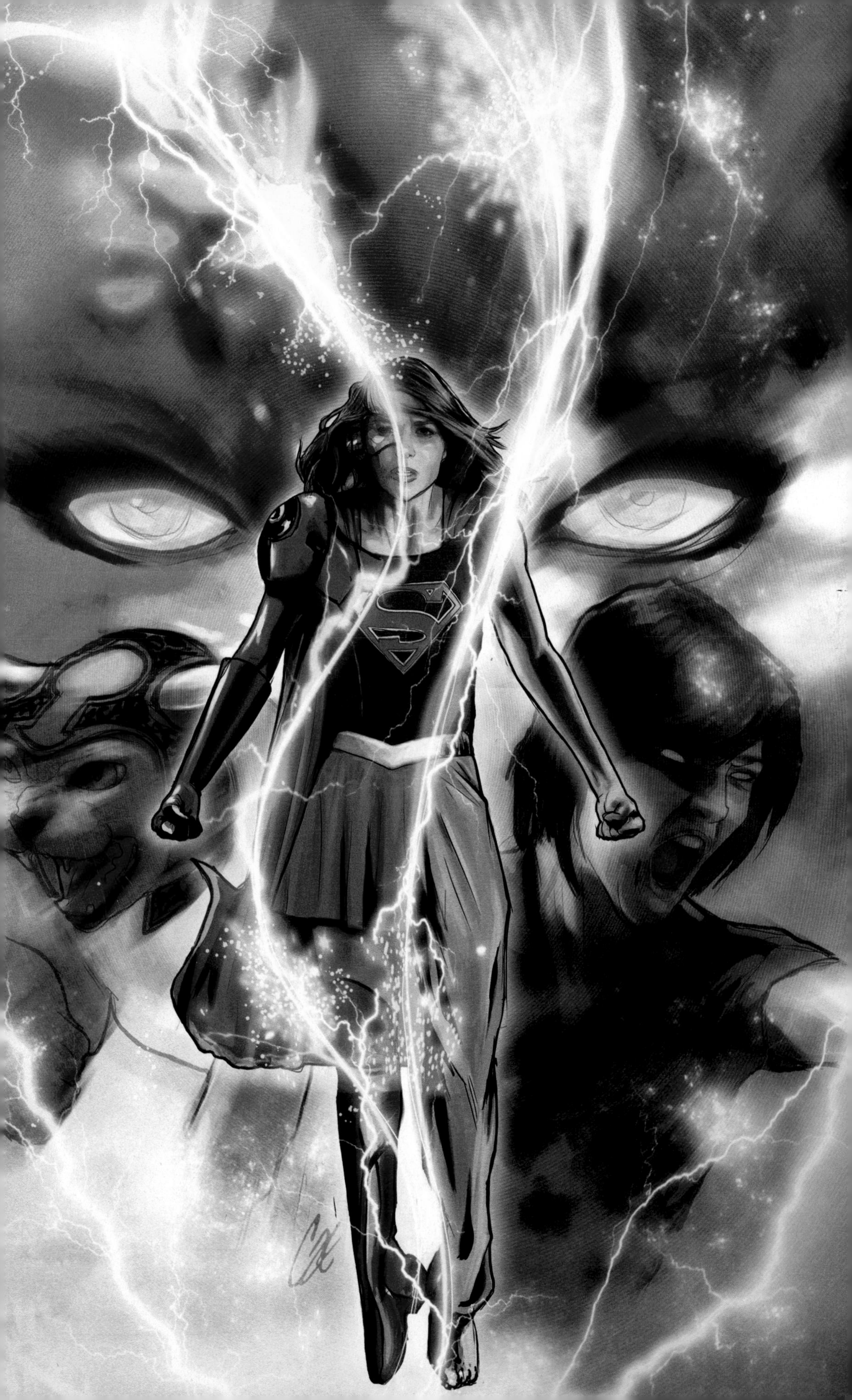

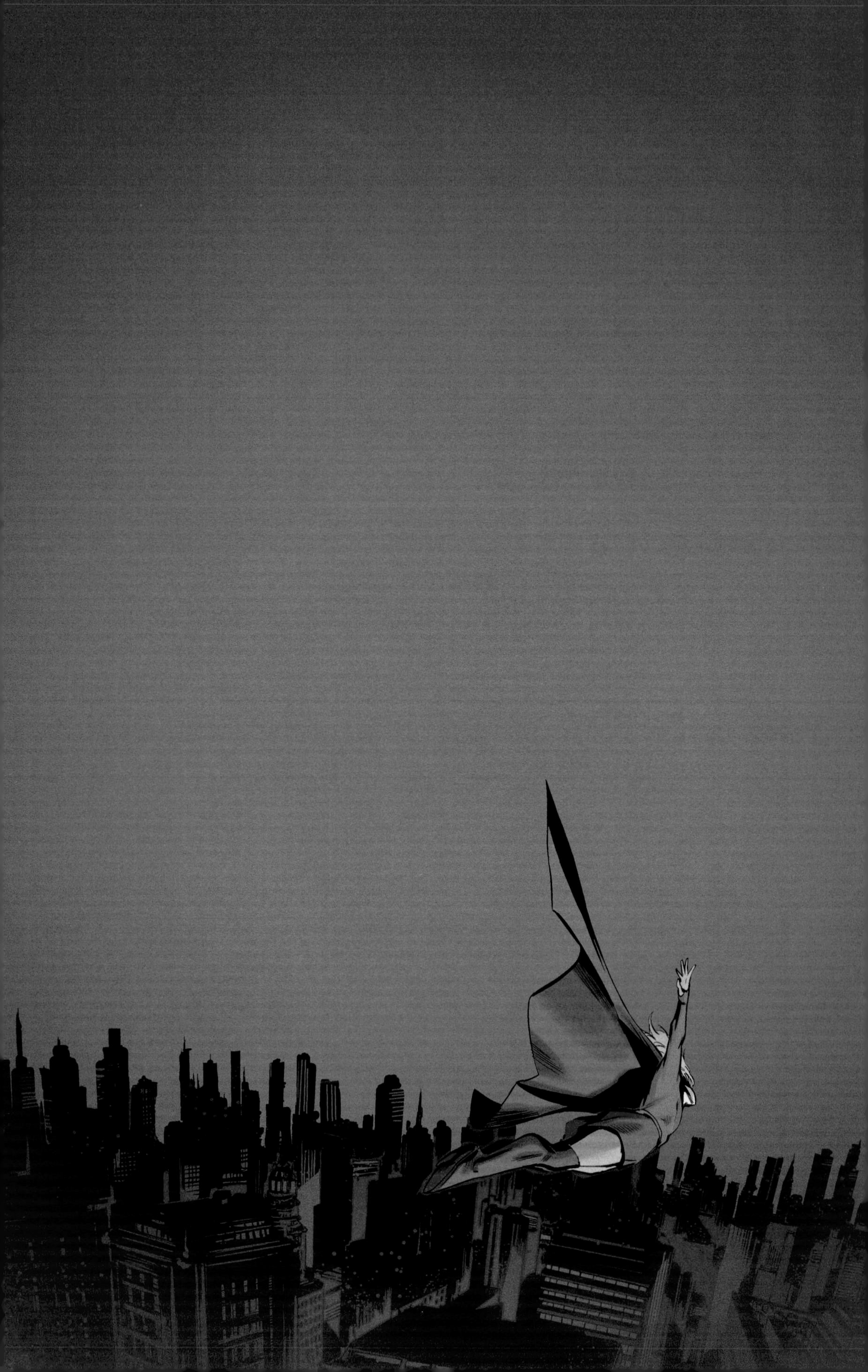

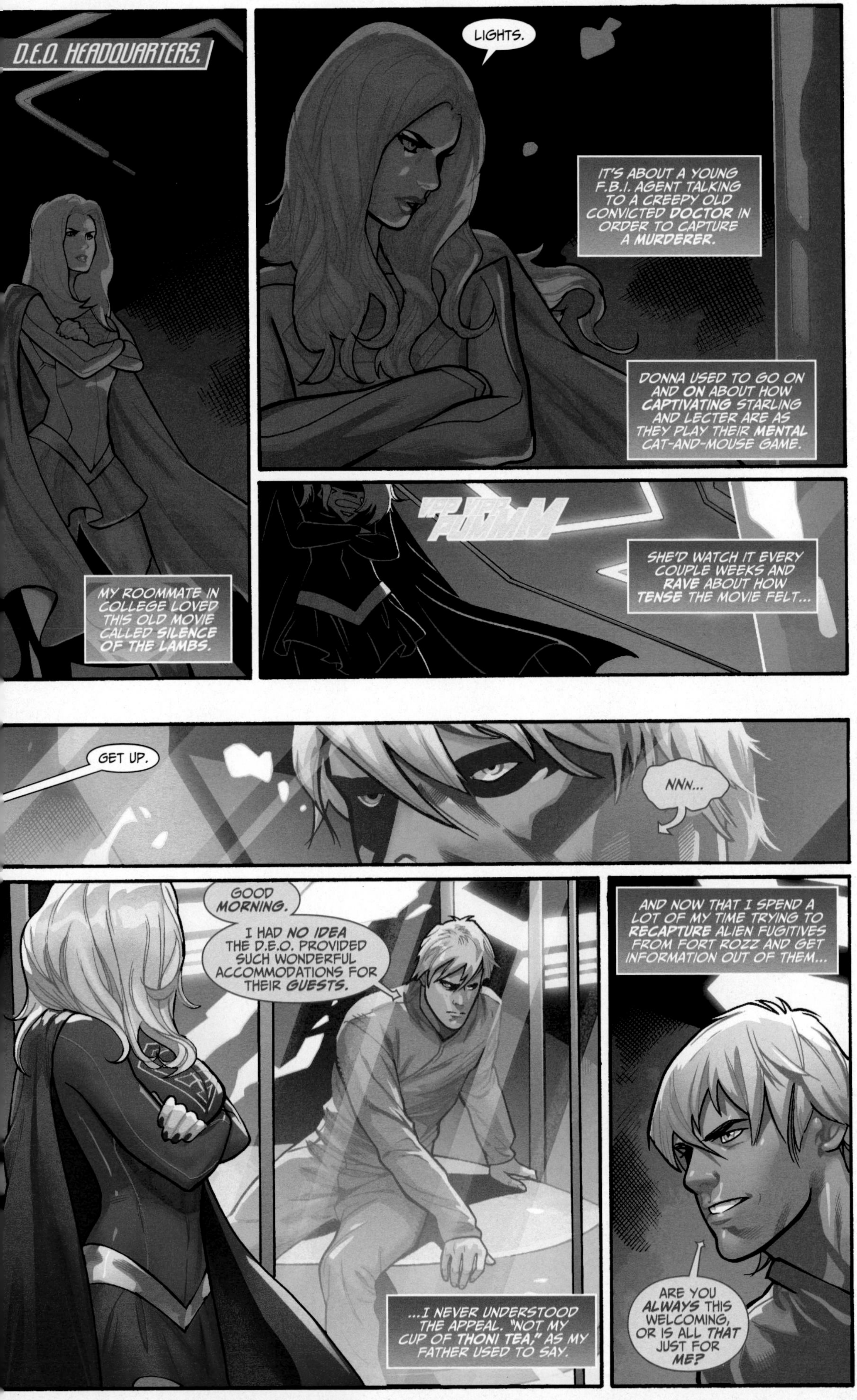
D.E.O. HEADQUARTERS.
MY ROOMMATE IN COLLEGE LOVED THIS OLD MOVIE CALLED SILENCE OF THE LAMBS.
LIGHTS.
IT'S ABOUT A YOUNG F.B.I. AGENT TALKING TO A CREEPY OLD CONVICTED DOCTOR IN ORDER TO CAPTURE A MURDERER.
DONNA USED TO GO ON AND ON ABOUT HOW CAPTIVATING STARLING AND LECTER ARE AS THEY PLAY THEIR MENTAL CAT-AND-MOUSE GAME.
SHE'D WATCH IT EVERY COUPLE WEEKS AND RAVE ABOUT HOW TENSE THE MOVIE FELT...
GET UP.
NNN...
GOOD MORNING.
I HAD NO IDEA THE D.E.O. PROVIDED SUCH WONDERFUL ACCOMMODATIONS FOR THEIR GUESTS.
...I NEVER UNDERSTOOD THE APPEAL. "NOT MY CUP OF THONI TEA," AS MY FATHER USED TO SAY.
AND NOW THAT I SPEND A LOT OF MY TIME TRYING TO RECAPTURE ALIEN FUGITIVES FROM FORT ROZZ AND GET INFORMATION OUT OF THEM...
ARE YOU ALWAYS THIS WELCOMING, OR IS ALL THAT JUST FOR ME?

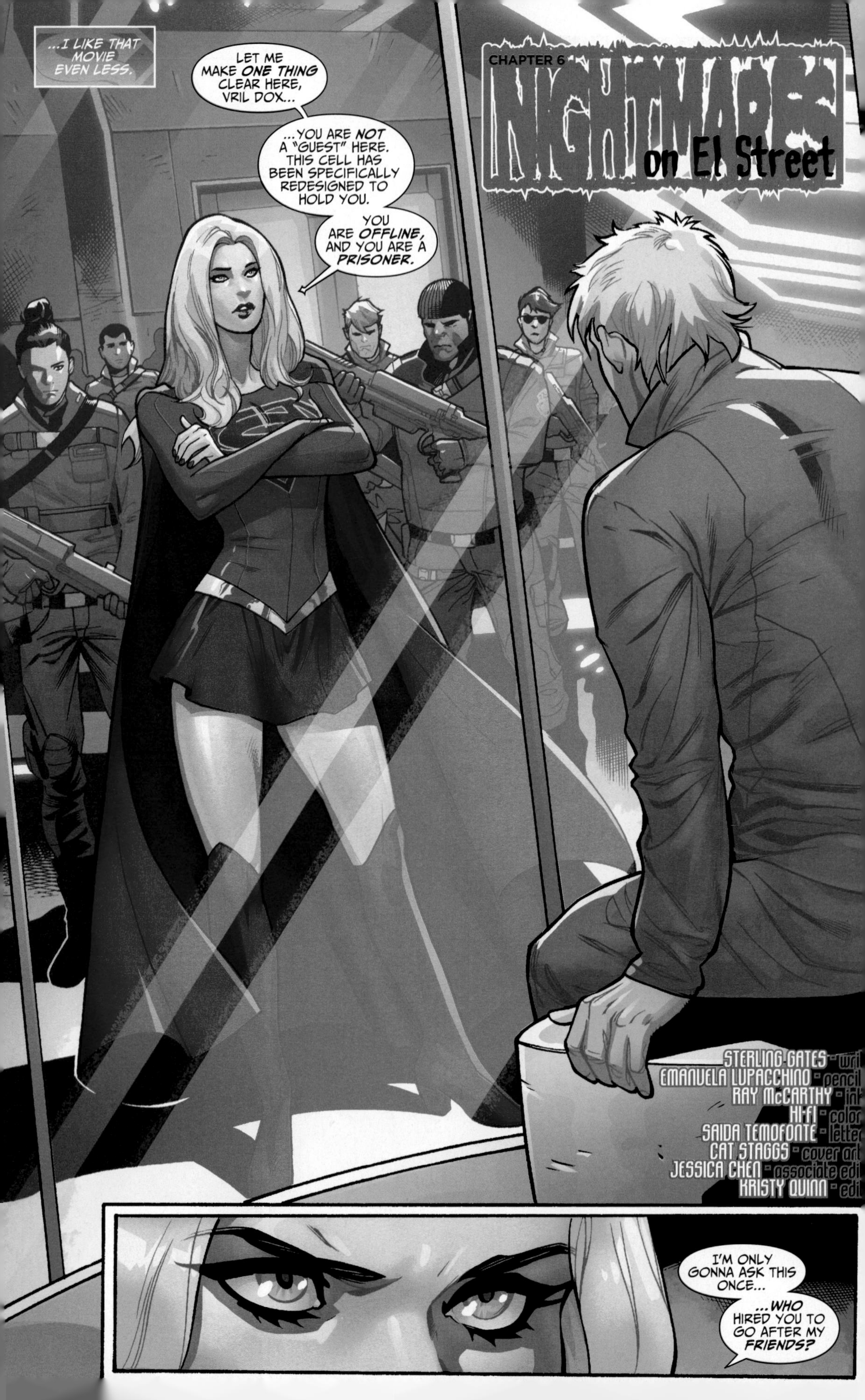
...I LIKE THAT MOVIE EVEN LESS.
LET ME MAKE ONE THING CLEAR HERE, VRIL DOX...
...YOU ARE NOT A "GUEST" HERE. THIS CELL HAS BEEN SPECIFICALLY REDESIGNED TO HOLD YOU.
YOU ARE OFFLINE, AND YOU ARE A PRISONER.
CHAPTER 6
NIGHTMARES on El Street
STERLING GATES - wri
EMANUELA LUPACCHINO - pencil
RAY McCARTHY - ink
HI-FI - color
SAIDA TEMOFONTE - letter
CAT STAGGS - cover art
JESSICA CHEN - associate edi
KRISTY QUINN - edi
I'M ONLY GONNA ASK THIS ONCE...
...WHO HIRED YOU TO GO AFTER MY FRIENDS?

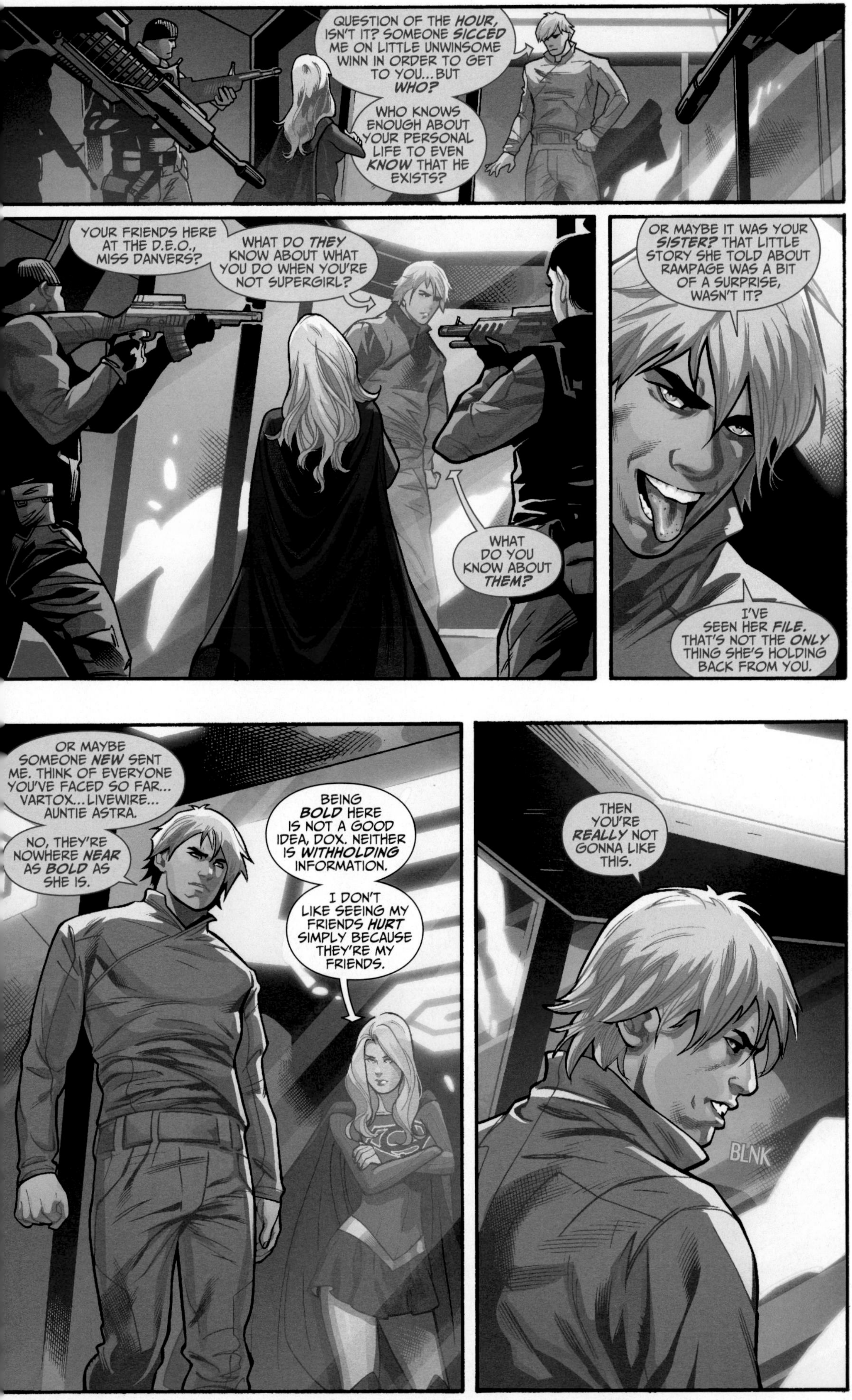
QUESTION OF THE HOUR, ISN'T IT? SOMEONE SICCED ME ON LITTLE UNWINSOME WINN IN ORDER TO GET TO YOU...BUT WHO?
WHO KNOWS ENOUGH ABOUT YOUR PERSONAL LIFE TO EVEN KNOW THAT HE EXISTS?
YOUR FRIENDS HERE AT THE D.E.O., MISS DANVERS?
WHAT DO THEY KNOW ABOUT WHAT YOU DO WHEN YOU'RE NOT SUPERGIRL?
WHAT DO YOU KNOW ABOUT THEM?
OR MAYBE IT WAS YOUR SISTER? THAT LITTLE STORY SHE TOLD ABOUT RAMPAGE WAS A BIT OF A SURPRISE, WASN'T IT?
I'VE SEEN HER FILE. THAT'S NOT THE ONLY THING SHE'S HOLDING BACK FROM YOU.
OR MAYBE SOMEONE NEW SENT ME. THINK OF EVERYONE YOU'VE FACED SO FAR... VARTOX...LIVEWIRE... AUNTIE ASTRA.
NO, THEY'RE NOWHERE NEAR AS BOLD AS SHE IS.
BEING BOLD HERE IS NOT A GOOD IDEA, DOX. NEITHER IS WITHHOLDING INFORMATION.
I DON'T LIKE SEEING MY FRIENDS HURT SIMPLY BECAUSE THEY'RE MY FRIENDS.
THEN YOU'RE REALLY NOT GONNA LIKE THIS.
BLNK

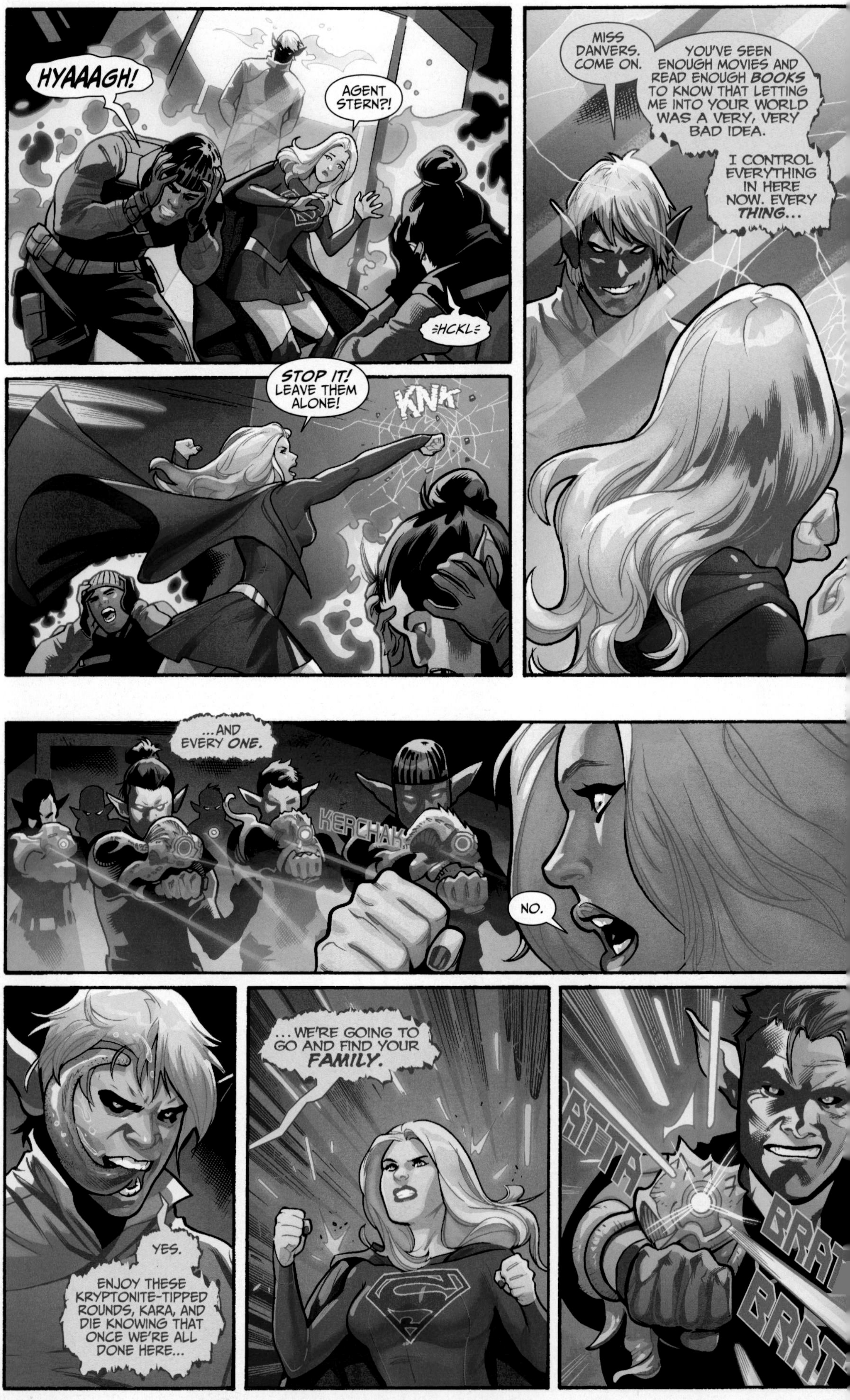
HYAAAGH!
AGENT STERN?!
HCKL
MISS DANVERS. COME ON.
YOU'VE SEEN ENOUGH MOVIES AND READ ENOUGH BOOKS TO KNOW THAT LETTING ME INTO YOUR WORLD WAS A VERY, VERY BAD IDEA.
I CONTROL EVERYTHING IN HERE NOW. EVERY THING...
STOP IT! LEAVE THEM ALONE!
KNK
...AND EVERY ONE.
KERCHAK
NO.
YES.
ENJOY THESE KRYPTONITE-TIPPED ROUNDS, KARA, AND DIE KNOWING THAT ONCE WE'RE ALL DONE HERE...
...WE'RE GOING TO GO AND FIND YOUR FAMILY.
BRAT
BRAT

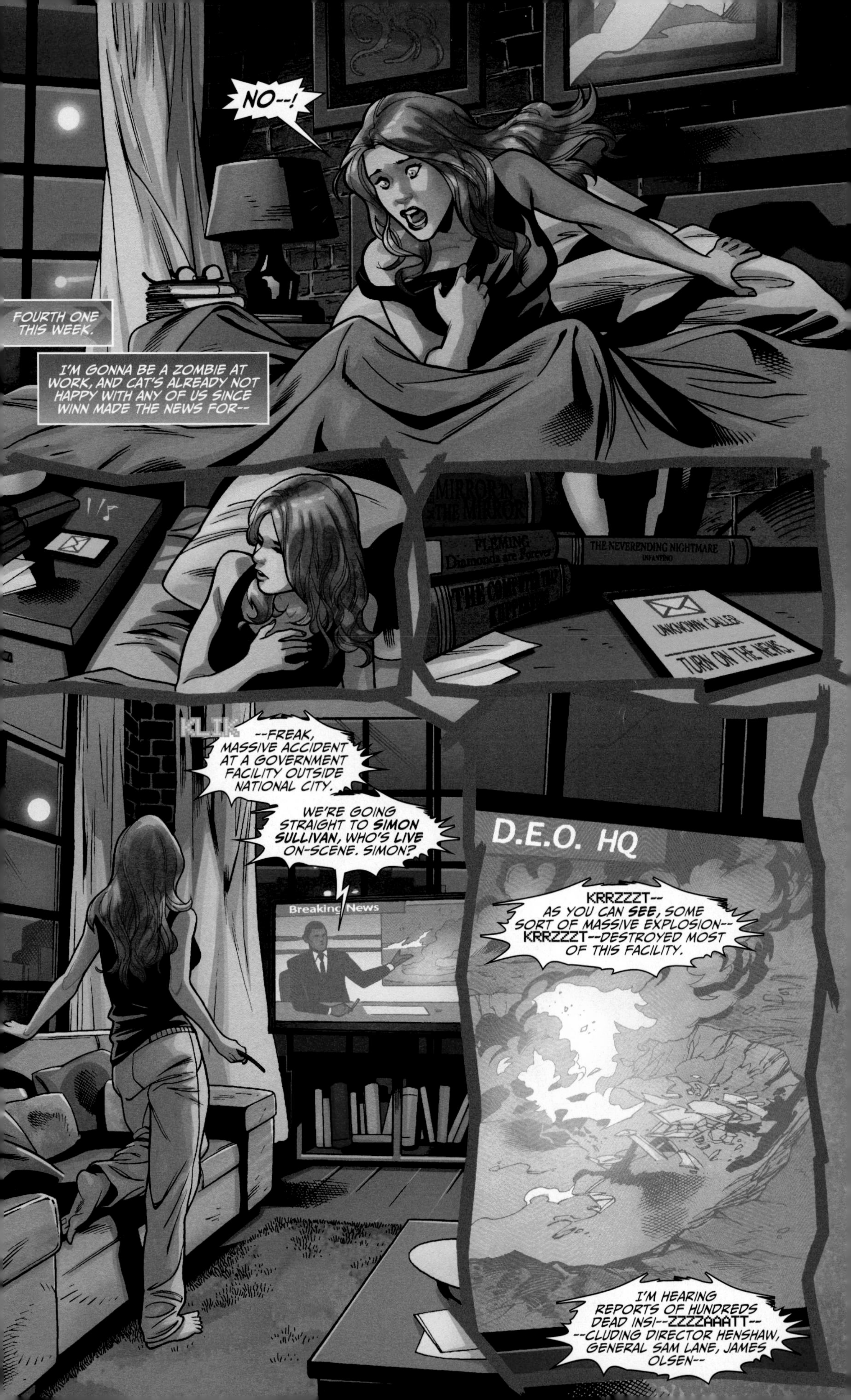
NO--!
FOURTH ONE THIS WEEK.
I'M GONNA BE A ZOMBIE AT WORK, AND CAT'S ALREADY NOT HAPPY WITH ANY OF US SINCE WINN MADE THE NEWS FOR--
MIRROR 'N THE MIRROR
FLEMING Diamonds are Forever
THE NEVERENDING NIGHTMARE INFANTINO
UNKNOWN CALLER
TURN ON THE NEWS.
KLIK
--FREAK, MASSIVE ACCIDENT AT A GOVERNMENT FACILITY OUTSIDE NATIONAL CITY.
WE'RE GOING STRAIGHT TO SIMON SULLIVAN, WHO'S LIVE ON-SCENE. SIMON?
Breaking News
D.E.O. HQ
KRZZZT-- AS YOU CAN SEE, SOME SORT OF MASSIVE EXPLOSION-- KRZZZT--DESTROYED MOST OF THIS FACILITY.
I'M HEARING REPORTS OF HUNDREDS DEAD INSI--ZZZZAAATT-- --CLUDING DIRECTOR HENSHAW, GENERAL SAM LANE, JAMES OLSEN--

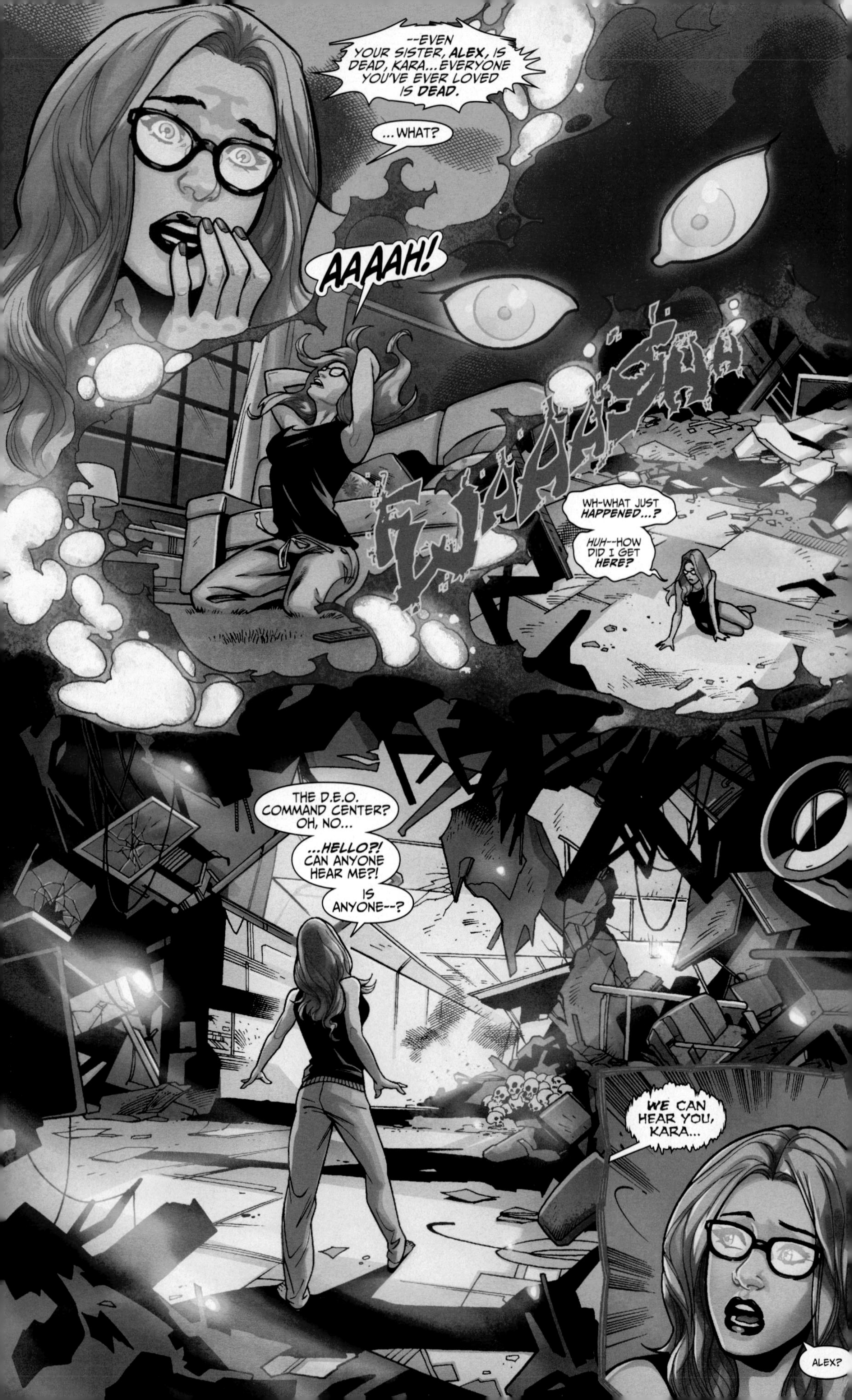
--EVEN YOUR SISTER, ALEX, IS DEAD, KARA...EVERYONE YOU'VE EVER LOVED IS DEAD.
...WHAT?
AAAAH!
FWAAASHH
WH-WHAT JUST HAPPENED...?
HUH--HOW DID I GET HERE?
THE D.E.O. COMMAND CENTER? OH, NO...
...HELLO?! CAN ANYONE HEAR ME?!
IS ANYONE--?
WE CAN HEAR YOU, KARA...
ALEX?

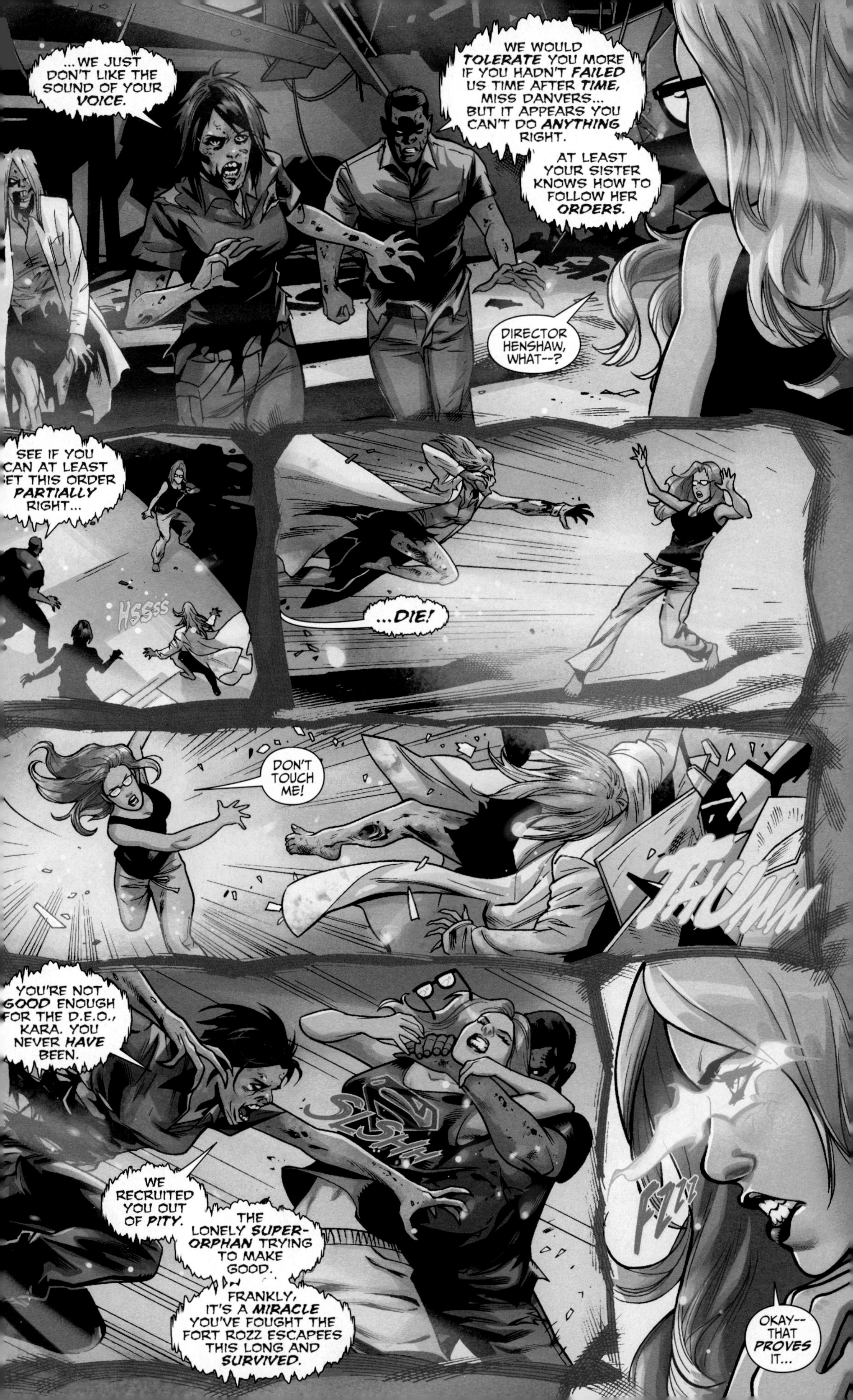
...WE JUST DON'T LIKE THE SOUND OF YOUR VOICE.
WE WOULD TOLERATE YOU MORE IF YOU HADN'T FAILED US TIME AFTER TIME, MISS DANVERS... BUT IT APPEARS YOU CAN'T DO ANYTHING RIGHT.
AT LEAST YOUR SISTER KNOWS HOW TO FOLLOW HER ORDERS.
DIRECTOR HENSHAW, WHAT--?
SEE IF YOU CAN AT LEAST GET THIS ORDER PARTIALLY RIGHT...
HSSSS
...DIE!
DON'T TOUCH ME!
THUMM
YOU'RE NOT GOOD ENOUGH FOR THE D.E.O., KARA. YOU NEVER HAVE BEEN.
SLSHH
WE RECRUITED YOU OUT OF PITY.
THE LONELY SUPER-ORPHAN TRYING TO MAKE GOOD.
FRANKLY, IT'S A MIRACLE YOU'VE FOUGHT THE FORT ROZZ ESCAPEES THIS LONG AND SURVIVED.
FZZZ
OKAY--THAT PROVES IT...

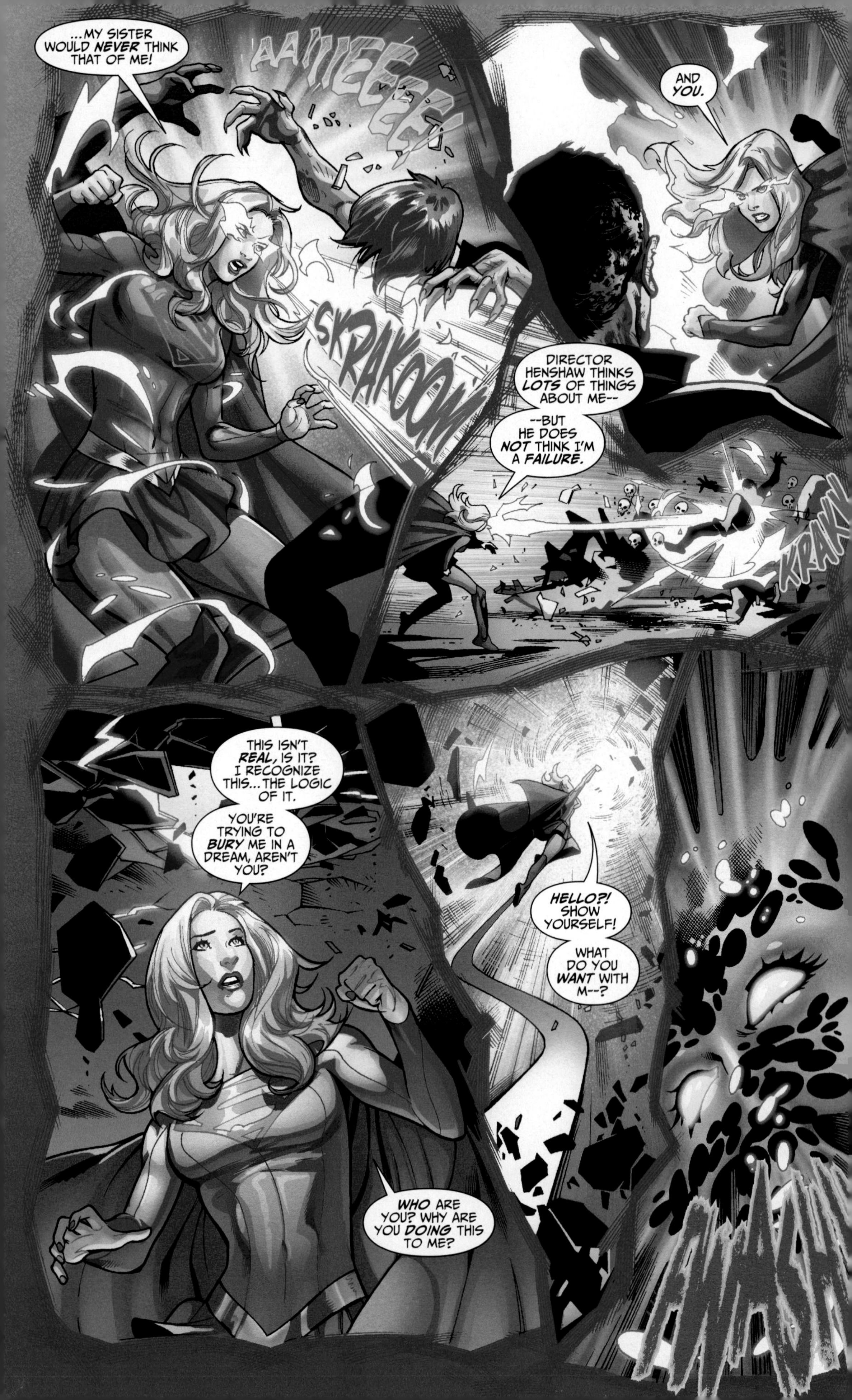
...MY SISTER WOULD NEVER THINK THAT OF ME!
AAIIIEEEGG
SKRAKOOM
AND YOU.
DIRECTOR HENSHAW THINKS LOTS OF THINGS ABOUT ME--
--BUT HE DOES NOT THINK I'M A FAILURE.
KRAK
THIS ISN'T REAL, IS IT? I RECOGNIZE THIS...THE LOGIC OF IT.
YOU'RE TRYING TO BURY ME IN A DREAM, AREN'T YOU?
WHO ARE YOU? WHY ARE YOU DOING THIS TO ME?
HELLO?! SHOW YOURSELF!
WHAT DO YOU WANT WITH M--?

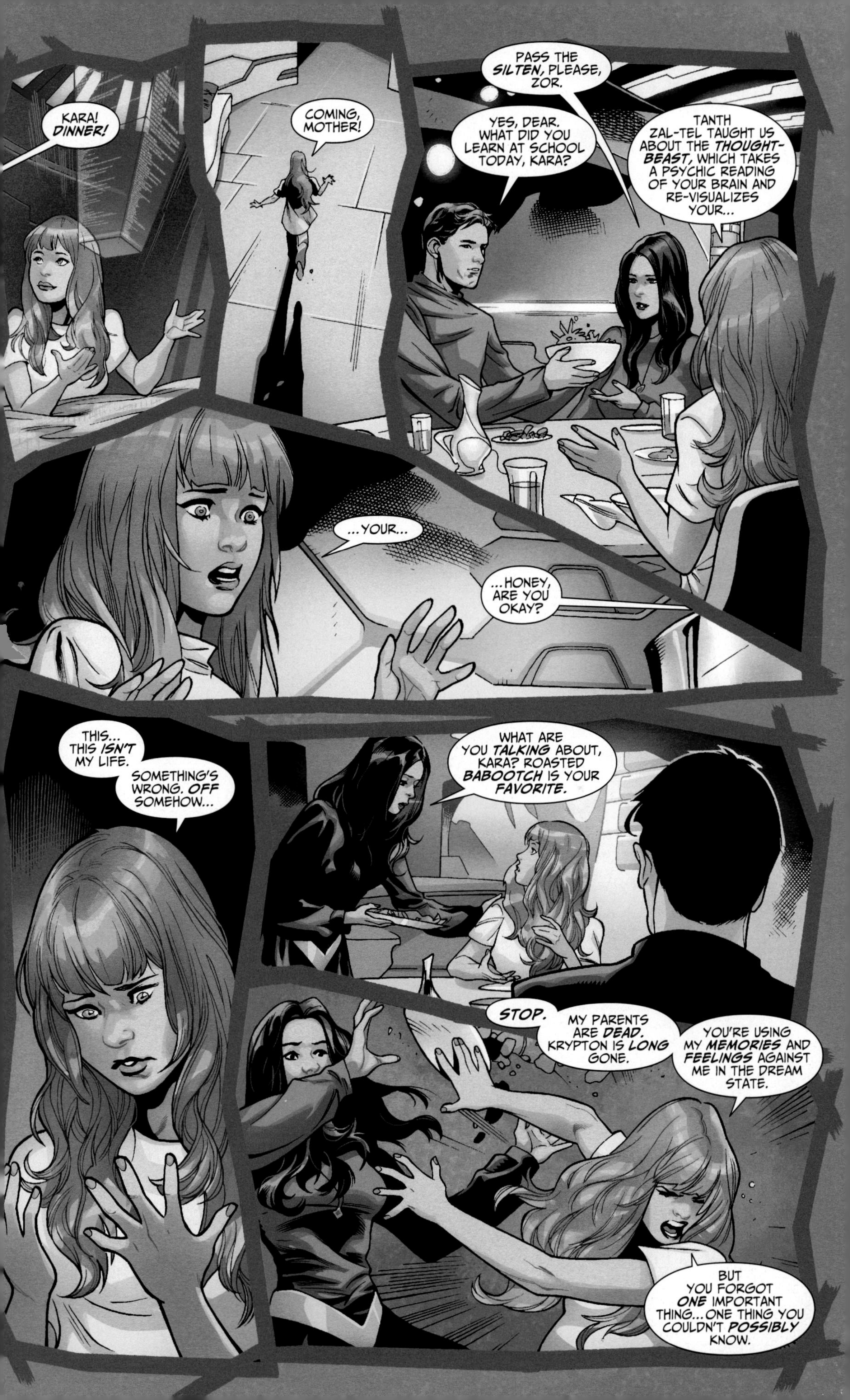
KARA! DINNER!
COMING, MOTHER!
PASS THE SILTEN, PLEASE, ZOR.
YES, DEAR. WHAT DID YOU LEARN AT SCHOOL TODAY, KARA?
TANTH ZAL-TEL TAUGHT US ABOUT THE THOUGHT-BEAST, WHICH TAKES A PSYCHIC READING OF YOUR BRAIN AND RE-VISUALIZES YOUR...
...YOUR...
...HONEY, ARE YOU OKAY?
THIS... THIS ISN'T MY LIFE.
SOMETHING'S WRONG. OFF SOMEHOW...
WHAT ARE YOU TALKING ABOUT, KARA? ROASTED BABOOTCH IS YOUR FAVORITE.
STOP.
MY PARENTS ARE DEAD. KRYPTON IS LONG GONE.
YOU'RE USING MY MEMORIES AND FEELINGS AGAINST ME IN THE DREAM STATE.
BUT YOU FORGOT ONE IMPORTANT THING...ONE THING YOU COULDN'T POSSIBLY KNOW.

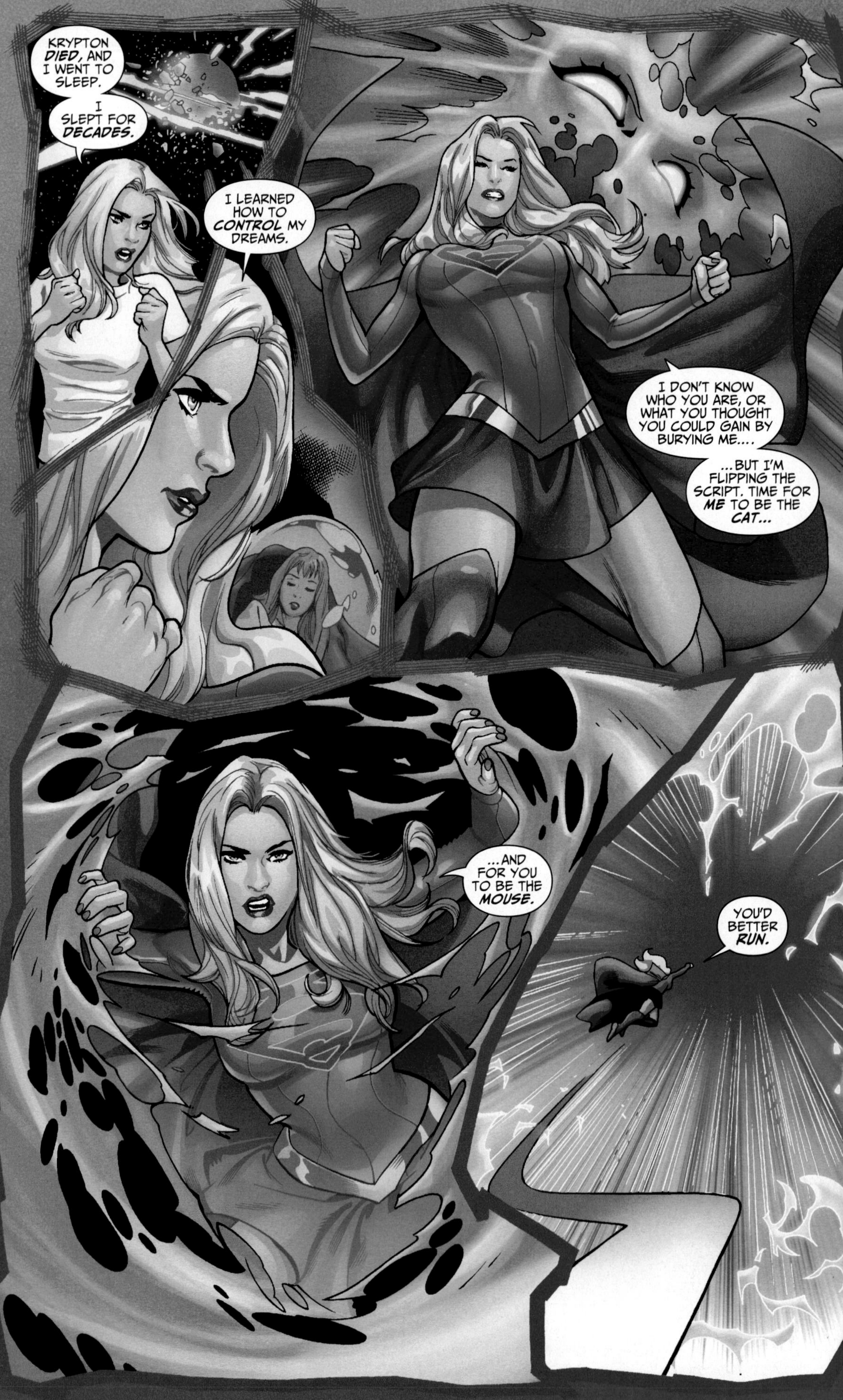
KRYPTON DIED, AND I WENT TO SLEEP.
I SLEPT FOR DECADES.
I LEARNED HOW TO CONTROL MY DREAMS.
I DON'T KNOW WHO YOU ARE, OR WHAT YOU THOUGHT YOU COULD GAIN BY BURYING ME....
...BUT I'M FLIPPING THE SCRIPT. TIME FOR ME TO BE THE CAT...
...AND FOR YOU TO BE THE MOUSE.
YOU'D BETTER RUN.

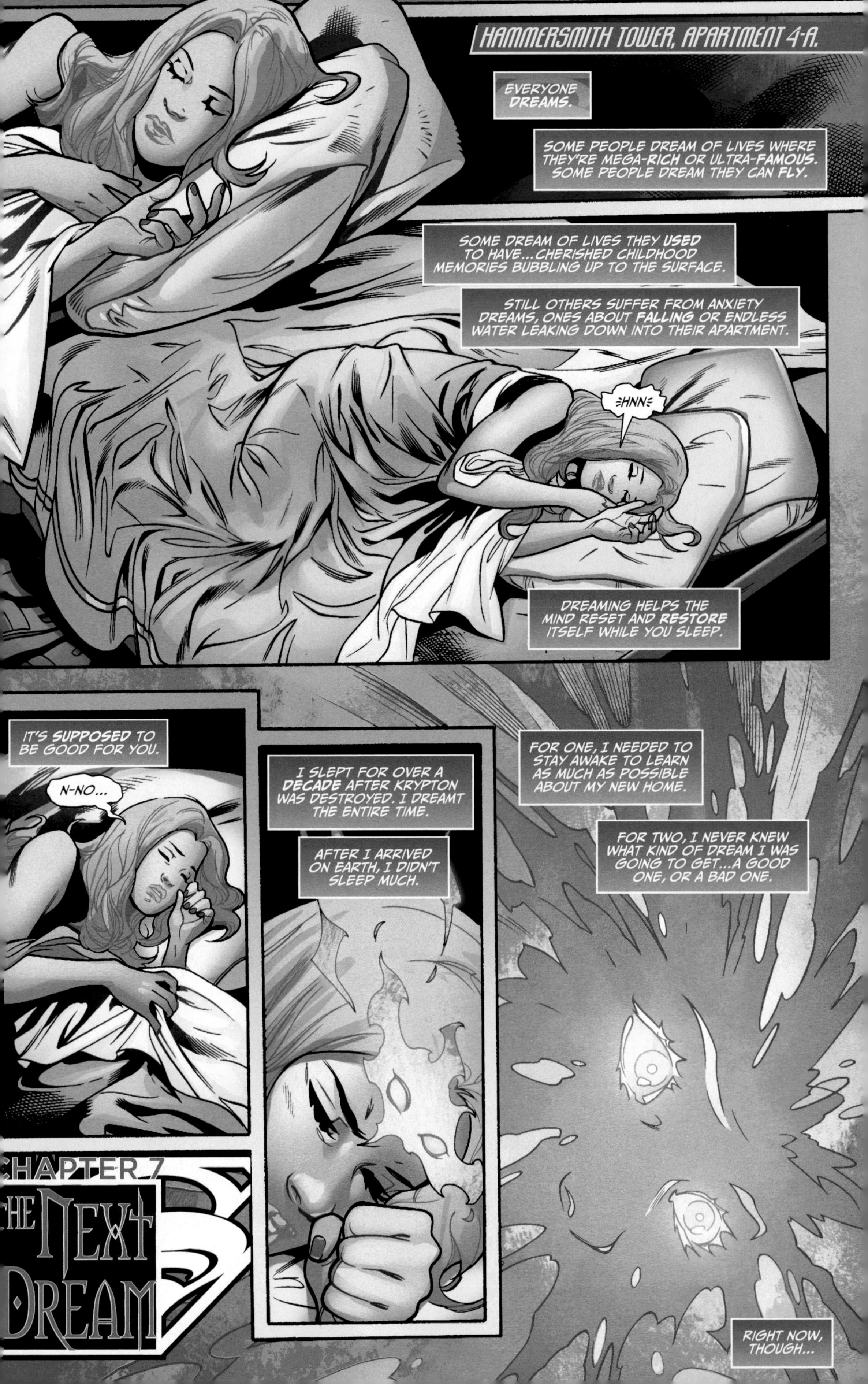
HAMMERSMITH TOWER, APARTMENT 4-A.
EVERYONE DREAMS.
SOME PEOPLE DREAM OF LIVES WHERE THEY'RE MEGA-RICH OR ULTRA-FAMOUS. SOME PEOPLE DREAM THEY CAN FLY.
SOME DREAM OF LIVES THEY USED TO HAVE...CHERISHED CHILDHOOD MEMORIES BUBBLING UP TO THE SURFACE.
STILL OTHERS SUFFER FROM ANXIETY DREAMS, ONES ABOUT FALLING OR ENDLESS WATER LEAKING DOWN INTO THEIR APARTMENT.
HNN
DREAMING HELPS THE MIND RESET AND RESTORE ITSELF WHILE YOU SLEEP.
IT'S SUPPOSED TO BE GOOD FOR YOU.
N-NO...
I SLEPT FOR OVER A DECADE AFTER KRYPTON WAS DESTROYED. I DREAMT THE ENTIRE TIME.
AFTER I ARRIVED ON EARTH, I DIDN'T SLEEP MUCH.
FOR ONE, I NEEDED TO STAY AWAKE TO LEARN AS MUCH AS POSSIBLE ABOUT MY NEW HOME.
FOR TWO, I NEVER KNEW WHAT KIND OF DREAM I WAS GOING TO GET...A GOOD ONE, OR A BAD ONE.
CHAPTER 7
THE NEXT DREAM
RIGHT NOW, THOUGH...

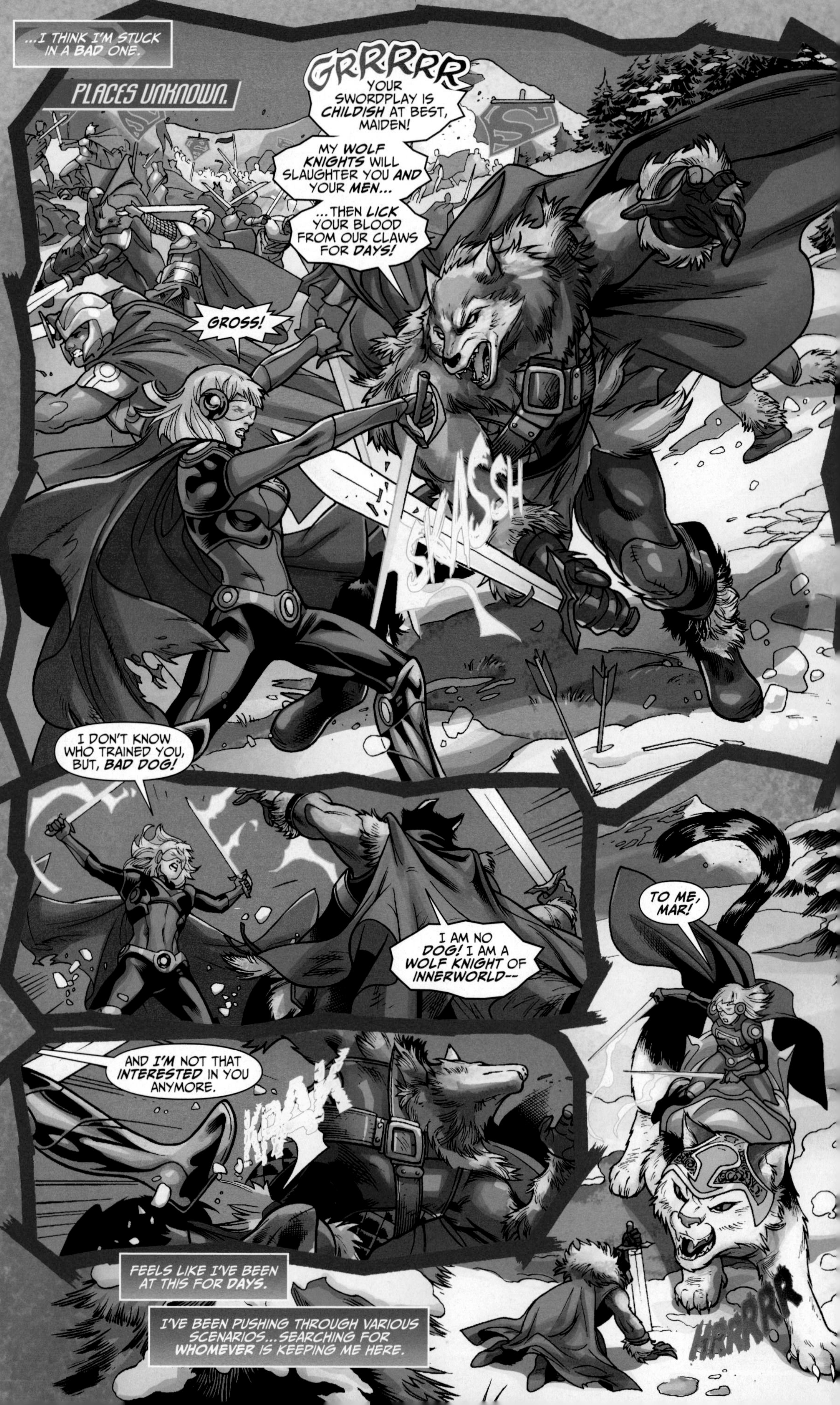
...I THINK I'M STUCK IN A BAD ONE.
PLACES UNKNOWN.
GRRRRR
YOUR SWORDPLAY IS CHILDISH AT BEST, MAIDEN!
MY WOLF KNIGHTS WILL SLAUGHTER YOU AND YOUR MEN...
...THEN LICK YOUR BLOOD FROM OUR CLAWS FOR DAYS!
GROSS!
SKASSH
I DON'T KNOW WHO TRAINED YOU, BUT, BAD DOG!
I AM NO DOG! I AM A WOLF KNIGHT OF INNERWORLD--
TO ME, MAR!
AND I'M NOT THAT INTERESTED IN YOU ANYMORE.
KRAK
FEELS LIKE I'VE BEEN AT THIS FOR DAYS.
I'VE BEEN PUSHING THROUGH VARIOUS SCENARIOS...SEARCHING FOR WHOMEVER IS KEEPING ME HERE.
HRRRRR

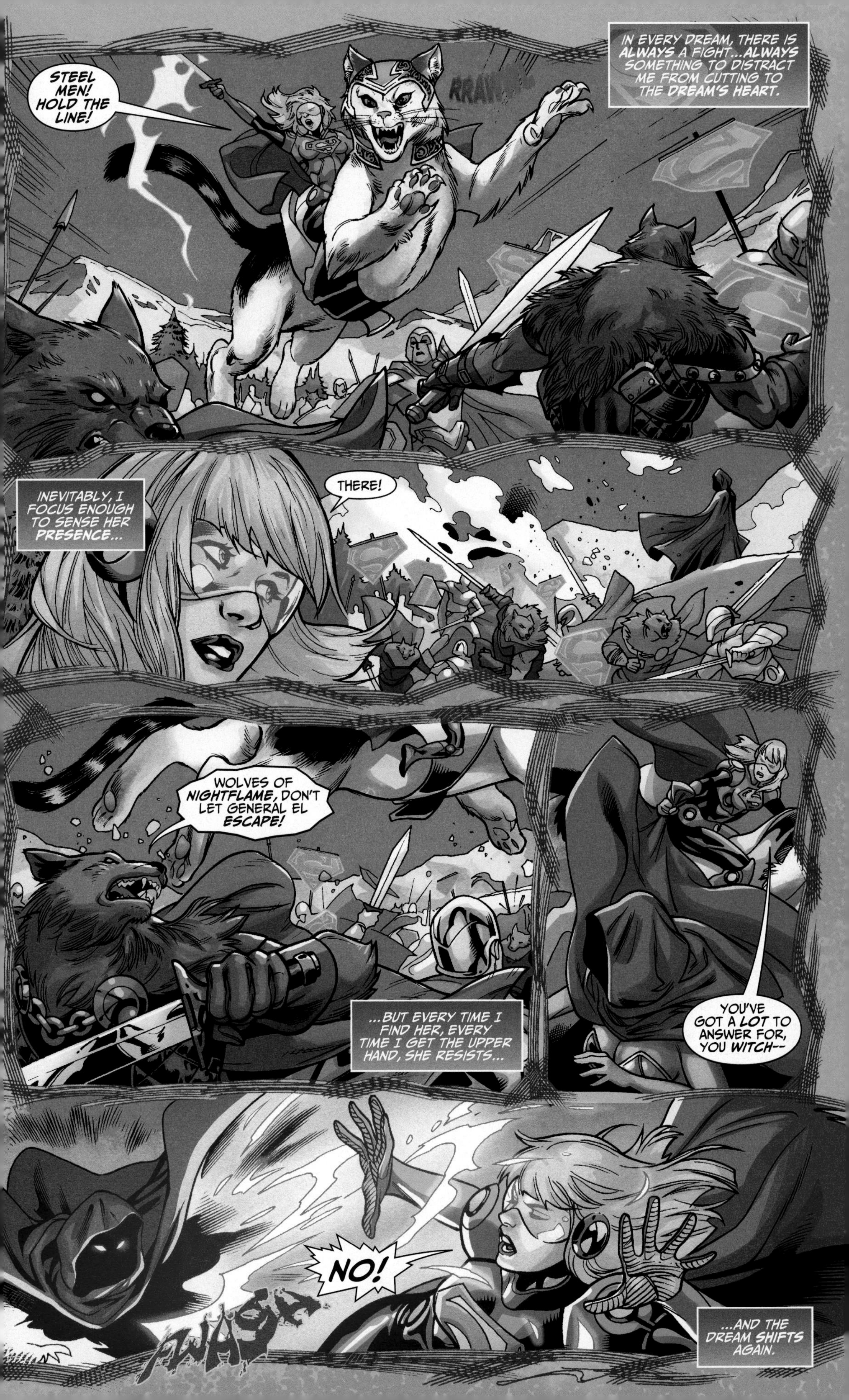
STEEL MEN! HOLD THE LINE!
IN EVERY DREAM, THERE IS ALWAYS A FIGHT...ALWAYS SOMETHING TO DISTRACT ME FROM CUTTING TO THE DREAM'S HEART.
INEVITABLY, I FOCUS ENOUGH TO SENSE HER PRESENCE...
THERE!
WOLVES OF NIGHTFLAME, DON'T LET GENERAL EL ESCAPE!
...BUT EVERY TIME I FIND HER, EVERY TIME I GET THE UPPER HAND, SHE RESISTS...
YOU'VE GOT A LOT TO ANSWER FOR, YOU WITCH--
NO!
...AND THE DREAM SHIFTS AGAIN.

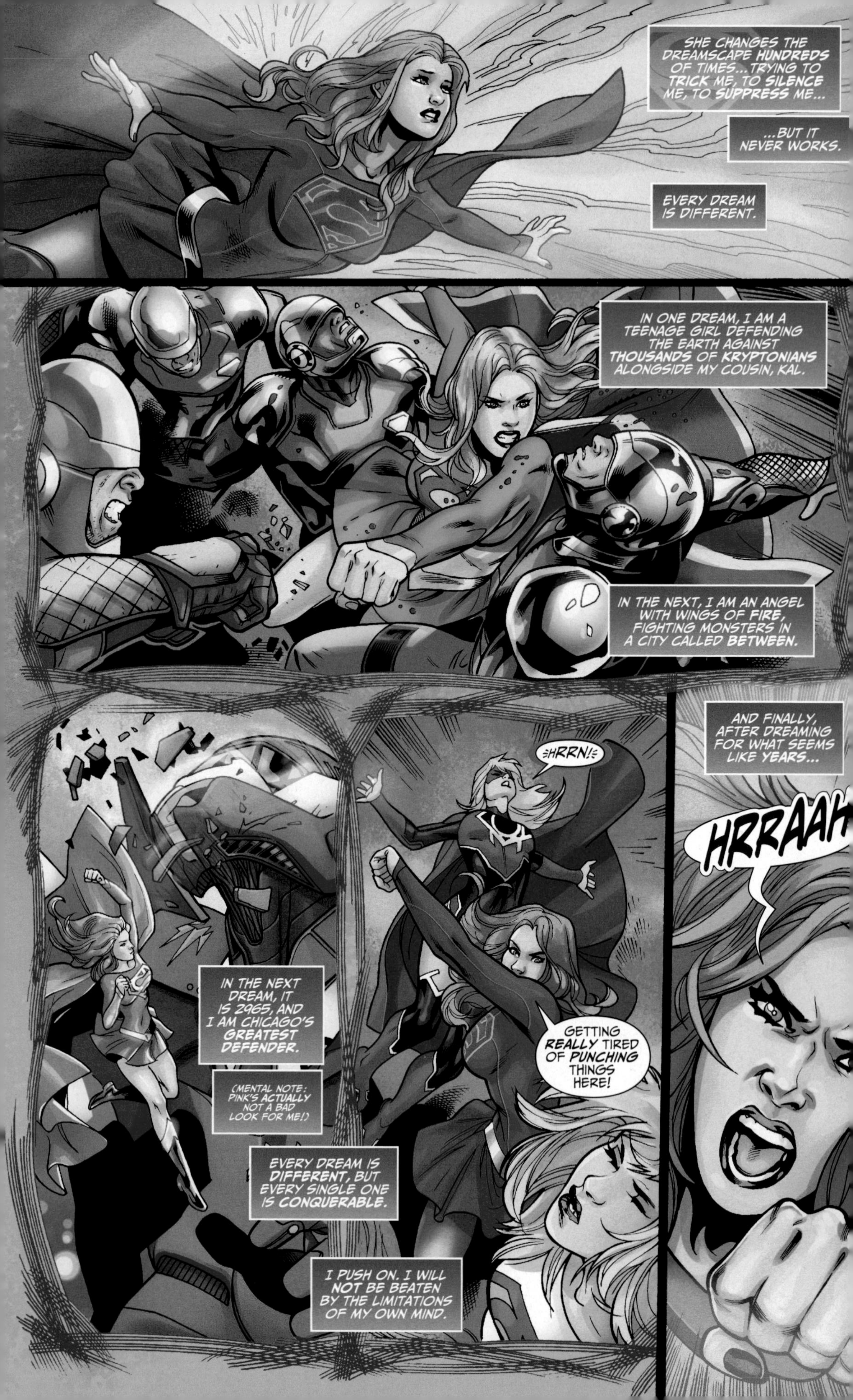
SHE CHANGES THE DREAMSCAPE HUNDREDS OF TIMES...TRYING TO TRICK ME, TO SILENCE ME, TO SUPPRESS ME...
...BUT IT NEVER WORKS.
EVERY DREAM IS DIFFERENT.
IN ONE DREAM, I AM A TEENAGE GIRL DEFENDING THE EARTH AGAINST THOUSANDS OF KRYPTONIANS ALONGSIDE MY COUSIN, KAL.
IN THE NEXT, I AM AN ANGEL WITH WINGS OF FIRE, FIGHTING MONSTERS IN A CITY CALLED BETWEEN.
IN THE NEXT DREAM, IT IS 2965, AND I AM CHICAGO'S GREATEST DEFENDER.
(MENTAL NOTE: PINK'S ACTUALLY NOT A BAD LOOK FOR ME!)
HRRN!
GETTING REALLY TIRED OF PUNCHING THINGS HERE!
EVERY DREAM IS DIFFERENT, BUT EVERY SINGLE ONE IS CONQUERABLE.
I PUSH ON. I WILL NOT BE BEATEN BY THE LIMITATIONS OF MY OWN MIND.
AND FINALLY, AFTER DREAMING FOR WHAT SEEMS LIKE YEARS...
HRRAAH

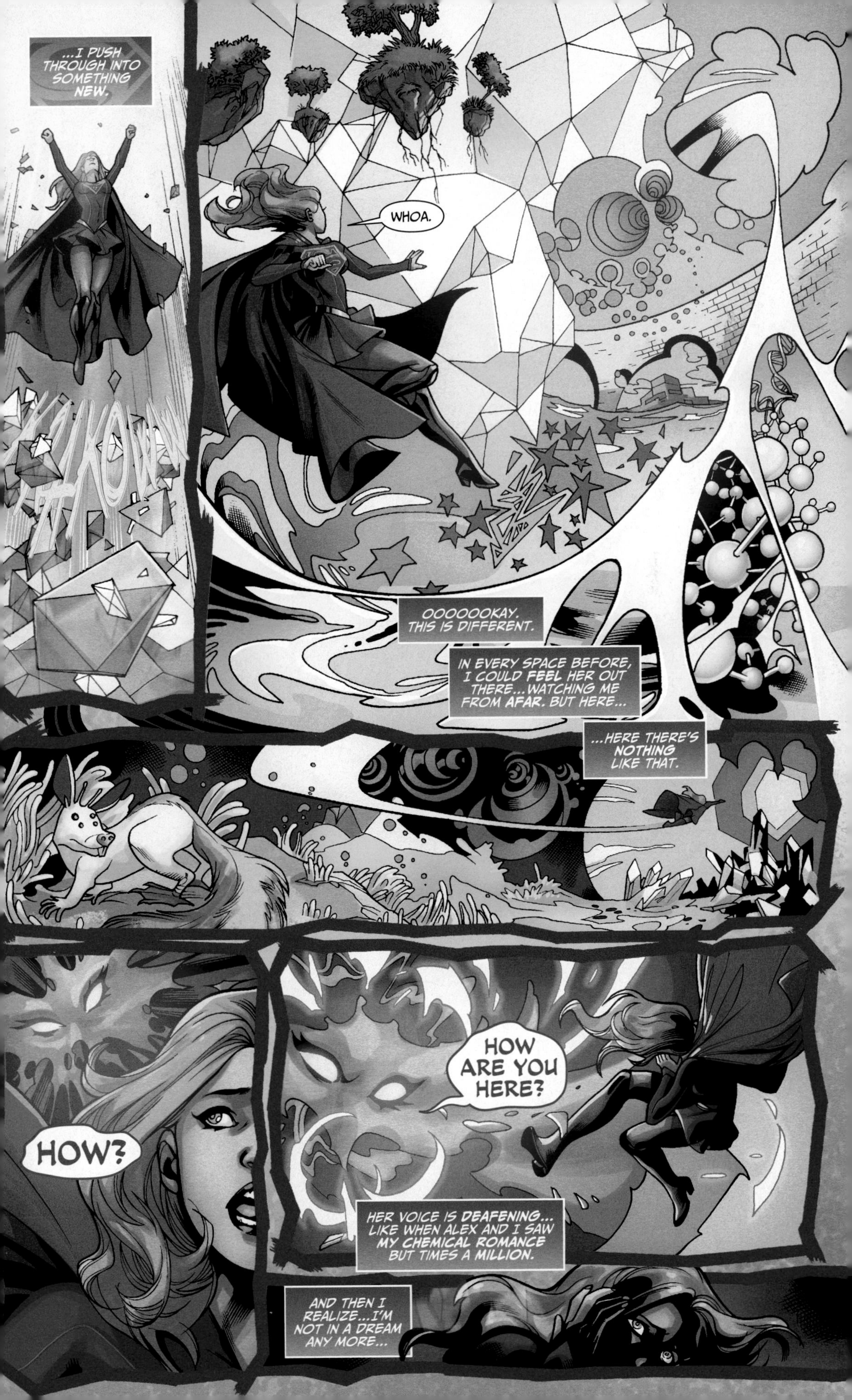
...I PUSH THROUGH INTO SOMETHING NEW.
KRAKOWW
WHOA.
OOOOOOKAY. THIS IS DIFFERENT.
IN EVERY SPACE BEFORE, I COULD FEEL HER OUT THERE...WATCHING ME FROM AFAR. BUT HERE...
...HERE THERE'S NOTHING LIKE THAT.
HOW?
HOW ARE YOU HERE?
HER VOICE IS DEAFENING... LIKE WHEN ALEX AND I SAW MY CHEMICAL ROMANCE BUT TIMES A MILLION.
AND THEN I REALIZE...I'M NOT IN A DREAM ANY MORE...

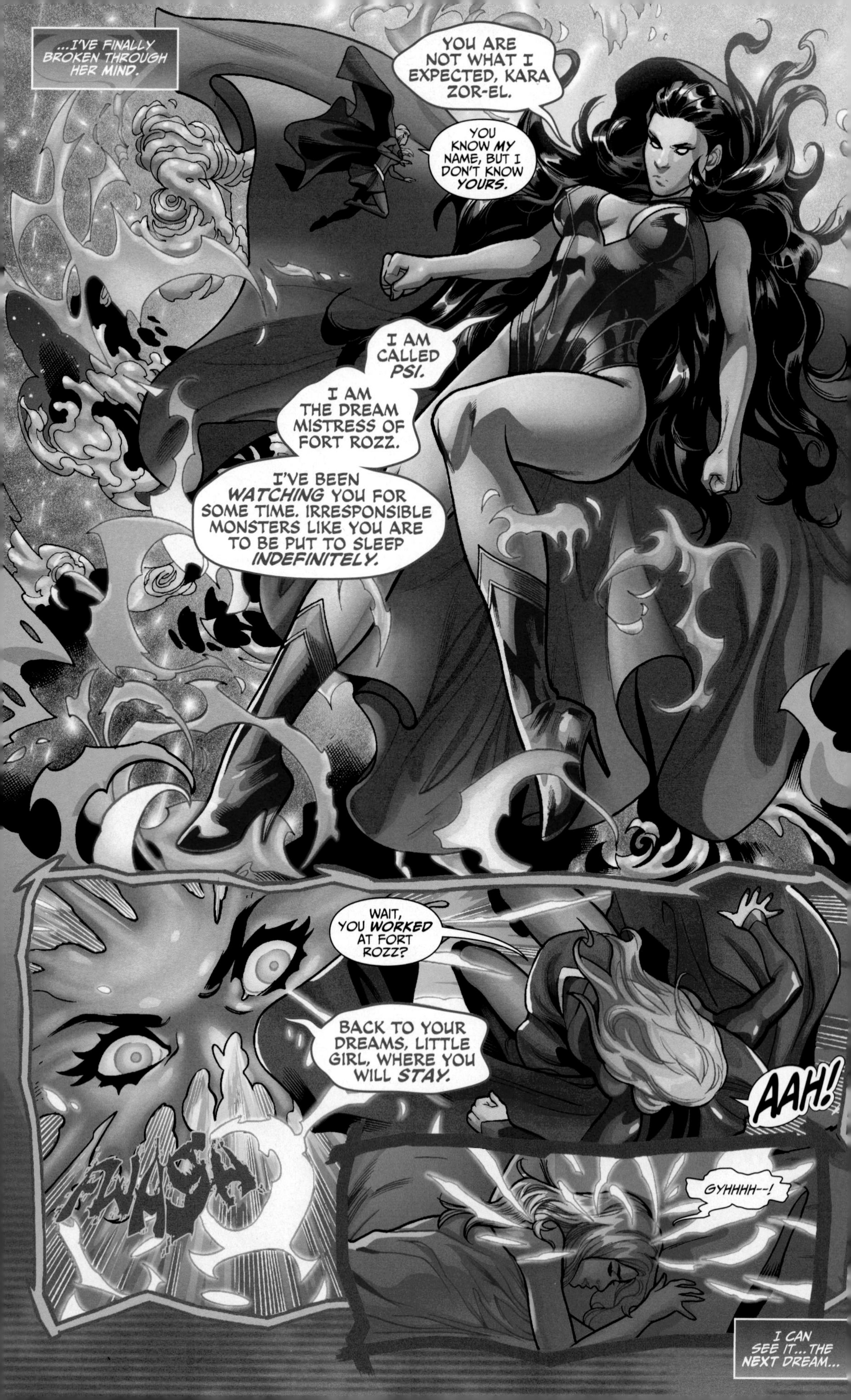

...I'VE FINALLY BROKEN THROUGH HER MIND.
YOU ARE NOT WHAT I EXPECTED, KARA ZOR-EL.
YOU KNOW MY NAME, BUT I DON'T KNOW YOURS.
I AM CALLED PSI.
I AM THE DREAM MISTRESS OF FORT ROZZ.
I'VE BEEN WATCHING YOU FOR SOME TIME. IRRESPONSIBLE MONSTERS LIKE YOU ARE TO BE PUT TO SLEEP INDEFINITELY.
WAIT, YOU WORKED AT FORT ROZZ?
BACK TO YOUR DREAMS, LITTLE GIRL, WHERE YOU WILL STAY.
AAH!
GYHHHH--!
I CAN SEE IT...THE NEXT DREAM...

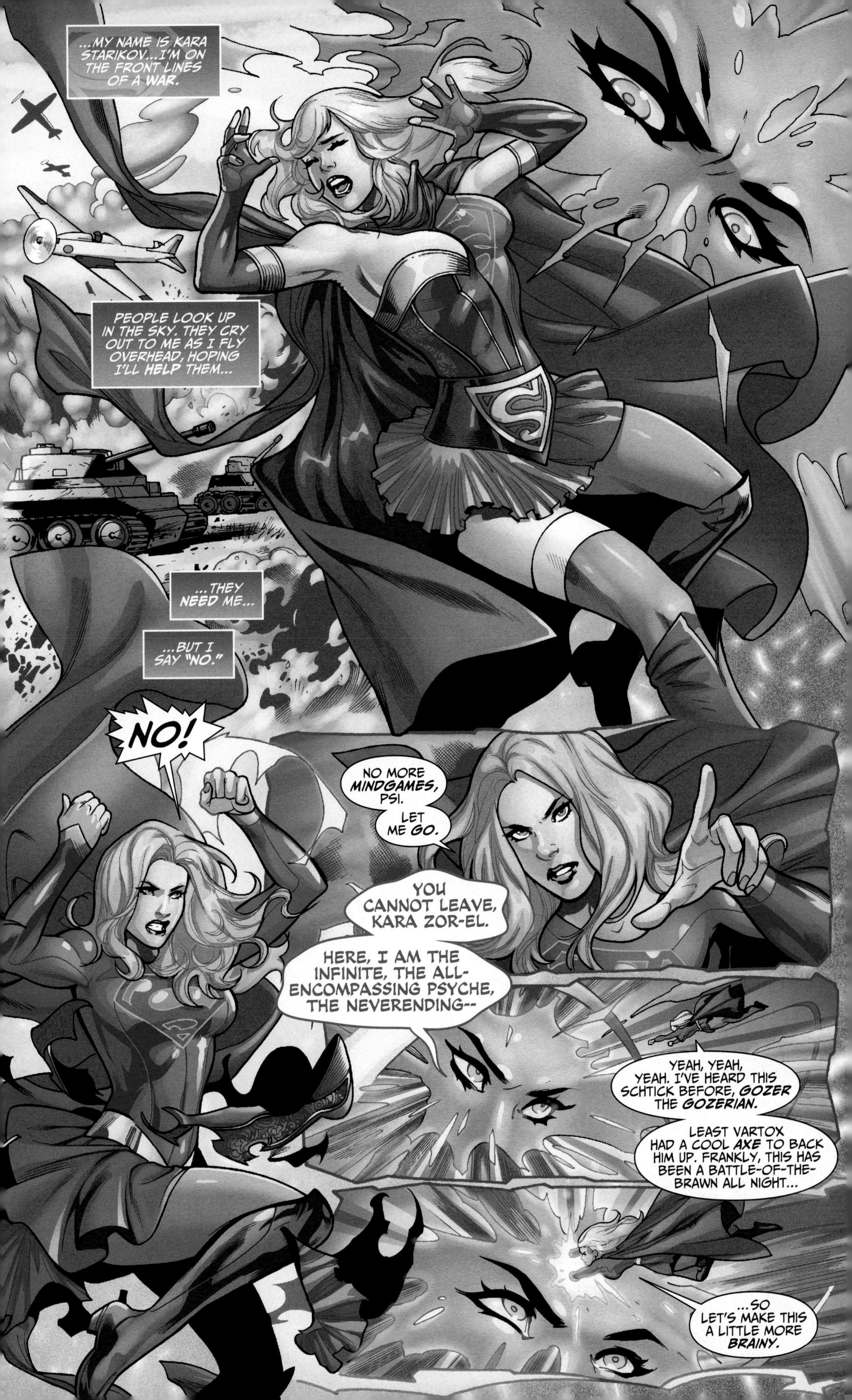

...MY NAME IS KARA STARIKOV...I'M ON THE FRONT LINES OF A WAR.
PEOPLE LOOK UP IN THE SKY. THEY CRY OUT TO ME AS I FLY OVERHEAD, HOPING I'LL HELP THEM...
...THEY NEED ME...
...BUT I SAY "NO."
NO!
NO MORE MINDGAMES, PSI.
LET ME GO.
YOU CANNOT LEAVE, KARA ZOR-EL.
HERE, I AM THE INFINITE, THE ALL-ENCOMPASSING PSYCHE, THE NEVERENDING--
YEAH, YEAH, YEAH. I'VE HEARD THIS SCHTICK BEFORE, GOZER THE GOZERIAN.
LEAST VARTOX HAD A COOL AXE TO BACK HIM UP. FRANKLY, THIS HAS BEEN A BATTLE-OF-THE-BRAWN ALL NIGHT...
...SO LET'S MAKE THIS A LITTLE MORE BRAINY.

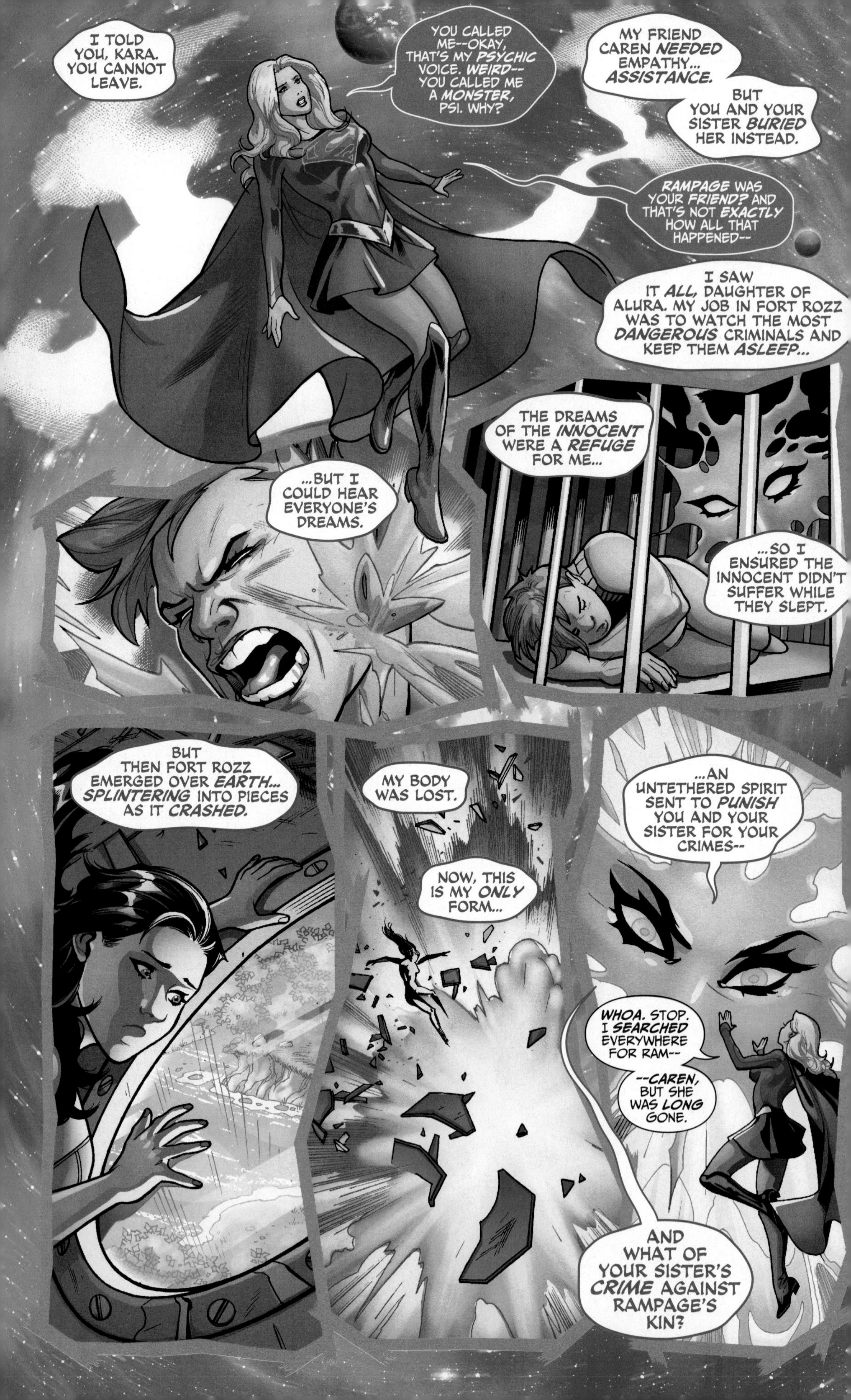
I TOLD YOU, KARA. YOU CANNOT LEAVE.
YOU CALLED ME--OKAY, THAT'S MY PSYCHIC VOICE. WEIRD--YOU CALLED ME A MONSTER, PSI. WHY?
MY FRIEND CAREN NEEDED EMPATHY... ASSISTANCE.
BUT YOU AND YOUR SISTER BURIED HER INSTEAD.
RAMPAGE WAS YOUR FRIEND? AND THAT'S NOT EXACTLY HOW ALL THAT HAPPENED--
I SAW IT ALL, DAUGHTER OF ALURA. MY JOB IN FORT ROZZ WAS TO WATCH THE MOST DANGEROUS CRIMINALS AND KEEP THEM ASLEEP...
...BUT I COULD HEAR EVERYONE'S DREAMS.
THE DREAMS OF THE INNOCENT WERE A REFUGE FOR ME...
...SO I ENSURED THE INNOCENT DIDN'T SUFFER WHILE THEY SLEPT.
BUT THEN FORT ROZZ EMERGED OVER EARTH... SPLINTERING INTO PIECES AS IT CRASHED.
MY BODY WAS LOST.
NOW, THIS IS MY ONLY FORM...
...AN UNTETHERED SPIRIT SENT TO PUNISH YOU AND YOUR SISTER FOR YOUR CRIMES--
WHOA. STOP. I SEARCHED EVERYWHERE FOR RAM--
--CAREN, BUT SHE WAS LONG GONE.
AND WHAT OF YOUR SISTER'S CRIME AGAINST RAMPAGE'S KIN?

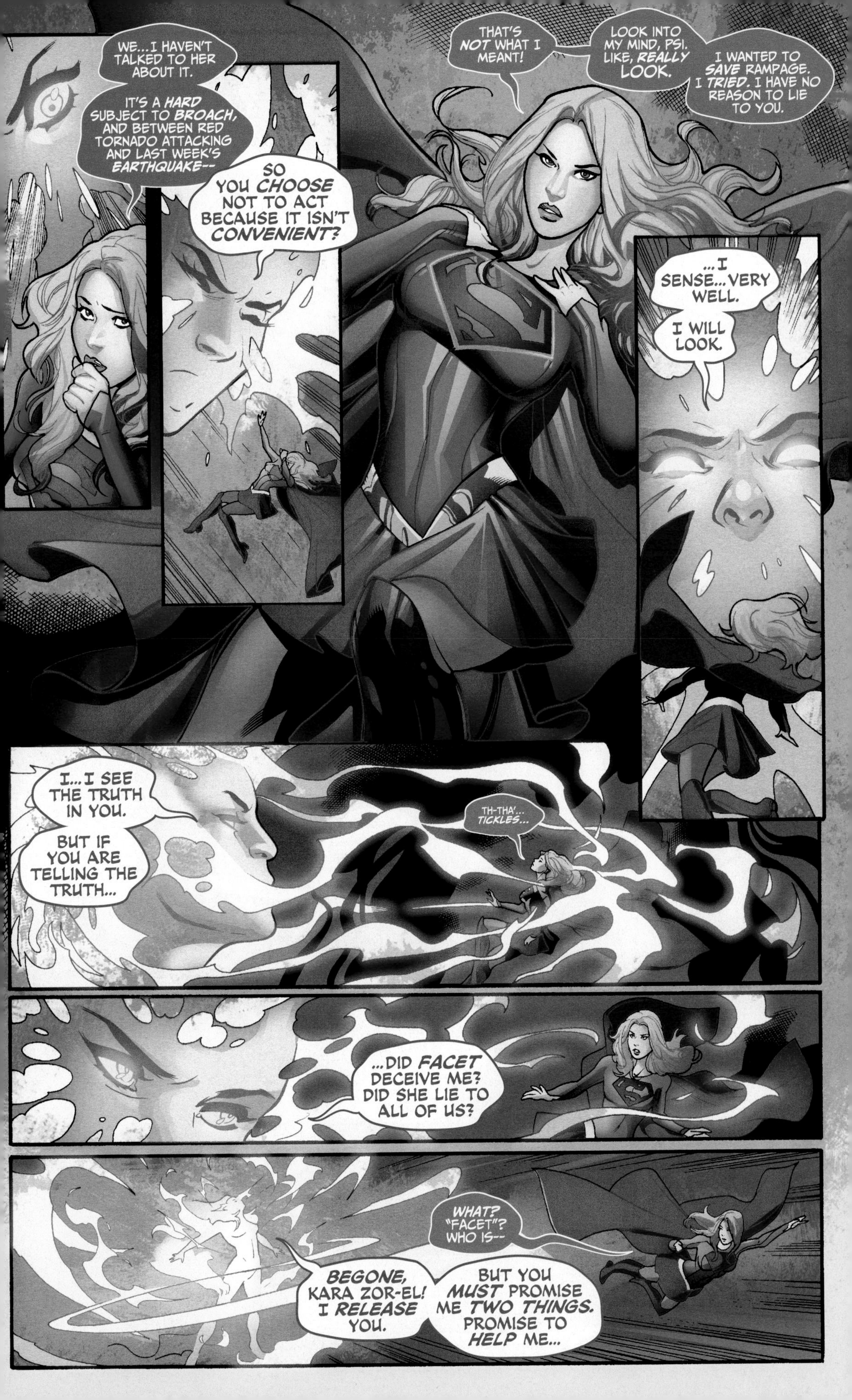
WE...I HAVEN'T TALKED TO HER ABOUT IT.
IT'S A HARD SUBJECT TO BROACH, AND BETWEEN RED TORNADO ATTACKING AND LAST WEEK'S EARTHQUAKE--
SO YOU CHOOSE NOT TO ACT BECAUSE IT ISN'T CONVENIENT?
THAT'S NOT WHAT I MEANT!
LOOK INTO MY MIND, PSI. LIKE, REALLY LOOK.
I WANTED TO SAVE RAMPAGE. I TRIED. I HAVE NO REASON TO LIE TO YOU.
...I SENSE...VERY WELL.
I WILL LOOK.
I...I SEE THE TRUTH IN YOU.
BUT IF YOU ARE TELLING THE TRUTH...
TH-THA'... TICKLES...
...DID FACET DECEIVE ME? DID SHE LIE TO ALL OF US?
WHAT? "FACET"? WHO IS--
BEGONE, KARA ZOR-EL! I RELEASE YOU.
BUT YOU MUST PROMISE ME TWO THINGS. PROMISE TO HELP ME...

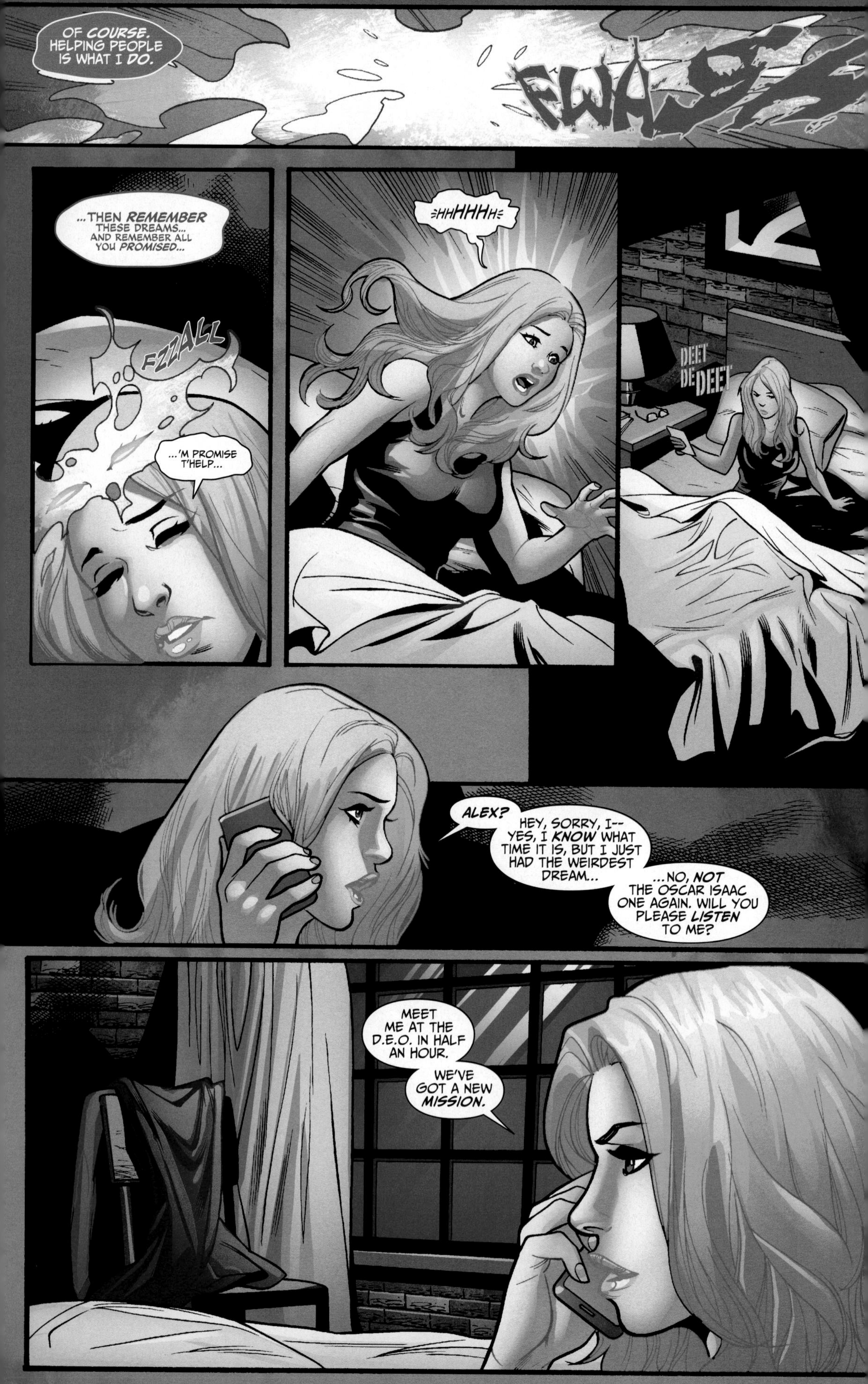
OF COURSE. HELPING PEOPLE IS WHAT I DO.
...THEN REMEMBER THESE DREAMS... AND REMEMBER ALL YOU PROMISED...
FZZALL
...'M PROMISE T'HELP...
HHHHHH
DEET DE DEET
ALEX?
HEY, SORRY, I-- YES, I KNOW WHAT TIME IT IS, BUT I JUST HAD THE WEIRDEST DREAM...
...NO, NOT THE OSCAR ISAAC ONE AGAIN. WILL YOU PLEASE LISTEN TO ME?
MEET ME AT THE D.E.O. IN HALF AN HOUR.
WE'VE GOT A NEW MISSION.

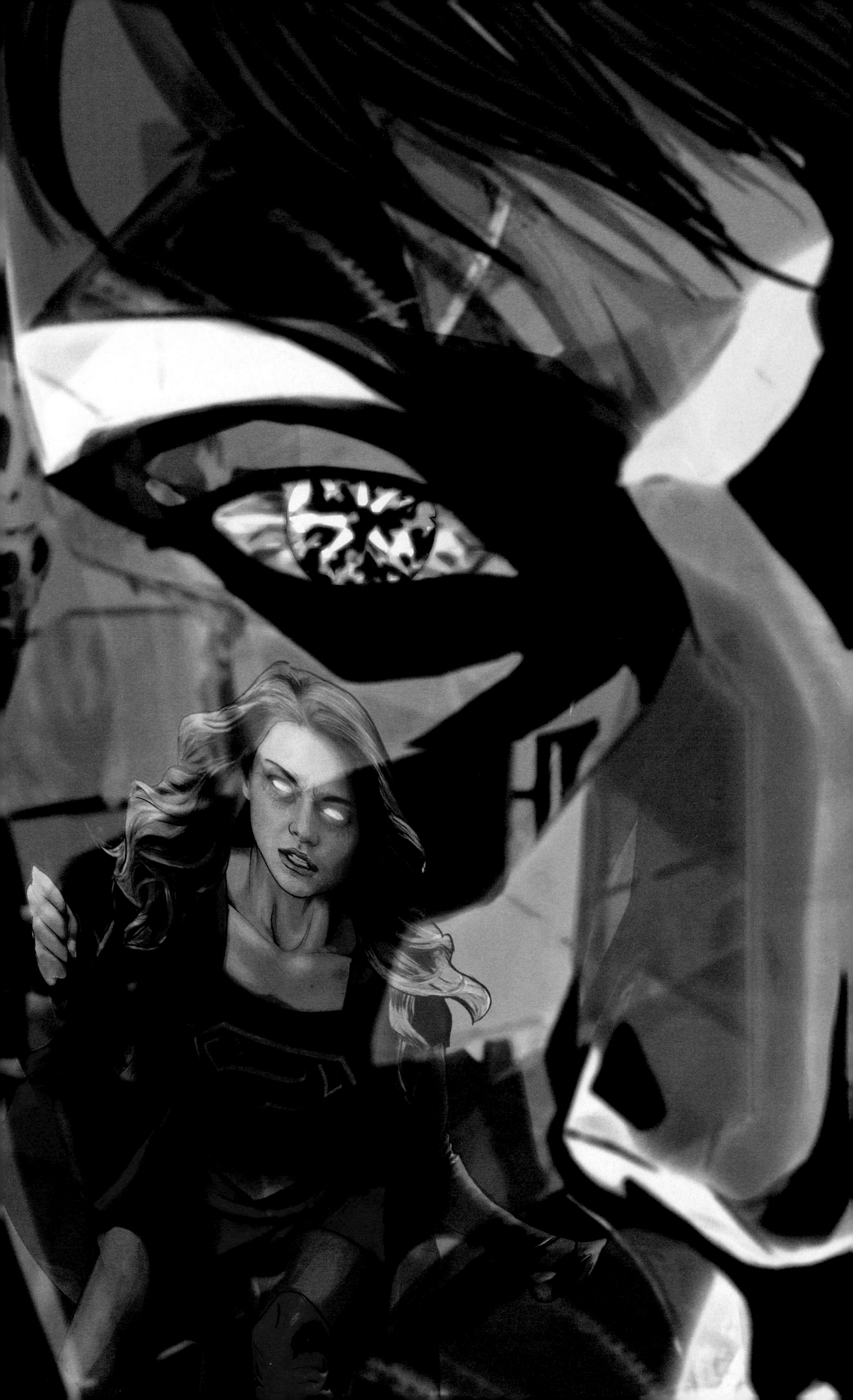

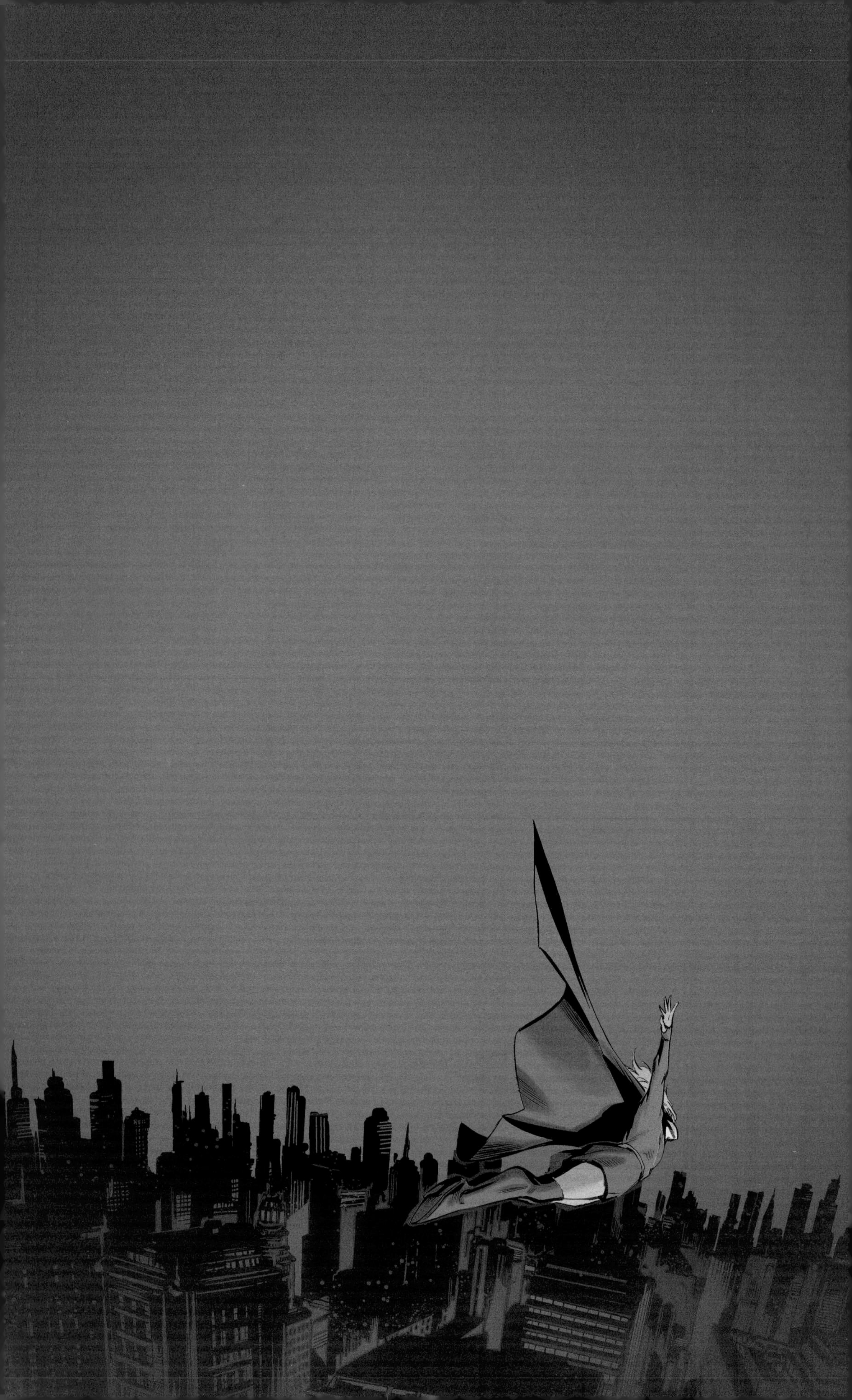

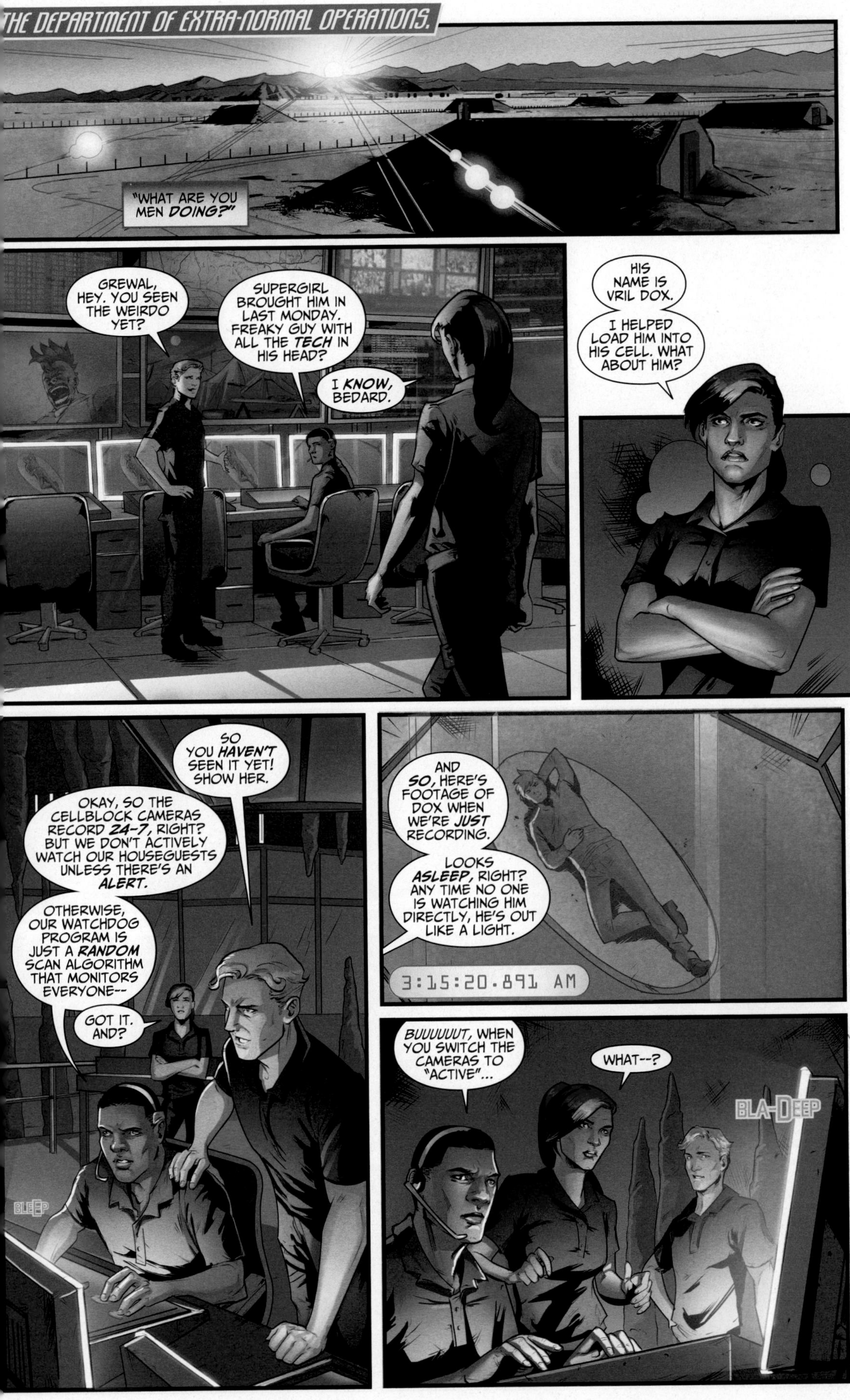
THE DEPARTMENT OF EXTRA-NORMAL OPERATIONS.
"WHAT ARE YOU MEN DOING?"
GREWAL, HEY. YOU SEEN THE WEIRDO YET?
SUPERGIRL BROUGHT HIM IN LAST MONDAY. FREAKY GUY WITH ALL THE TECH IN HIS HEAD?
I KNOW, BEDARD.
HIS NAME IS VRIL DOX.
I HELPED LOAD HIM INTO HIS CELL. WHAT ABOUT HIM?
SO YOU HAVEN'T SEEN IT YET! SHOW HER.
OKAY, SO THE CELLBLOCK CAMERAS RECORD 24-7, RIGHT? BUT WE DON'T ACTIVELY WATCH OUR HOUSEGUESTS UNLESS THERE'S AN ALERT.
OTHERWISE, OUR WATCHDOG PROGRAM IS JUST A RANDOM SCAN ALGORITHM THAT MONITORS EVERYONE--
GOT IT. AND?
BLEEP
AND SO, HERE'S FOOTAGE OF DOX WHEN WE'RE JUST RECORDING.
LOOKS ASLEEP, RIGHT? ANY TIME NO ONE IS WATCHING HIM DIRECTLY, HE'S OUT LIKE A LIGHT.
3:15:20.891 AM
BUUUUUUT, WHEN YOU SWITCH THE CAMERAS TO "ACTIVE"...
WHAT--?
BLA-DEEP

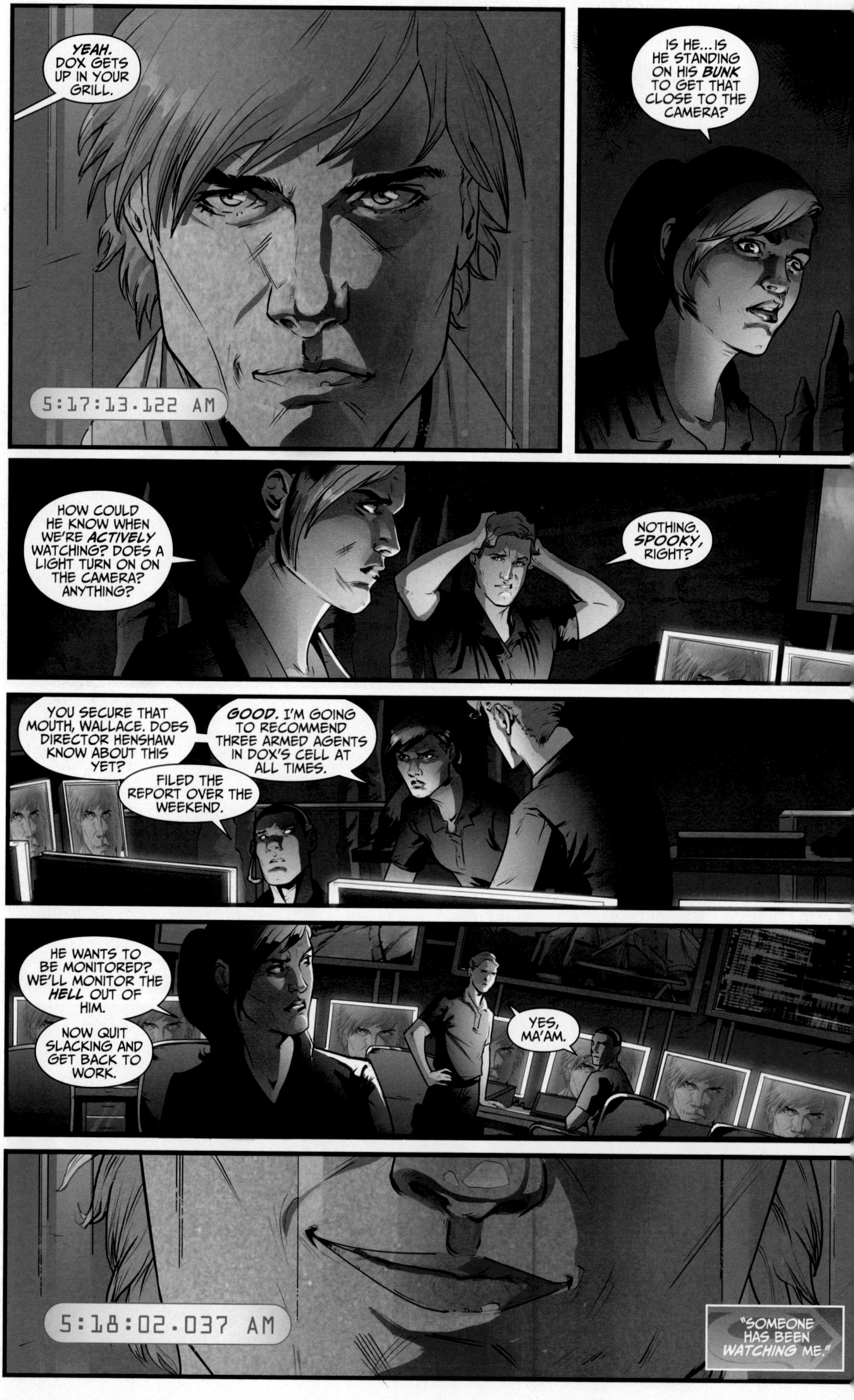
YEAH. DOX GETS UP IN YOUR GRILL.
5:17:13.122 AM
IS HE...IS HE STANDING ON HIS BUNK TO GET THAT CLOSE TO THE CAMERA?
HOW COULD HE KNOW WHEN WE'RE ACTIVELY WATCHING? DOES A LIGHT TURN ON ON THE CAMERA? ANYTHING?
NOTHING. SPOOKY, RIGHT?
YOU SECURE THAT MOUTH, WALLACE. DOES DIRECTOR HENSHAW KNOW ABOUT THIS YET?
FILED THE REPORT OVER THE WEEKEND.
GOOD. I'M GOING TO RECOMMEND THREE ARMED AGENTS IN DOX'S CELL AT ALL TIMES.
HE WANTS TO BE MONITORED? WE'LL MONITOR THE HELL OUT OF HIM.
NOW QUIT SLACKING AND GET BACK TO WORK.
YES, MA'AM.
5:18:02.037 AM
"SOMEONE HAS BEEN WATCHING ME."

"WATCHING YOU" HOW, KARA?

CHAPTER 8

SISTERY MYSTERY (REPRISE)

AND IS THAT WHY WE'RE OUT HERE ON A FIVE A.M. DRIVE TO DESTINATIONS UNKNOWN?

I-I... ...YOU KNOW, I'VE NEVER RIDDEN IN ONE OF THESE BEFORE? THEY'RE CRAMPED. FLYING'S WAY BETTER.

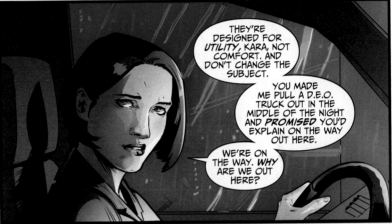

THEY'RE DESIGNED FOR UTILITY, KARA, NOT COMFORT. AND DON'T CHANGE THE SUBJECT.

YOU MADE ME PULL A D.E.O. TRUCK OUT IN THE MIDDLE OF THE NIGHT AND PROMISED YOU'D EXPLAIN ON THE WAY OUT HERE.

WE'RE ON THE WAY. WHY ARE WE OUT HERE?

BECAUSE OF RAMPAGE.

"RAMPAGE WAS LIVING A QUIET LIFE...FORGOTTEN, OUT OF THE WAY. JUST SOMEONE TRYING TO FADE INTO THE BACKGROUND.

STERLING GATES - writer
CARMEN CARNERO - artist
SANDRA MOLINA - colorist
SAIDA TEMOFONTE - letterer
CAT STAGGS - cover artist
JESSICA CHEN - associate editor
KRISTY QUINN - editor

"SHE COULD'VE KILLED ME IN THE SEWERS, BUT SHE DIDN'T.

WHY NOT?

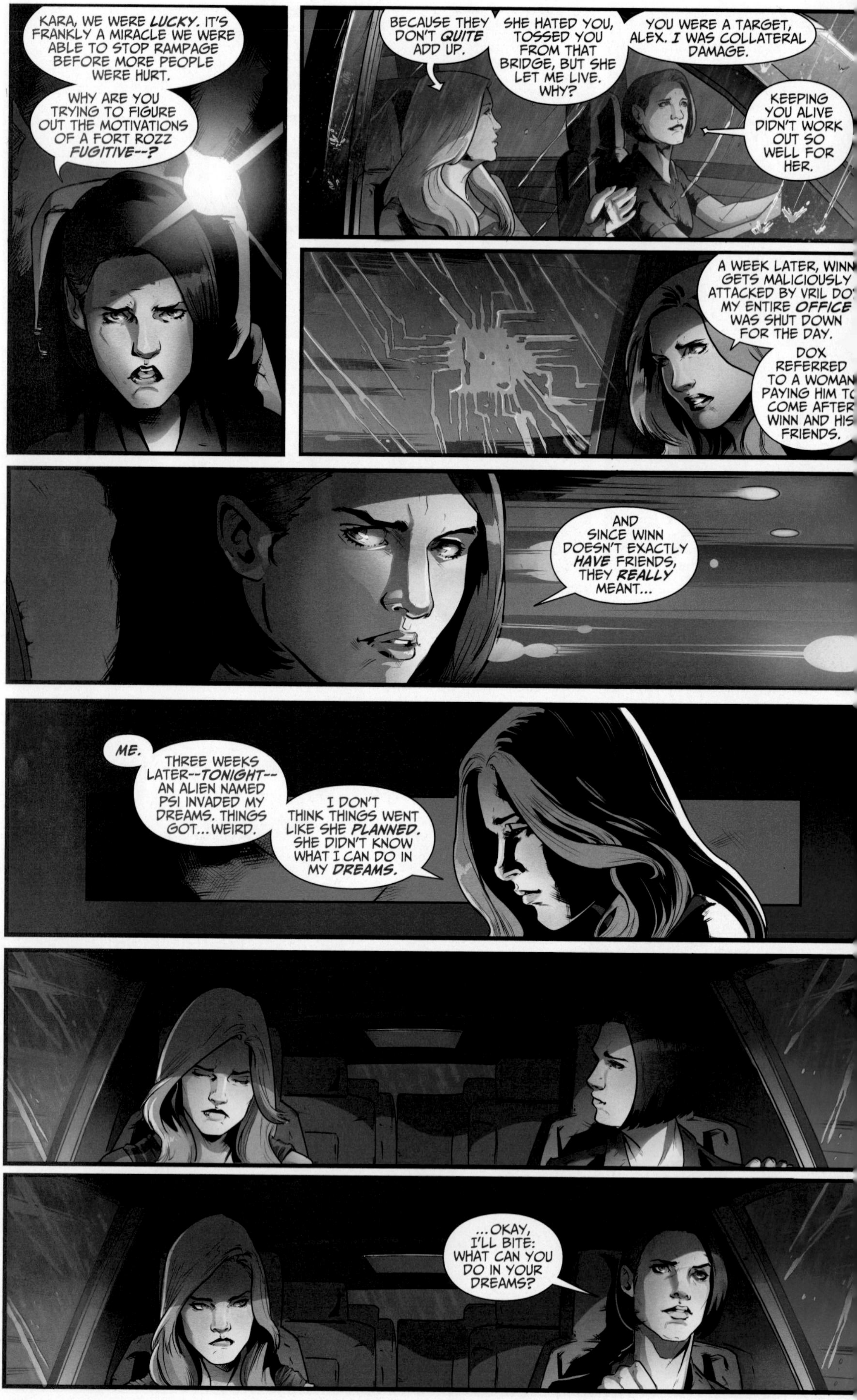
KARA, WE WERE LUCKY. IT'S FRANKLY A MIRACLE WE WERE ABLE TO STOP RAMPAGE BEFORE MORE PEOPLE WERE HURT.
WHY ARE YOU TRYING TO FIGURE OUT THE MOTIVATIONS OF A FORT ROZZ FUGITIVE--?
BECAUSE THEY DON'T QUITE ADD UP.
SHE HATED YOU, TOSSED YOU FROM THAT BRIDGE, BUT SHE LET ME LIVE. WHY?
YOU WERE A TARGET, ALEX. I WAS COLLATERAL DAMAGE.
KEEPING YOU ALIVE DIDN'T WORK OUT SO WELL FOR HER.
A WEEK LATER, WINN GETS MALICIOUSLY ATTACKED BY VRIL DOX. MY ENTIRE OFFICE WAS SHUT DOWN FOR THE DAY.
DOX REFERRED TO A WOMAN PAYING HIM TO COME AFTER WINN AND HIS FRIENDS.
AND SINCE WINN DOESN'T EXACTLY HAVE FRIENDS, THEY REALLY MEANT...
ME.
THREE WEEKS LATER--TONIGHT--AN ALIEN NAMED PSI INVADED MY DREAMS. THINGS GOT...WEIRD.
I DON'T THINK THINGS WENT LIKE SHE PLANNED. SHE DIDN'T KNOW WHAT I CAN DO IN MY DREAMS.
...OKAY, I'LL BITE: WHAT CAN YOU DO IN YOUR DREAMS?

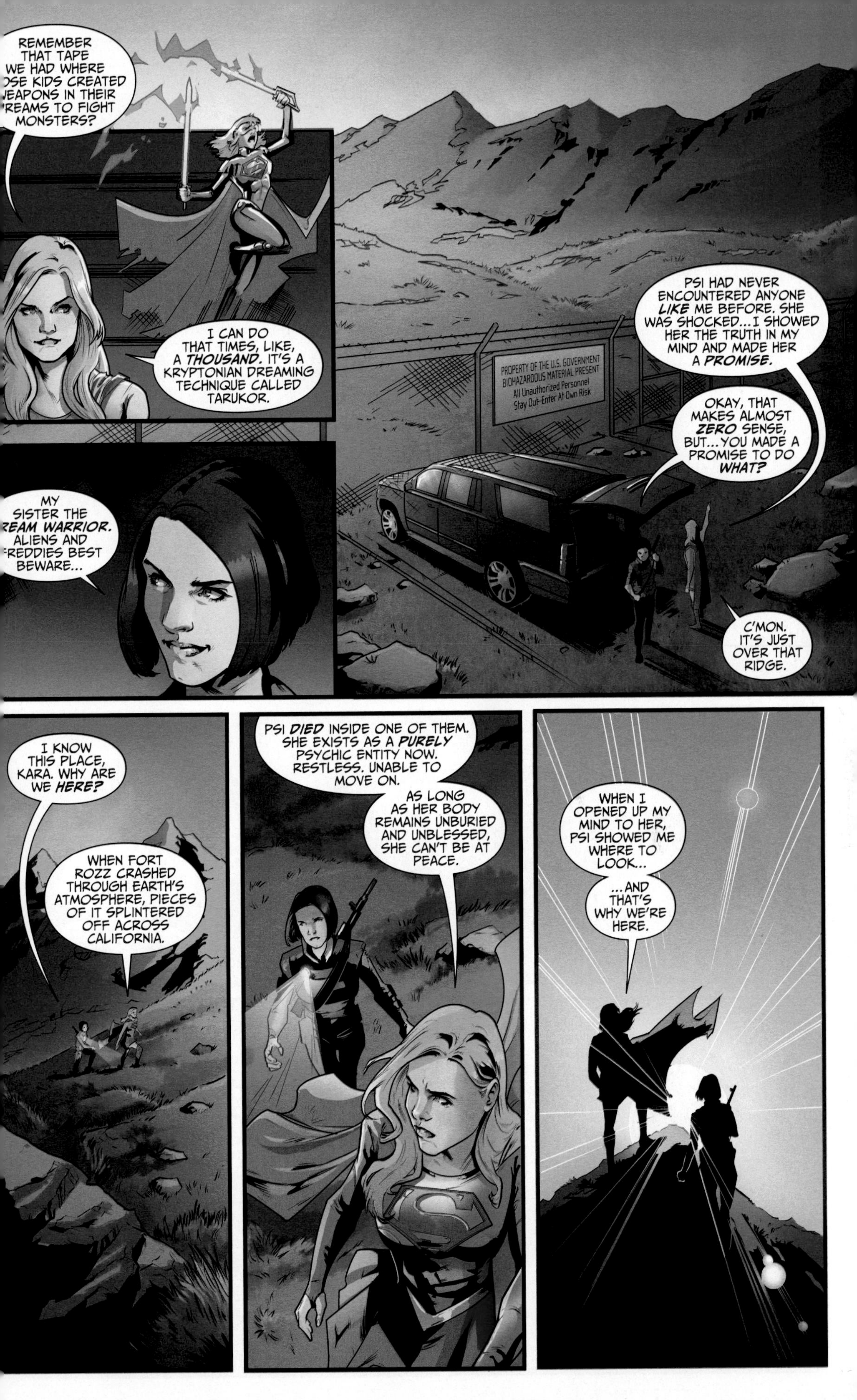

REMEMBER THAT TAPE WE HAD WHERE OSE KIDS CREATED WEAPONS IN THEIR REAMS TO FIGHT MONSTERS?
I CAN DO THAT TIMES, LIKE, A THOUSAND. IT'S A KRYPTONIAN DREAMING TECHNIQUE CALLED TARUKOR.
MY SISTER THE REAM WARRIOR. ALIENS AND FREDDIES BEST BEWARE...
PSI HAD NEVER ENCOUNTERED ANYONE LIKE ME BEFORE. SHE WAS SHOCKED...I SHOWED HER THE TRUTH IN MY MIND AND MADE HER A PROMISE.
PROPERTY OF THE U.S. GOVERNMENT
BIOHAZARDOUS MATERIAL PRESENT
All Unauthorized Personnel
Stay Out-Enter At Own Risk
OKAY, THAT MAKES ALMOST ZERO SENSE, BUT...YOU MADE A PROMISE TO DO WHAT?
C'MON. IT'S JUST OVER THAT RIDGE.
I KNOW THIS PLACE, KARA. WHY ARE WE HERE?
WHEN FORT ROZZ CRASHED THROUGH EARTH'S ATMOSPHERE, PIECES OF IT SPLINTERED OFF ACROSS CALIFORNIA.
PSI DIED INSIDE ONE OF THEM. SHE EXISTS AS A PURELY PSYCHIC ENTITY NOW. RESTLESS. UNABLE TO MOVE ON.
AS LONG AS HER BODY REMAINS UNBURIED AND UNBLESSED, SHE CAN'T BE AT PEACE.
WHEN I OPENED UP MY MIND TO HER, PSI SHOWED ME WHERE TO LOOK...
...AND THAT'S WHY WE'RE HERE.

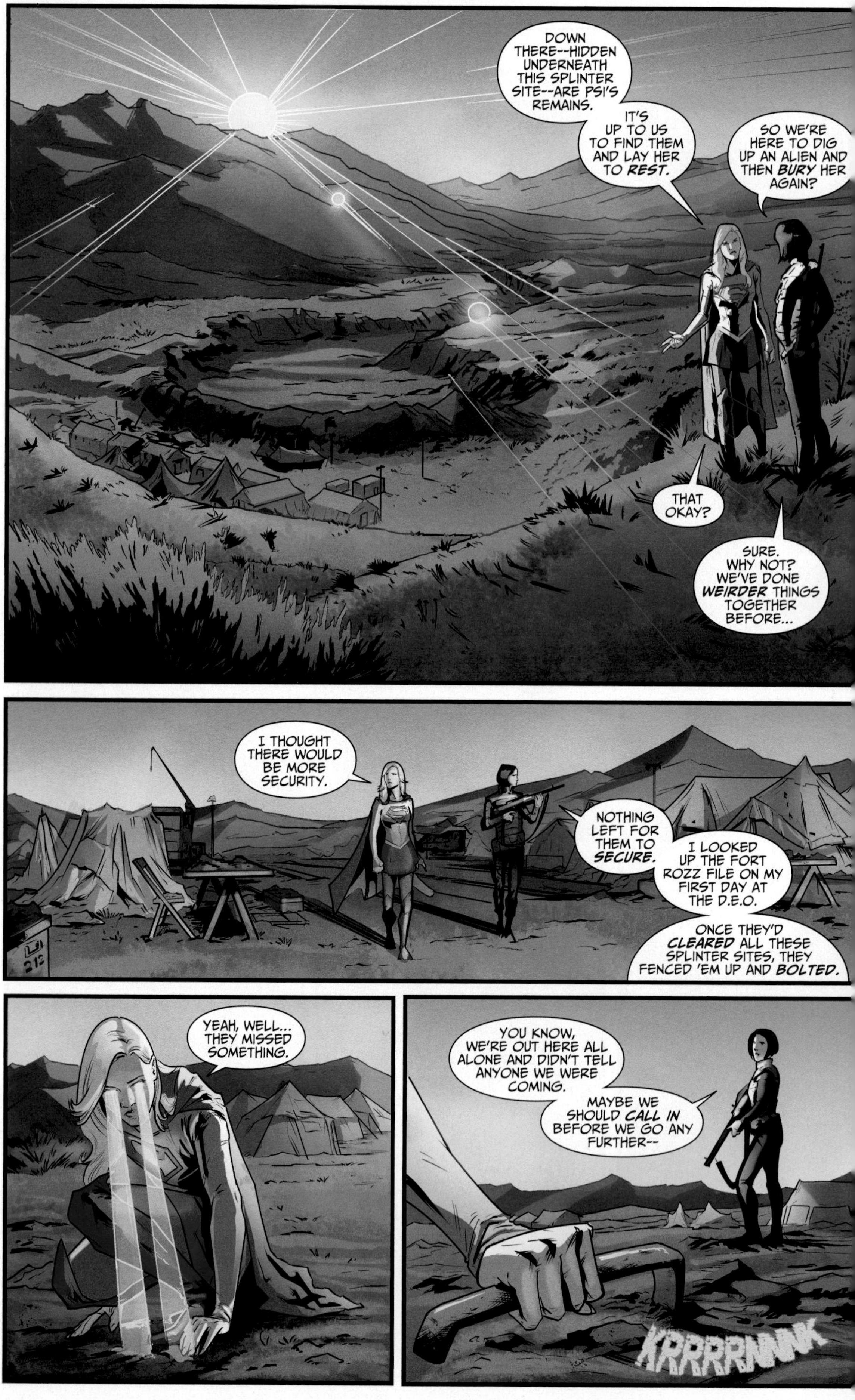
DOWN THERE--HIDDEN UNDERNEATH THIS SPLINTER SITE--ARE PSI'S REMAINS.
IT'S UP TO US TO FIND THEM AND LAY HER TO REST.
SO WE'RE HERE TO DIG UP AN ALIEN AND THEN BURY HER AGAIN?
THAT OKAY?
SURE. WHY NOT? WE'VE DONE WEIRDER THINGS TOGETHER BEFORE...
I THOUGHT THERE WOULD BE MORE SECURITY.
NOTHING LEFT FOR THEM TO SECURE.
I LOOKED UP THE FORT ROZZ FILE ON MY FIRST DAY AT THE D.E.O.
ONCE THEY'D CLEARED ALL THESE SPLINTER SITES, THEY FENCED 'EM UP AND BOLTED.
YEAH, WELL... THEY MISSED SOMETHING.
YOU KNOW, WE'RE OUT HERE ALL ALONE AND DIDN'T TELL ANYONE WE WERE COMING.
MAYBE WE SHOULD CALL IN BEFORE WE GO ANY FURTHER--
KRRRRNNNK

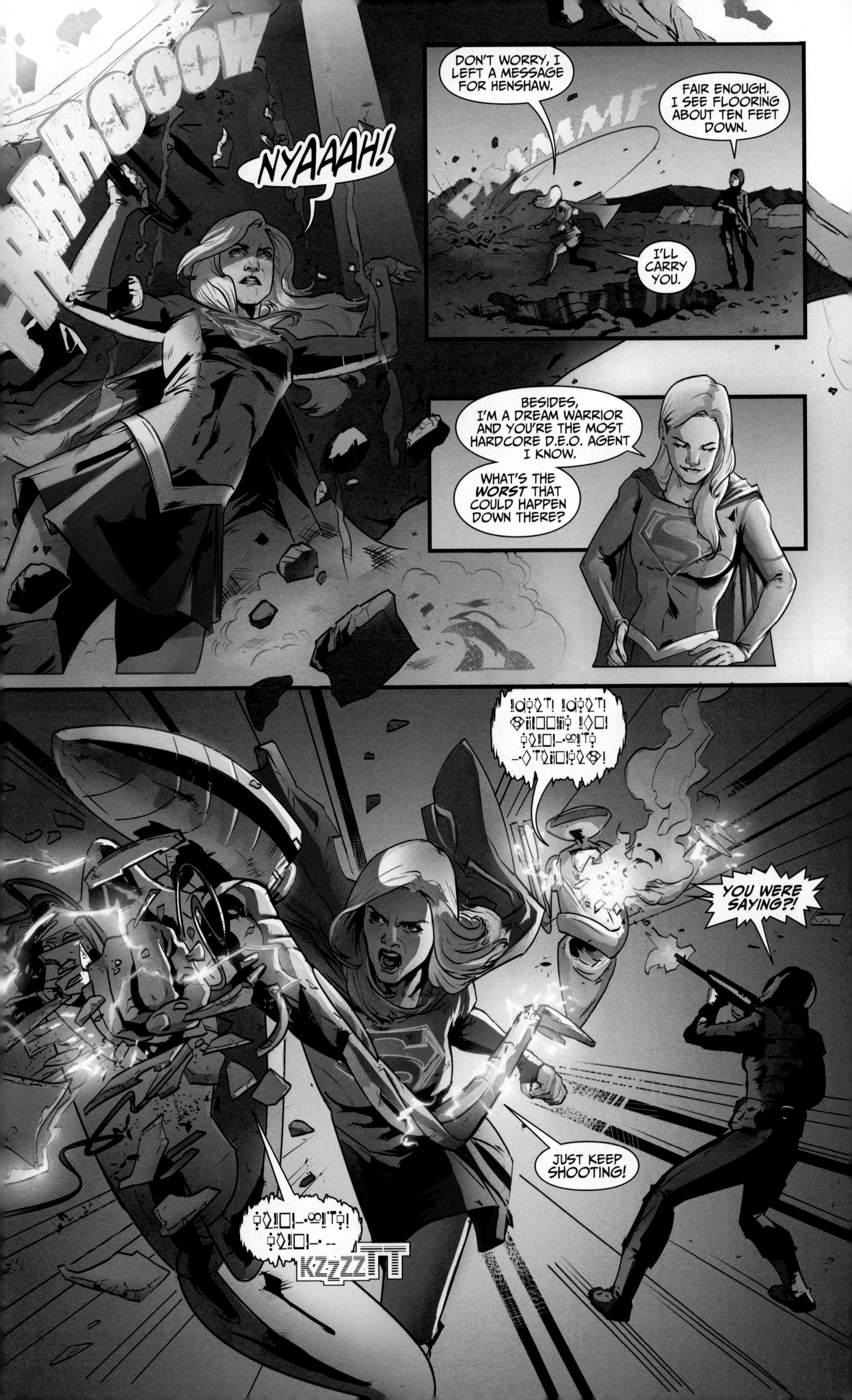
PRROOOW
NYAAAH!
DON'T WORRY, I LEFT A MESSAGE FOR HENSHAW.
FAIR ENOUGH. I SEE FLOORING ABOUT TEN FEET DOWN.
I'LL CARRY YOU.
BESIDES, I'M A DREAM WARRIOR AND YOU'RE THE MOST HARDCORE D.E.O. AGENT I KNOW.
WHAT'S THE WORST THAT COULD HAPPEN DOWN THERE?
YOU WERE SAYING?!
JUST KEEP SHOOTING!
KZZZZTT

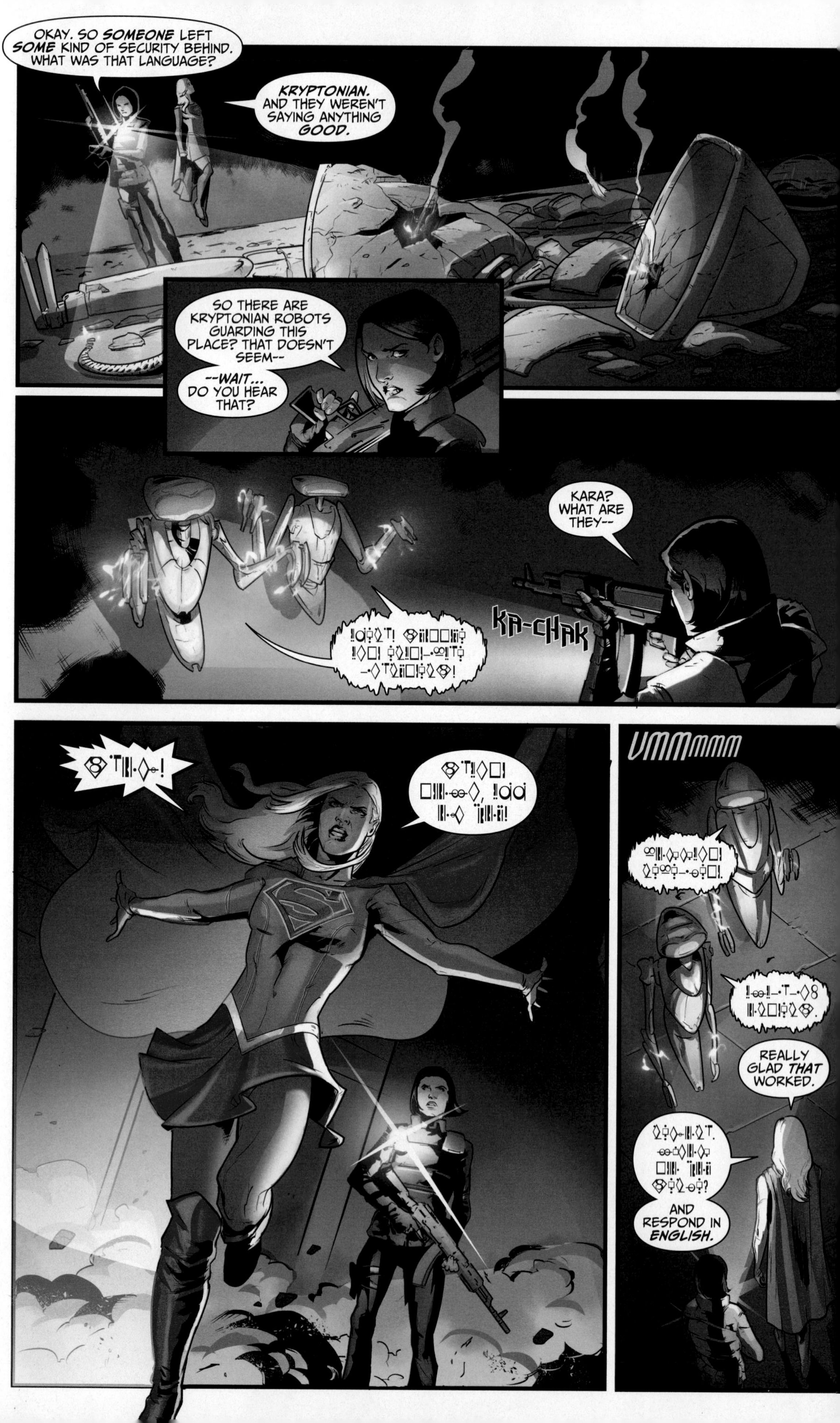

OKAY. SO SOMEONE LEFT SOME KIND OF SECURITY BEHIND. WHAT WAS THAT LANGUAGE?
KRYPTONIAN. AND THEY WEREN'T SAYING ANYTHING GOOD.
SO THERE ARE KRYPTONIAN ROBOTS GUARDING THIS PLACE? THAT DOESN'T SEEM--
--WAIT... DO YOU HEAR THAT?
KARA? WHAT ARE THEY--
KA-CHAK
VMMmmm
REALLY GLAD THAT WORKED.
AND RESPOND IN ENGLISH.

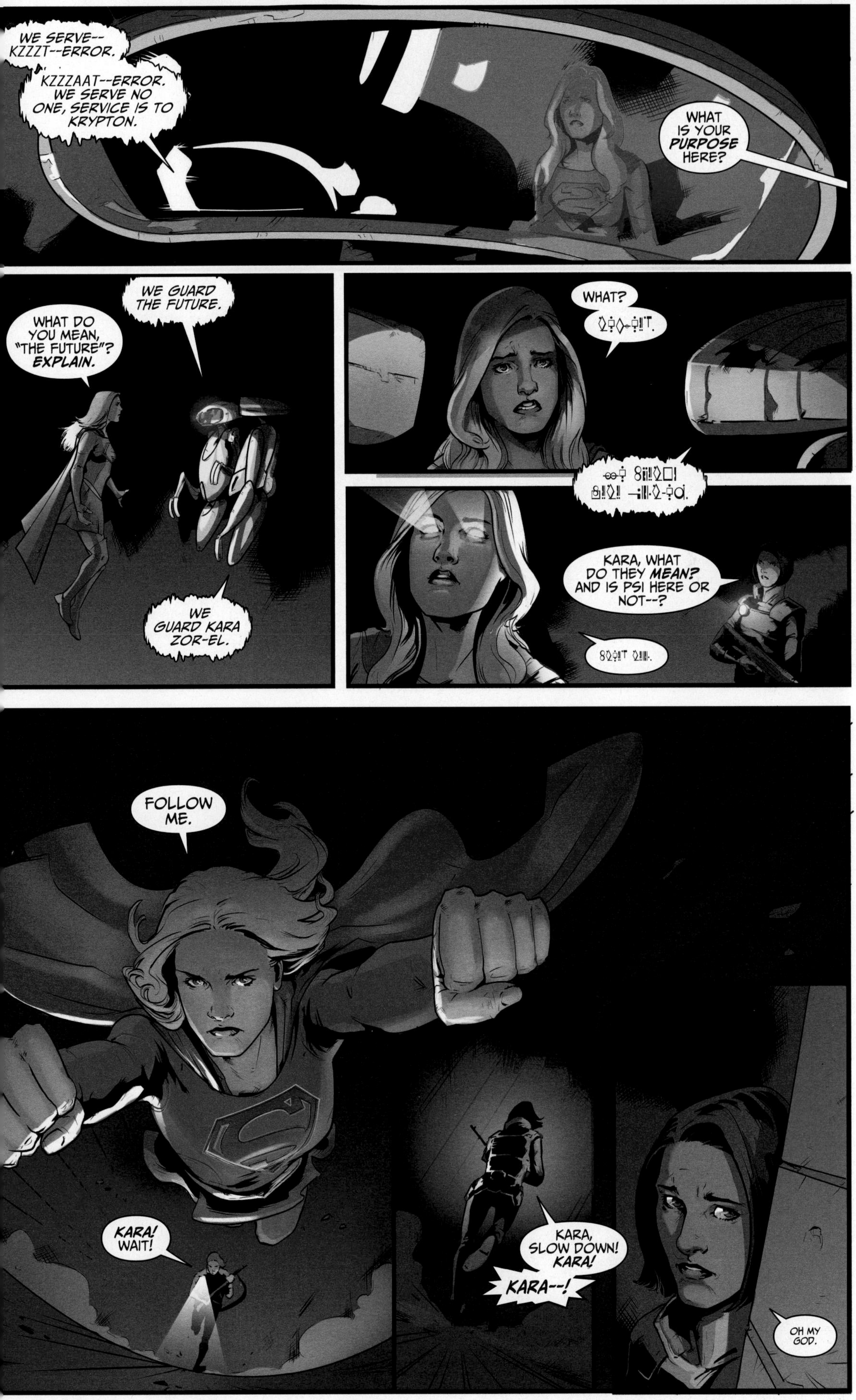
WE SERVE--KZZZT--ERROR.
KZZZAAT--ERROR. WE SERVE NO ONE, SERVICE IS TO KRYPTON.
WHAT IS YOUR **PURPOSE** HERE?
WE GUARD THE FUTURE.
WHAT DO YOU MEAN, "THE FUTURE"? **EXPLAIN.**
WE GUARD KARA ZOR-EL.
WHAT?
KARA, WHAT DO THEY **MEAN?** AND IS PSI HERE OR NOT--?
FOLLOW ME.
KARA! WAIT!
KARA, SLOW DOWN! **KARA!**
KARA--!
OH MY GOD.

LOOK AT THIS.

LOOK AT THIS!

KRYPTONIAN SUNSTONES OF MY FAMILY. PICTURES OF *US* AS KIDS! MY FIRST DAY AT CATCO!

MY FIRST DAY AS SUPERGIRL! I'VE BEEN SO *CAREFUL*, BUT THEY HAVE PICTURES OF ALL OF IT.

ALL OF IT!

"...AND THEY'VE GONE TO GREAT LENGTHS TO LEAD US *HERE*."

YES, MASTER FACET. SHE IS IN PLACE.

AWAITING YOUR ORDERS.

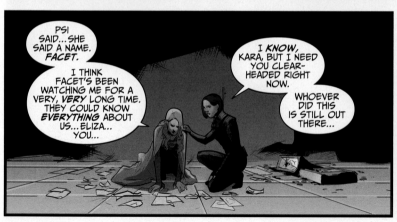

PSI SAID...SHE SAID A NAME. *FACET*.

I THINK FACET'S BEEN WATCHING ME FOR A VERY, *VERY* LONG TIME. THEY COULD KNOW *EVERYTHING* ABOUT US...ELIZA... YOU...

I *KNOW*, KARA, BUT I NEED YOU CLEAR-HEADED RIGHT NOW.

WHOEVER DID THIS IS STILL OUT THERE...

MYSTERIES INFURIATE ME.

ALEX! HERE COME TWO MORE!

SKRZAK

CLARK *LOVES* THEM. HE SAYS READING MYSTERIES GROWING UP IS HALF THE REASON HE BECAME A REPORTER.

SKSSH

I SEE 'EM, I SEE 'EM!

AT LEAST THEY COME APART PRETTY *EASILY*!

SKLAZZ

AGATHA CHRISTIE, JIM THOMPSON, DASHIELL WHAT'S-HIS-NAME... THEY TAUGHT KAL HOW TO UNCOVER THE HIDDEN TRUTHS IN PEOPLE.

I JUST WANT THE WORLD TO BE *STRAIGHTFORWARD*. TO BE *CLEAR*.

SURE, IF YOU HAVE *SUPER-STRENGTH* AND *STEEL-HARD SKIN*...(WHICH I DON'T.)

WHAT IF PEOPLE WORE THE TRUTH ON THEIR SLEEVES...WHAT IF THEY WERE SELF-EVIDENTLY *BAD* OR *GOOD*?

ALEX, STAY LOW!

SKRADOWWWW

INSTEAD, PEOPLE HIDE THINGS ABOUT THEMSELVES BECAUSE THEY'RE AFRAID. AFRAID OF WHAT OTHERS WILL FIND...

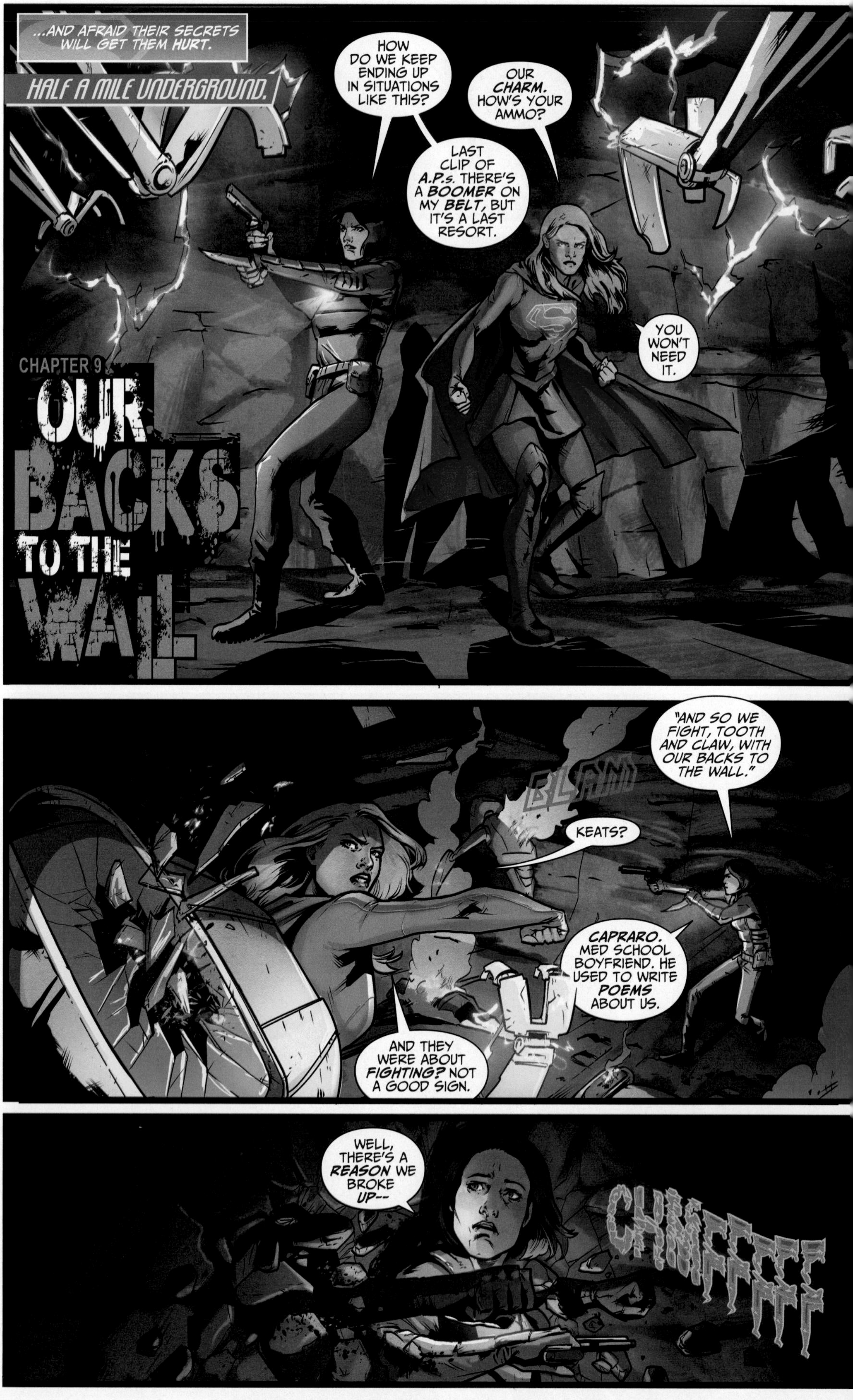
...AND AFRAID THEIR SECRETS WILL GET THEM HURT.
HALF A MILE UNDERGROUND.
HOW DO WE KEEP ENDING UP IN SITUATIONS LIKE THIS?
OUR CHARM. HOW'S YOUR AMMO?
LAST CLIP OF A.P.s. THERE'S A BOOMER ON MY BELT, BUT IT'S A LAST RESORT.
YOU WON'T NEED IT.
CHAPTER 9
OUR BACKS TO THE WALL
"AND SO WE FIGHT, TOOTH AND CLAW, WITH OUR BACKS TO THE WALL."
BLAM
KEATS?
CAPRARO. MED SCHOOL BOYFRIEND. HE USED TO WRITE POEMS ABOUT US.
AND THEY WERE ABOUT FIGHTING? NOT A GOOD SIGN.
WELL, THERE'S A REASON WE BROKE UP--
CHUFFFFF

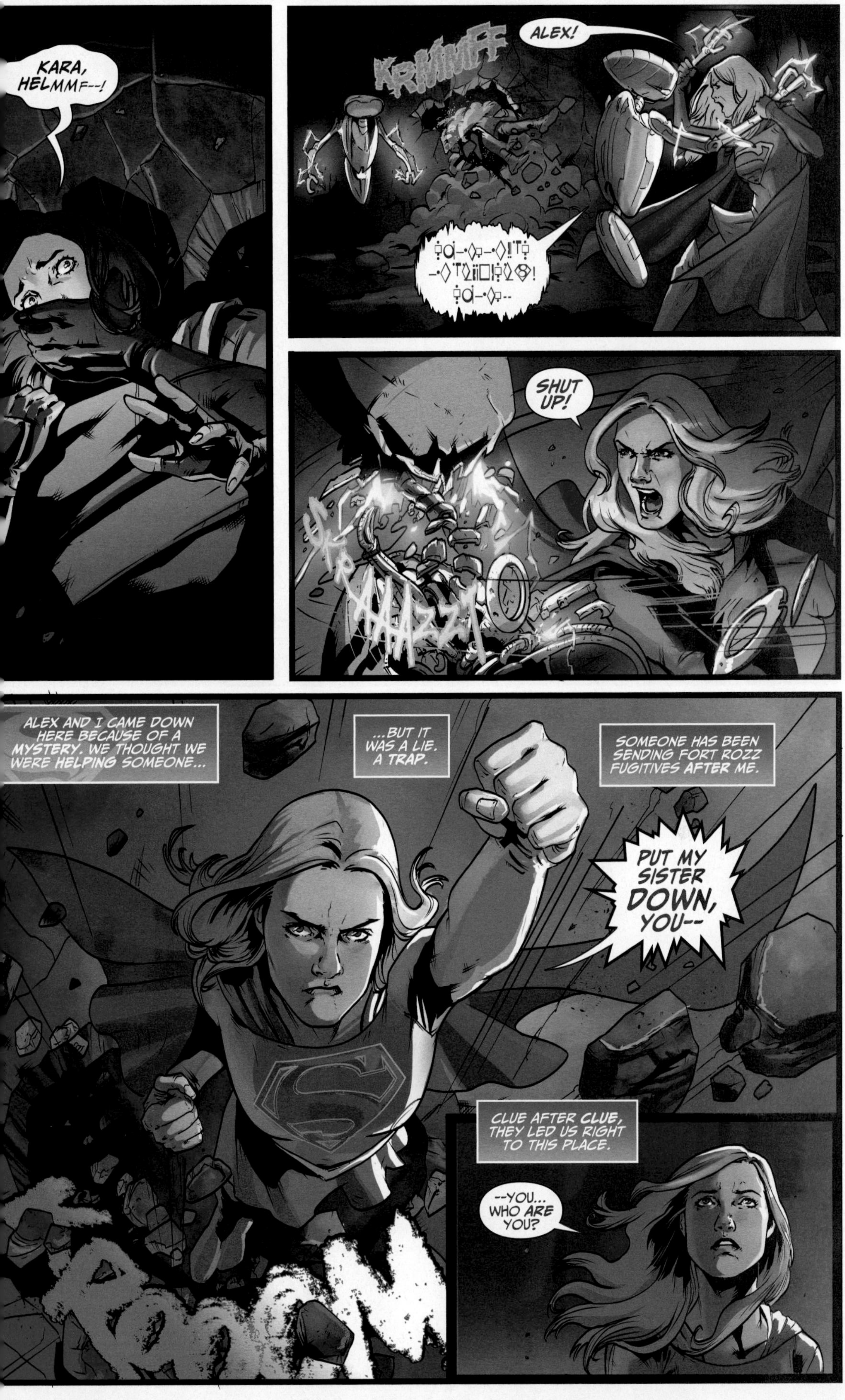
KARA, HELMMF--!
KRMMFF
ALEX!
SHUT UP!
ALEX AND I CAME DOWN HERE BECAUSE OF A MYSTERY. WE THOUGHT WE WERE HELPING SOMEONE...
...BUT IT WAS A LIE. A TRAP.
SOMEONE HAS BEEN SENDING FORT ROZZ FUGITIVES AFTER ME.
PUT MY SISTER DOWN, YOU--
CLUE AFTER CLUE, THEY LED US RIGHT TO THIS PLACE.
--YOU... WHO ARE YOU?

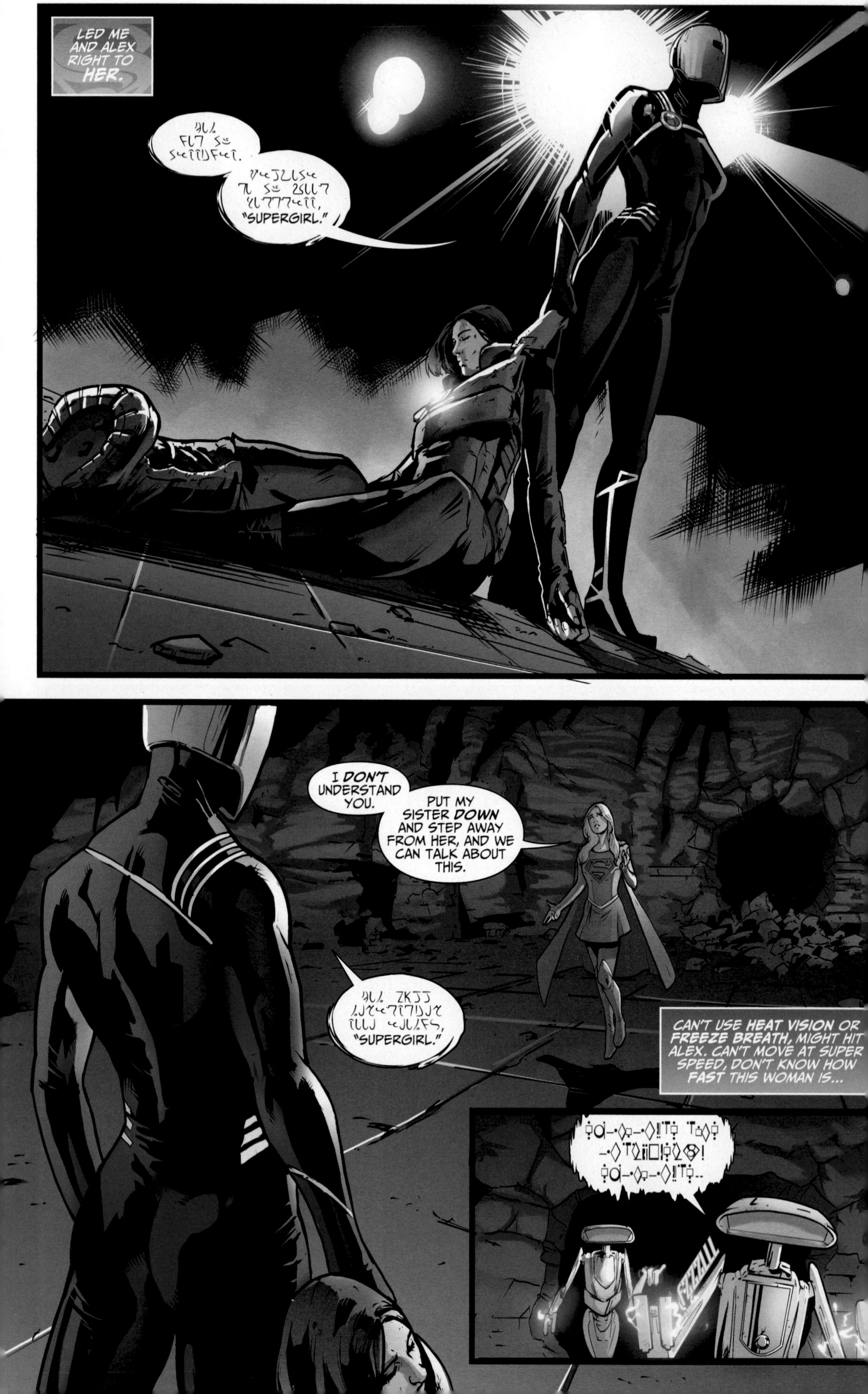
LED ME AND ALEX RIGHT TO HER.
"SUPERGIRL."
I DON'T UNDERSTAND YOU.
PUT MY SISTER DOWN AND STEP AWAY FROM HER, AND WE CAN TALK ABOUT THIS.
"SUPERGIRL."
CAN'T USE HEAT VISION OR FREEZE BREATH, MIGHT HIT ALEX. CAN'T MOVE AT SUPER SPEED, DON'T KNOW HOW FAST THIS WOMAN IS...

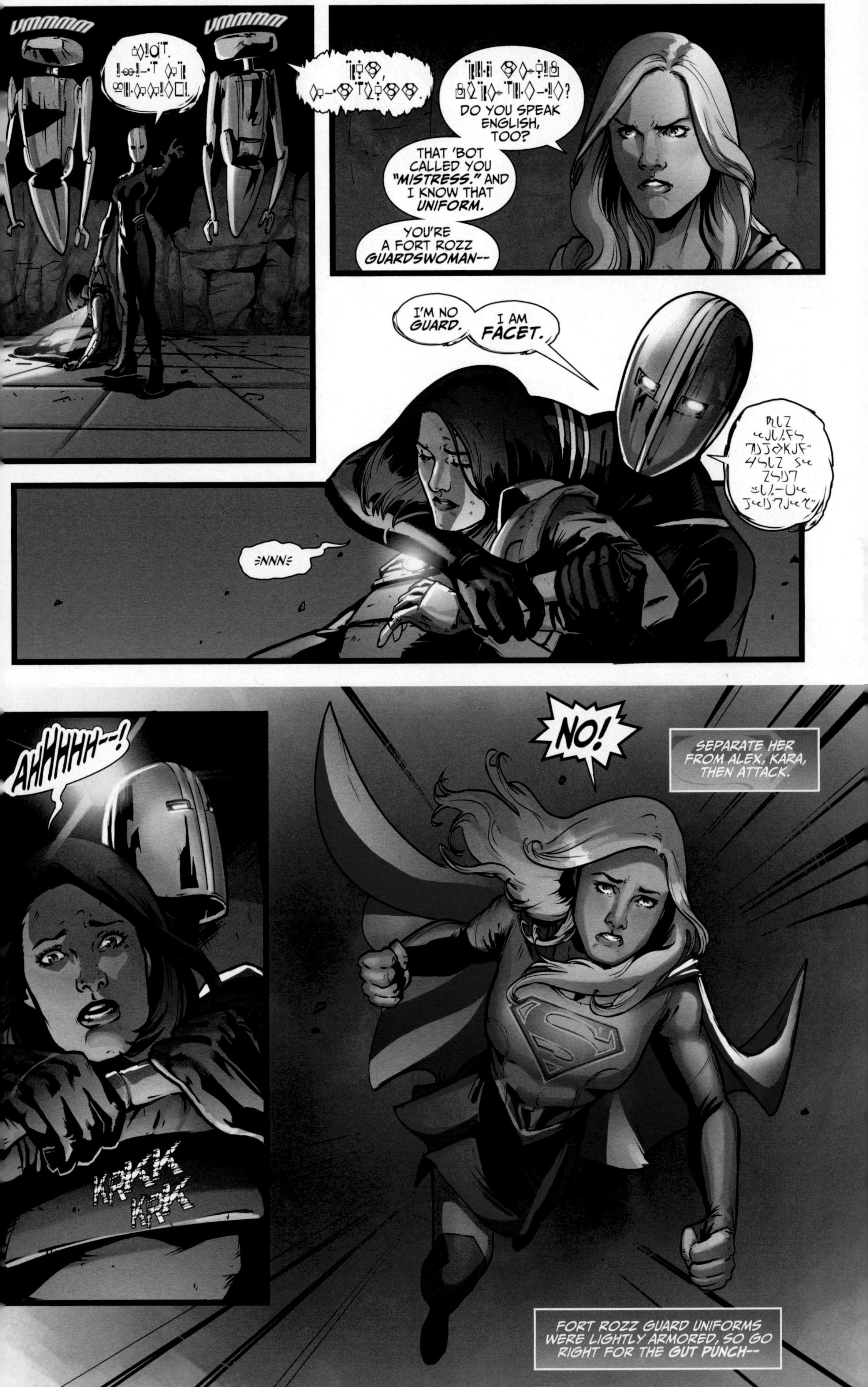

VMMMM
VMMMM
DO YOU SPEAK ENGLISH, TOO?
THAT 'BOT CALLED YOU "MISTRESS." AND I KNOW THAT UNIFORM.
YOU'RE A FORT ROZZ GUARDSWOMAN--
I'M NO GUARD.
I AM FACET.
NNN
AHHHHH--!
KRAK KRAK
NO!
SEPARATE HER FROM ALEX, KARA, THEN ATTACK.
FORT ROZZ GUARD UNIFORMS WERE LIGHTLY ARMORED, SO GO RIGHT FOR THE GUT PUNCH--

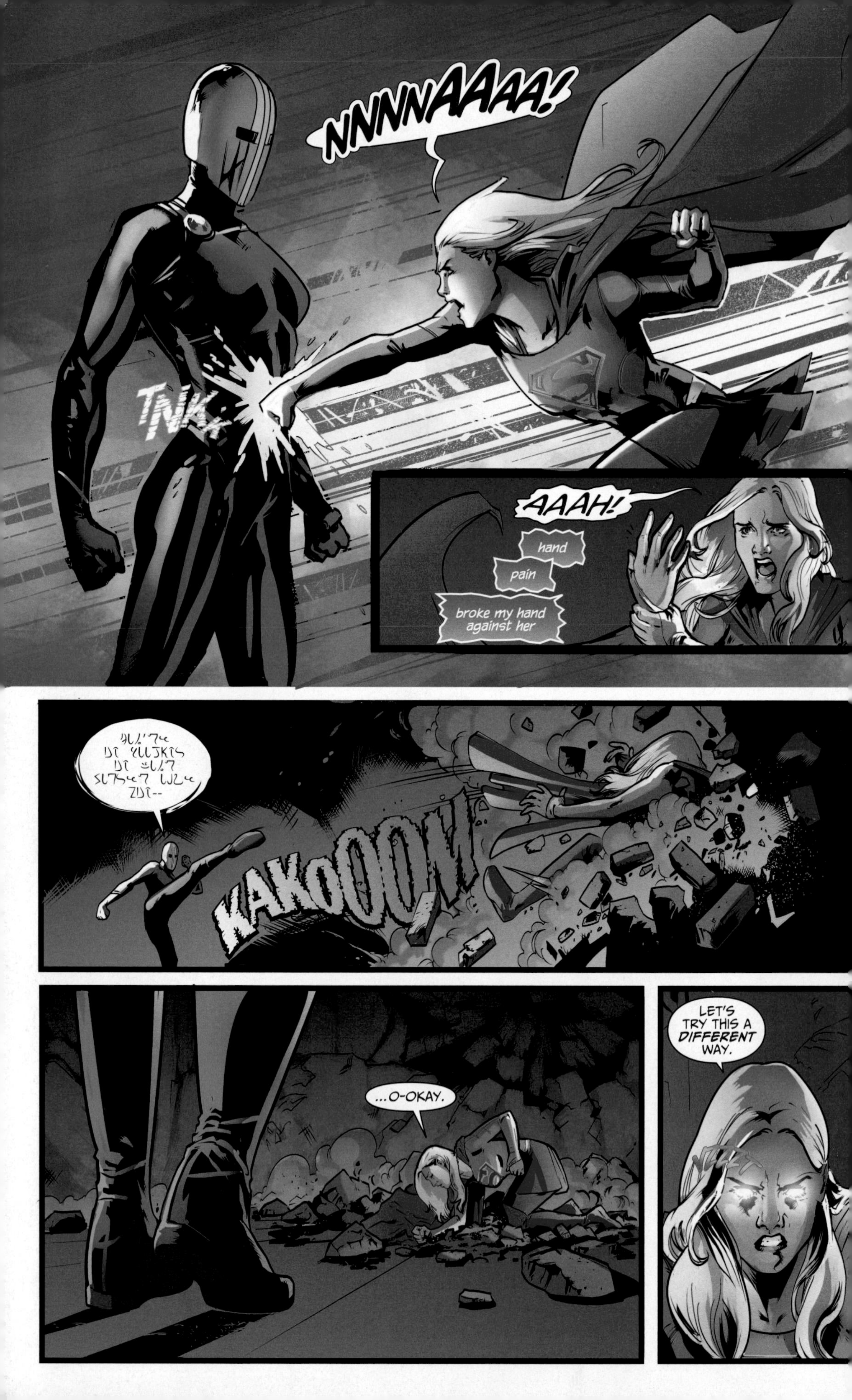

NNNNAAAA!
TNK
AAAH!
hand
pain
broke my hand against her
KAKOOOOM
...O-OKAY.
LET'S TRY THIS A DIFFERENT WAY.

I FOUGHT THE RED TORNADO LIKE THIS.

POURED ALL MY ANGER, ALL MY DISAPPOINTMENT... ALL MY HEAT INTO IT.

RED TORNADO MELTED. I COULDN'T USE MY POWERS FOR A DAY AFTER THAT.

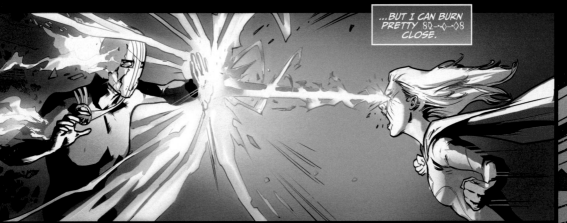

I CAN'T BURN THAT HOT HERE, I STILL HAVE TO GET ALEX TO SAFETY...

HRRAAH!

...BUT I CAN BURN PRETTY 8◊-◊-◊8 CLOSE.

N'YAAAHHHHH!!!

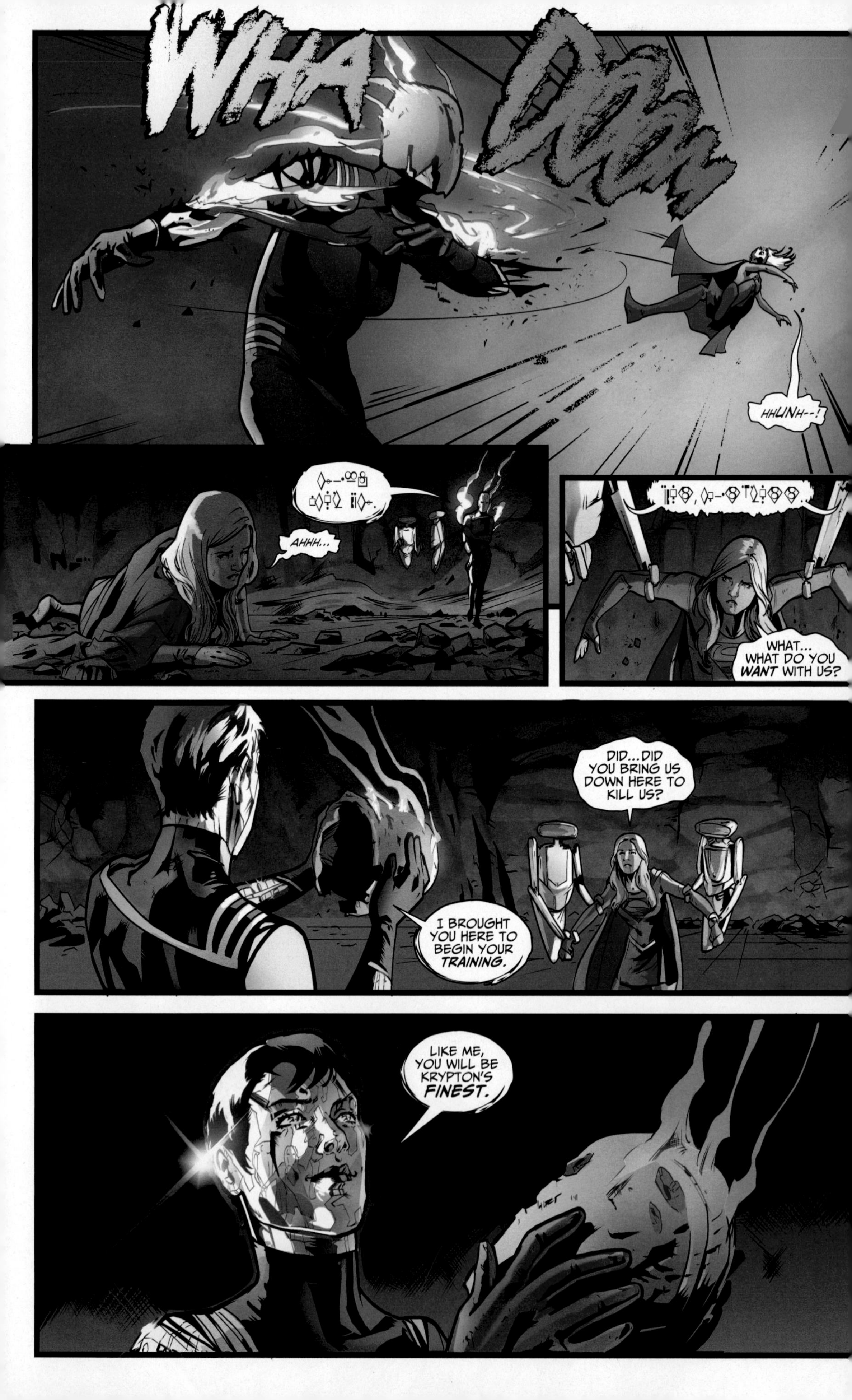
WHA DOOM
HHUNH--!
AHHH...
WHAT... WHAT DO YOU WANT WITH US?
DID...DID YOU BRING US DOWN HERE TO KILL US?
I BROUGHT YOU HERE TO BEGIN YOUR TRAINING.
LIKE ME, YOU WILL BE KRYPTON'S FINEST.

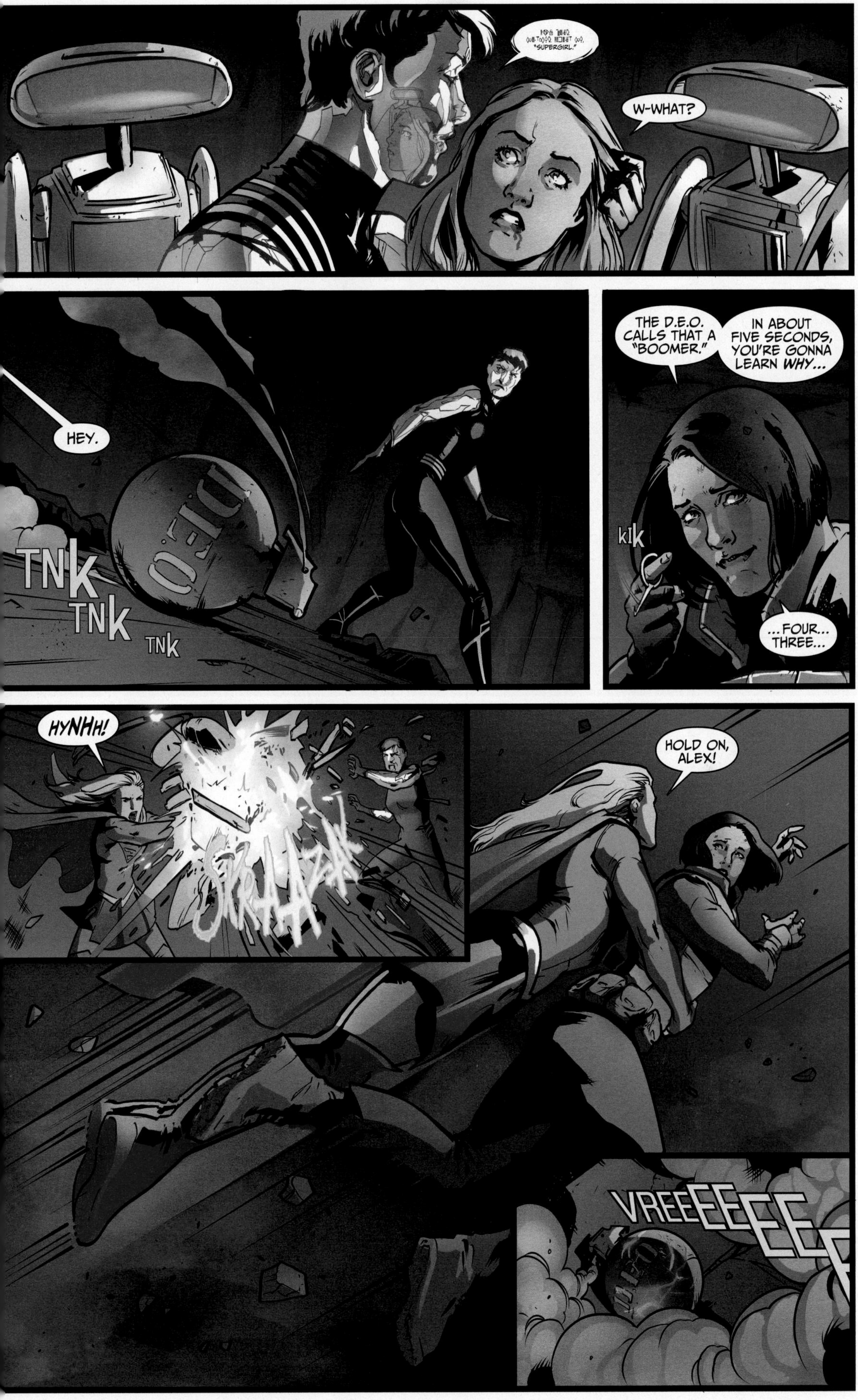
"SUPERGIRL."
W-WHAT?
HEY.
TNK TNK TNK
THE D.E.O. CALLS THAT A "BOOMER."
IN ABOUT FIVE SECONDS, YOU'RE GONNA LEARN WHY...
KIK
...FOUR... THREE...
HYNHH!
SKRAAZAK
HOLD ON, ALEX!
VREEEEEEEE

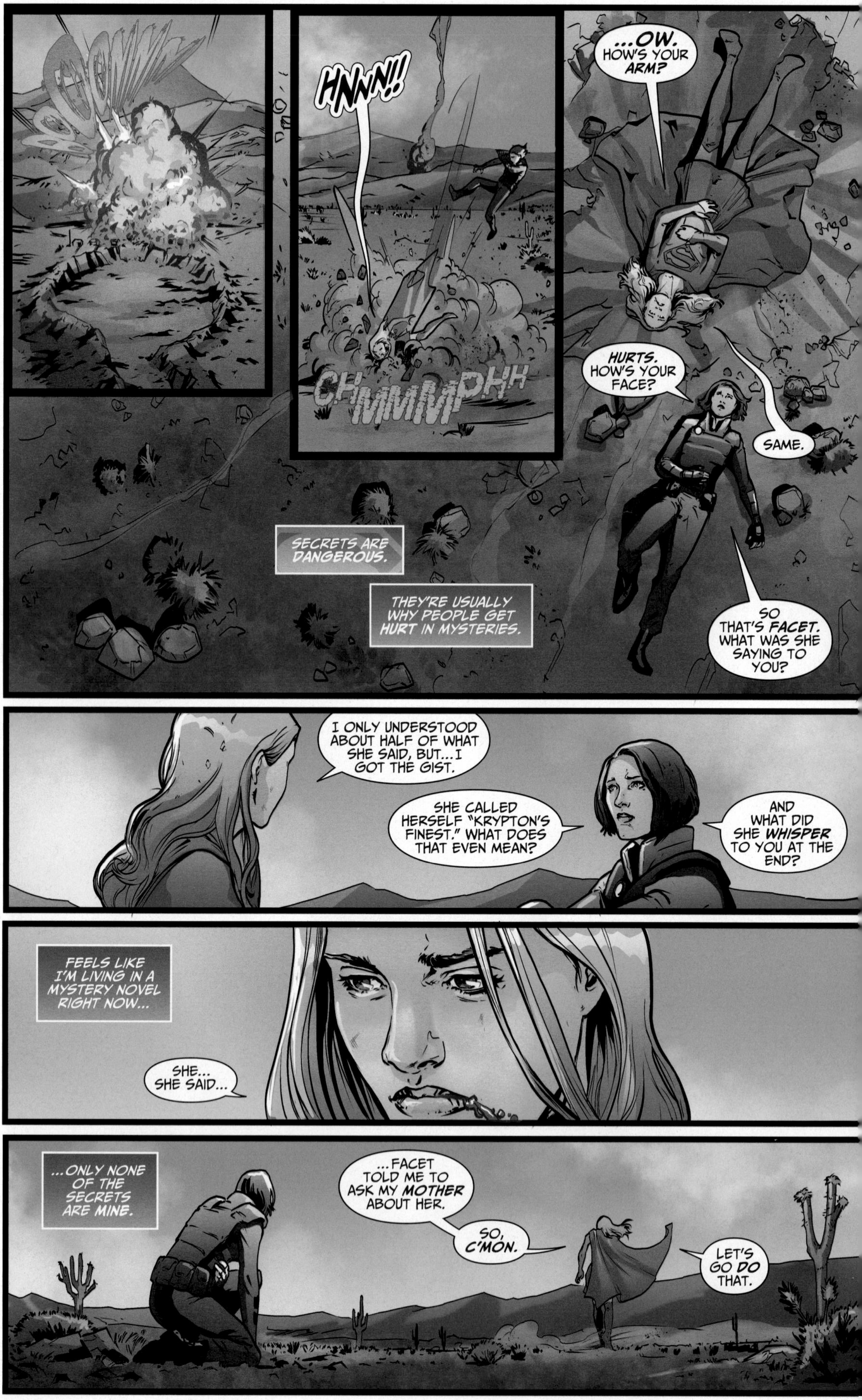
HNNN!!
CHMMMPHH
...OW. HOW'S YOUR ARM?
HURTS. HOW'S YOUR FACE?
SAME.
SECRETS ARE DANGEROUS.
THEY'RE USUALLY WHY PEOPLE GET HURT IN MYSTERIES.
SO THAT'S FACET. WHAT WAS SHE SAYING TO YOU?
I ONLY UNDERSTOOD ABOUT HALF OF WHAT SHE SAID, BUT...I GOT THE GIST.
SHE CALLED HERSELF "KRYPTON'S FINEST." WHAT DOES THAT EVEN MEAN?
AND WHAT DID SHE WHISPER TO YOU AT THE END?
FEELS LIKE I'M LIVING IN A MYSTERY NOVEL RIGHT NOW...
SHE... SHE SAID...
...ONLY NONE OF THE SECRETS ARE MINE.
...FACET TOLD ME TO ASK MY MOTHER ABOUT HER.
SO, C'MON.
LET'S GO DO THAT.

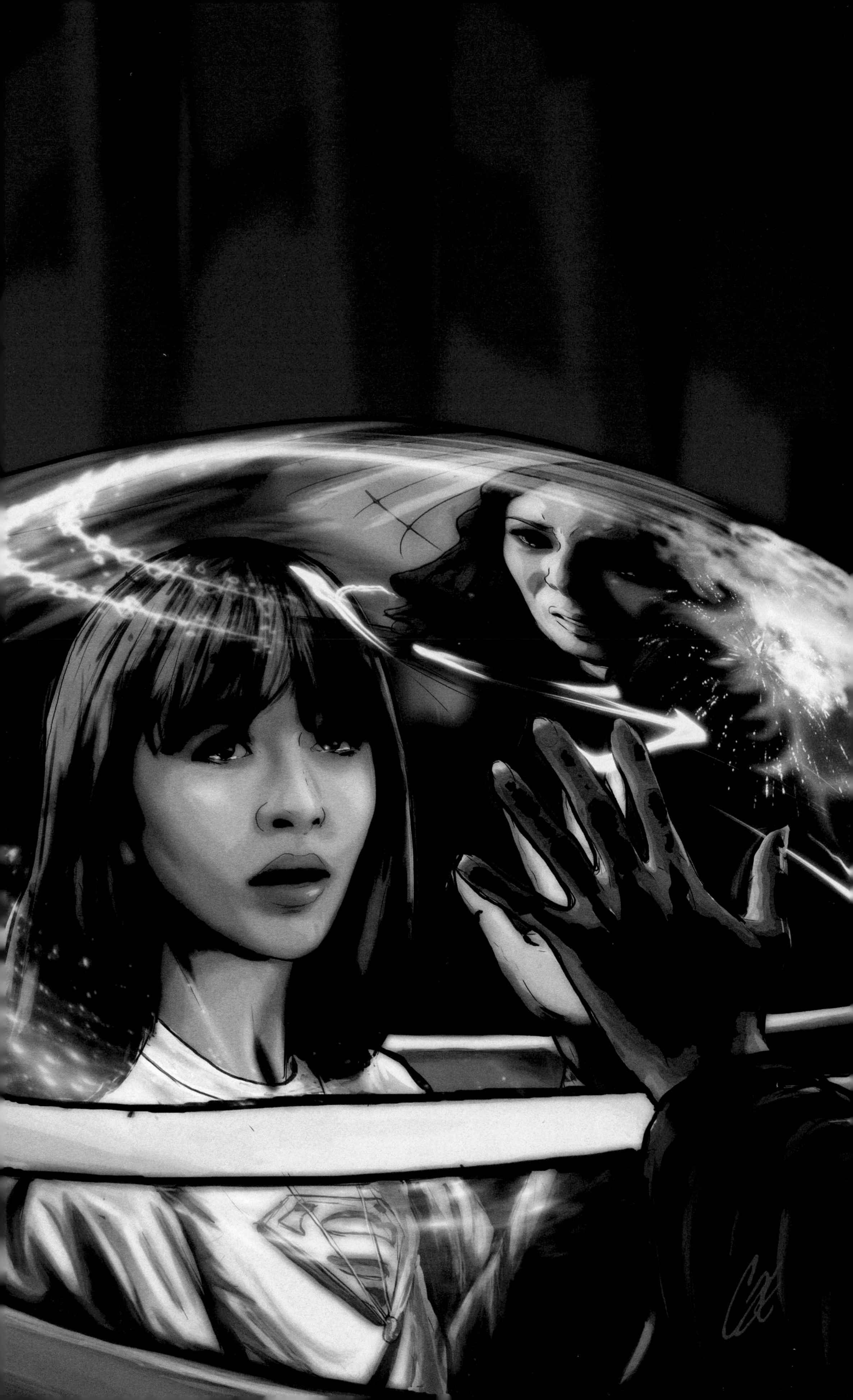

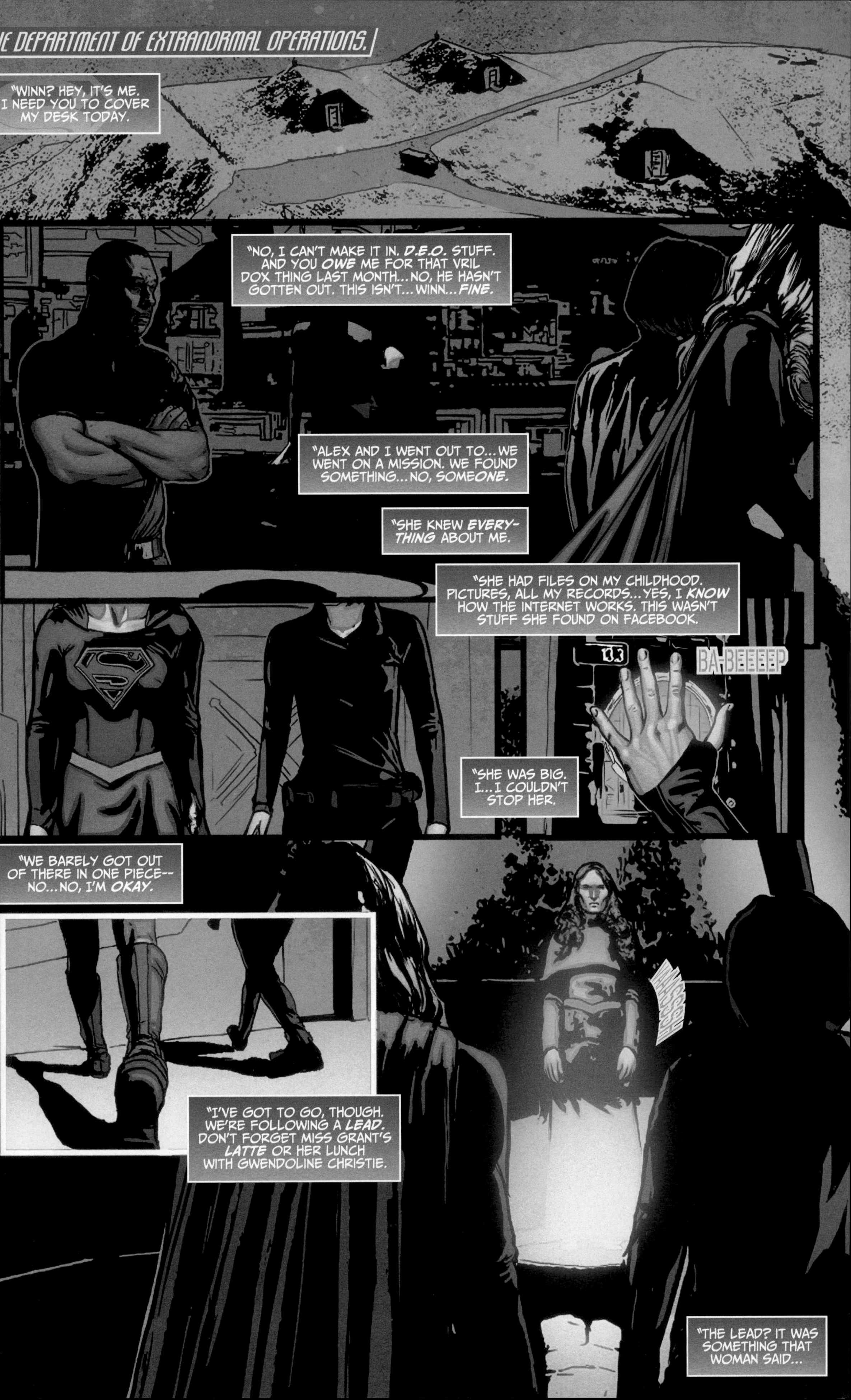
...E DEPARTMENT OF EXTRANORMAL OPERATIONS.
"WINN? HEY, IT'S ME. I NEED YOU TO COVER MY DESK TODAY.
"NO, I CAN'T MAKE IT IN. D.E.O. STUFF. AND YOU OWE ME FOR THAT VRIL DOX THING LAST MONTH...NO, HE HASN'T GOTTEN OUT. THIS ISN'T...WINN...FINE.
"ALEX AND I WENT OUT TO...WE WENT ON A MISSION. WE FOUND SOMETHING...NO, SOMEONE.
"SHE KNEW EVERYTHING ABOUT ME.
"SHE HAD FILES ON MY CHILDHOOD. PICTURES, ALL MY RECORDS...YES, I KNOW HOW THE INTERNET WORKS. THIS WASN'T STUFF SHE FOUND ON FACEBOOK.
BA-BEEEEP
"SHE WAS BIG. I...I COULDN'T STOP HER.
"WE BARELY GOT OUT OF THERE IN ONE PIECE--NO...NO, I'M OKAY.
"I'VE GOT TO GO, THOUGH. WE'RE FOLLOWING A LEAD. DON'T FORGET MISS GRANT'S LATTE OR HER LUNCH WITH GWENDOLINE CHRISTIE.
"THE LEAD? IT WAS SOMETHING THAT WOMAN SAID...

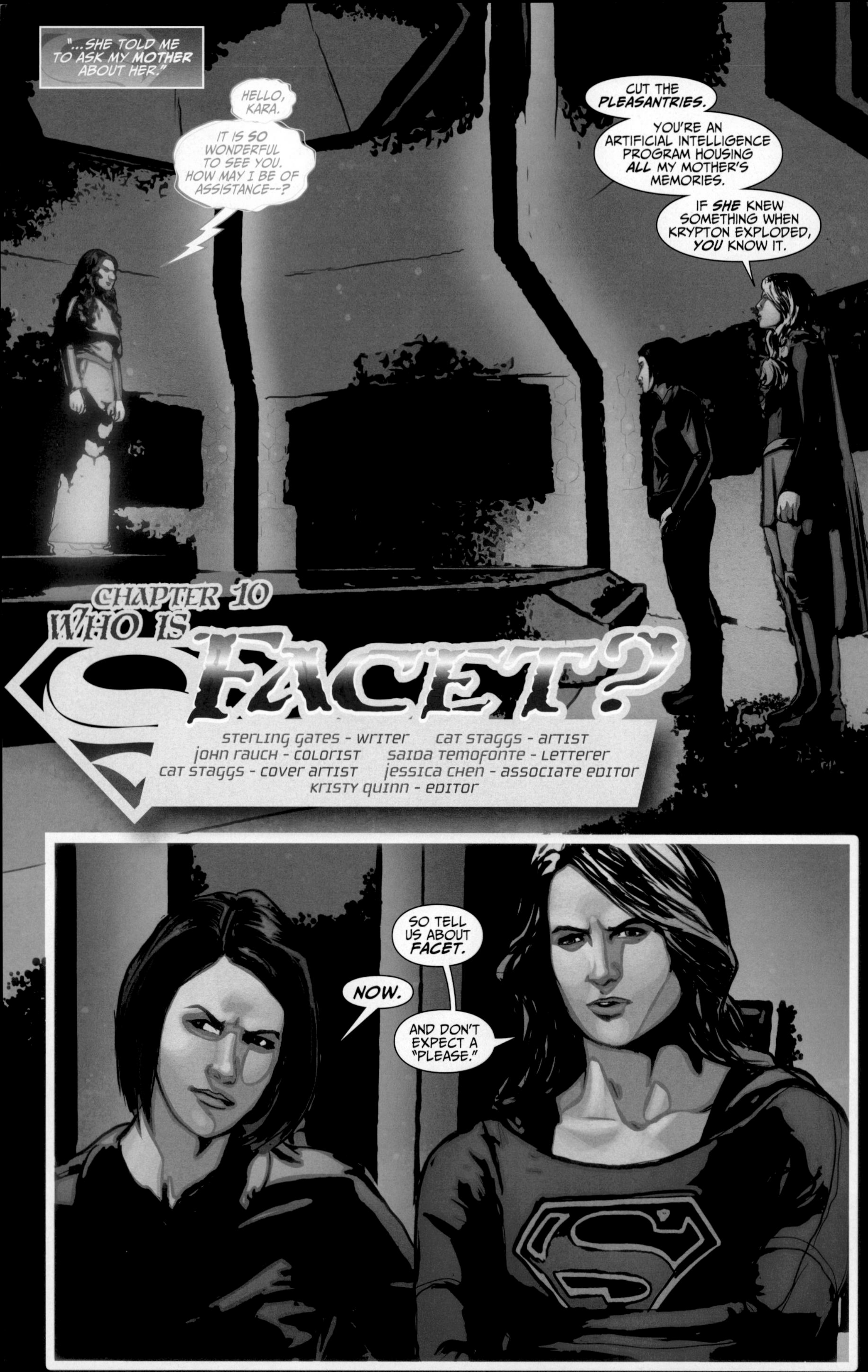
"...SHE TOLD ME TO ASK MY MOTHER ABOUT HER."
HELLO, KARA.
IT IS SO WONDERFUL TO SEE YOU. HOW MAY I BE OF ASSISTANCE--?
CUT THE PLEASANTRIES.
YOU'RE AN ARTIFICIAL INTELLIGENCE PROGRAM HOUSING ALL MY MOTHER'S MEMORIES.
IF SHE KNEW SOMETHING WHEN KRYPTON EXPLODED, YOU KNOW IT.
CHAPTER 10
WHO IS FACET?
STERLING GATES - WRITER
CAT STAGGS - ARTIST
JOHN RAUCH - COLORIST
SAIDA TEMOFONTE - LETTERER
CAT STAGGS - COVER ARTIST
JESSICA CHEN - ASSOCIATE EDITOR
KRISTY QUINN - EDITOR
SO TELL US ABOUT FACET.
NOW.
AND DON'T EXPECT A "PLEASE."

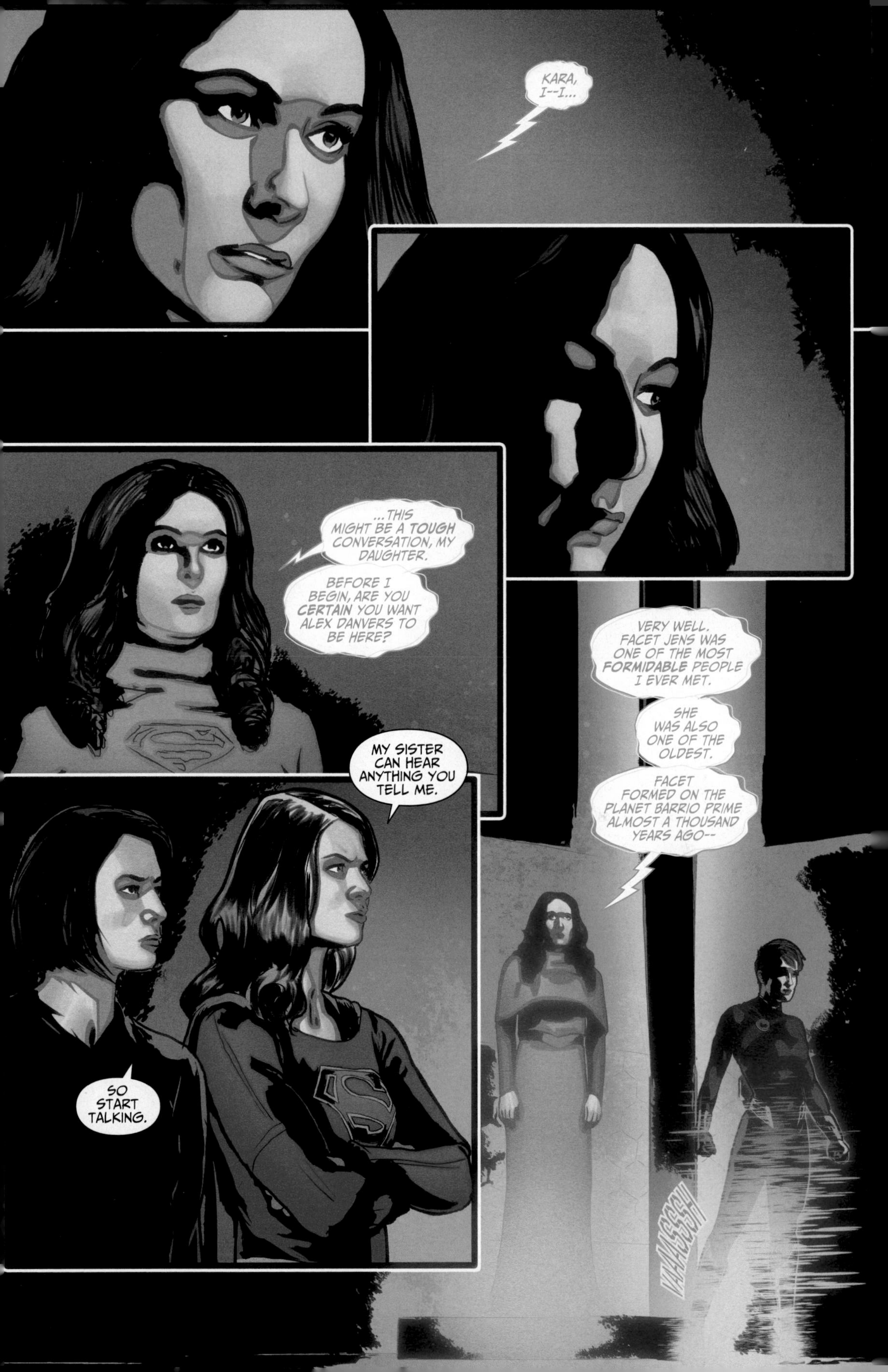

KARA, I--I...
...THIS MIGHT BE A TOUGH CONVERSATION, MY DAUGHTER.
BEFORE I BEGIN, ARE YOU CERTAIN YOU WANT ALEX DANVERS TO BE HERE?
MY SISTER CAN HEAR ANYTHING YOU TELL ME.
SO START TALKING.
VERY WELL. FACET JENS WAS ONE OF THE MOST FORMIDABLE PEOPLE I EVER MET.
SHE WAS ALSO ONE OF THE OLDEST.
FACET FORMED ON THE PLANET BARRIO PRIME ALMOST A THOUSAND YEARS AGO--
VVVASSSH

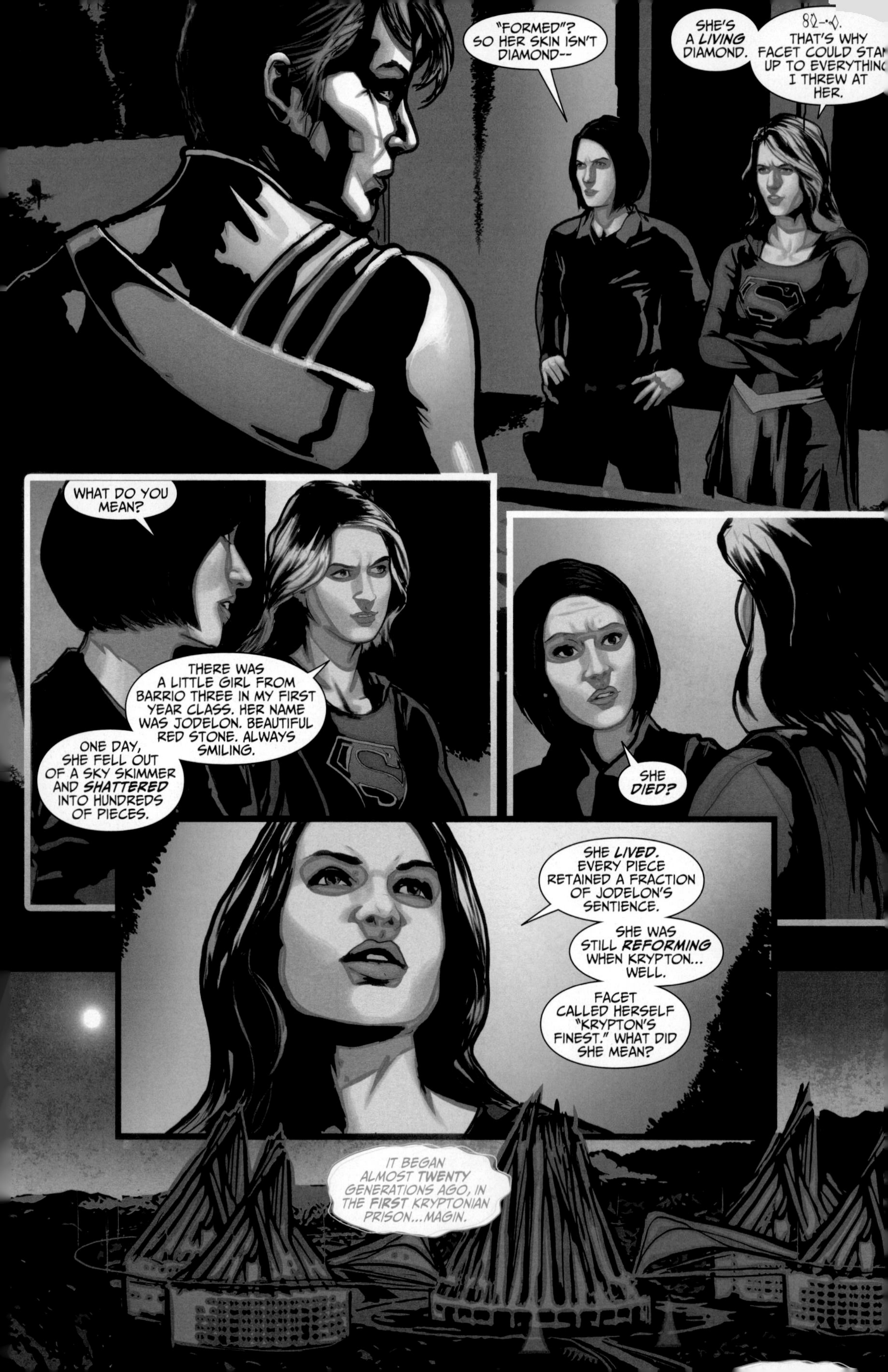

"FORMED"? SO HER SKIN ISN'T DIAMOND--
SHE'S A LIVING DIAMOND.
THAT'S WHY FACET COULD STAN UP TO EVERYTHING I THREW AT HER.
WHAT DO YOU MEAN?
THERE WAS A LITTLE GIRL FROM BARRIO THREE IN MY FIRST YEAR CLASS. HER NAME WAS JODELON. BEAUTIFUL RED STONE. ALWAYS SMILING.
ONE DAY, SHE FELL OUT OF A SKY SKIMMER AND SHATTERED INTO HUNDREDS OF PIECES.
SHE DIED?
SHE LIVED. EVERY PIECE RETAINED A FRACTION OF JODELON'S SENTIENCE.
SHE WAS STILL REFORMING WHEN KRYPTON... WELL.
FACET CALLED HERSELF "KRYPTON'S FINEST." WHAT DID SHE MEAN?
IT BEGAN ALMOST TWENTY GENERATIONS AGO, IN THE FIRST KRYPTONIAN PRISON...MAGIN.

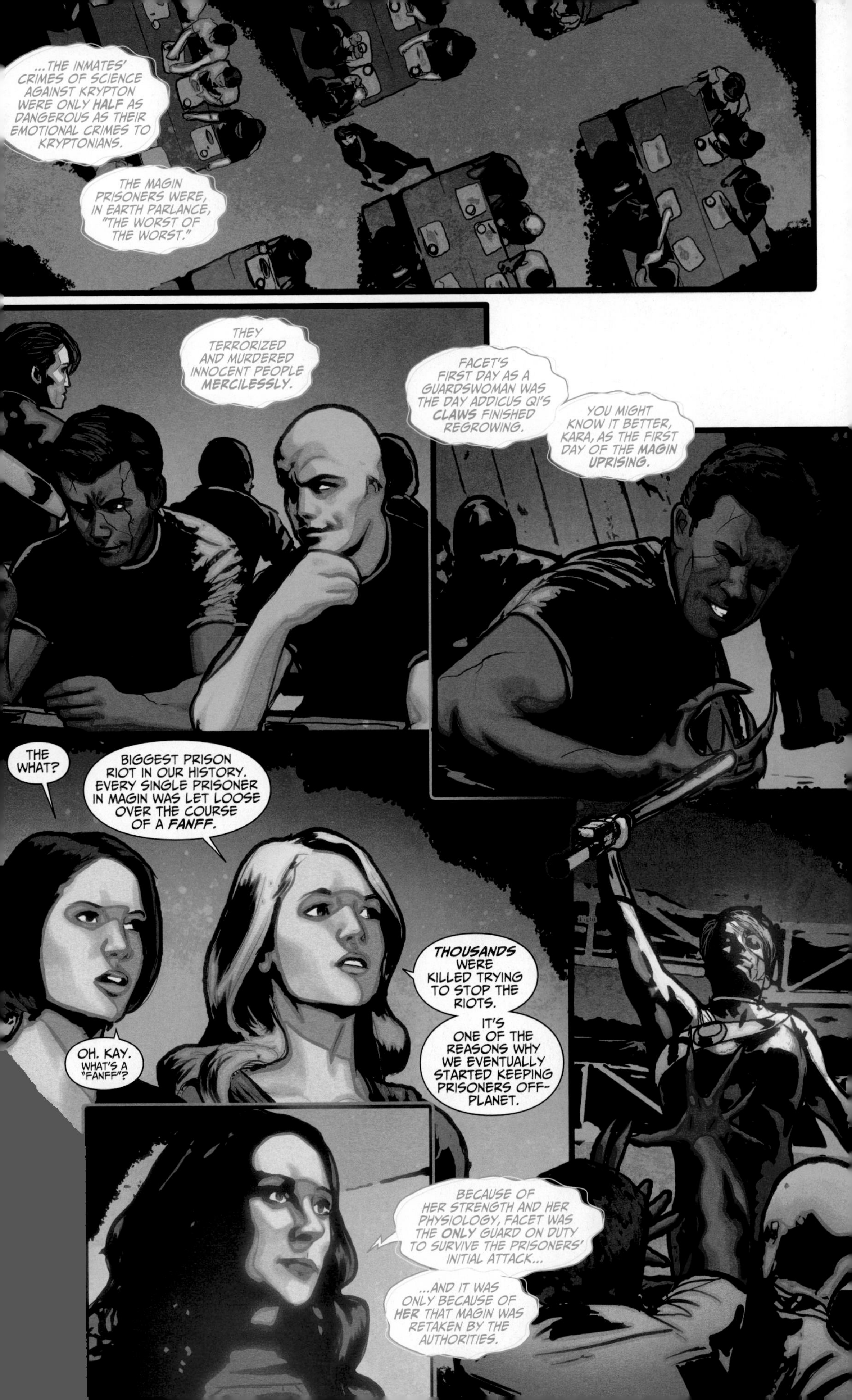
...THE INMATES' CRIMES OF SCIENCE AGAINST KRYPTON WERE ONLY HALF AS DANGEROUS AS THEIR EMOTIONAL CRIMES TO KRYPTONIANS.
THE MAGIN PRISONERS WERE, IN EARTH PARLANCE, "THE WORST OF THE WORST."
THEY TERRORIZED AND MURDERED INNOCENT PEOPLE MERCILESSLY.
FACET'S FIRST DAY AS A GUARDSWOMAN WAS THE DAY ADDICUS QI'S CLAWS FINISHED REGROWING.
YOU MIGHT KNOW IT BETTER, KARA, AS THE FIRST DAY OF THE MAGIN UPRISING.
THE WHAT?
BIGGEST PRISON RIOT IN OUR HISTORY. EVERY SINGLE PRISONER IN MAGIN WAS LET LOOSE OVER THE COURSE OF A FANFF.
OH. KAY. WHAT'S A "FANFF"?
THOUSANDS WERE KILLED TRYING TO STOP THE RIOTS.
IT'S ONE OF THE REASONS WHY WE EVENTUALLY STARTED KEEPING PRISONERS OFF-PLANET.
BECAUSE OF HER STRENGTH AND HER PHYSIOLOGY, FACET WAS THE ONLY GUARD ON DUTY TO SURVIVE THE PRISONERS' INITIAL ATTACK...
...AND IT WAS ONLY BECAUSE OF HER THAT MAGIN WAS RETAKEN BY THE AUTHORITIES.

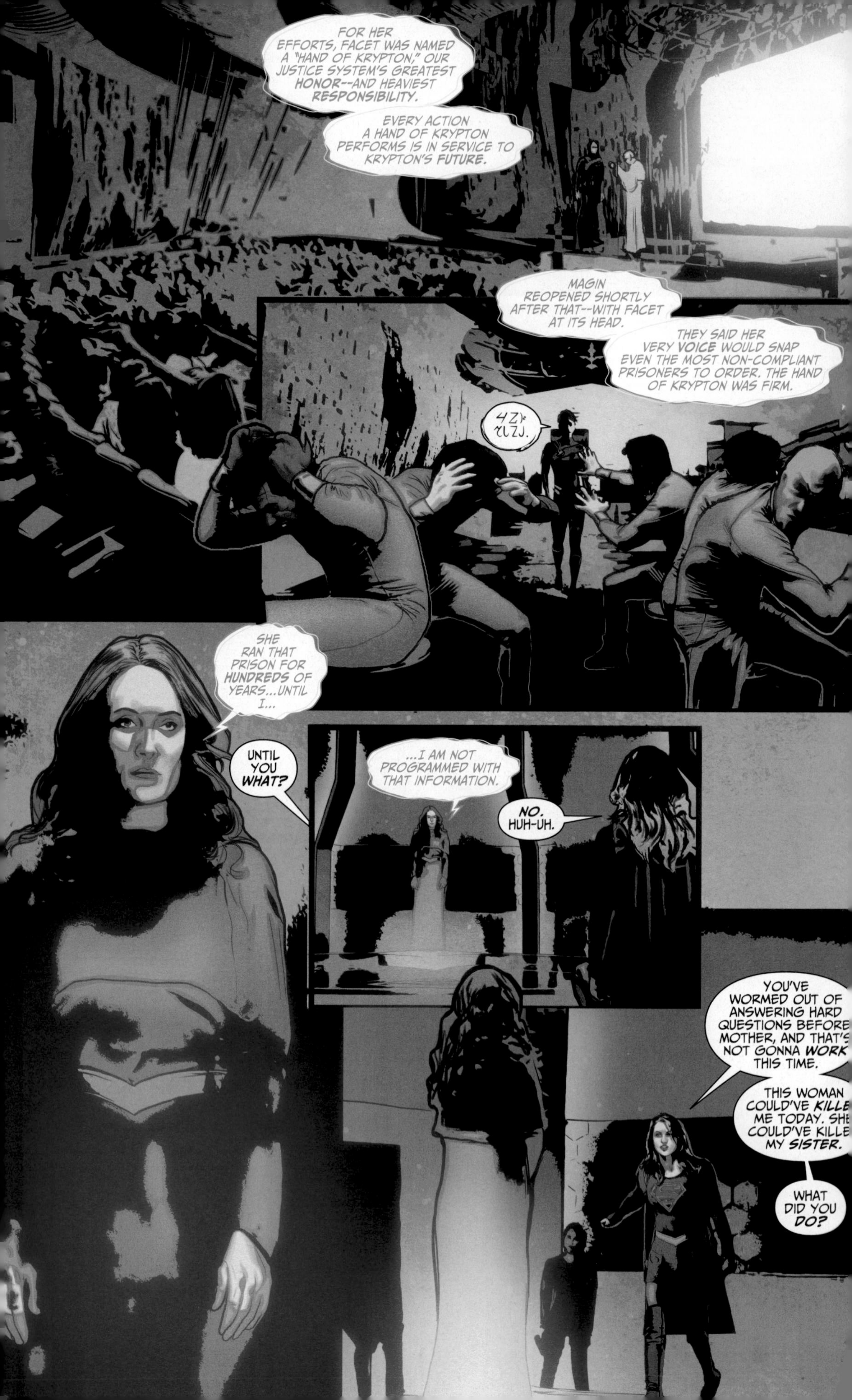

FOR HER EFFORTS, FACET WAS NAMED A "HAND OF KRYPTON," OUR JUSTICE SYSTEM'S GREATEST HONOR--AND HEAVIEST RESPONSIBILITY.
EVERY ACTION A HAND OF KRYPTON PERFORMS IS IN SERVICE TO KRYPTON'S FUTURE.
MAGIN REOPENED SHORTLY AFTER THAT--WITH FACET AT ITS HEAD.
THEY SAID HER VERY VOICE WOULD SNAP EVEN THE MOST NON-COMPLIANT PRISONERS TO ORDER. THE HAND OF KRYPTON WAS FIRM.
SHE RAN THAT PRISON FOR HUNDREDS OF YEARS...UNTIL I...
UNTIL YOU WHAT?
...I AM NOT PROGRAMMED WITH THAT INFORMATION.
NO. HUH-UH.
YOU'VE WORMED OUT OF ANSWERING HARD QUESTIONS BEFORE MOTHER, AND THAT'S NOT GONNA WORK THIS TIME.
THIS WOMAN COULD'VE KILLED ME TODAY. SHE COULD'VE KILLED MY SISTER.
WHAT DID YOU DO?

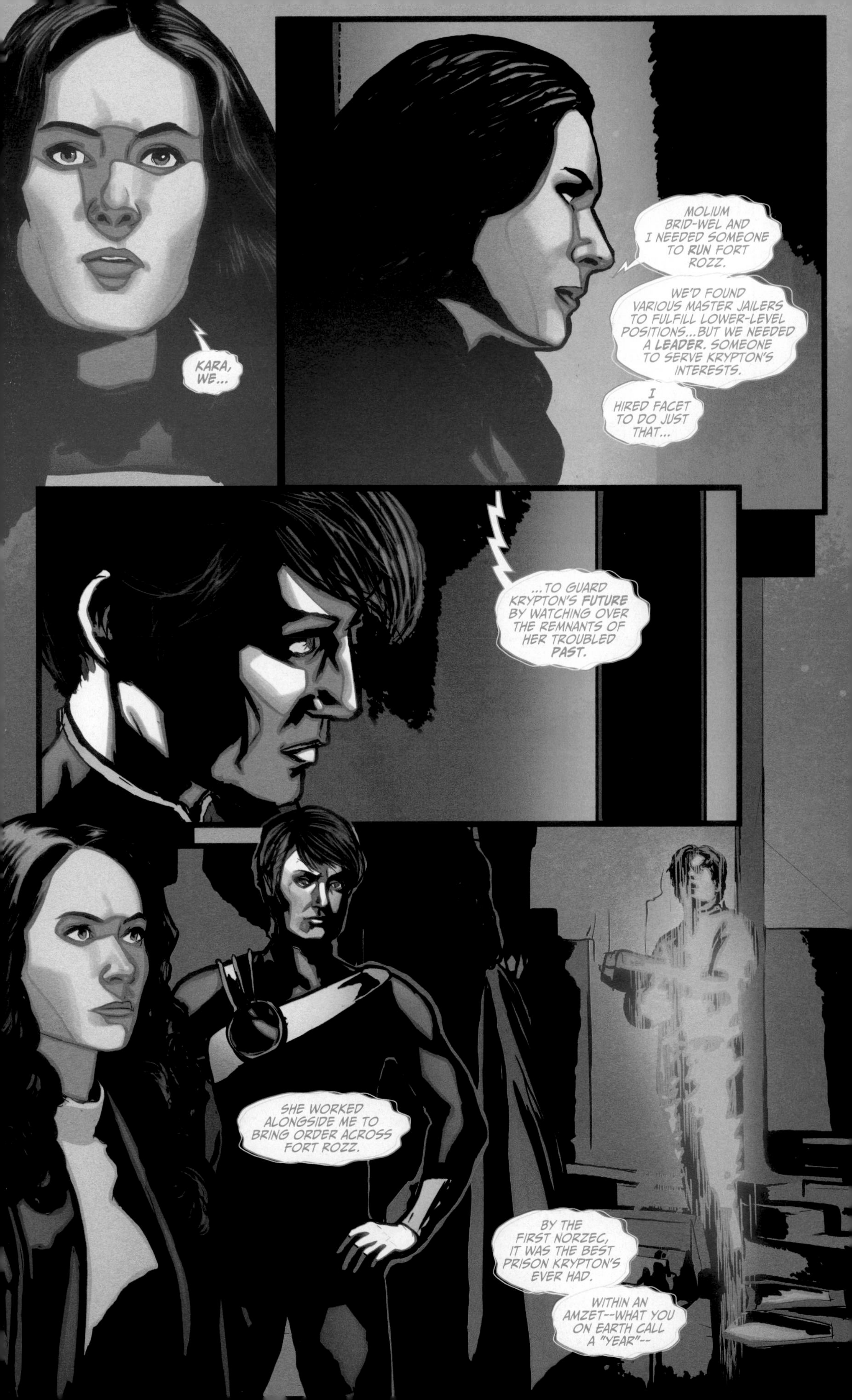
KARA, WE...
MOLIUM BRID-WEL AND I NEEDED SOMEONE TO RUN FORT ROZZ.
WE'D FOUND VARIOUS MASTER JAILERS TO FULFILL LOWER-LEVEL POSITIONS...BUT WE NEEDED A LEADER. SOMEONE TO SERVE KRYPTON'S INTERESTS.
I HIRED FACET TO DO JUST THAT...
...TO GUARD KRYPTON'S FUTURE BY WATCHING OVER THE REMNANTS OF HER TROUBLED PAST.
SHE WORKED ALONGSIDE ME TO BRING ORDER ACROSS FORT ROZZ.
BY THE FIRST NORZEC, IT WAS THE BEST PRISON KRYPTON'S EVER HAD.
WITHIN AN AMZET--WHAT YOU ON EARTH CALL A "YEAR"--

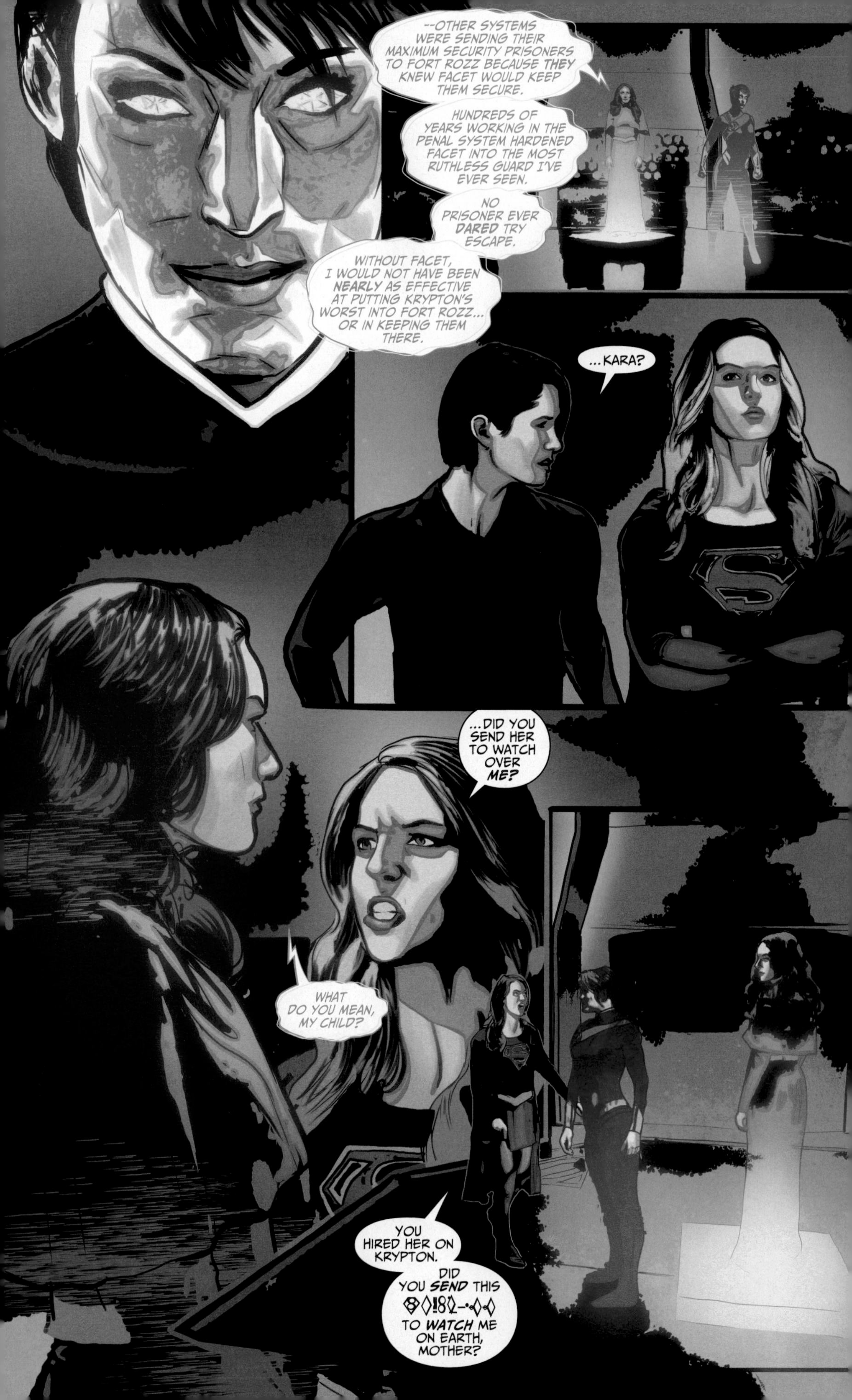
--OTHER SYSTEMS WERE SENDING THEIR MAXIMUM SECURITY PRISONERS TO FORT ROZZ BECAUSE **THEY** KNEW FACET WOULD KEEP THEM SECURE.
HUNDREDS OF YEARS WORKING IN THE PENAL SYSTEM HARDENED FACET INTO THE MOST RUTHLESS GUARD I'VE EVER SEEN.
NO PRISONER EVER **DARED** TRY ESCAPE.
WITHOUT FACET, I WOULD NOT HAVE BEEN **NEARLY** AS EFFECTIVE AT PUTTING KRYPTON'S WORST INTO FORT ROZZ... OR IN KEEPING THEM THERE.
...KARA?
...DID YOU SEND HER TO WATCH OVER ***ME?***
WHAT DO YOU MEAN, MY CHILD?
YOU HIRED HER ON KRYPTON.
DID YOU ***SEND*** THIS
TO ***WATCH*** ME ON EARTH, MOTHER?

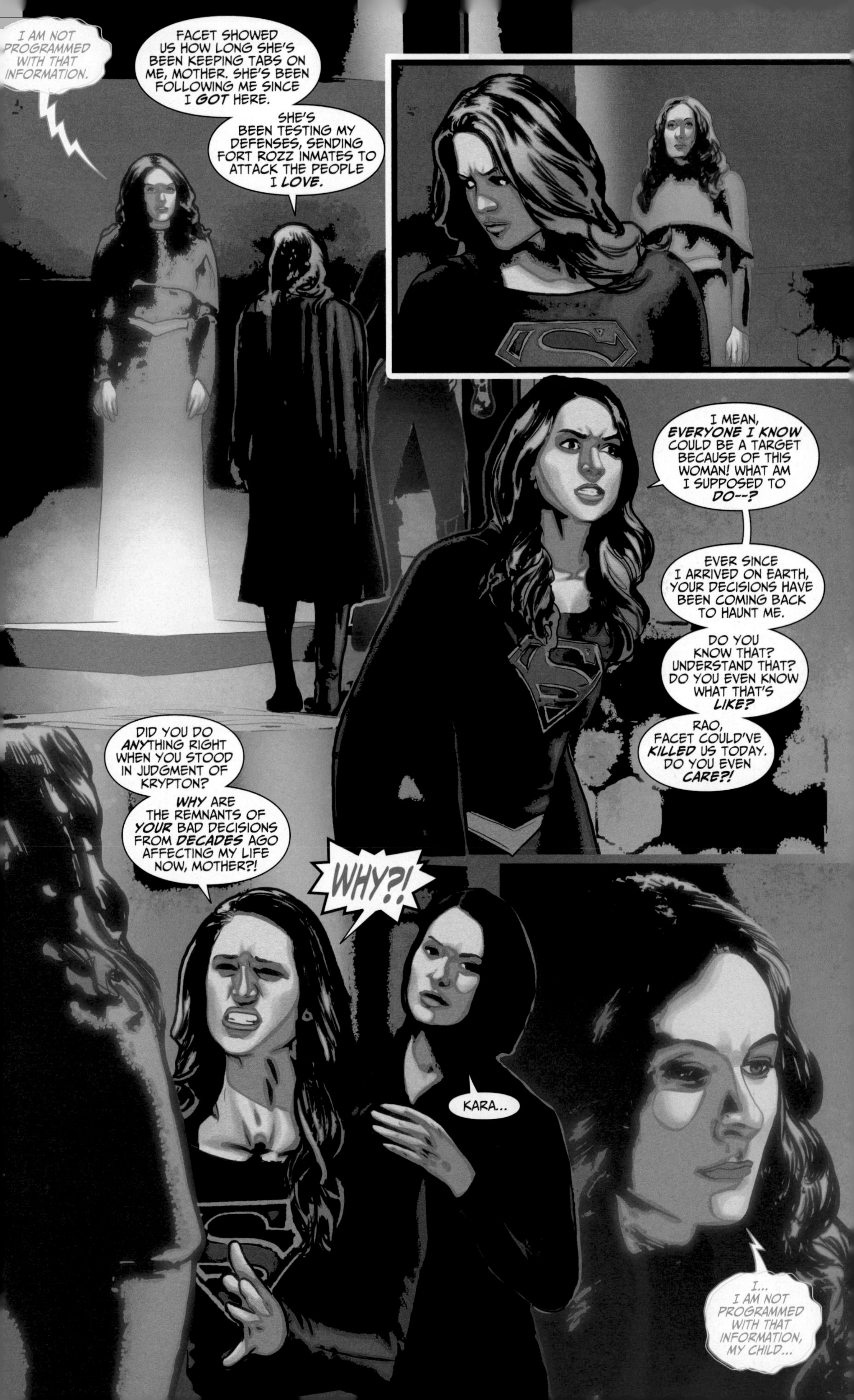

I AM NOT PROGRAMMED WITH THAT INFORMATION.
FACET SHOWED US HOW LONG SHE'S BEEN KEEPING TABS ON ME, MOTHER. SHE'S BEEN FOLLOWING ME SINCE I GOT HERE.
SHE'S BEEN TESTING MY DEFENSES, SENDING FORT ROZZ INMATES TO ATTACK THE PEOPLE I LOVE.
I MEAN, EVERYONE I KNOW COULD BE A TARGET BECAUSE OF THIS WOMAN! WHAT AM I SUPPOSED TO DO--?
EVER SINCE I ARRIVED ON EARTH, YOUR DECISIONS HAVE BEEN COMING BACK TO HAUNT ME.
DO YOU KNOW THAT? UNDERSTAND THAT? DO YOU EVEN KNOW WHAT THAT'S LIKE?
RAO, FACET COULD'VE KILLED US TODAY. DO YOU EVEN CARE?!
DID YOU DO ANYTHING RIGHT WHEN YOU STOOD IN JUDGMENT OF KRYPTON?
WHY ARE THE REMNANTS OF YOUR BAD DECISIONS FROM DECADES AGO AFFECTING MY LIFE NOW, MOTHER?!
WHY?!
KARA...
I... I AM NOT PROGRAMMED WITH THAT INFORMATION, MY CHILD...

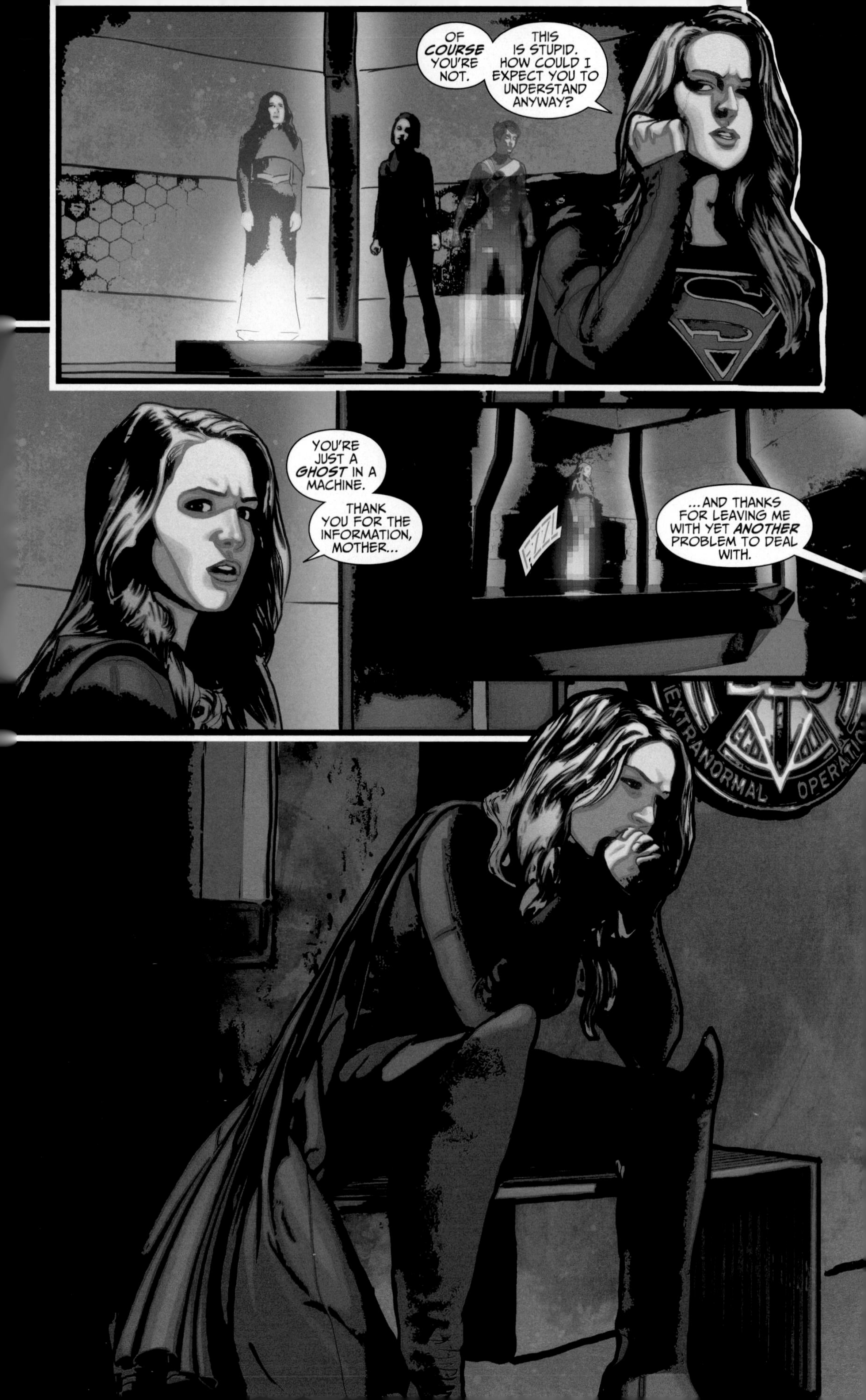
OF COURSE YOU'RE NOT.
THIS IS STUPID. HOW COULD I EXPECT YOU TO UNDERSTAND ANYWAY?
YOU'RE JUST A GHOST IN A MACHINE.
THANK YOU FOR THE INFORMATION, MOTHER...
FZZL
...AND THANKS FOR LEAVING ME WITH YET ANOTHER PROBLEM TO DEAL WITH.

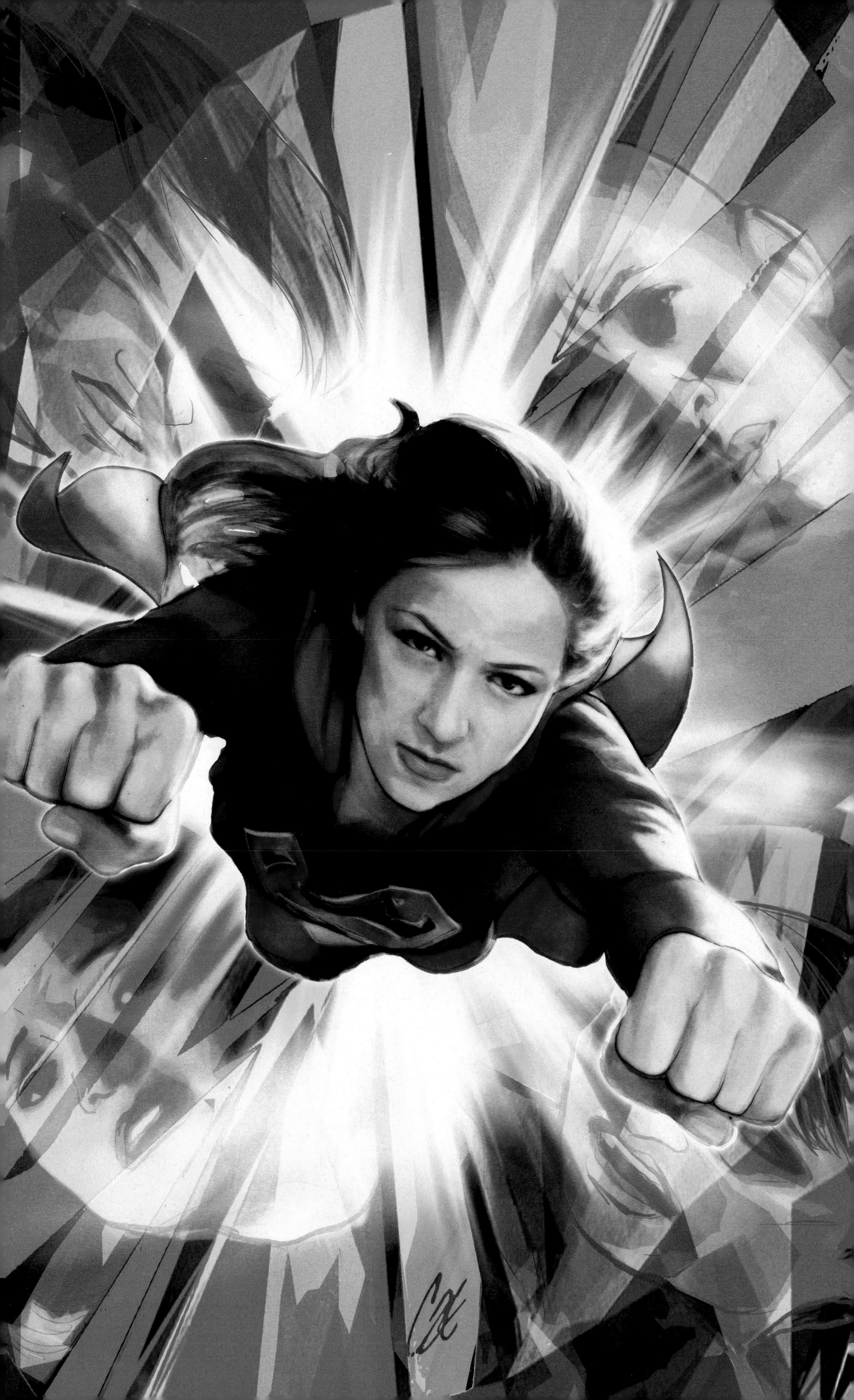

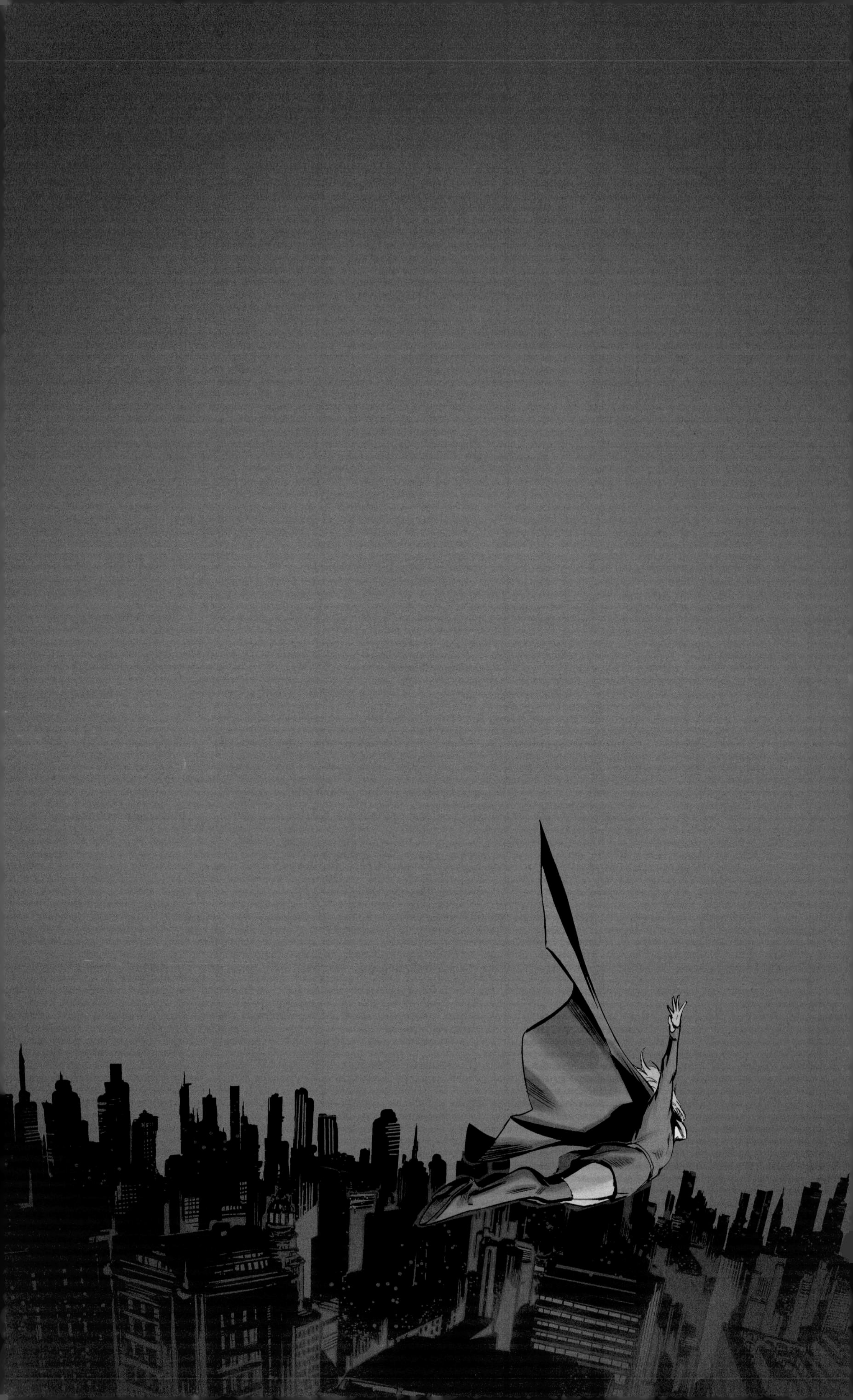

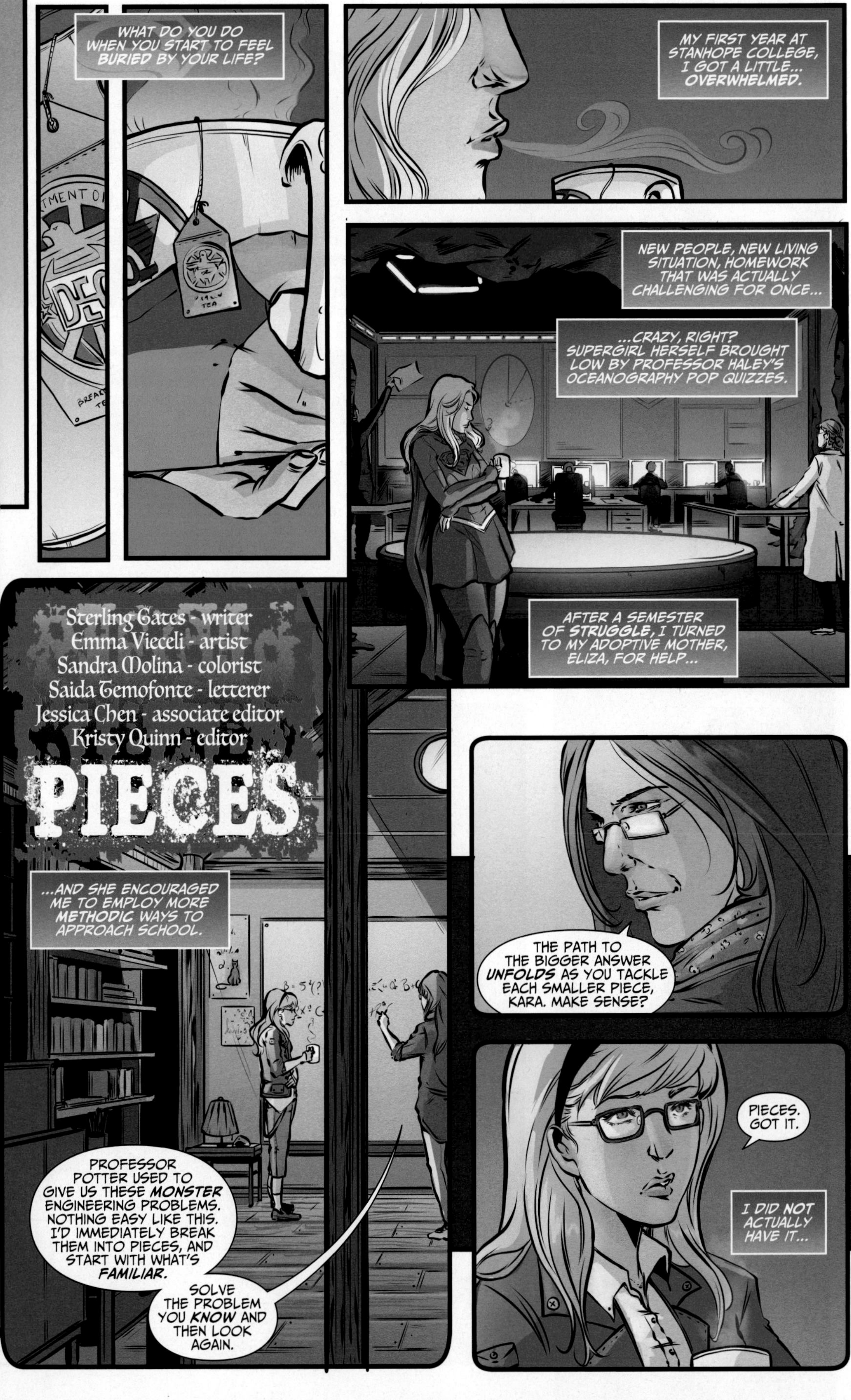
WHAT DO YOU DO WHEN YOU START TO FEEL BURIED BY YOUR LIFE?
MY FIRST YEAR AT STANHOPE COLLEGE, I GOT A LITTLE... OVERWHELMED.
NEW PEOPLE, NEW LIVING SITUATION, HOMEWORK THAT WAS ACTUALLY CHALLENGING FOR ONCE...
...CRAZY, RIGHT? SUPERGIRL HERSELF BROUGHT LOW BY PROFESSOR HALEY'S OCEANOGRAPHY POP QUIZZES.
AFTER A SEMESTER OF STRUGGLE, I TURNED TO MY ADOPTIVE MOTHER, ELIZA, FOR HELP...
Sterling Gates - writer
Emma Vieceli - artist
Sandra Molina - colorist
Saida Temofonte - letterer
Jessica Chen - associate editor
Kristy Quinn - editor
PIECES
...AND SHE ENCOURAGED ME TO EMPLOY MORE METHODIC WAYS TO APPROACH SCHOOL.
PROFESSOR POTTER USED TO GIVE US THESE MONSTER ENGINEERING PROBLEMS. NOTHING EASY LIKE THIS. I'D IMMEDIATELY BREAK THEM INTO PIECES, AND START WITH WHAT'S FAMILIAR.
SOLVE THE PROBLEM YOU KNOW AND THEN LOOK AGAIN.
THE PATH TO THE BIGGER ANSWER UNFOLDS AS YOU TACKLE EACH SMALLER PIECE, KARA. MAKE SENSE?
PIECES. GOT IT.
I DID NOT ACTUALLY HAVE IT...

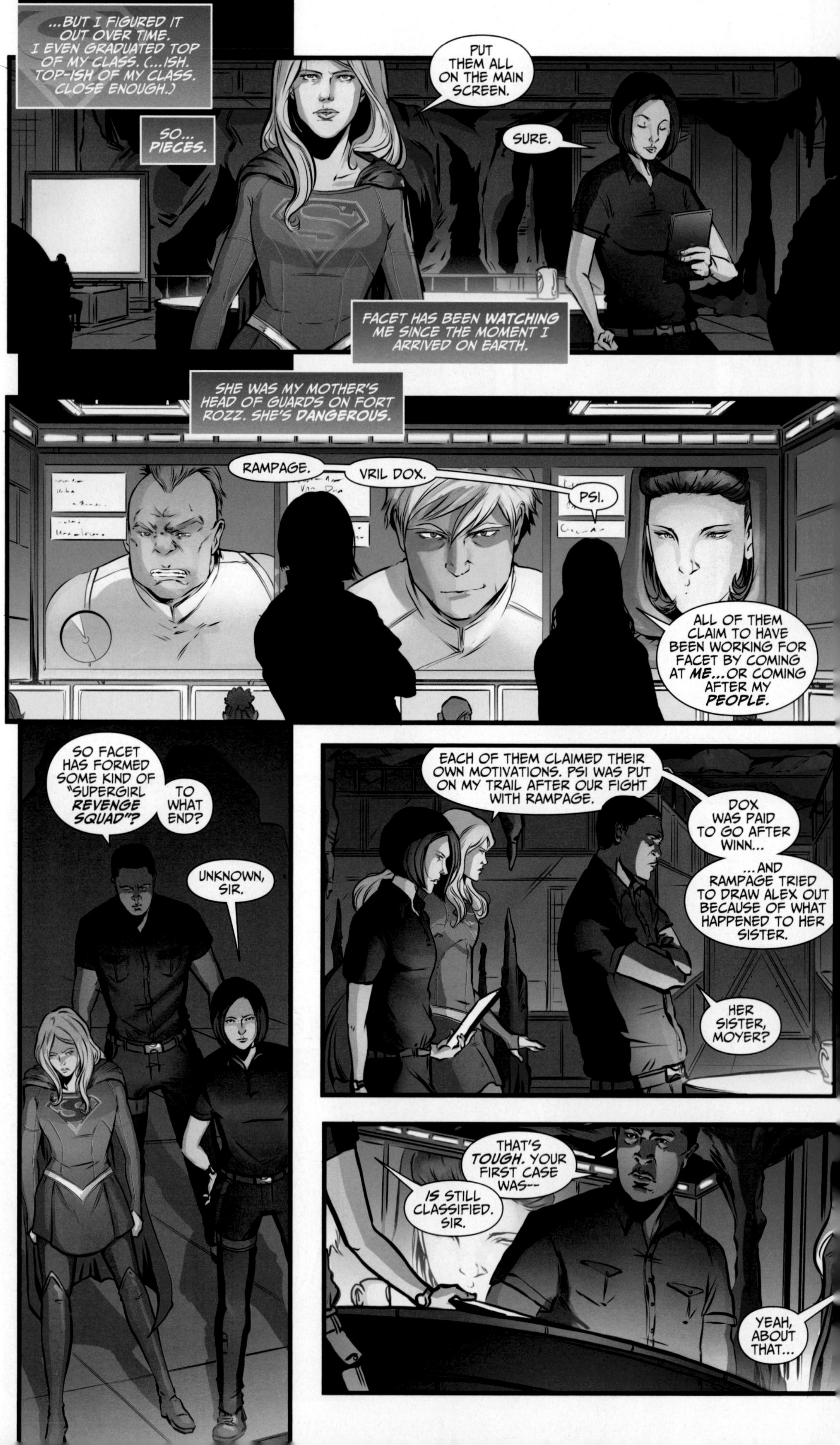
...BUT I FIGURED IT OUT OVER TIME. I EVEN GRADUATED TOP OF MY CLASS. (...ISH. TOP-ISH OF MY CLASS. CLOSE ENOUGH.)
PUT THEM ALL ON THE MAIN SCREEN.
SO... PIECES.
SURE.
FACET HAS BEEN WATCHING ME SINCE THE MOMENT I ARRIVED ON EARTH.
SHE WAS MY MOTHER'S HEAD OF GUARDS ON FORT ROZZ. SHE'S DANGEROUS.
RAMPAGE.
VRIL DOX.
PSI.
ALL OF THEM CLAIM TO HAVE BEEN WORKING FOR FACET BY COMING AT ME...OR COMING AFTER MY PEOPLE.
SO FACET HAS FORMED SOME KIND OF "SUPERGIRL REVENGE SQUAD"?
TO WHAT END?
UNKNOWN, SIR.
EACH OF THEM CLAIMED THEIR OWN MOTIVATIONS. PSI WAS PUT ON MY TRAIL AFTER OUR FIGHT WITH RAMPAGE.
DOX WAS PAID TO GO AFTER WINN...
...AND RAMPAGE TRIED TO DRAW ALEX OUT BECAUSE OF WHAT HAPPENED TO HER SISTER.
HER SISTER, MOYER?
THAT'S TOUGH. YOUR FIRST CASE WAS--
IS STILL CLASSIFIED. SIR.
YEAH, ABOUT THAT...

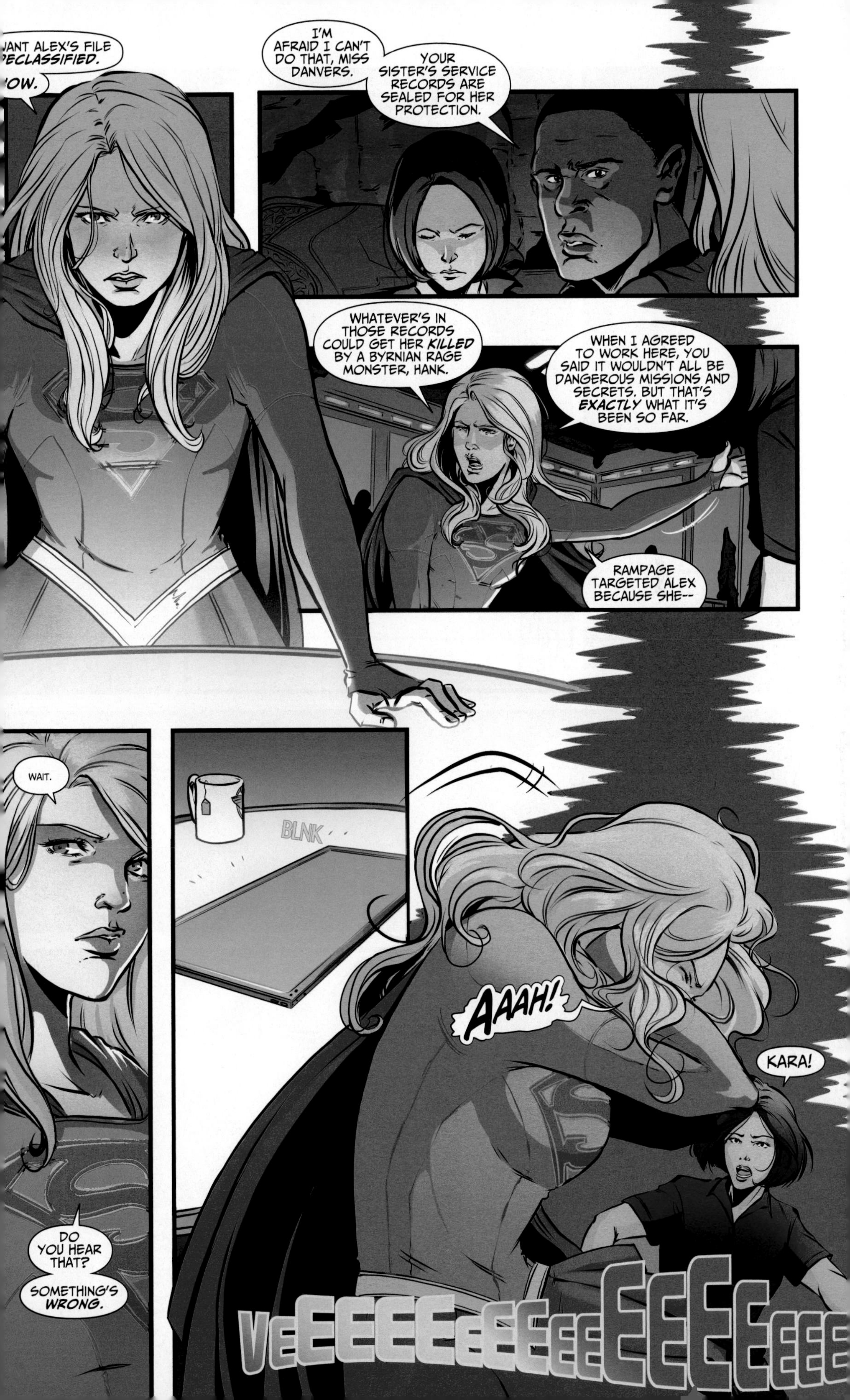

WANT ALEX'S FILE DECLASSIFIED.
NOW.
I'M AFRAID I CAN'T DO THAT, MISS DANVERS.
YOUR SISTER'S SERVICE RECORDS ARE SEALED FOR HER PROTECTION.
WHATEVER'S IN THOSE RECORDS COULD GET HER KILLED BY A BYRNIAN RAGE MONSTER, HANK.
WHEN I AGREED TO WORK HERE, YOU SAID IT WOULDN'T ALL BE DANGEROUS MISSIONS AND SECRETS. BUT THAT'S EXACTLY WHAT IT'S BEEN SO FAR.
RAMPAGE TARGETED ALEX BECAUSE SHE--
WAIT.
DO YOU HEAR THAT?
SOMETHING'S WRONG.
BLNK
AAAH!
KARA!
VEEEEEeEEeeeEEEEeee

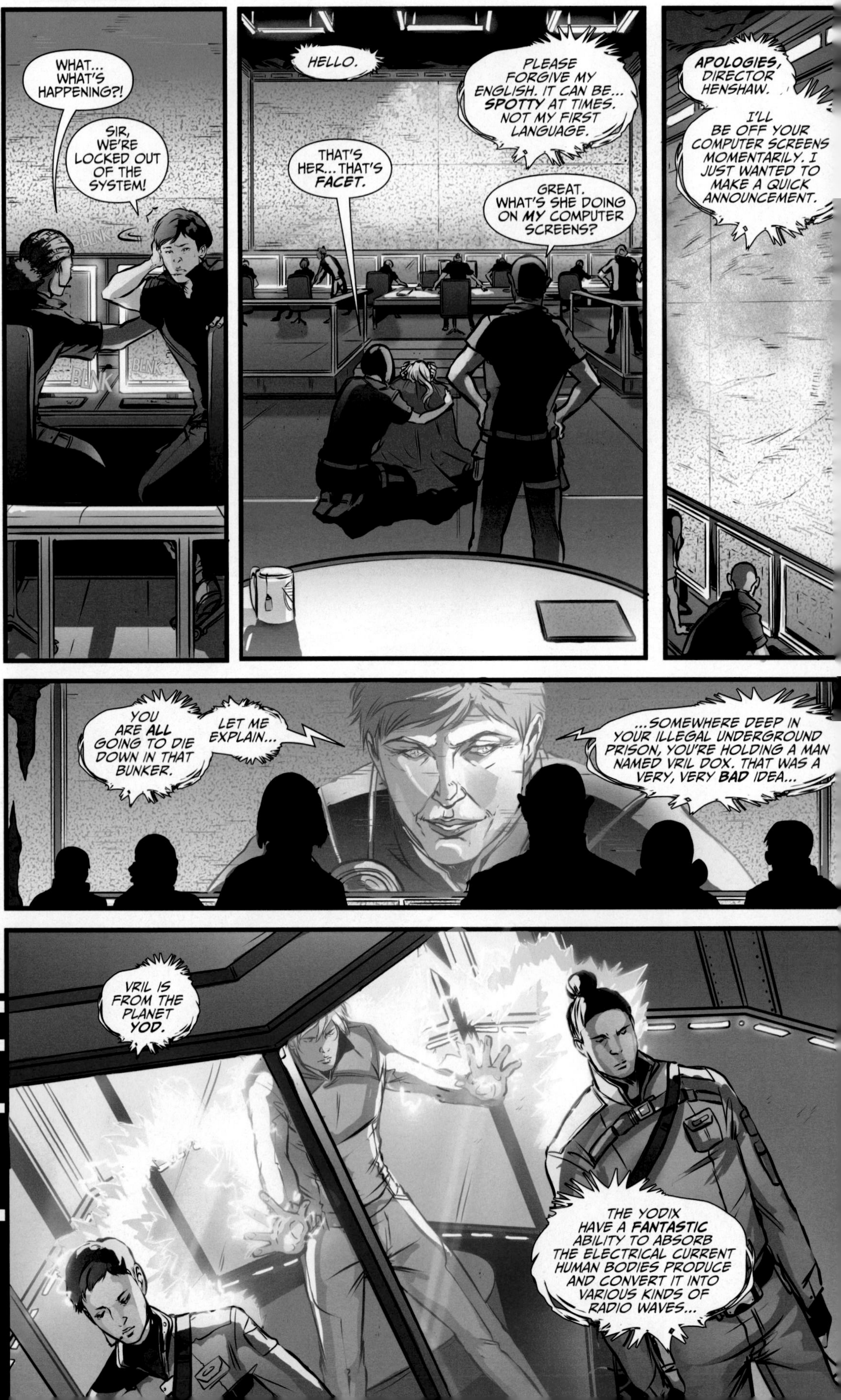
WHAT... WHAT'S HAPPENING?!
SIR, WE'RE LOCKED OUT OF THE SYSTEM!
BLNK
BLNK
BLNK
HELLO.
PLEASE FORGIVE MY ENGLISH. IT CAN BE... SPOTTY AT TIMES. NOT MY FIRST LANGUAGE.
THAT'S HER...THAT'S FACET.
GREAT. WHAT'S SHE DOING ON MY COMPUTER SCREENS?
APOLOGIES, DIRECTOR HENSHAW.
I'LL BE OFF YOUR COMPUTER SCREENS MOMENTARILY. I JUST WANTED TO MAKE A QUICK ANNOUNCEMENT.
YOU ARE ALL GOING TO DIE DOWN IN THAT BUNKER.
LET ME EXPLAIN...
...SOMEWHERE DEEP IN YOUR ILLEGAL UNDERGROUND PRISON, YOU'RE HOLDING A MAN NAMED VRIL DOX. THAT WAS A VERY, VERY BAD IDEA...
VRIL IS FROM THE PLANET YOD.
THE YODIX HAVE A FANTASTIC ABILITY TO ABSORB THE ELECTRICAL CURRENT HUMAN BODIES PRODUCE AND CONVERT IT INTO VARIOUS KINDS OF RADIO WAVES...

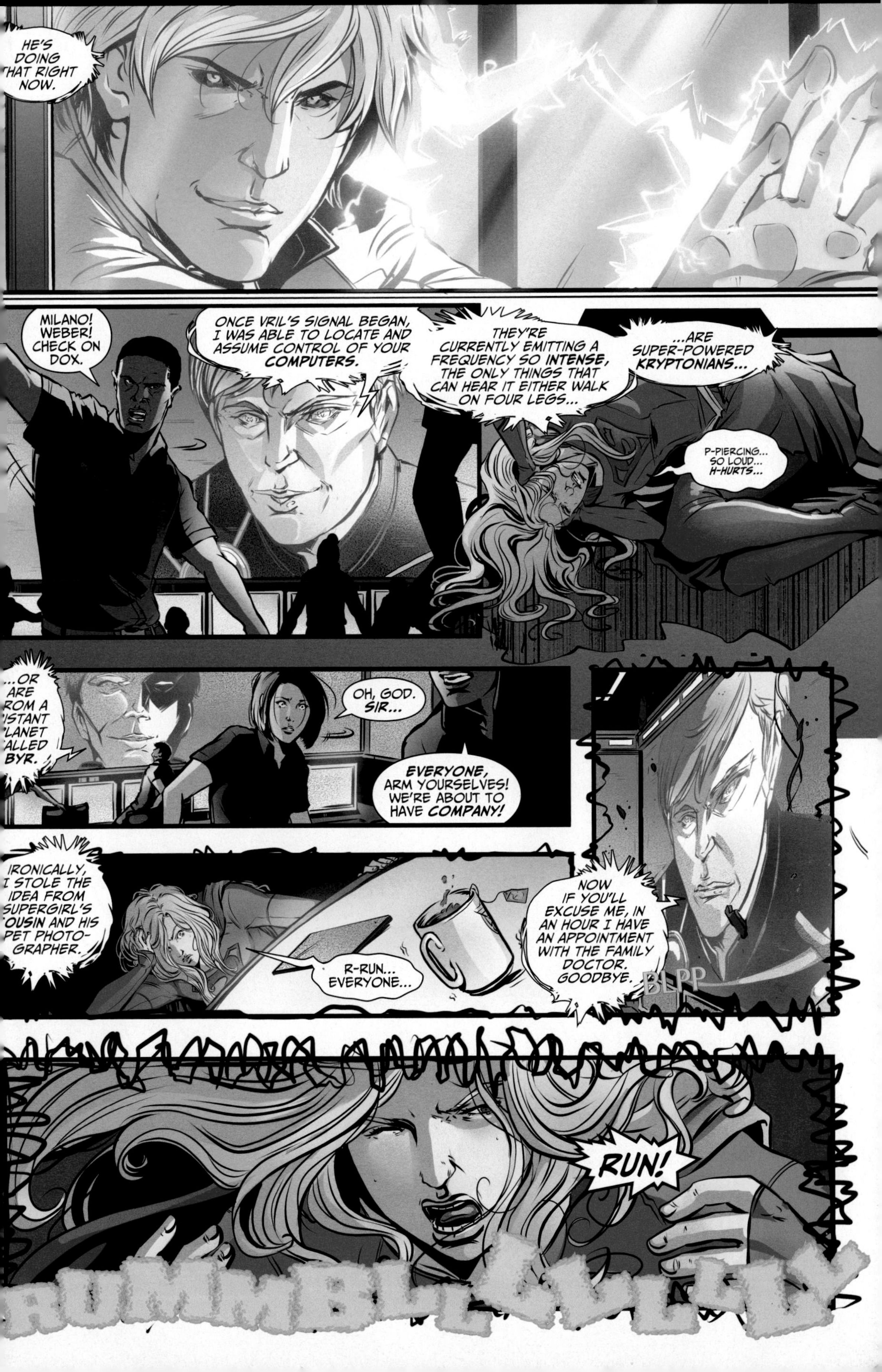
HE'S DOING THAT RIGHT NOW.
MILANO! WEBER! CHECK ON DOX.
ONCE VRIL'S SIGNAL BEGAN, I WAS ABLE TO LOCATE AND ASSUME CONTROL OF YOUR COMPUTERS.
THEY'RE CURRENTLY EMITTING A FREQUENCY SO INTENSE, THE ONLY THINGS THAT CAN HEAR IT EITHER WALK ON FOUR LEGS...
...ARE SUPER-POWERED KRYPTONIANS...
P-PIERCING... SO LOUD... H-HURTS...
OH, GOD. SIR...
EVERYONE, ARM YOURSELVES! WE'RE ABOUT TO HAVE COMPANY!
IRONICALLY, I STOLE THE IDEA FROM SUPERGIRL'S COUSIN AND HIS PET PHOTO-GRAPHER.
R-RUN... EVERYONE...
NOW IF YOU'LL EXCUSE ME, IN AN HOUR I HAVE AN APPOINTMENT WITH THE FAMILY DOCTOR. GOODBYE.
BLPP
RUN!
RUMMBLLLLLLY

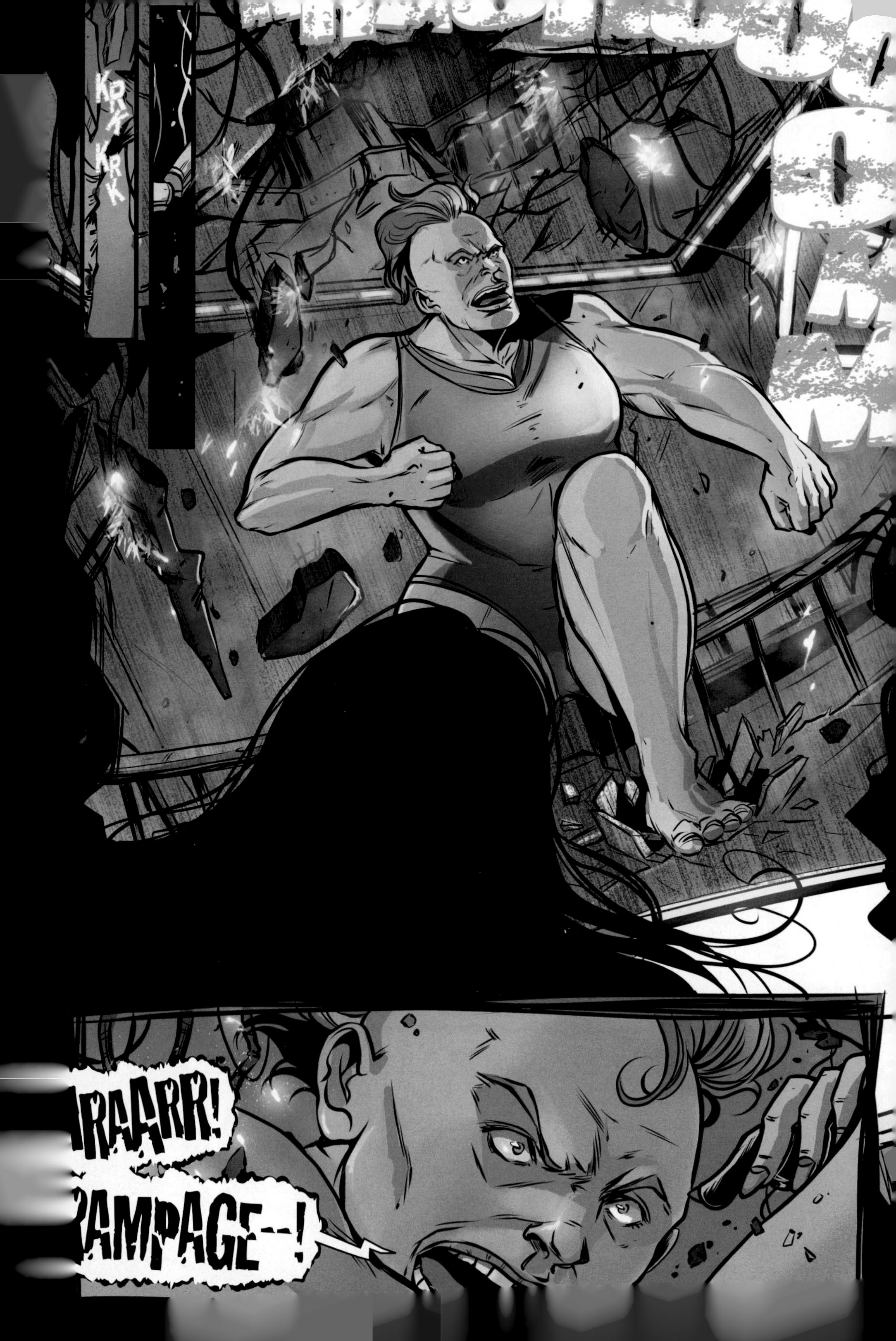
KRK KRK
RAARR!
RAMPAGE--!

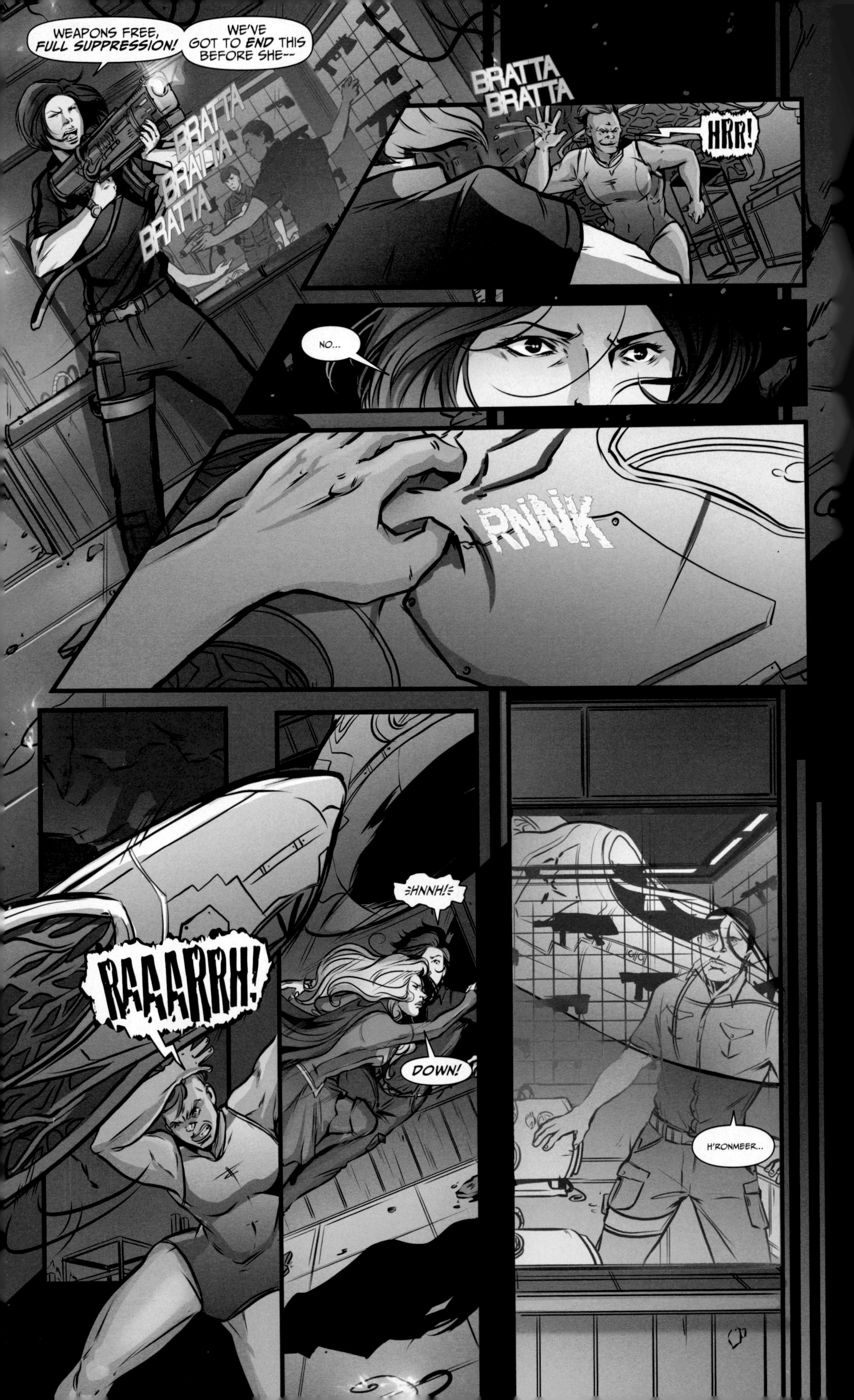
WEAPONS FREE, FULL SUPPRESSION!
WE'VE GOT TO END THIS BEFORE SHE--
BRATTA BRATTA BRATTA BRATTA
BRATTA BRATTA
HRR!
NO...
RNNK
RAAARRH!
HNNH!
DOWN!
H'RONMEER...

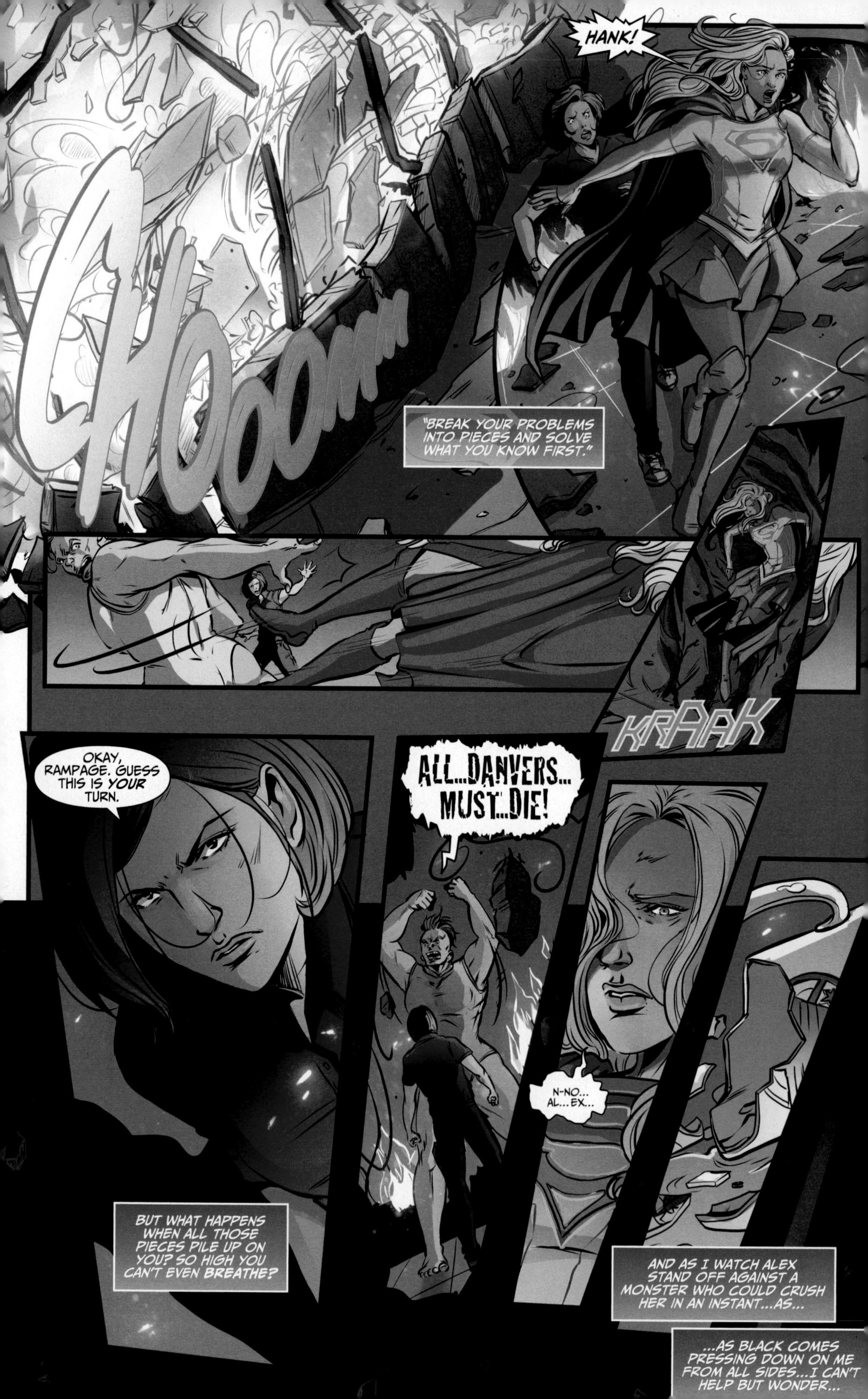
HANK!
CHOOOM
"BREAK YOUR PROBLEMS INTO PIECES AND SOLVE WHAT YOU KNOW FIRST."
KRAAK
OKAY, RAMPAGE. GUESS THIS IS YOUR TURN.
ALL...DANVERS... MUST...DIE!
N-NO... AL...EX...
BUT WHAT HAPPENS WHEN ALL THOSE PIECES PILE UP ON YOU? SO HIGH YOU CAN'T EVEN BREATHE?
AND AS I WATCH ALEX STAND OFF AGAINST A MONSTER WHO COULD CRUSH HER IN AN INSTANT...AS...
...AS BLACK COMES PRESSING DOWN ON ME FROM ALL SIDES...I CAN'T HELP BUT WONDER...

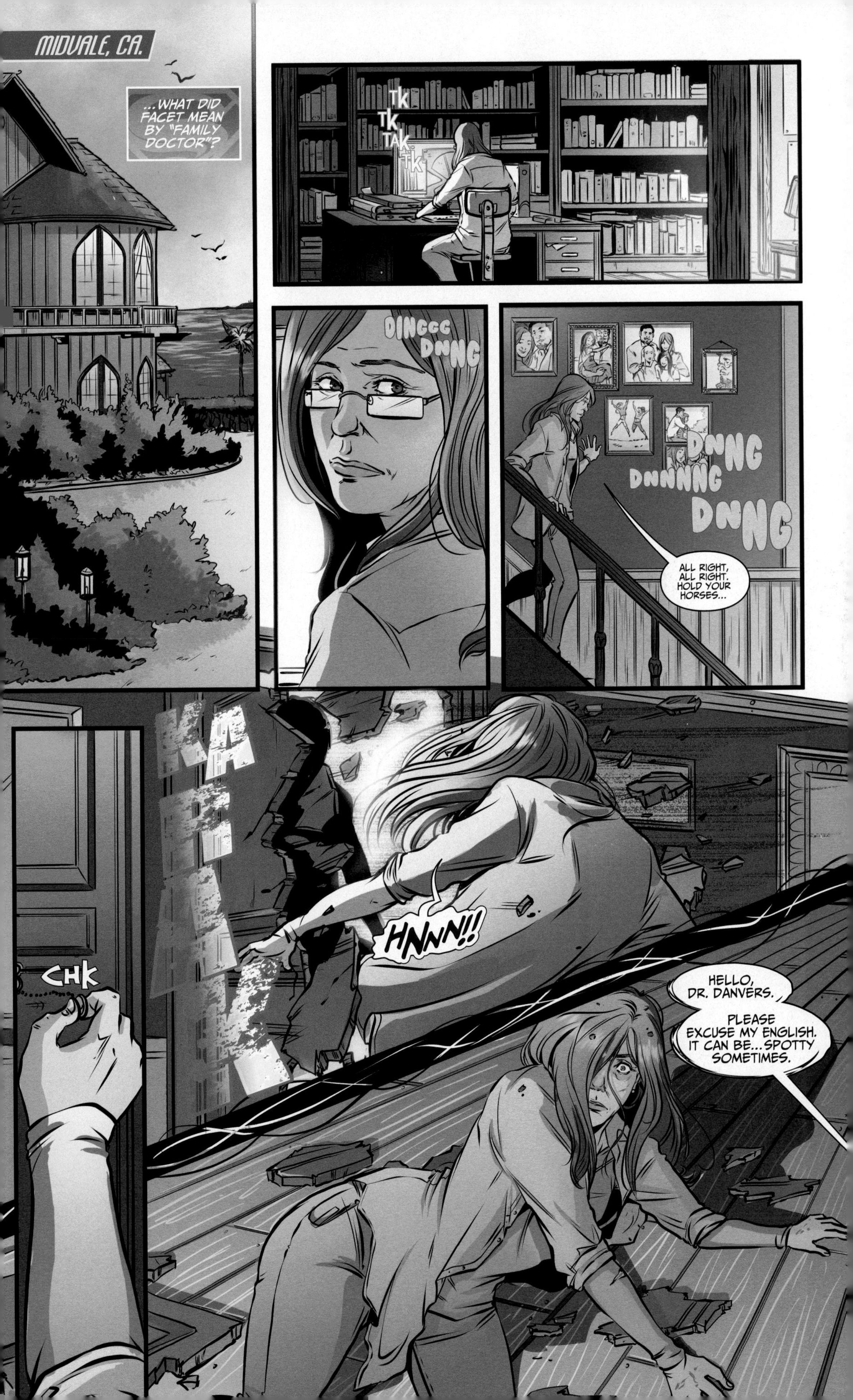
MIDVALE, CA.
...WHAT DID FACET MEAN BY "FAMILY DOCTOR"?
TK TK TAK TK
DINGGG DNNG
DNNG DNNNNG DNNG
ALL RIGHT, ALL RIGHT. HOLD YOUR HORSES...
CHK
HNNN!!
HELLO, DR. DANVERS.
PLEASE EXCUSE MY ENGLISH. IT CAN BE...SPOTTY SOMETIMES.

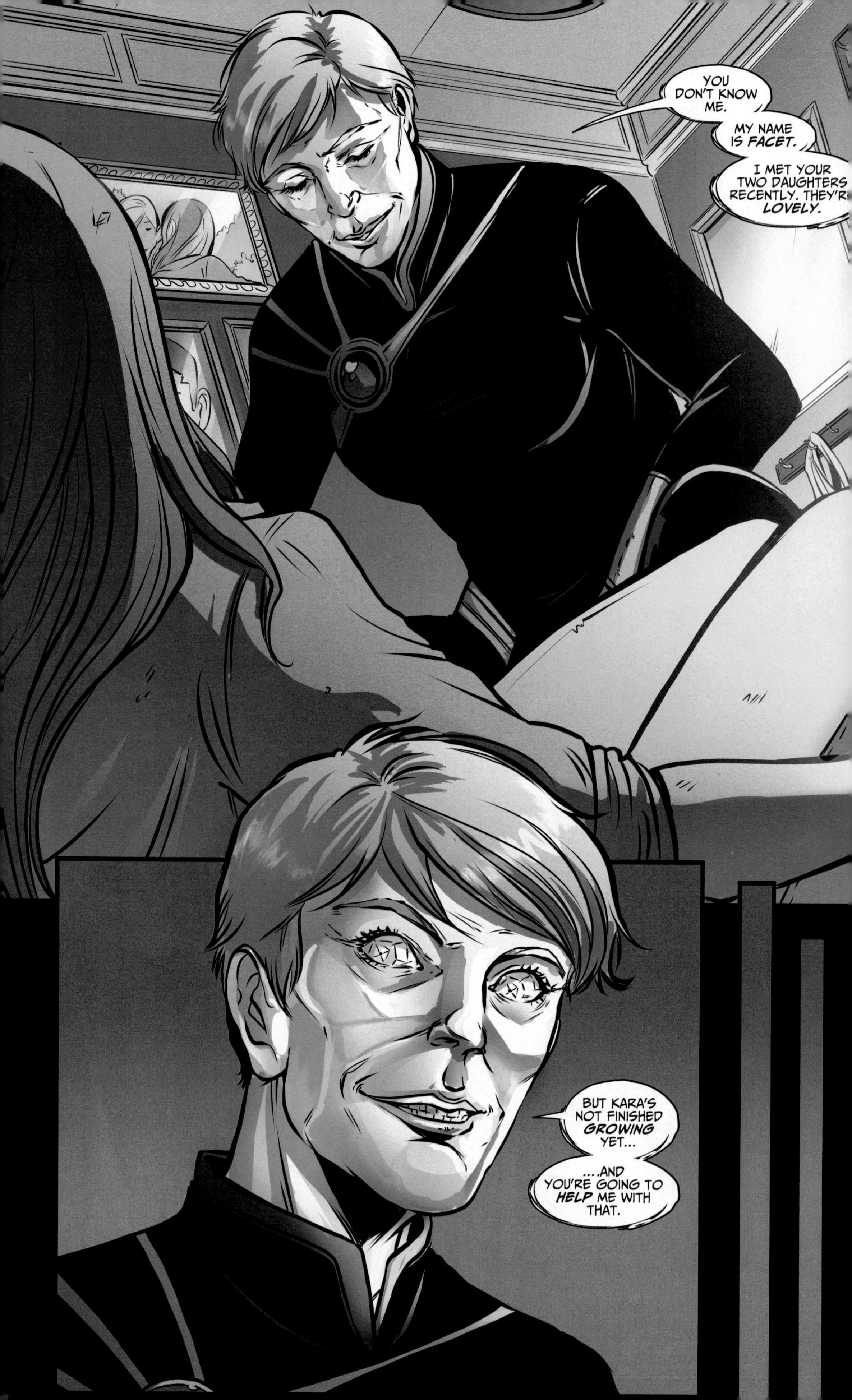
YOU DON'T KNOW ME.
MY NAME IS FACET.
I MET YOUR TWO DAUGHTERS RECENTLY. THEY'RE LOVELY.
BUT KARA'S NOT FINISHED GROWING YET...
...AND YOU'RE GOING TO HELP ME WITH THAT.

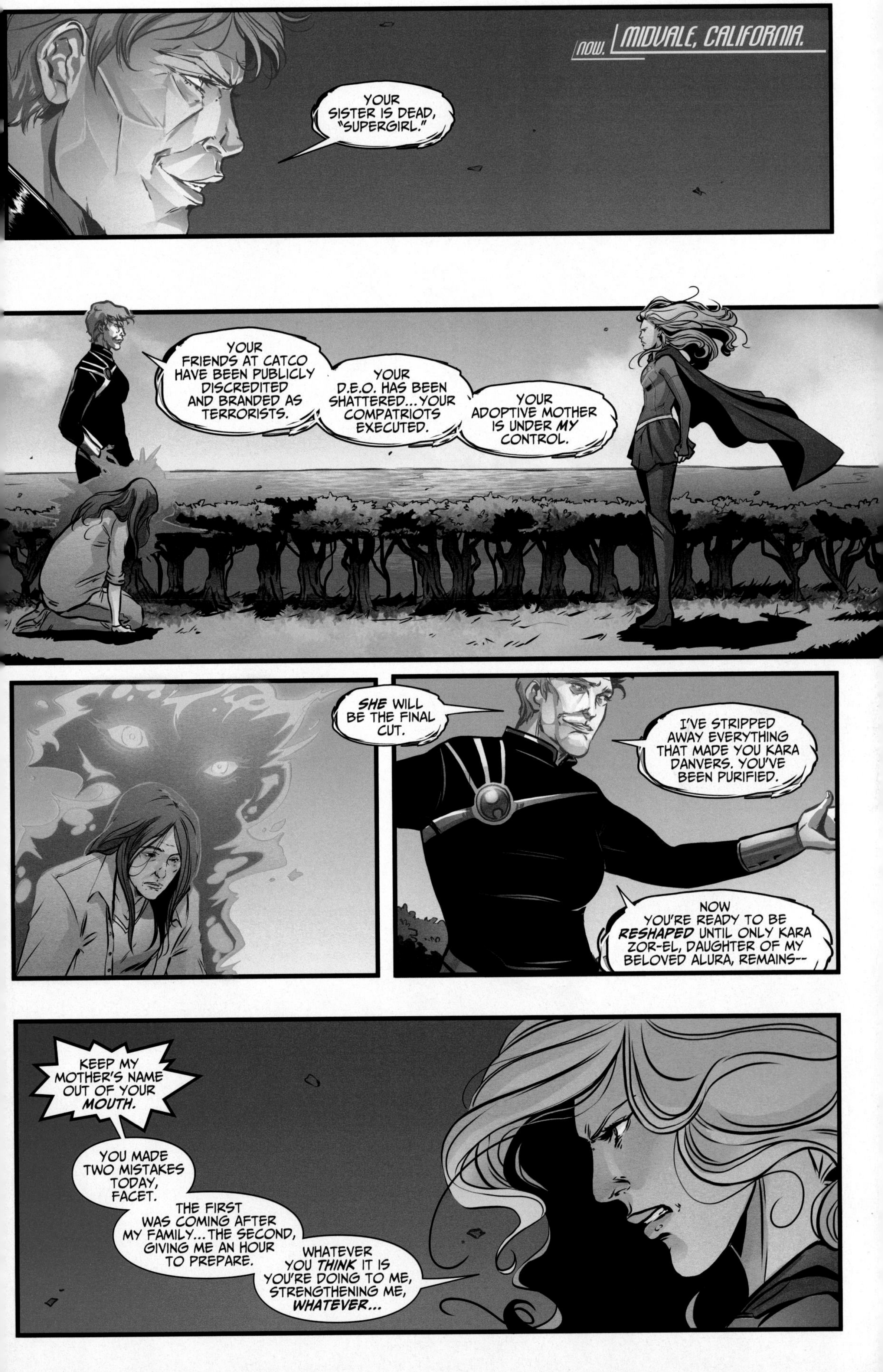
NOW. MIDVALE, CALIFORNIA.
YOUR SISTER IS DEAD, "SUPERGIRL."
YOUR FRIENDS AT CATCO HAVE BEEN PUBLICLY DISCREDITED AND BRANDED AS TERRORISTS.
YOUR D.E.O. HAS BEEN SHATTERED...YOUR COMPATRIOTS EXECUTED.
YOUR ADOPTIVE MOTHER IS UNDER *MY* CONTROL.
SHE WILL BE THE FINAL CUT.
I'VE STRIPPED AWAY EVERYTHING THAT MADE YOU KARA DANVERS. YOU'VE BEEN PURIFIED.
NOW YOU'RE READY TO BE *RESHAPED* UNTIL ONLY KARA ZOR-EL, DAUGHTER OF MY BELOVED ALURA, REMAINS--
KEEP MY MOTHER'S NAME OUT OF YOUR *MOUTH.*
YOU MADE TWO MISTAKES TODAY, FACET.
THE FIRST WAS COMING AFTER MY FAMILY...THE SECOND, GIVING ME AN HOUR TO PREPARE.
WHATEVER YOU *THINK* IT IS YOU'RE DOING TO ME, STRENGTHENING ME, *WHATEVER...*

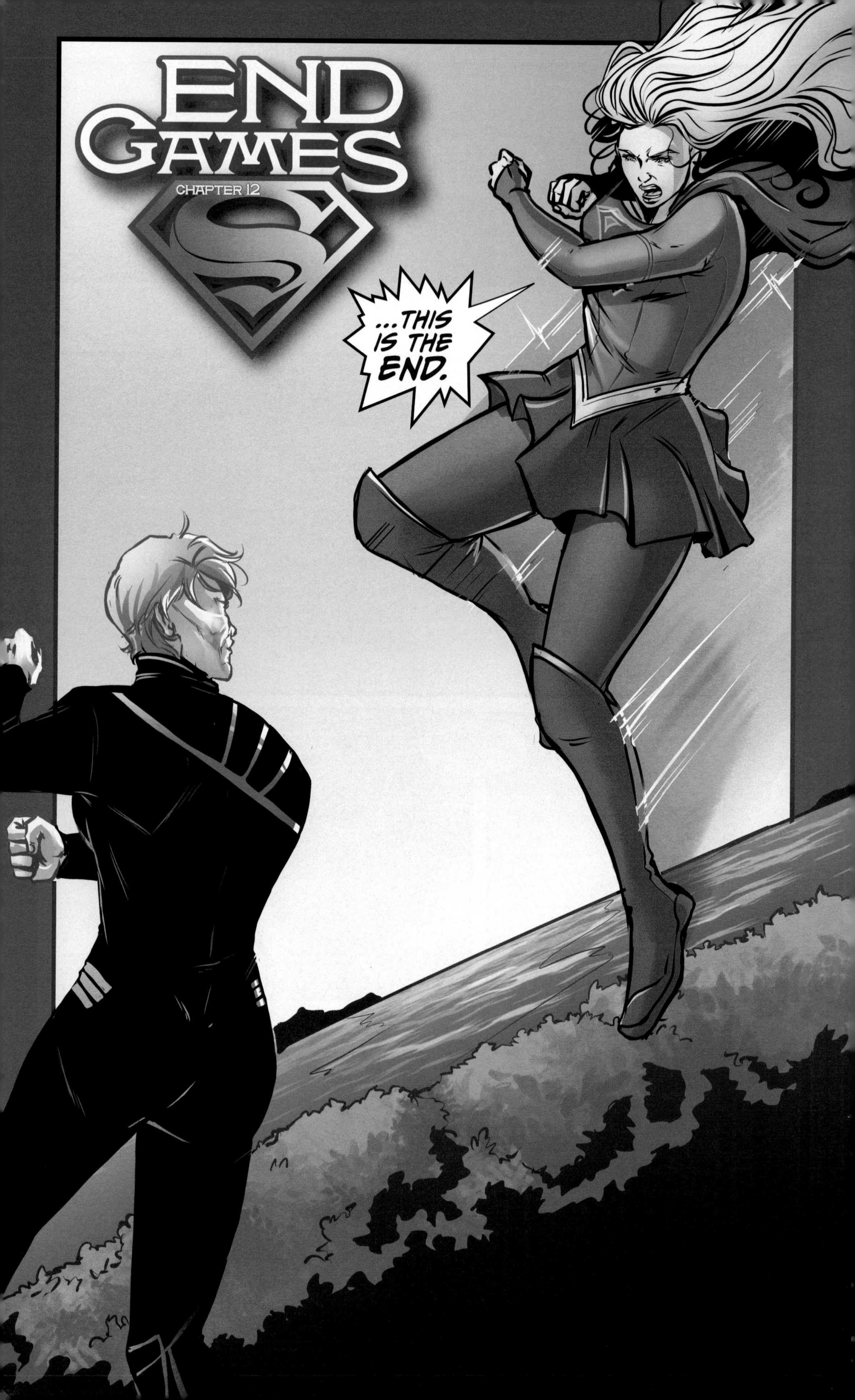
END GAMES
CHAPTER 12
...THIS IS THE END.

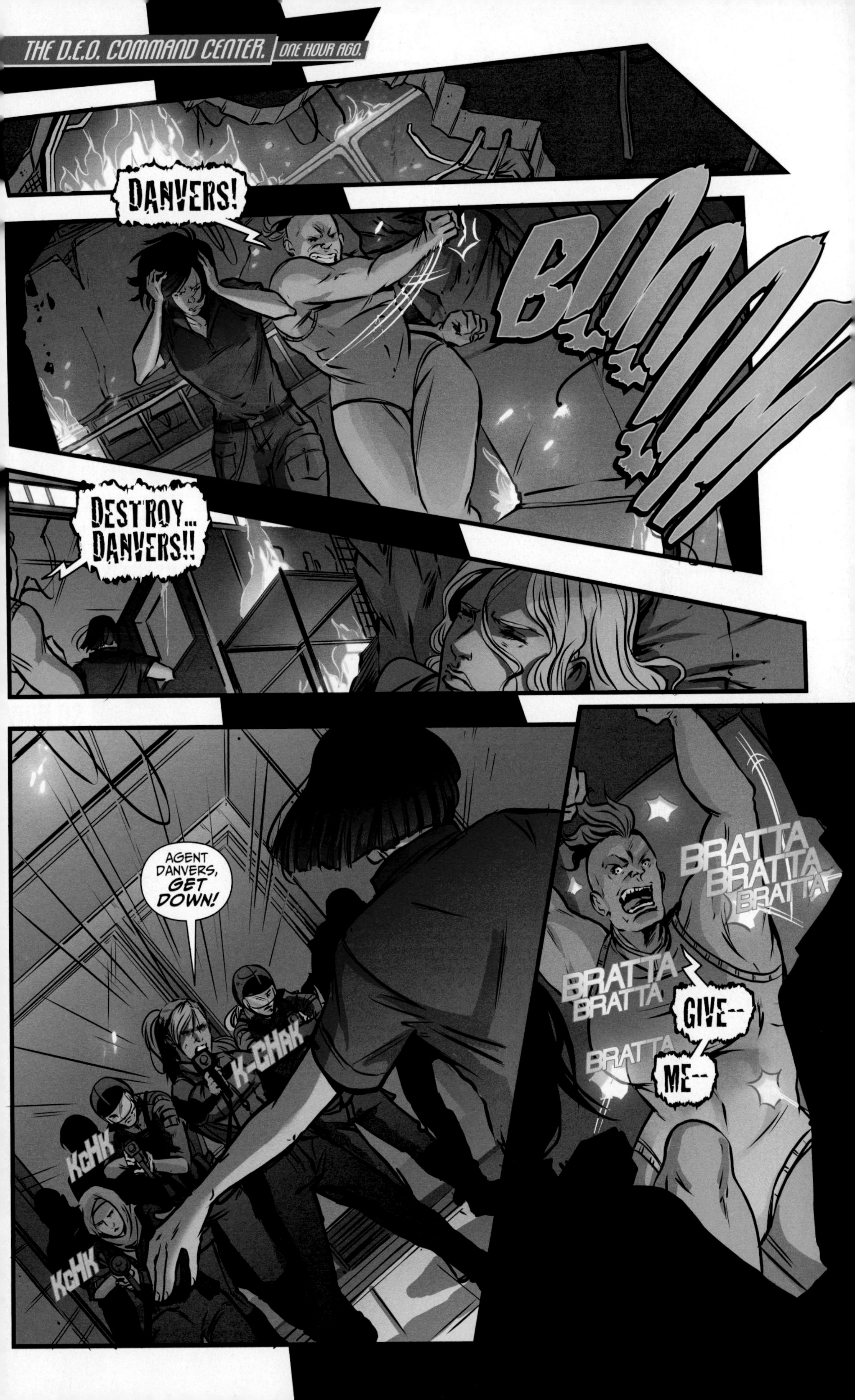
THE D.E.O. COMMAND CENTER.
ONE HOUR AGO.
DANVERS!
BOOOM
DESTROY... DANVERS!!
AGENT DANVERS, GET DOWN!
K-CHAK
KcHK
KcHK
BRATTA BRATTA BRATTA
BRATTA BRATTA
GIVE--
BRATTA
ME--

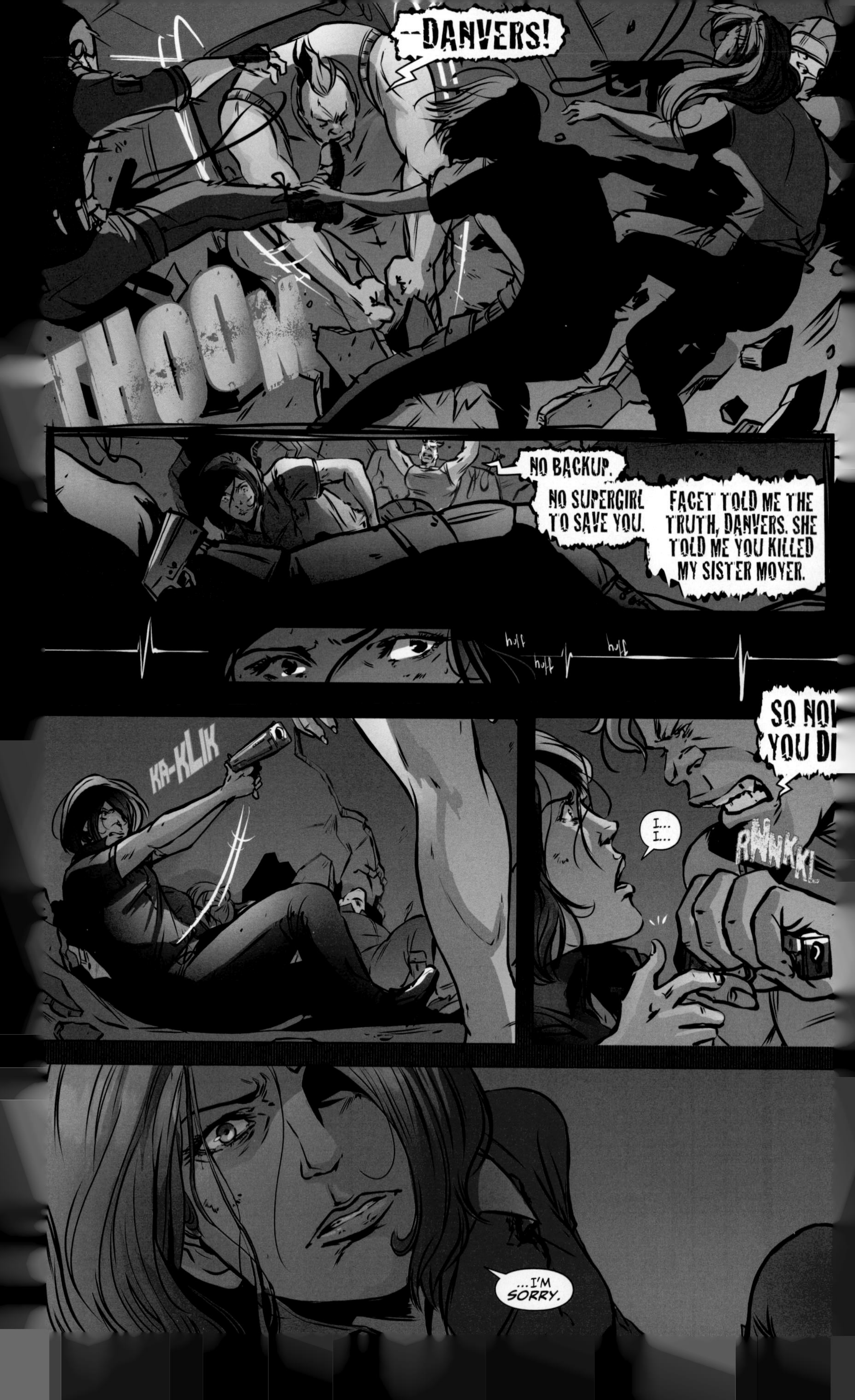

--DANVERS!
THOOM
NO BACKUP.
NO SUPERGIRL TO SAVE YOU.
FACET TOLD ME THE TRUTH, DANVERS. SHE TOLD ME YOU KILLED MY SISTER MOYER.
huff
huff
huff
KA-KLIK
SO NOW YOU DI
I... I...
RWNKK!
...I'M SORRY.

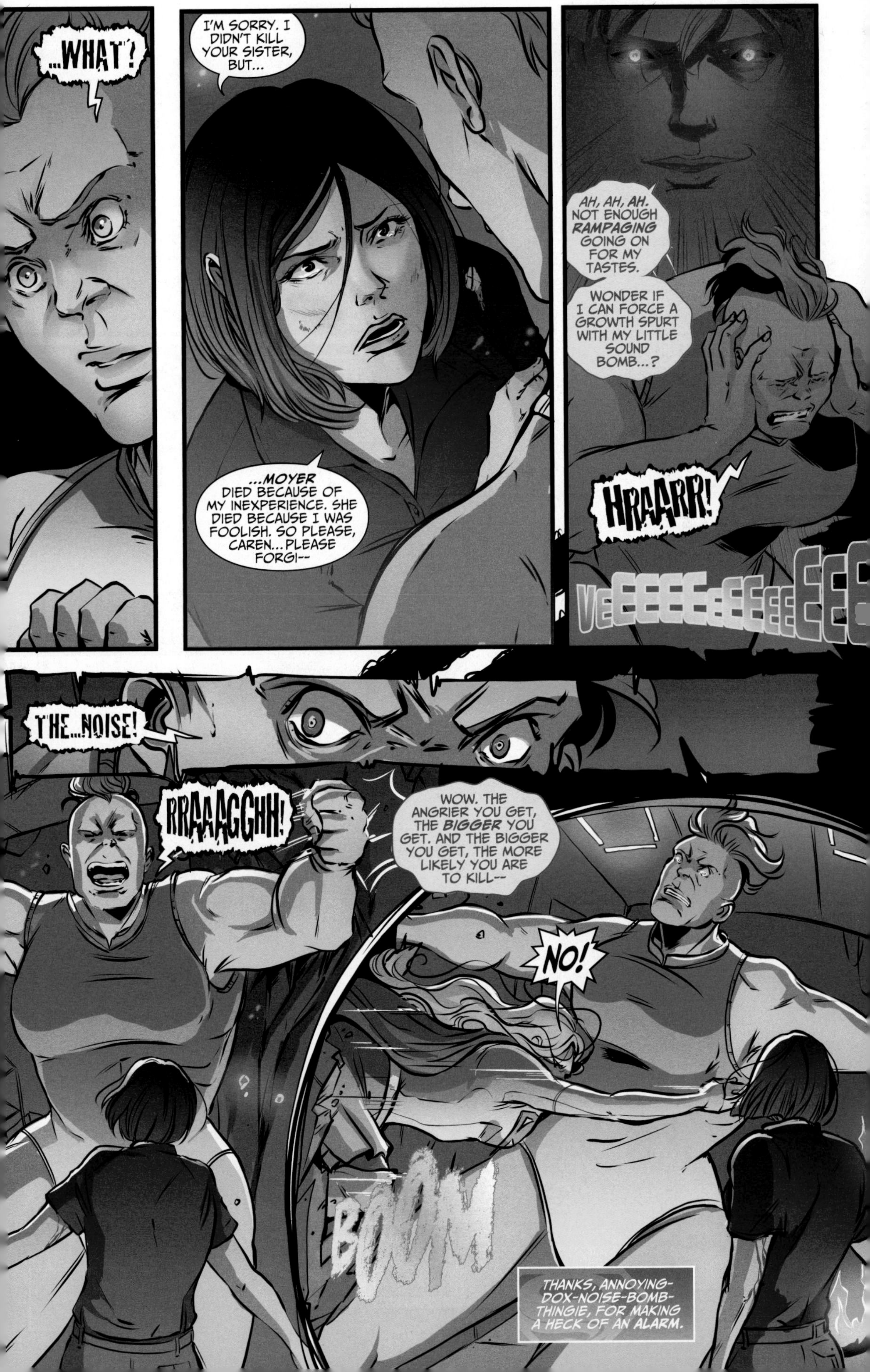

...WHAT?
I'M SORRY. I DIDN'T KILL YOUR SISTER, BUT...
...MOYER DIED BECAUSE OF MY INEXPERIENCE. SHE DIED BECAUSE I WAS FOOLISH. SO PLEASE, CAREN...PLEASE FORGI--
AH, AH, AH. NOT ENOUGH RAMPAGING GOING ON FOR MY TASTES.
WONDER IF I CAN FORCE A GROWTH SPURT WITH MY LITTLE SOUND BOMB...?
HRAARR!
VEEEEEEEEEEEEE
THE...NOISE!
RRAAAGGHH!
WOW. THE ANGRIER YOU GET, THE BIGGER YOU GET. AND THE BIGGER YOU GET, THE MORE LIKELY YOU ARE TO KILL--
NO!
BOOM
THANKS, ANNOYING-DOX-NOISE-BOMB-THINGIE, FOR MAKING A HECK OF AN ALARM.

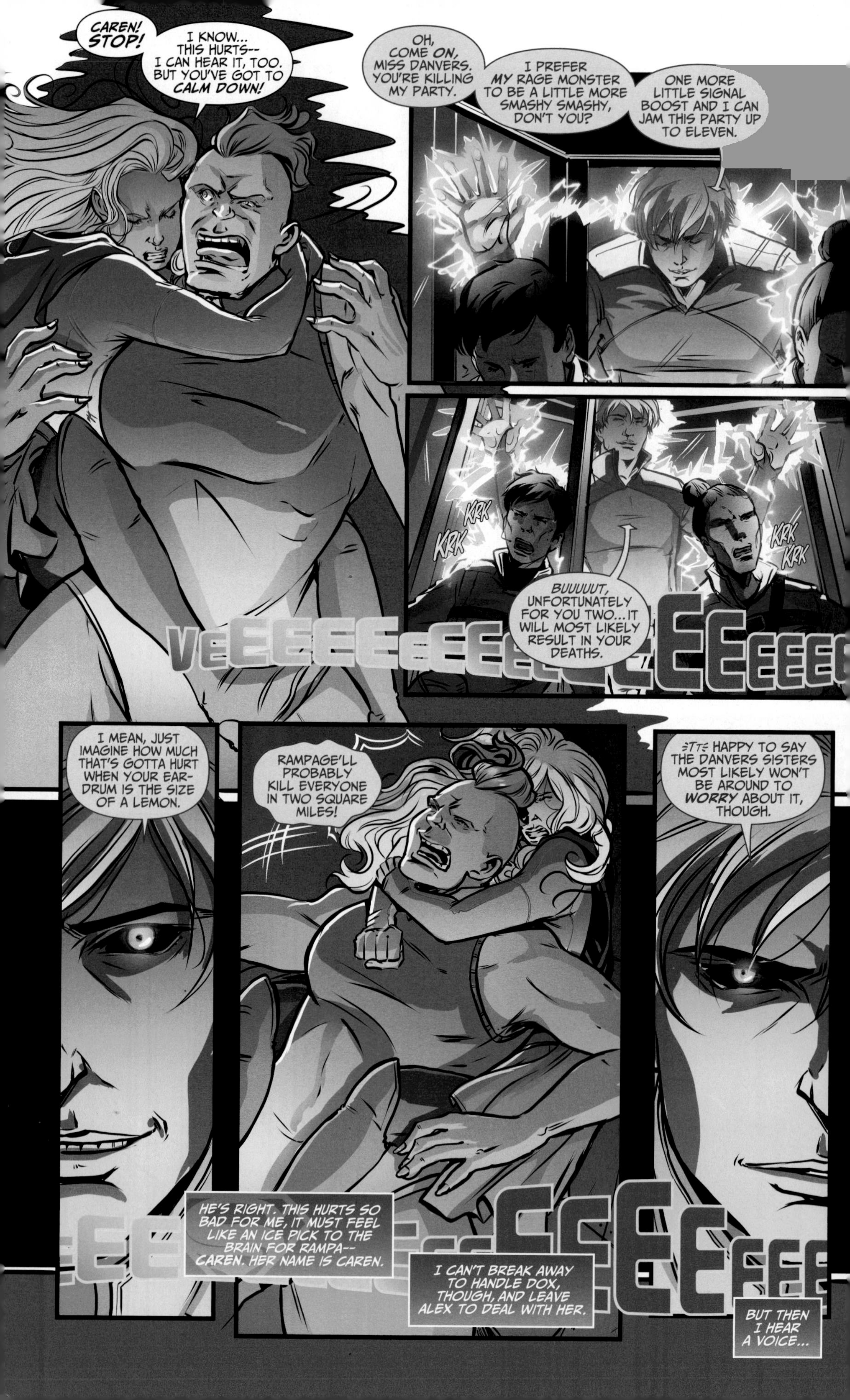
CAREN! STOP!
I KNOW... THIS HURTS-- I CAN HEAR IT, TOO. BUT YOU'VE GOT TO CALM DOWN!
OH, COME ON, MISS DANVERS. YOU'RE KILLING MY PARTY.
I PREFER MY RAGE MONSTER TO BE A LITTLE MORE SMASHY SMASHY, DON'T YOU?
ONE MORE LITTLE SIGNAL BOOST AND I CAN JAM THIS PARTY UP TO ELEVEN.
KRK KRK
KRK KRK
BUUUUT, UNFORTUNATELY FOR YOU TWO... IT WILL MOST LIKELY RESULT IN YOUR DEATHS.
I MEAN, JUST IMAGINE HOW MUCH THAT'S GOTTA HURT WHEN YOUR EAR-DRUM IS THE SIZE OF A LEMON.
RAMPAGE'LL PROBABLY KILL EVERYONE IN TWO SQUARE MILES!
HAPPY TO SAY THE DANVERS SISTERS MOST LIKELY WON'T BE AROUND TO WORRY ABOUT IT, THOUGH.
HE'S RIGHT. THIS HURTS SO BAD FOR ME, IT MUST FEEL LIKE AN ICE PICK TO THE BRAIN FOR RAMPA-- CAREN. HER NAME IS CAREN.
I CAN'T BREAK AWAY TO HANDLE DOX, THOUGH, AND LEAVE ALEX TO DEAL WITH HER.
BUT THEN I HEAR A VOICE...

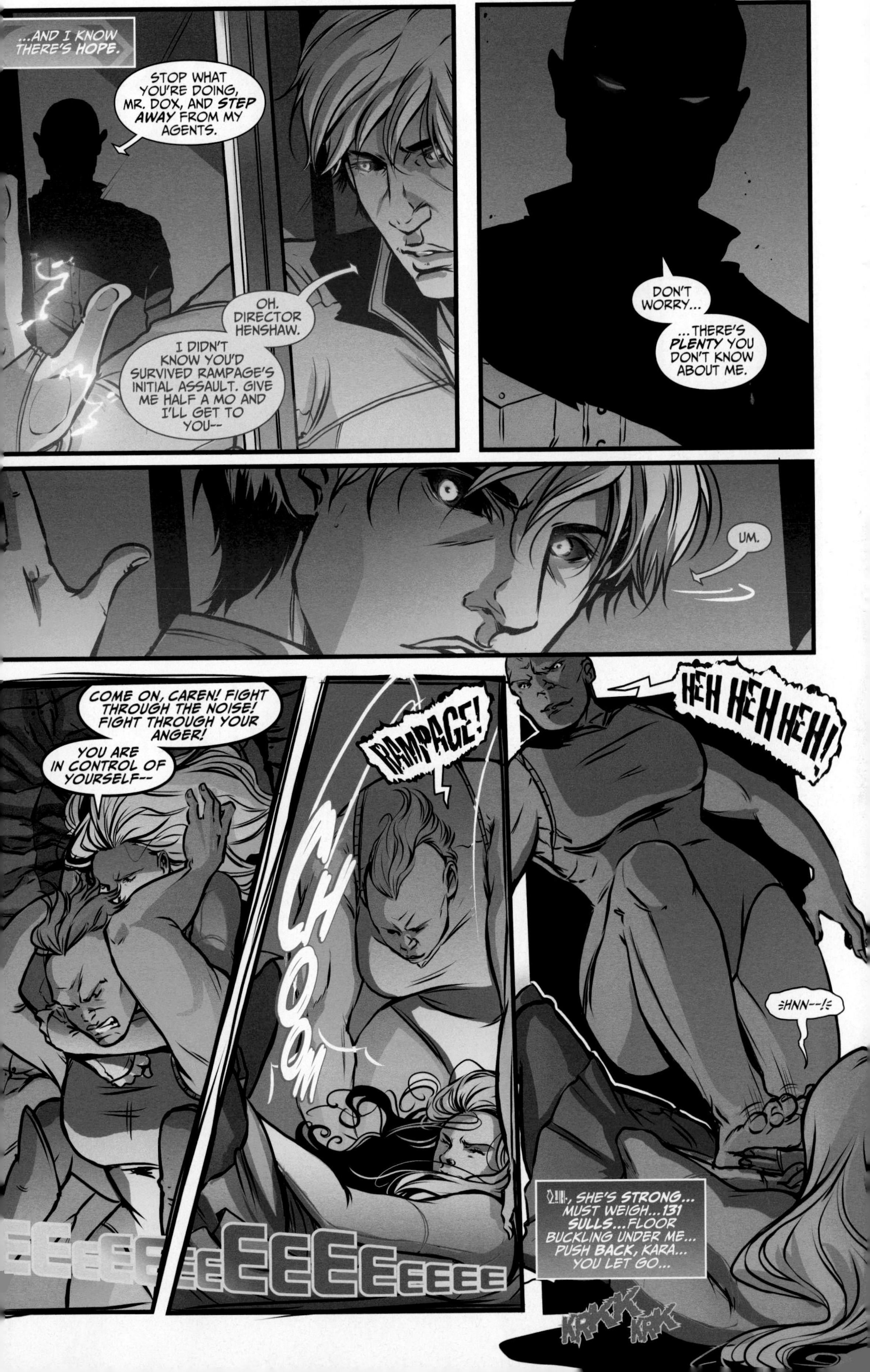

...AND I KNOW THERE'S HOPE.
STOP WHAT YOU'RE DOING, MR. DOX, AND STEP AWAY FROM MY AGENTS.
OH. DIRECTOR HENSHAW.
I DIDN'T KNOW YOU'D SURVIVED RAMPAGE'S INITIAL ASSAULT. GIVE ME HALF A MO AND I'LL GET TO YOU--
DON'T WORRY...
...THERE'S PLENTY YOU DON'T KNOW ABOUT ME.
UM.
COME ON, CAREN! FIGHT THROUGH THE NOISE! FIGHT THROUGH YOUR ANGER!
YOU ARE IN CONTROL OF YOURSELF--
EEEEEEEEEEEEEEEE
RAMPAGE!
CHOOOM
HEH HEH HEH HEH!
HNN--!
, SHE'S STRONG... MUST WEIGH...131 SULLS...FLOOR BUCKLING UNDER ME... PUSH BACK, KARA... YOU LET GO...
KRKK KRK

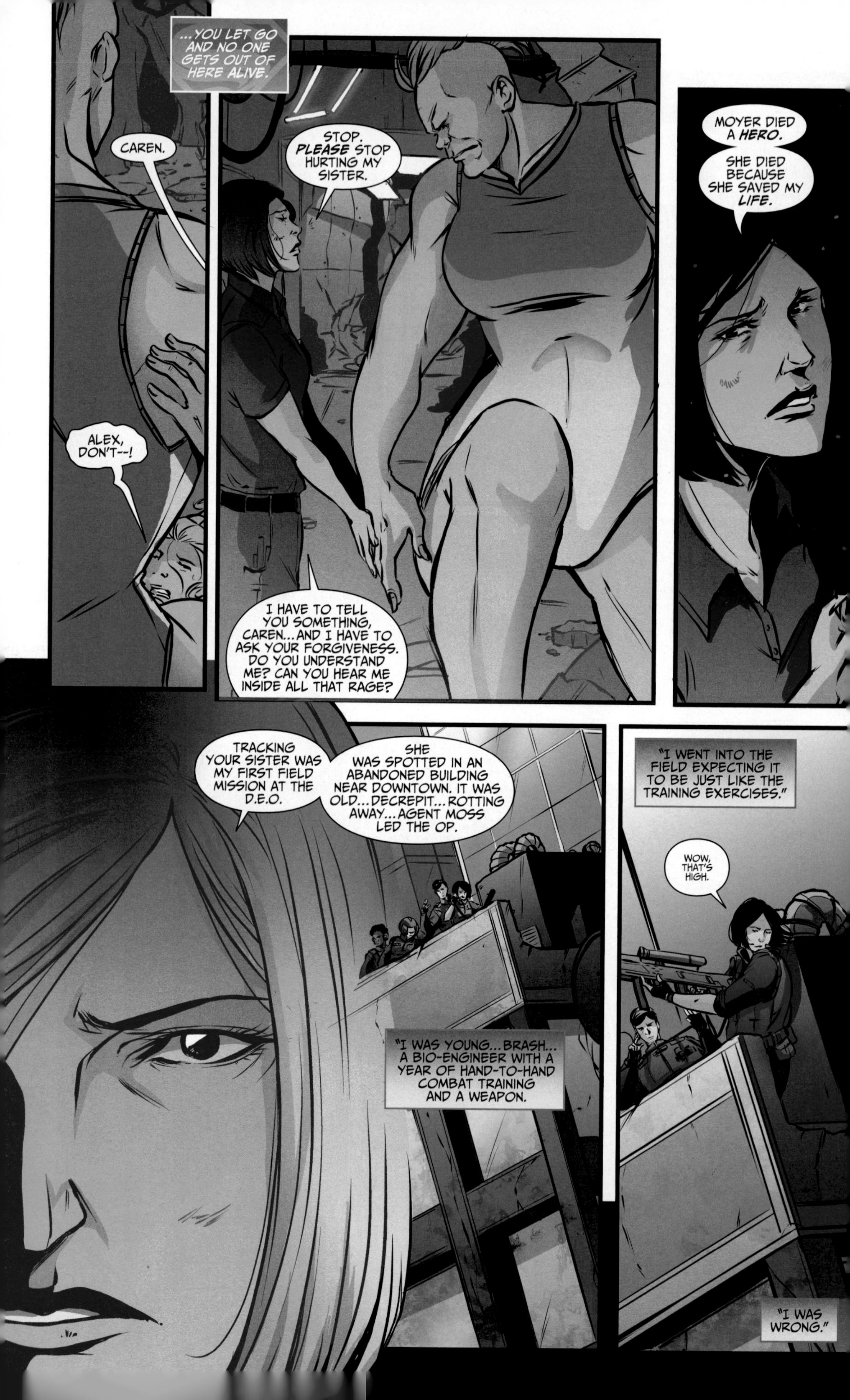
...YOU LET GO AND NO ONE GETS OUT OF HERE ALIVE.
CAREN.
ALEX, DON'T--!
STOP. PLEASE STOP HURTING MY SISTER.
I HAVE TO TELL YOU SOMETHING, CAREN...AND I HAVE TO ASK YOUR FORGIVENESS. DO YOU UNDERSTAND ME? CAN YOU HEAR ME INSIDE ALL THAT RAGE?
MOYER DIED A HERO.
SHE DIED BECAUSE SHE SAVED MY LIFE.
TRACKING YOUR SISTER WAS MY FIRST FIELD MISSION AT THE D.E.O.
SHE WAS SPOTTED IN AN ABANDONED BUILDING NEAR DOWNTOWN. IT WAS OLD...DECREPIT...ROTTING AWAY...AGENT MOSS LED THE OP.
"I WAS YOUNG...BRASH... A BIO-ENGINEER WITH A YEAR OF HAND-TO-HAND COMBAT TRAINING AND A WEAPON.
"I WENT INTO THE FIELD EXPECTING IT TO BE JUST LIKE THE TRAINING EXERCISES."
WOW, THAT'S HIGH.
"I WAS WRONG."

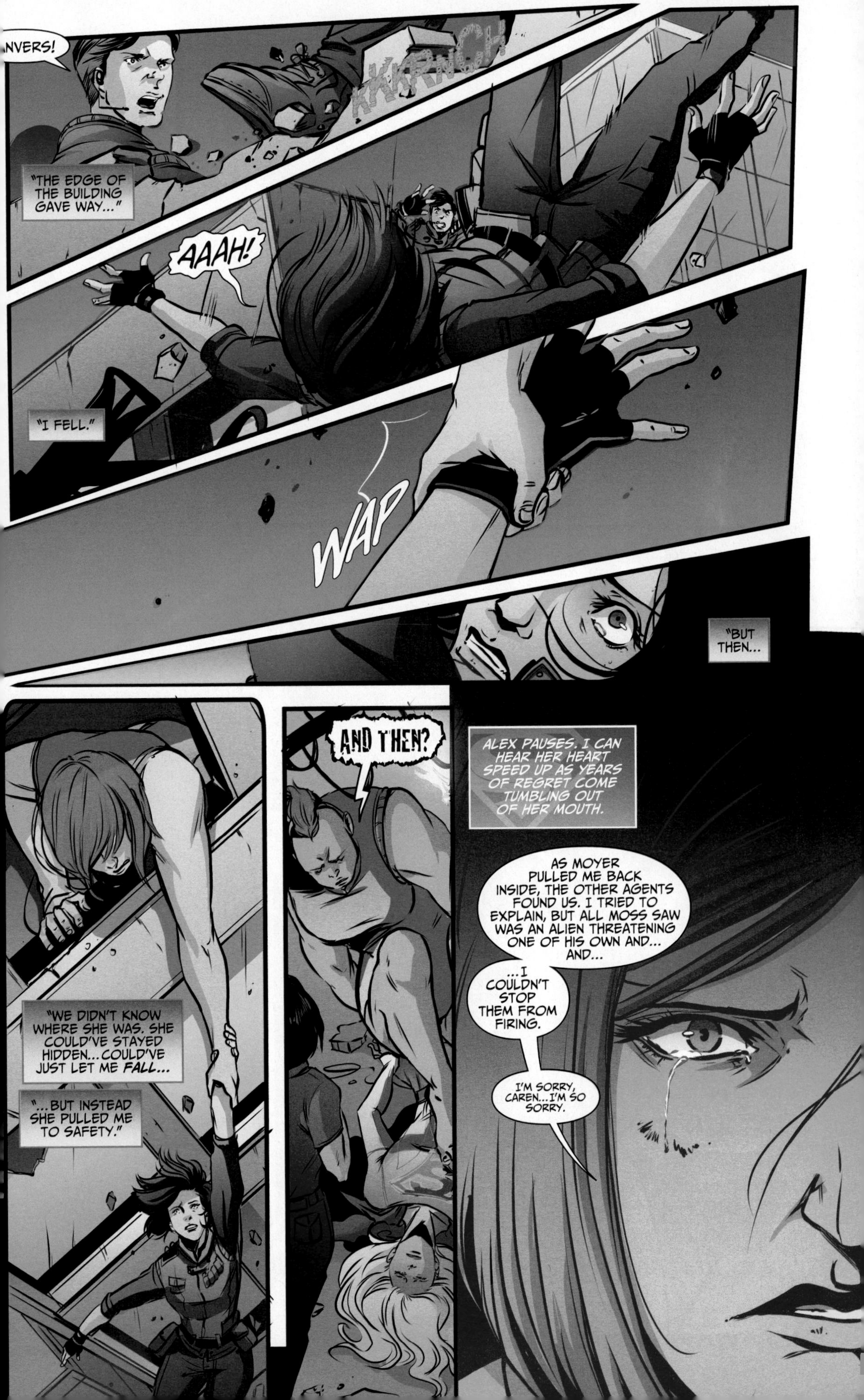

NVERS!
KKKRNCH!
"THE EDGE OF THE BUILDING GAVE WAY..."
AAAH!
"I FELL."
WAP
"BUT THEN...
AND THEN?
ALEX PAUSES. I CAN HEAR HER HEART SPEED UP AS YEARS OF REGRET COME TUMBLING OUT OF HER MOUTH.
"WE DIDN'T KNOW WHERE SHE WAS. SHE COULD'VE STAYED HIDDEN...COULD'VE JUST LET ME FALL...
"...BUT INSTEAD SHE PULLED ME TO SAFETY."
AS MOYER PULLED ME BACK INSIDE, THE OTHER AGENTS FOUND US. I TRIED TO EXPLAIN, BUT ALL MOSS SAW WAS AN ALIEN THREATENING ONE OF HIS OWN AND... AND...
...I COULDN'T STOP THEM FROM FIRING.
I'M SORRY, CAREN...I'M SO SORRY.

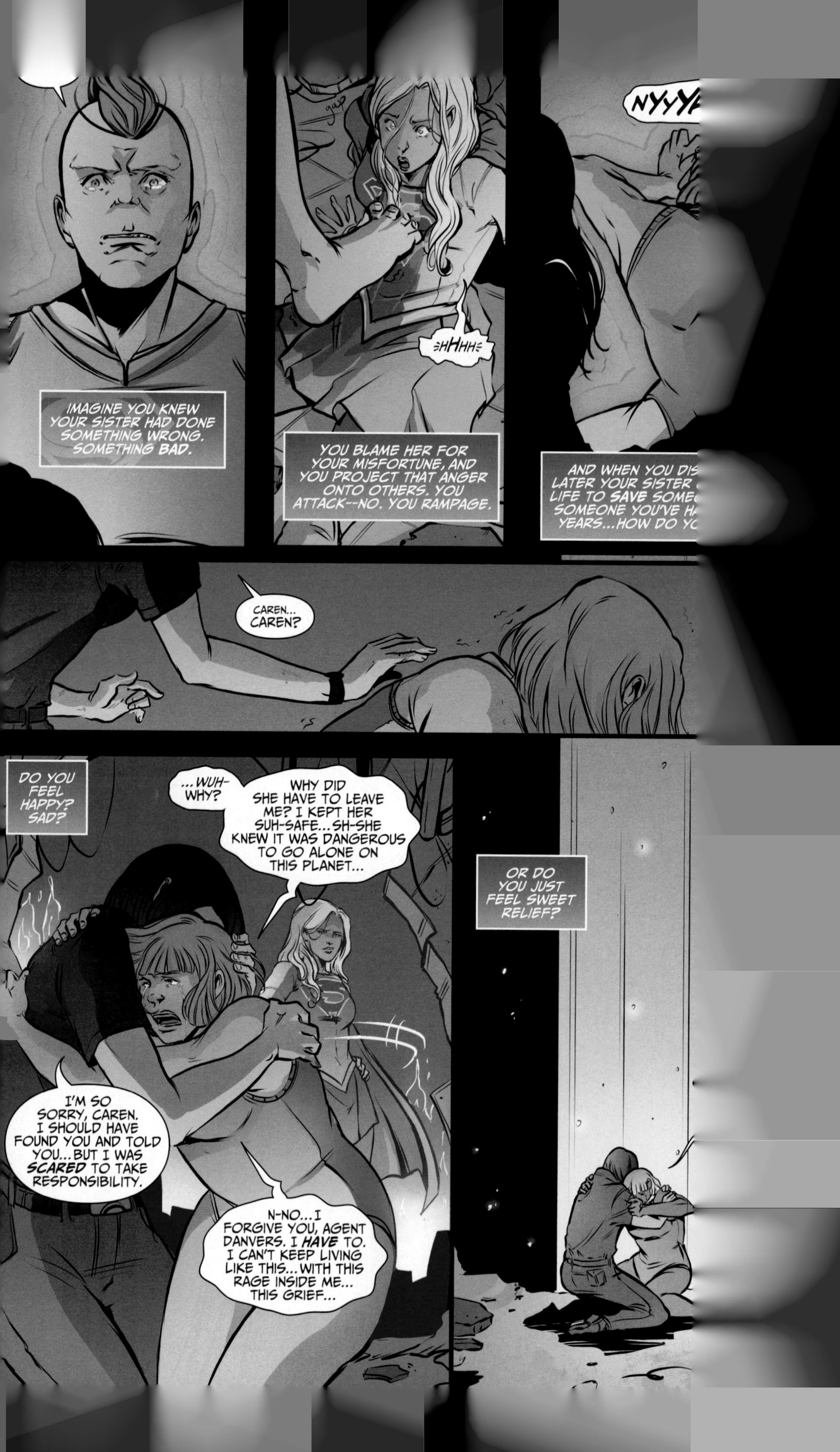
IMAGINE YOU KNEW YOUR SISTER HAD DONE SOMETHING WRONG. SOMETHING BAD.
SHHHH
YOU BLAME HER FOR YOUR MISFORTUNE, AND YOU PROJECT THAT ANGER ONTO OTHERS. YOU ATTACK--NO. YOU RAMPAGE.
NYYYA
AND WHEN YOU DIS
LATER YOUR SISTER
LIFE TO SAVE SOME
SOMEONE YOU'VE HA
YEARS...HOW DO YO
CAREN... CAREN?
DO YOU FEEL HAPPY? SAD?
...WUH-WHY?
WHY DID SHE HAVE TO LEAVE ME? I KEPT HER SUH-SAFE...SH-SHE KNEW IT WAS DANGEROUS TO GO ALONE ON THIS PLANET...
I'M SO SORRY, CAREN. I SHOULD HAVE FOUND YOU AND TOLD YOU...BUT I WAS SCARED TO TAKE RESPONSIBILITY.
N-NO...I FORGIVE YOU, AGENT DANVERS. I HAVE TO. I CAN'T KEEP LIVING LIKE THIS...WITH THIS RAGE INSIDE ME... THIS GRIEF...
OR DO YOU JUST FEEL SWEET RELIEF?

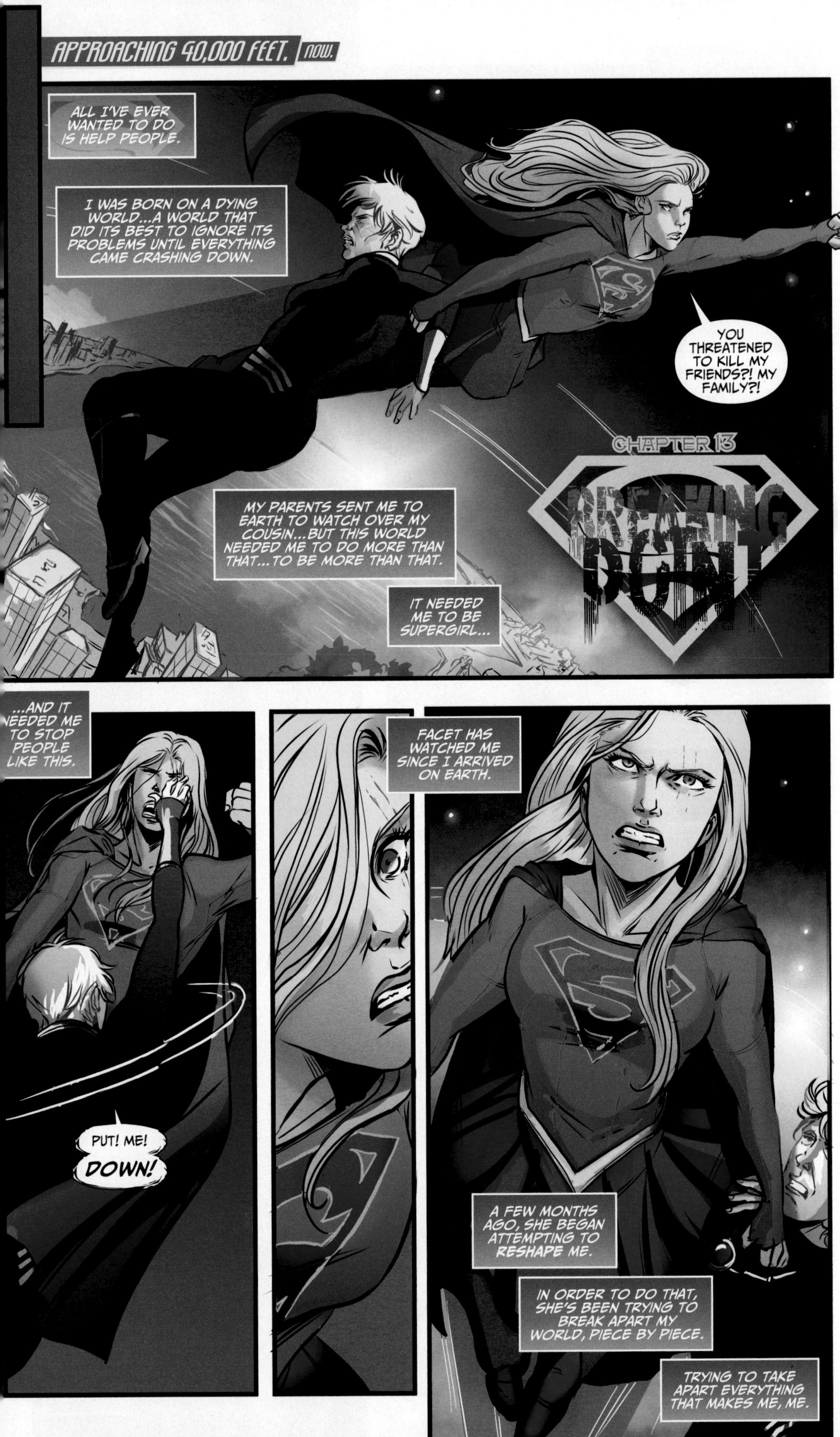
APPROACHING 40,000 FEET. NOW.
ALL I'VE EVER WANTED TO DO IS HELP PEOPLE.
I WAS BORN ON A DYING WORLD...A WORLD THAT DID ITS BEST TO IGNORE ITS PROBLEMS UNTIL EVERYTHING CAME CRASHING DOWN.
YOU THREATENED TO KILL MY FRIENDS?! MY FAMILY?!
CHAPTER 13
BREAKING POINT
MY PARENTS SENT ME TO EARTH TO WATCH OVER MY COUSIN...BUT THIS WORLD NEEDED ME TO DO MORE THAN THAT...TO BE MORE THAN THAT.
IT NEEDED ME TO BE SUPERGIRL...
...AND IT NEEDED ME TO STOP PEOPLE LIKE THIS.
PUT! ME! DOWN!
FACET HAS WATCHED ME SINCE I ARRIVED ON EARTH.
A FEW MONTHS AGO, SHE BEGAN ATTEMPTING TO RESHAPE ME.
IN ORDER TO DO THAT, SHE'S BEEN TRYING TO BREAK APART MY WORLD, PIECE BY PIECE.
TRYING TO TAKE APART EVERYTHING THAT MAKES ME, ME.

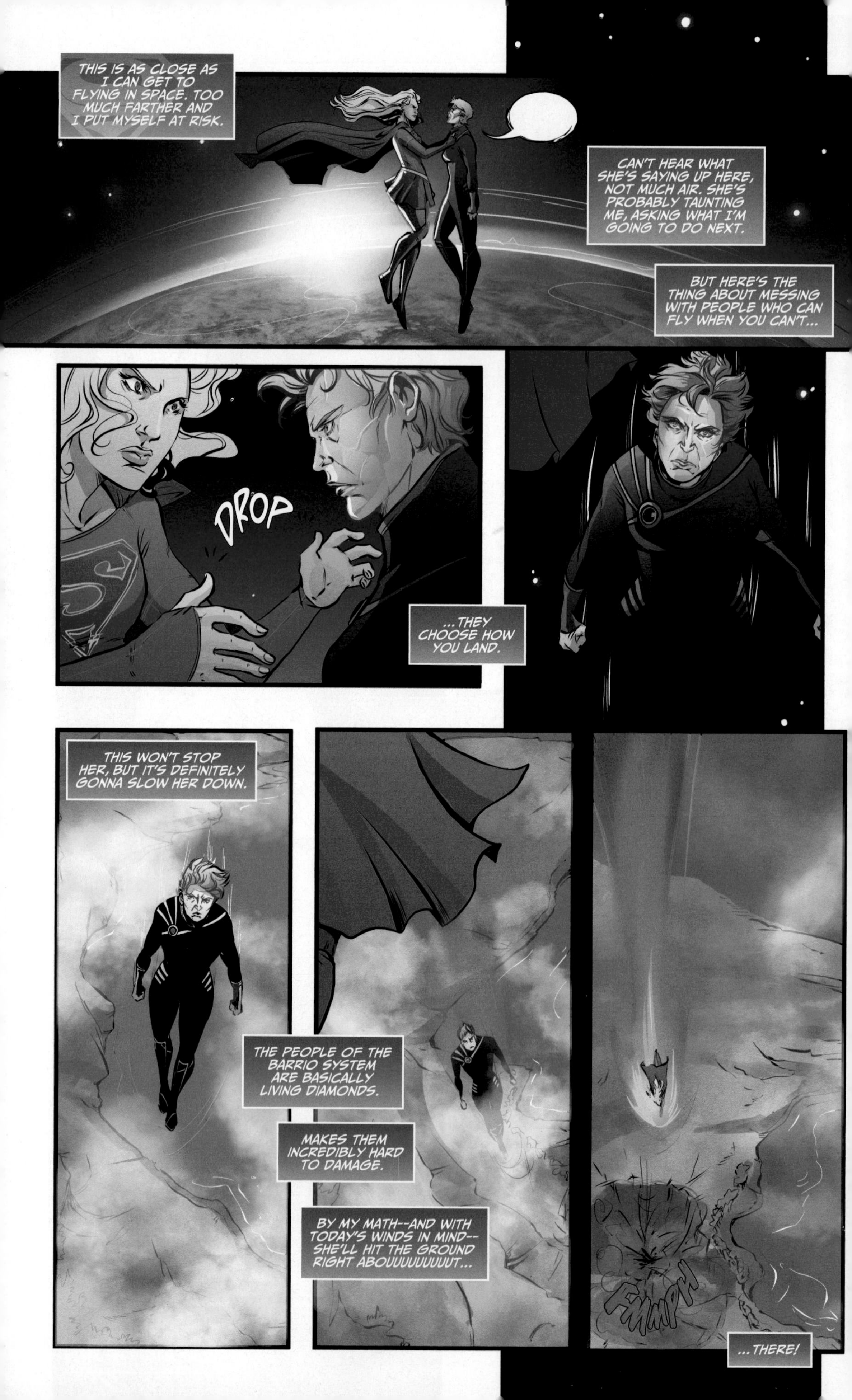
THIS IS AS CLOSE AS I CAN GET TO FLYING IN SPACE. TOO MUCH FARTHER AND I PUT MYSELF AT RISK.
CAN'T HEAR WHAT SHE'S SAYING UP HERE, NOT MUCH AIR. SHE'S PROBABLY TAUNTING ME, ASKING WHAT I'M GOING TO DO NEXT.
BUT HERE'S THE THING ABOUT MESSING WITH PEOPLE WHO CAN FLY WHEN YOU CAN'T...
DROP
...THEY CHOOSE HOW YOU LAND.
THIS WON'T STOP HER, BUT IT'S DEFINITELY GONNA SLOW HER DOWN.
THE PEOPLE OF THE BARRIO SYSTEM ARE BASICALLY LIVING DIAMONDS.
MAKES THEM INCREDIBLY HARD TO DAMAGE.
BY MY MATH--AND WITH TODAY'S WINDS IN MIND--SHE'LL HIT THE GROUND RIGHT ABOUUUUUUUUT...
FWMPH
...THERE!

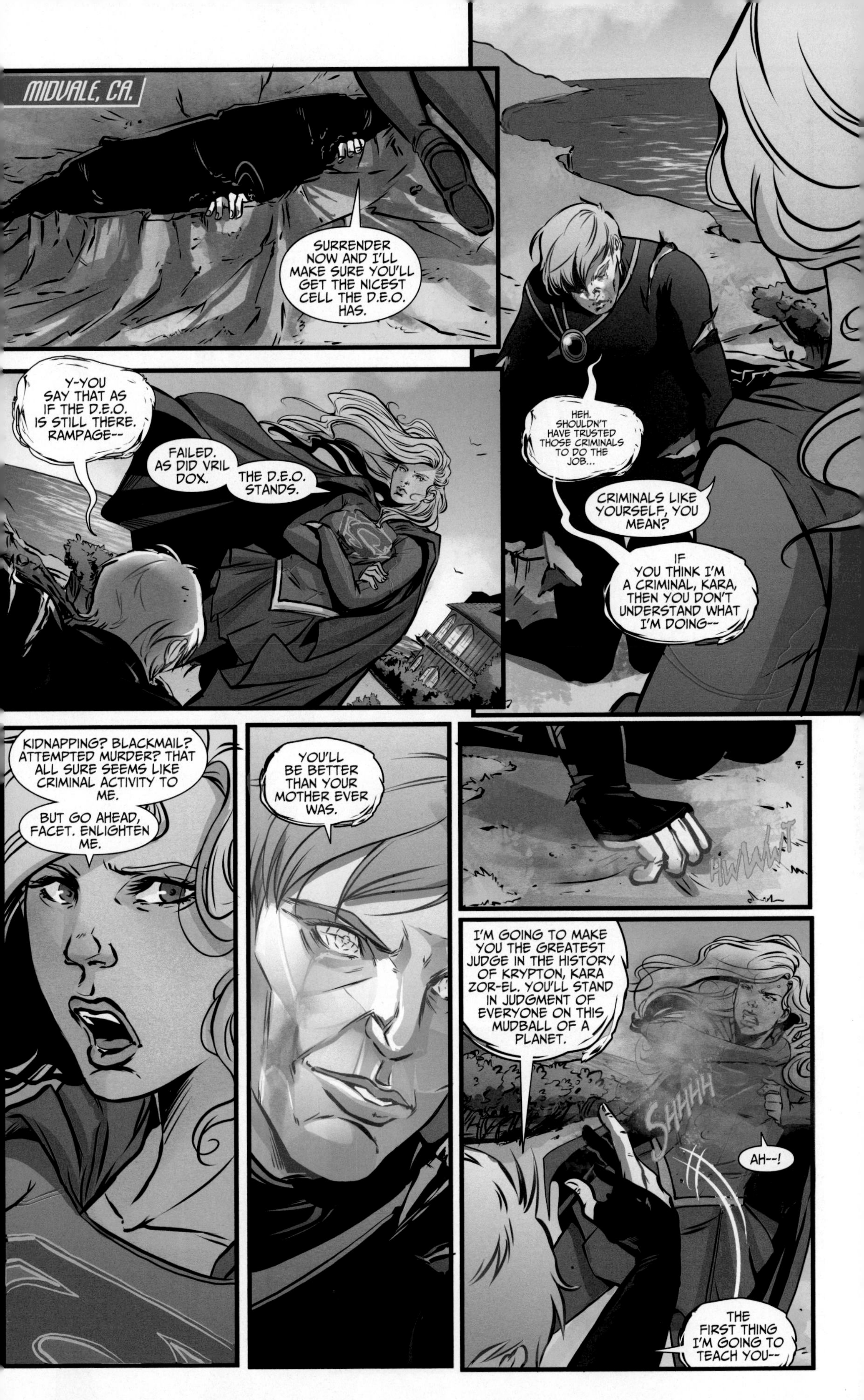
MIDVALE, CA.
SURRENDER NOW AND I'LL MAKE SURE YOU'LL GET THE NICEST CELL THE D.E.O. HAS.
Y-YOU SAY THAT AS IF THE D.E.O. IS STILL THERE. RAMPAGE--
FAILED. AS DID VRIL DOX.
THE D.E.O. STANDS.
HEH. SHOULDN'T HAVE TRUSTED THOSE CRIMINALS TO DO THE JOB...
CRIMINALS LIKE YOURSELF, YOU MEAN?
IF YOU THINK I'M A CRIMINAL, KARA, THEN YOU DON'T UNDERSTAND WHAT I'M DOING--
KIDNAPPING? BLACKMAIL? ATTEMPTED MURDER? THAT ALL SURE SEEMS LIKE CRIMINAL ACTIVITY TO ME.
BUT GO AHEAD, FACET. ENLIGHTEN ME.
YOU'LL BE BETTER THAN YOUR MOTHER EVER WAS.
I'M GOING TO MAKE YOU THE GREATEST JUDGE IN THE HISTORY OF KRYPTON, KARA ZOR-EL. YOU'LL STAND IN JUDGMENT OF EVERYONE ON THIS MUDBALL OF A PLANET.
SHHHH
AH--!
THE FIRST THING I'M GOING TO TEACH YOU--

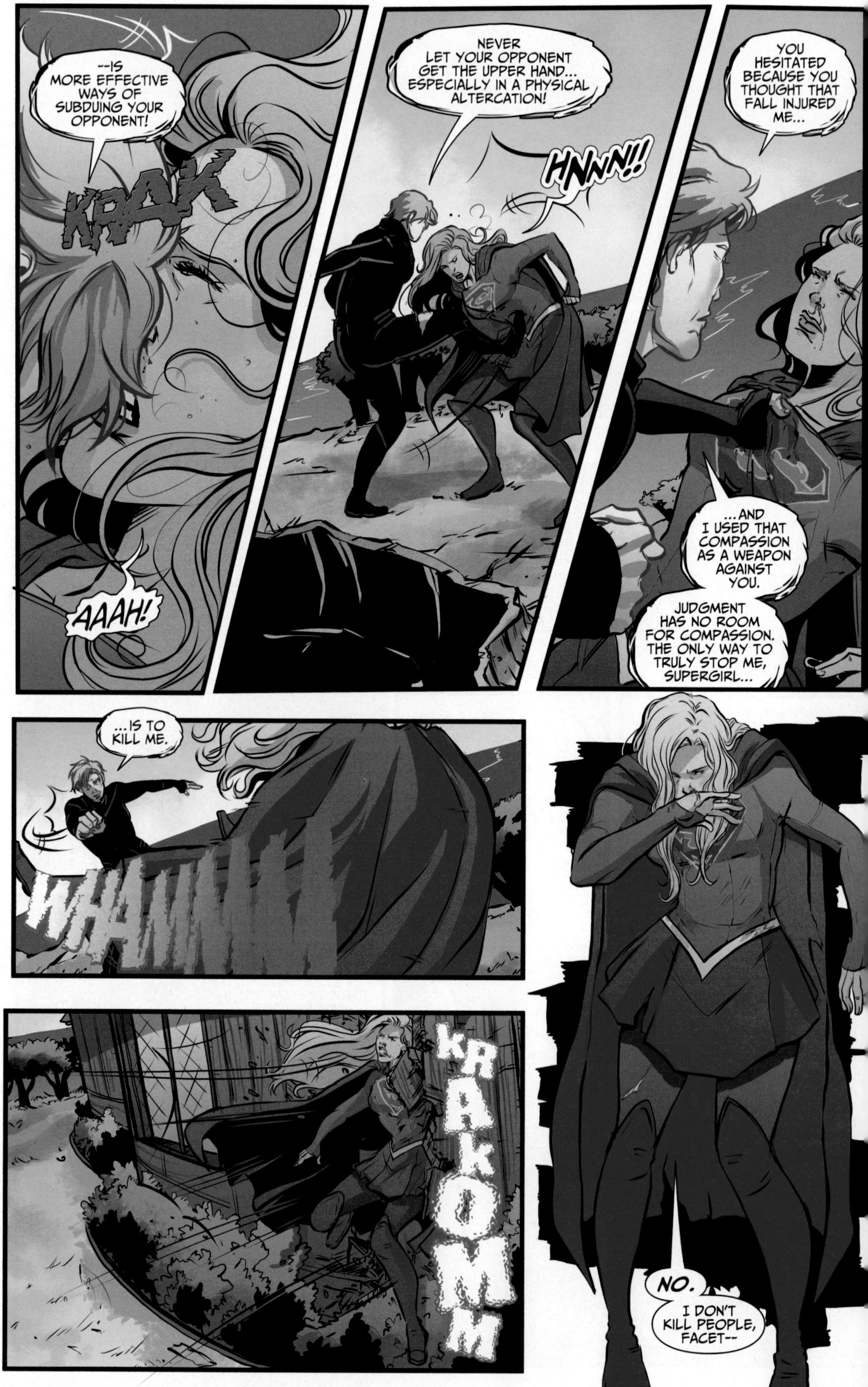
--IS MORE EFFECTIVE WAYS OF SUBDUING YOUR OPPONENT!
KRAK
AAAH!
NEVER LET YOUR OPPONENT GET THE UPPER HAND... ESPECIALLY IN A PHYSICAL ALTERCATION!
HNNN!!
YOU HESITATED BECAUSE YOU THOUGHT THAT FALL INJURED ME...
...AND I USED THAT COMPASSION AS A WEAPON AGAINST YOU.
JUDGMENT HAS NO ROOM FOR COMPASSION. THE ONLY WAY TO TRULY STOP ME, SUPERGIRL...
...IS TO KILL ME.
KRAKOMM
NO.
I DON'T KILL PEOPLE, FACET--

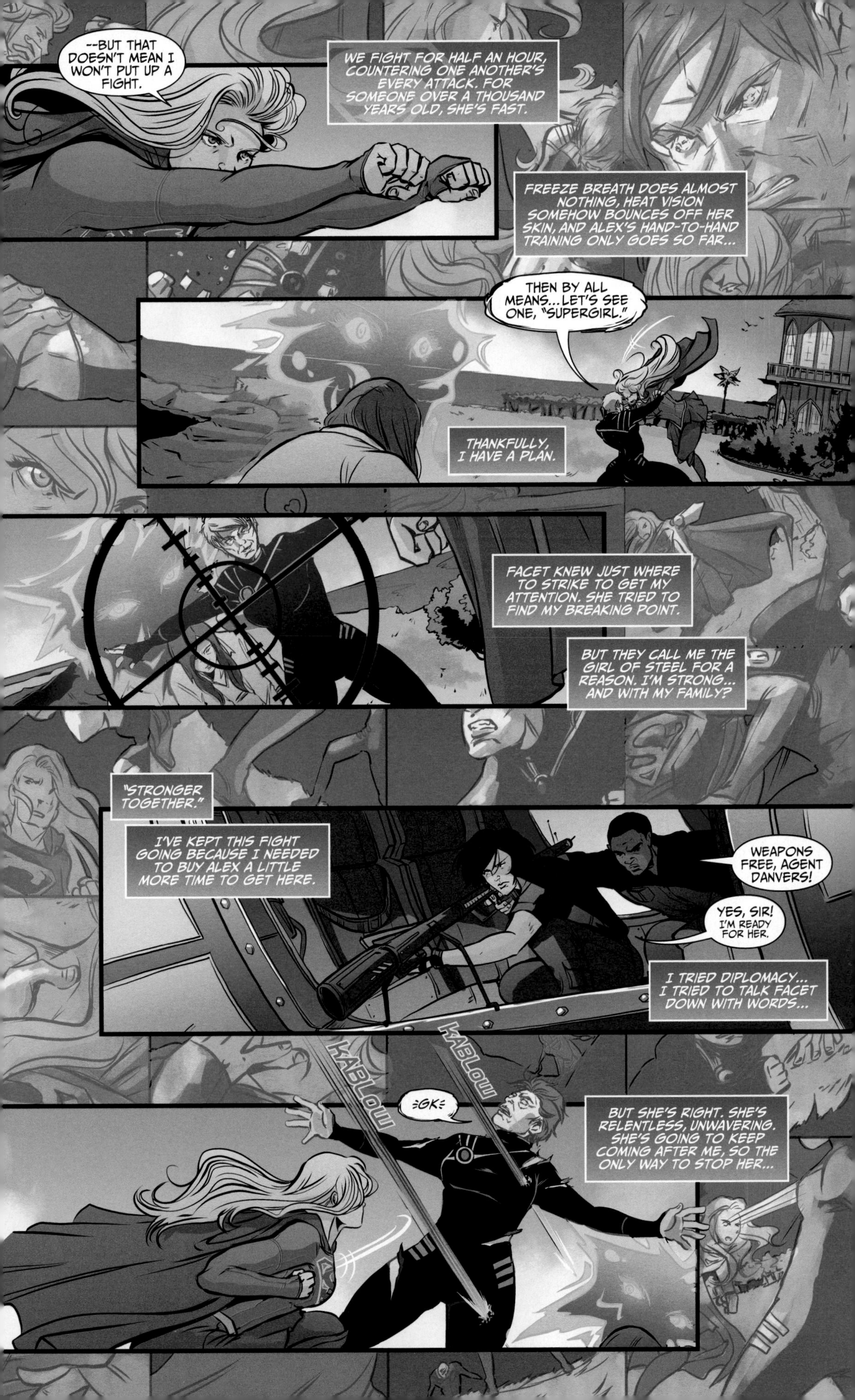
--BUT THAT DOESN'T MEAN I WON'T PUT UP A FIGHT.
WE FIGHT FOR HALF AN HOUR, COUNTERING ONE ANOTHER'S EVERY ATTACK. FOR SOMEONE OVER A THOUSAND YEARS OLD, SHE'S FAST.
FREEZE BREATH DOES ALMOST NOTHING, HEAT VISION SOMEHOW BOUNCES OFF HER SKIN, AND ALEX'S HAND-TO-HAND TRAINING ONLY GOES SO FAR...
THEN BY ALL MEANS...LET'S SEE ONE, "SUPERGIRL."
THANKFULLY, I HAVE A PLAN.
FACET KNEW JUST WHERE TO STRIKE TO GET MY ATTENTION. SHE TRIED TO FIND MY BREAKING POINT.
BUT THEY CALL ME THE GIRL OF STEEL FOR A REASON. I'M STRONG... AND WITH MY FAMILY?
"STRONGER TOGETHER."
I'VE KEPT THIS FIGHT GOING BECAUSE I NEEDED TO BUY ALEX A LITTLE MORE TIME TO GET HERE.
WEAPONS FREE, AGENT DANVERS!
YES, SIR! I'M READY FOR HER.
I TRIED DIPLOMACY... I TRIED TO TALK FACET DOWN WITH WORDS...
KABLOU
KABLOU
GK
BUT SHE'S RIGHT. SHE'S RELENTLESS, UNWAVERING. SHE'S GOING TO KEEP COMING AFTER ME, SO THE ONLY WAY TO STOP HER...

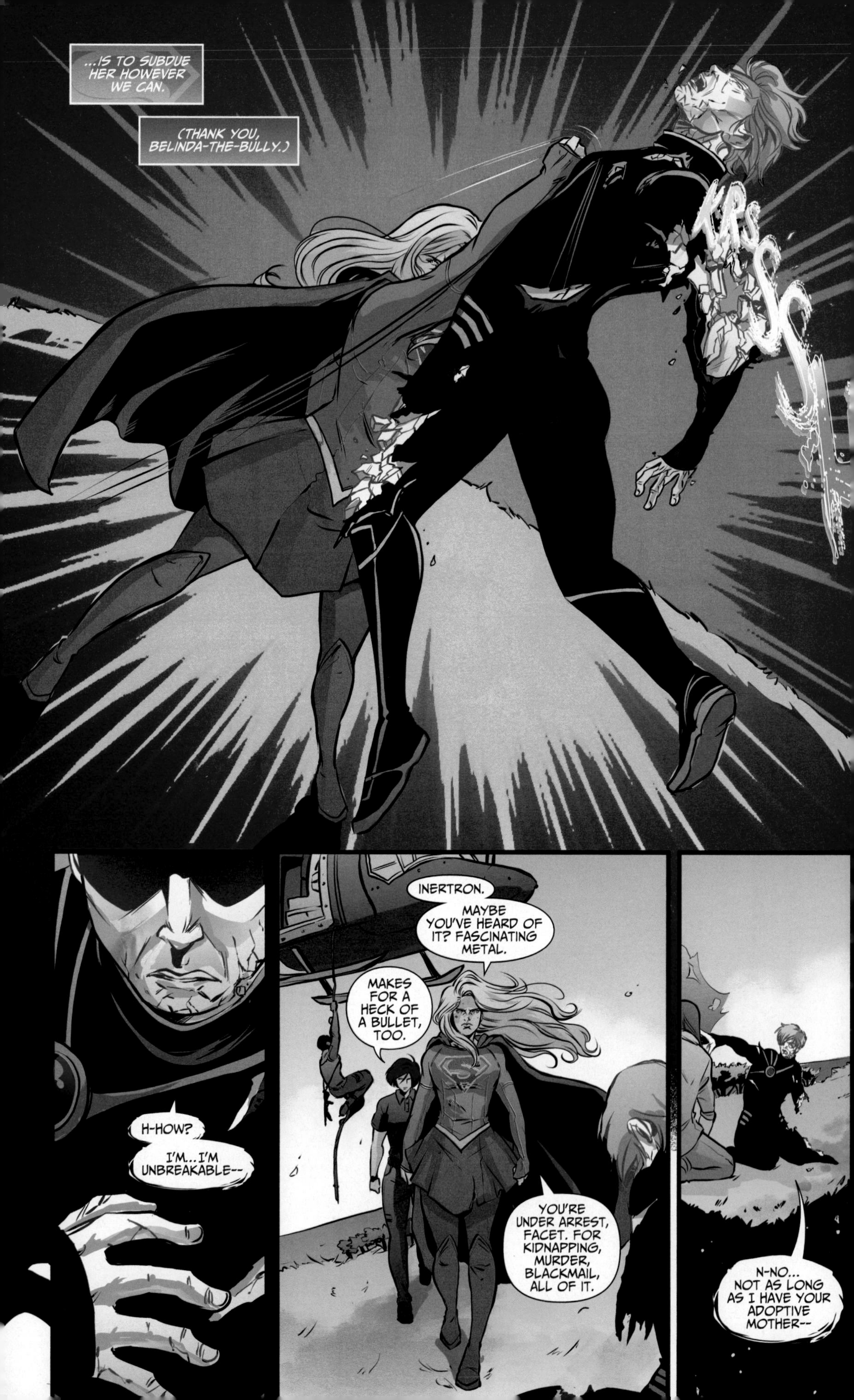

...IS TO SUBDUE HER HOWEVER WE CAN.
(THANK YOU, BELINDA-THE-BULLY.)
KRSSSH
H-HOW?
I'M...I'M UNBREAKABLE--
INERTRON.
MAYBE YOU'VE HEARD OF IT? FASCINATING METAL.
MAKES FOR A HECK OF A BULLET, TOO.
YOU'RE UNDER ARREST, FACET. FOR KIDNAPPING, MURDER, BLACKMAIL, ALL OF IT.
N-NO... NOT AS LONG AS I HAVE YOUR ADOPTIVE MOTHER--

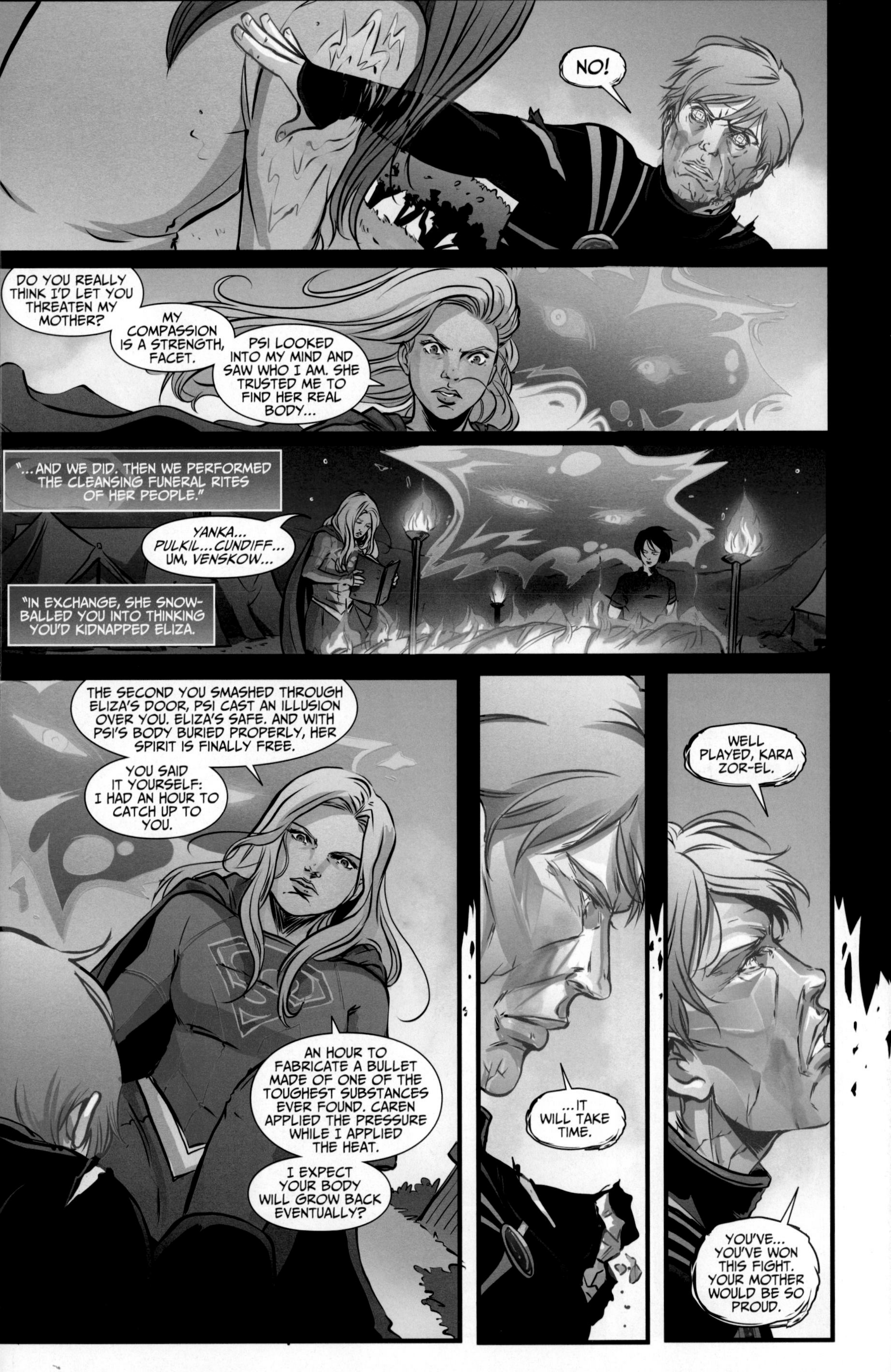
NO!
DO YOU REALLY THINK I'D LET YOU THREATEN MY MOTHER?
MY COMPASSION IS A STRENGTH, FACET.
PSI LOOKED INTO MY MIND AND SAW WHO I AM. SHE TRUSTED ME TO FIND HER REAL BODY...
"...AND WE DID. THEN WE PERFORMED THE CLEANSING FUNERAL RITES OF HER PEOPLE."
YANKA... PULKIL...CUNDIFF... UM, VENSKOW...
"IN EXCHANGE, SHE SNOW-BALLED YOU INTO THINKING YOU'D KIDNAPPED ELIZA.
THE SECOND YOU SMASHED THROUGH ELIZA'S DOOR, PSI CAST AN ILLUSION OVER YOU. ELIZA'S SAFE. AND WITH PSI'S BODY BURIED PROPERLY, HER SPIRIT IS FINALLY FREE.
YOU SAID IT YOURSELF: I HAD AN HOUR TO CATCH UP TO YOU.
AN HOUR TO FABRICATE A BULLET MADE OF ONE OF THE TOUGHEST SUBSTANCES EVER FOUND. CAREN APPLIED THE PRESSURE WHILE I APPLIED THE HEAT.
I EXPECT YOUR BODY WILL GROW BACK EVENTUALLY?
...IT WILL TAKE TIME.
WELL PLAYED, KARA ZOR-EL.
YOU'VE... YOU'VE WON THIS FIGHT. YOUR MOTHER WOULD BE SO PROUD.

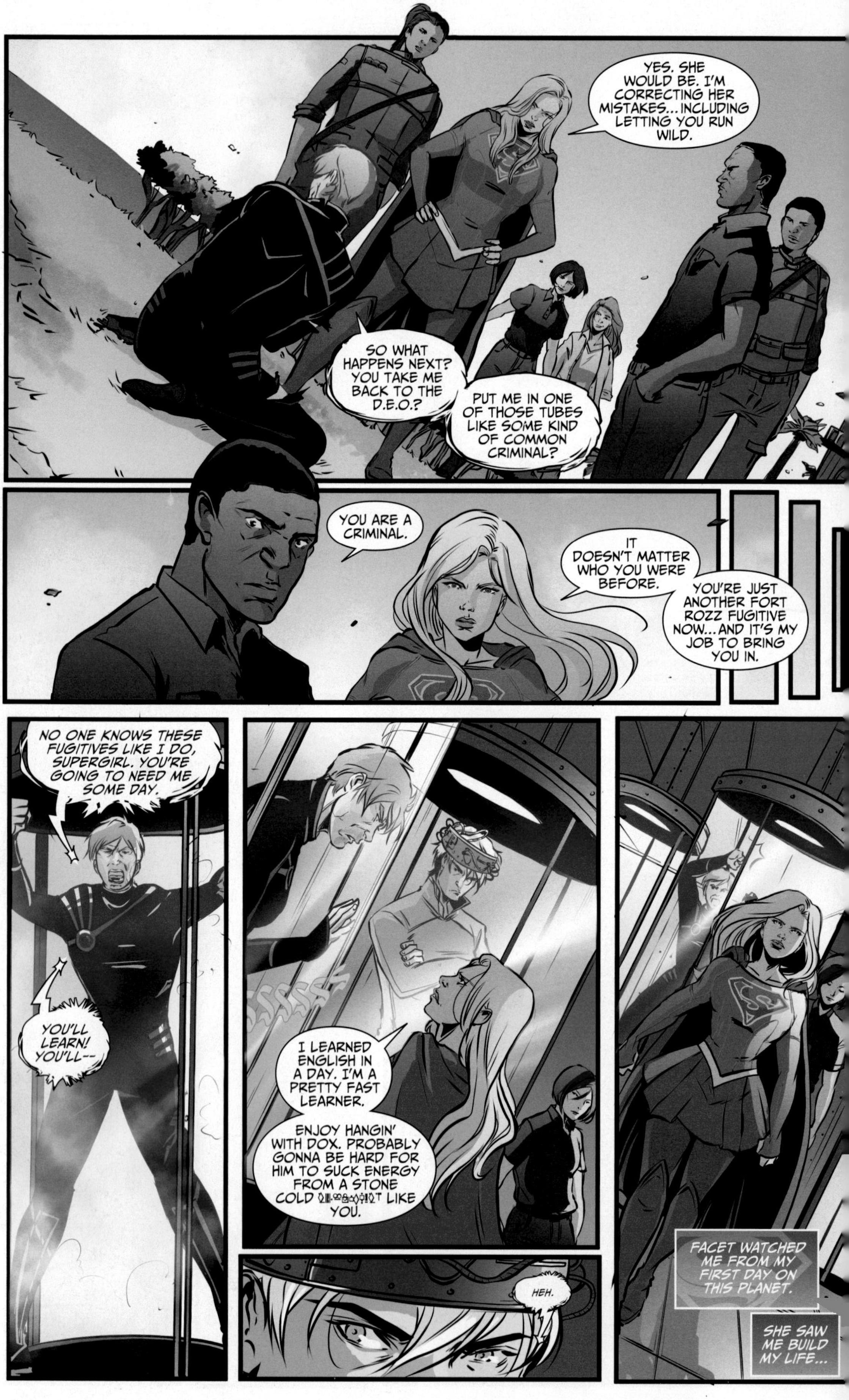
YES. SHE WOULD BE. I'M CORRECTING HER MISTAKES...INCLUDING LETTING YOU RUN WILD.
SO WHAT HAPPENS NEXT? YOU TAKE ME BACK TO THE D.E.O.?
PUT ME IN ONE OF THOSE TUBES LIKE SOME KIND OF COMMON CRIMINAL?
YOU ARE A CRIMINAL.
IT DOESN'T MATTER WHO YOU WERE BEFORE.
YOU'RE JUST ANOTHER FORT ROZZ FUGITIVE NOW...AND IT'S MY JOB TO BRING YOU IN.
NO ONE KNOWS THESE FUGITIVES LIKE I DO, SUPERGIRL. YOU'RE GOING TO NEED ME SOME DAY.
YOU'LL LEARN! YOU'LL--
I LEARNED ENGLISH IN A DAY. I'M A PRETTY FAST LEARNER.
ENJOY HANGIN' WITH DOX. PROBABLY GONNA BE HARD FOR HIM TO SUCK ENERGY FROM A STONE COLD LIKE YOU.
HEH.
FACET WATCHED ME FROM MY FIRST DAY ON THIS PLANET.
SHE SAW ME BUILD MY LIFE...

...FIND A JOB...

--MAKE THAT A DOUBLE LATTE, KEER-AH. I COULD USE THE EXTRA KICK TODAY.

YES, MISS GRANT.

...SHE WATCHED ME MAKE FRIENDS.

COME ON, RABIAH, THAT WAS MY LOOT--WHAT? OH. SORRY.

COME ON, RAZZLERDAZZLER130!

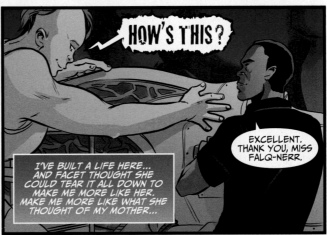

HOW'S THIS?

EXCELLENT. THANK YOU, MISS FALQ-NERR.

I'VE BUILT A LIFE HERE... AND FACET THOUGHT SHE COULD TEAR IT ALL DOWN TO MAKE ME MORE LIKE HER. MAKE ME MORE LIKE WHAT SHE THOUGHT OF MY MOTHER...

...BUT I'M NOT ALURA. I'M ME.

WHEN I GOT TO EARTH, I HID MY GIFTS... SUPPRESSED WHAT MADE ME SPECIAL IN ORDER TO FIT IN.

--WE'VE GOT "SCREAM," "CONTACT," ORRRR THE TOM CRUISE CLASSIC, "ALL THE RIGHT MOVES." Y'KNOW, IF YOU PAUSE IT JUST RIGHT, YOU CAN SEE--

BUT THAT TIME IS OVER. I'M PROUD OF WHO I AM. WHO I'VE BECOME.

RACE YOU THERE!

MY PARENTS DIED SO I COULD LIVE...AND TO LIVE HOW SOMEONE ELSE CHOOSES FOR ME WOULD DISHONOR THEIR MEMORY.

I WON'T DO THAT. I'M SUPERGIRL...

IT'S HANK.

I'VE GOTTA CHANGE BEFORE WE GO.

DA-DEET

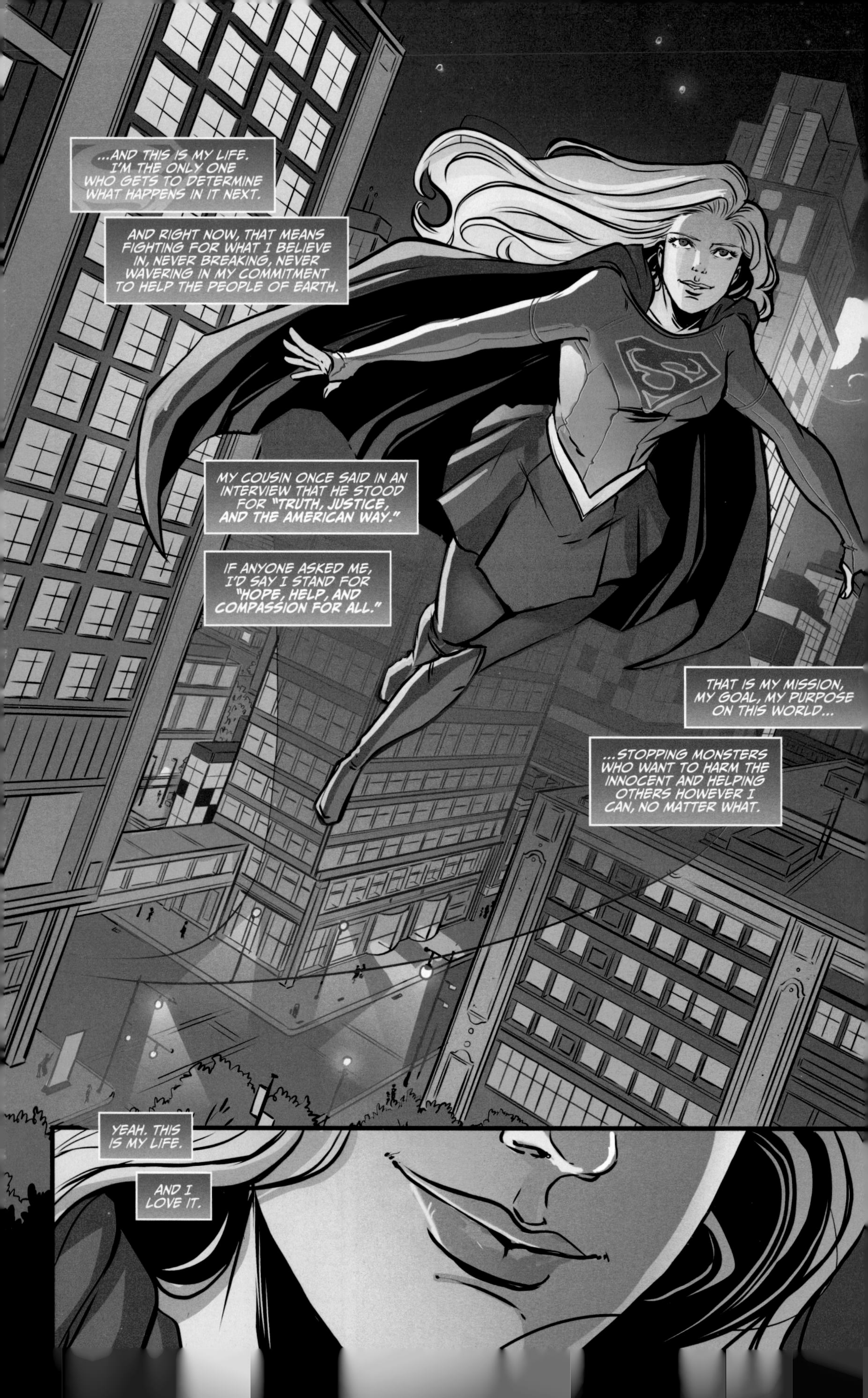
...AND THIS IS MY LIFE. I'M THE ONLY ONE WHO GETS TO DETERMINE WHAT HAPPENS IN IT NEXT.
AND RIGHT NOW, THAT MEANS FIGHTING FOR WHAT I BELIEVE IN, NEVER BREAKING, NEVER WAVERING IN MY COMMITMENT TO HELP THE PEOPLE OF EARTH.
MY COUSIN ONCE SAID IN AN INTERVIEW THAT HE STOOD FOR "TRUTH, JUSTICE, AND THE AMERICAN WAY."
IF ANYONE ASKED ME, I'D SAY I STAND FOR "HOPE, HELP, AND COMPASSION FOR ALL."
THAT IS MY MISSION, MY GOAL, MY PURPOSE ON THIS WORLD...
...STOPPING MONSTERS WHO WANT TO HARM THE INNOCENT AND HELPING OTHERS HOWEVER I CAN, NO MATTER WHAT.
YEAH. THIS IS MY LIFE.
AND I LOVE IT.